AZ
OF 21ST
CENTURY
CARS

TONY LEWIN

AZ
OF 21ST
CENTURY
CARS

MERRELL
LONDON · NEW YORK

ABOUT THIS BOOK

The *A–Z of 21st-Century Cars* is a brand new, authoritative and accessible guide to cars, car design and the global car industry. With more than 300 meticulously researched entries and over 1500 photographs and portraits, it provides insightful analyses of a host of key car designs, detailed histories of the world's most important carmakers and brands, and profiles of the leading designers responsible for shaping the vehicles on our roads today.

A carefully structured system of entries, divided into Designers, Marques and Models, makes this book simple to use and the information easy to find, and cross-references enable the reader to research more widely around a given topic. The entries are arranged **alphabetically** to facilitate quick reference, while browsers will appreciate the wealth of detail and background information that comes with each article.

A simple **colour-coded system** of entries ensures instant access to the required material:

Entries relating to **designers and design studios** are colour-coded green, and include sidebars with biographical details and key designs.

Entries relating to **marques** are coded blue. They cover key developments in each company's history, prominent personalities and the most important production and concept cars influencing its current models. Comprehensive sidebars document the major events and the most significant models in the evolution of each brand.

Entries relating to specific car **models** are colour-coded red. They include technical specifications and a full design evaluation as well as individual model histories, the dates of key generation changes and an assessment of the model's influence on other designs and designers and the broader car market.

Names preceded by the **icon »** in the text refer to entries on other designers, marques or models.

For the sake of clarity in all areas, the **terminology** in this guide is given in international English, using the terms, phrases and acronyms employed by the professional car-design community. A full explanation of these specialized expressions is provided in the **Glossary**, beginning on page 534.

References to the **model years** of products generally relate to the date the design first appeared in public, often at a motor show, rather than the date of market launch. With many North American models in particular, the initial show appearance may be as much as two years ahead of the eventual production model.

Measurements are given in the metric units employed across all levels of the global car business; for the convenience of readers in the United Kingdom and the United States, imperial conversions are also included.

Given that **CO_2 emissions** are fast becoming the standard by which a vehicle's environmental friendliness – and its taxation class – is measured, we also wherever possible give each model's European mandated CO_2 figure in terms of grams per kilometre. Equivalent data has not yet been recorded for vehicles sold in North America.

And, finally, with the international auto industry in the midst of yet more major realignments, we have provided a handy guide to which brands belong to which manufacturing groups – at least at the time of going to press (May 2011). **Who Owns Whom** is on pages 532–33.

INTRODUCTION

For all its familiarity and everyday usefulness, the automobile is one of the most mysterious inventions of the industrial age. It is churned out by the million from huge, heartless factories, yet we have somehow managed to endow it with a personality, a cultural life of its own. Each car is different, and each has developed its own mythology. People get fired up about cars, either positively or negatively, in a way that they generally don't about cameras, washing machines or other consumer products.

Just what it is that triggers this intimate connection is something best left to psychologists to explain. Yet in the real world it is the car designer who comes closest to understanding the subconscious forces at work, creating shapes that not only are practical and pretty but also play on the emotions of the customer, and bit by bit build up the aura of a brand.

But how, exactly, does the designer do this? What trick of line or light makes an Aston Martin exciting? Why is a BMW sporty, an Audi efficient and a Mercedes superior? How can premium brands, such as Lexus and Infiniti, be created from scratch? And would a Ferrari with a Fiat badge seem quite so exotic? In this book we try to answer all these questions and more, unpacking the mysterious mix of style, substance, reputation and romance that turns base metal into something more special.

In the century and a quarter that has elapsed since Karl Benz filed German patent number 37435 for his 'Vehicle with Gas Engine Drive' in 1886, the automobile has transformed itself from that wobbly-wheeled, horse-scaring contraption into a near-essential of modern life, something that has penetrated every corner of the globe and touched the lives of all but the most isolated people on the planet. In that process it has by turns served as a powerful symbol of personal freedom, a vehicle for individual self-expression and a flag-waving statement of lifestyle choice – witness the California celebrity circuit's endorsement of the Toyota Prius hybrid.

The zeal with which these roles have been taken up is testament to the energy and the passion bound up in automobile culture. In the highly design-conscious society that we now inhabit, the car has become much more than mere transport; for many, it has acquired the status of a personal manifesto, a statement of belief or aesthetic preference. More than any other mass-produced artefact, cars carry a powerful symbolic value. Extravagant or economical, discreet or flashy, soft or hard, each projects a different persona. Like it or not, these personalities are evident everywhere and at all times – even when the car itself is not in use. Whether in motion or parked on the street, cars are the most visible form of design in our public spaces: their shapes are an important ingredient in our visual environment. Car design matters to everyone, not just to carmakers and car users.

This guide seeks to steer the reader through a dozen decades of automobile design evolution, focusing most closely on the more recent generations in which the foundations for today's models were laid. By deconstructing the aesthetic as well as the engineering elements that make up a car design, we can see how automotive style has developed over the years. We chart the major advances

2009 BMW VISION EFFICIENTDYNAMICS CONCEPT

2008 CITROËN HYPNOS CONCEPT

7

in design, explore the thinking of the designers (from Pininfarina and Bertone to Giorgetto Giugiaro and Chris Bangle) who were brave enough to make those big steps, and examine the philosophies of such companies as Citroën, Alfa Romeo and BMW that had the courage to build those designs. We take a close look, too, at companies that have built up a rock-solid identity by the systematic application of strict design criteria, such as Audi.

We can in turn employ this background knowledge to understand how today's designers and product planners are able, much as artists are, to harness shapes and proportions, surfaces and graphics to influence the customer's emotions. Here we discuss how, as demonstrated by the Jaguar XJ, the shape of the side windows can control the look of the whole car; how, as in the Range Rover Sport, the angles of the pillars can be manipulated to make a car look lower and sportier; how a low-level light catcher can make a fat car look thin; and, as exemplified by Audi, how LED light patterns are the new jewellery to project brand identity.

The stakes are high, but the rewards of getting it right are immense: a hot-selling product that hits the bullseye and keeps the factories turning profitably day and night. Sceptical? Just consider some historical examples: the crisply stylish Volkswagen Golf in the 1970s, Peugeot's warm and feminine 205 of 1983, and the post-millennium Mini Cooper, with its huge array of colours, stripes and accessories, perfect for an urban elite eager to personalize its transport. Each was astutely judged and instantly successful and, even today, designers are constantly striving to replicate the phenomenon of such models as these, which so brilliantly captured the zeitgeist.

It is these in particular that we celebrate in this book: the models and the designers that changed the course of car design, that altered the outlook and the expectations of the man or woman in the street, that inspired interest where previously there was none. That spark of excitement is essential, for without the shared passion and commitment of designer and customer, cars would rate no higher than washing machines in terms of the desire they generate.

On a more practical note, we have faced some tough choices in whittling down the many thousands of eligible models to the more manageable 150 or so that made the final cut for this book. Such choices are necessarily subjective, and there will be many who will argue fiercely in favour of some of the designs we have had to leave out, or even contest the inclusion of others.

Likewise, it would be possible to put a strong case for the inclusion of such marques as Austin, Plymouth and Oldsmobile, which were influential in the twentieth century but did not survive past the millennium and into the twenty-first century as is our prime focus here. Where to draw the line is always a conundrum.

Still more exasperating is not to be able to mention more than a relative handful of the several thousand designers whose creativity and imagination over the decades have made the automobile spectrum such a rich and vibrant one. The sad fact is that too many of these major talents go unrecognized, their work being credited to the chief designer or the design director of the moment – someone who may have done little more than oversee a design programme or represent the design division in meetings with senior management. So our apologies go out in advance to all those designers whose work is shown in this book but who have not been credited by name. In recent years and with the increasing internationalization of design there are signs of greater openness in crediting individual designers, especially among American and European companies, and we look forward to including many more names in later editions of this book.

This is indeed an auspicious time to be publishing a book of this kind. With the auto industry in the midst of its worst-ever economic crisis but with major new opportunities presenting themselves in the shape of eco-friendly electric cars, there is the sense that we are on the cusp of a new era, one in which car design must respond to ethical and environmental expectations as well as aesthetic values. The next edition of the *A-Z of 21st-Century Cars* could look very different indeed.

2006-GENERATION AUDI R8

2009 INFINITI ESSENCE CONCEPT

DESIGNERS

MARQUES

18	ABARTH	150	FERRARI	309	MCLAREN	442	SAAB
19	AC	160	FIAT	312	MAHINDRA	447	SALEEN
20	ACURA	168	FIRST AUTO WORKS	313	MARUTI	448	SAMSUNG
22	ALFA ROMEO	174	FORD	314	MASERATI	449	SATURN
29	ARTEGA			319	MAYBACH	452	SCION
32	ASTON MARTIN	196	GAZ	322	MAZDA	454	SEAT
40	AUDI	197	GEELY	326	MERCEDES-BENZ	456	SKODA
		198	GENERAL MOTORS	340	MERCURY	460	SMART
60	BENTLEY	205	GREAT WALL	341	MG ROVER	466	SPYKER
66	BMW			342	MINI	467	SSANGYONG
81	BRILLIANCE	213	HINDUSTAN	346	MITSUBISHI	472	SUBARU
82	BRISTOL	216	HOLDEN	352	MORGAN	473	SUZUKI
84	BUGATTI	218	HONDA				
88	BUICK	230	HUMMER	358	NISSAN	476	TATA
91	BYD AUTO	232	HYUNDAI			478	TESLA
				372	OPEL/VAUXHALL	479	THINK
94	CADILLAC	240	INFINITI			482	TOYOTA
100	CATERHAM	242	ISUZU	378	PAGANI	492	TVR
103	CHERY			380	PAYKAN		
104	CHEVROLET	246	JAGUAR	381	PERODUA	496	UAZ
112	CHRYSLER	256	JEEP	382	PEUGEOT		
118	CITROËN			400	PONTIAC	502	VENTURI
		262	KIA	404	PORSCHE	503	VOLGA
132	DACIA	264	KOENIGSEGG	413	PROTON	504	VOLKSWAGEN
133	DAEWOO	266	KTM			514	VOLVO
134	DAIHATSU			420	RENAULT		
138	DODGE	268	LADA	433	ROEWE	528	WESTFIELD
144	DONKERVOORT	270	LAMBORGHINI	434	ROLLS-ROYCE	529	WIESMANN
		276	LANCIA				
		280	LAND ROVER			531	ZIL
		286	LEXUS				
		292	LINCOLN				
		298	LOTUS				
		304	LTI				

MODELS

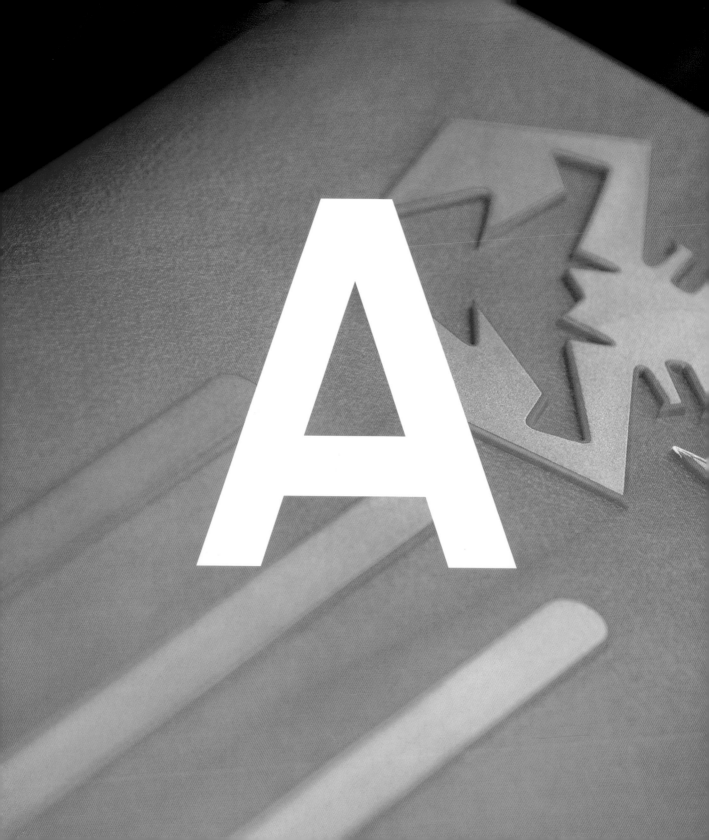

ABARTH

ITALY | FOUNDED 1947 | SPORTS BRAND OF FIAT | ABARTHCARS.CO.UK

Austrian-born Karl Abarth (1908–1979) began his career as a motorcycle engineer and became a successful racer in the 1930s. After the Second World War he moved to Italy to work on the highly complex Cisitalia Grand Prix racing car with a team assembled by Ferdinand Porsche. His own fledgling operation was already under way, and when the Cisitalia project ran out of cash and collapsed, Abarth set up a racing team using its equipment and vehicles.

Soon Abarth began winning races, and with the launch of the popular Fiat 600 in 1955 he had an eager market for his tuning kits and aftermarket exhaust systems developed on the racetrack. The conversion kits, which would be delivered to the owners in large wooden crates, contained all that was needed virtually to double the standard car's power output. Abarth's racing cars – especially the stunning »Zagato-bodied 750 GT – dominated the smaller classes across Europe, and extravagant streamlined models that had been specially rebodied by such designers as »Bertone began breaking speed records, too.

In 1971 Abarth sold his operation to »Fiat. It became in effect the Italian company's rally team, going on to win a string of international rallies and championships with such classics as the Fiat 131. After the death of its founder in 1979, however, the Abarth organization gradually lost its way as an independent engineering entity.

It was only with the sweeping changes brought in by Fiat CEO Sergio Marchionne from 2007 that Abarth became a serious brand once again. The famous scorpion emblem – chosen by Karl Abarth as his birth sign was Scorpio – reappeared on a tuned »Fiat Grande Punto in 2007, and it made an emotional return to the reborn »Fiat 500 the following year. With 200 horsepower in a tiny car, Signor Abarth would have approved.

HISTORY

1922	Karl Abarth (KA) apprenticed to Italian motorcycle maker
1925	KA begins motorcycle testing and racing
1929	First Abarth-branded motorcycle
1930	KA becomes European champion
1947	Begins tuning work on cars
1948	Joins Cisitalia Grand Prix project
1949	Cisitalia collapses; KA founds racing team
1950	KA founds aftermarket performance exhausts business
1970	Three world rally manufacturer's titles
1971	Abarth absorbed by Fiat
1979	KA dies
1980s	Rally success with Lancia team
2007	Abarth relaunched as performance brand by Fiat

PRINCIPAL MODELS

1955	Fiat Abarth 750 GT Zagato
1958	Fiat 500 Abarth
1969	Fiat Abarth 2000 Sport Spider
2007	Fiat Abarth Grande Punto
2008	Fiat Abarth 500

KARL ABARTH AND THE 1965 ABARTH RANGE

2007 FIAT ABARTH GRANDE PUNTO

2008 FIAT ABARTH 500

AC

GREAT BRITAIN | FOUNDED 1904 | SPECIALIST SPORTS CARS

AC is one of the car industry's most enduring paradoxes. Britain's oldest car company and the producer of the Cobra, one of the most iconic sports cars of all time, it was also responsible for one of the least charismatic vehicles ever conceived: the dismal and dangerous single-seater motorized tricycle for invalid drivers. AC's business history is peppered with crises and changes of ownership, and its post-2000 position is sustained more by the enthusiasm of individuals than the flow of investment or profits.

In its earliest days AC was known for its high-quality small vehicles, but the company soon progressed, via elegant sports saloons and tourers, to the highly desirable Ace roadster in the 1950s. Sensing the powerful appeal of the discreet, six-cylinder Ace, American sports-car legend Carroll Shelby began fitting large tuned American V8 engines to create the thundering, fire-breathing Cobra – and so it was that the most enduring of AC's designs was born.

Extreme performance enthusiasts rushed to experience the thrill of huge horsepower in a simple, lightweight two-seater, and soon Cobras were a regular sight at Le Mans 24 Hours, and dominating sports-car racing. A complicated series of deals and interrelationships saw Ford take effective control of AC in the 1980s, only for the company to go independent – and lose the right to use the Cobra name – a decade later. AC never really recovered from these setbacks, but what is now known as the MkVI could be set for a minor comeback as a handcrafted, Corvette-engined Cobra replica produced in Germany for wealthy enthusiast clients.

HISTORY

1920s	Production of small and medium cars
1930s	Production of sports tourers and saloons
1950s	Production of sports cars and invalid cars
1965	Wins sports car world championship
1986	Ford Motor Company and Autokraft take control
1992	Autokraft assumes full control
1997	Alan Lubinsky acquires company
2005	UK operations moved to Malta
2008	Maltese operation closes
2009	Gullwing resumes production in Germany

PRINCIPAL MODELS

1950s	Ace, Aceca, Greyhound
1962	Cobra
1968	Frua 428 coupé
1978	3000 ME
1985	Cobra MkIV
2009	MkVI from Gullwing
2011	MkVI shown at Geneva show

1950s ACE

1950s ACECA

1962 COBRA

2011 MKVI

ACURA

JAPAN | FOUNDED 1986 | PREMIUM CARS AND SUVS | ACURA.COM

Almost unknown outside North America, Acura nevertheless has the distinction of having led the industry when it launched in 1986 as the premium brand of Japan's »Honda. This was the first time a volume carmaker had developed an upscale brand in-house rather than by acquiring another company. Indeed, Acura was one of the first brands to be the invention of marketing experts rather than of engineers or entrepreneurs.

Acura's formula of smarter and more luxurious derivatives of Honda products, backed by superb customer service, proved an immediate success, and by the end of the decade both »Nissan and »Toyota had responded with their own newly cultivated premium marques, »Infiniti and »Lexus respectively. Unlike its competitors, however, Acura has not expanded outside North America and Hong Kong.

Such prominent sporty models as the aluminium-construction, mid-engined NSX supercar gave Acura a high profile in the 1990s. This racy image was reflected at a more affordable level by the Integra Type R, a highly tuned small coupé that developed a cult following among tuners and enthusiasts across the United States and, in its Honda form, in Europe and Japan. Many key technical innovations associated with Honda – such as the super-handling all-wheel-drive system – actually debuted on Acura models, but despite its engineering credibility the brand began to lose its way stylistically.

The 2007 Advanced Sports Car concept, although front-engined and very different in its design language, was tipped as a replacement for the NSX but was cancelled in 2008. Instead, Acura began to strengthen its visual identity with a controversial uniform frontal style and heavy grille; this was most extreme of all on the California-designed ZDX sports crossover, Acura's answer to the equally controversial »BMW X6.

2005 RL

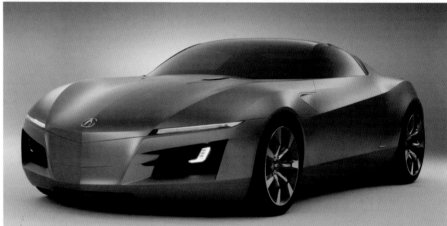

2007 ADVANCED SPORTS CAR CONCEPT

HISTORY AND PRINCIPAL MODELS

1986	Launches in USA with Legend premium sedan
1991	NSX supercar
1997	Integra Type R
2001	MDX crossover
2005	NSX production ceases. RL premium sedan
2007	Advanced Sports Car concept
2009	ZDX sports crossover; FC Sport concept

ALFONSO ALBAISA
CUBA/UNITED STATES | BORN 1964 | CAR DESIGNER AND ARCHITECT

CV	
1988	BA in industrial design, Pratt Institute, New York. Starts working at Nissan Design America (NDA)
2000	Design director, NDA studio, San Diego
2005	Director, NDA studio. Secondments to Nissan design studio, Atsugi, Japan
2007	Vice president of design, Nissan Design Europe, London
2010	Vice president of design, NDA

KEY DESIGNS	
2002	Nissan 350Z; Nissan Quest concept
2003	Nissan Altima and Maxima
2004	Nissan Farmington Hills studio (architect)
2006	Nissan Urge showcar
2007	Nissan GT-R
2009	Nissan Qazana showcar
2010	Nissan Qashqai and Juke

2002 NISSAN 350Z

2009 NISSAN QAZANA SHOWCAR

As a seven-year-old growing up in Miami, Alfonso Albaisa was inspired to become a car designer by the sight of a black Jaguar E-Type convertible. He joined »Nissan upon graduation from the Pratt Institute in New York City in 1988, having been offered a position during his final year, and has risen to become one of the major influences in the company's worldwide design activities.

Albaisa's most formative years were those spent in California, at Nissan's San Diego studio, and on secondment to Japan. In 2007 he cited the 2002 Quest concept – a long, sinuous multi-seater – as one of his favourite designs; this sensitive and voluptuous take on the normally box-like large minivan morphed into a production model the following year with many of its innovative style elements intact. That in itself was a key achievement, considering the complex approvals process governing the relationships between Nissan's many global design centres.

The ability to get forward-looking and sometimes confrontational designs through Nissan's management process has stood Albaisa in good stead: a stream of strong designs, including the Porsche-challenging »Nissan GT-R sports car in Japan and the »Nissan Qashqai and Juke crossovers in Europe, have been rewarded with sales success. In 2010, after three successful years leading Nissan Design Europe in London, Albaisa was named vice president of design at Nissan Design America.

ALFA ROMEO

ITALY | FOUNDED 1910 | SPORTING CARS | ALFAROMEO.COM

When it comes to passion and an exotic aura at an affordable price, there is only one carmaker that fits the bill: Alfa Romeo. Even the name has a romantic ring to it, redolent of everything glamorous and Italian; it's one of the few names that can be uttered in the same breath as Maserati or Ferrari (indeed, there is a connection with Ferrari, as the cars that formed the basis of Enzo Ferrari's first racing team were Grand Prix Alfa Romeos). The bloodline may have long since blurred, but instilled in every Alfa Romeo is the implicit promise that this is something a bit more special, a bit more touched by genius, than the average car. What is more, this emotional connection has remained remarkably resilient over the years, despite the many crises the company has suffered and despite a succession of poor products in the leaner times.

At the core of Alfa Romeo's appeal is the combination of beautiful exterior design (usually with the signature of »Bertone, »Pininfarina or »Giorgetto Giugiaro) and finely honed sports-car engineering under the skin. Although many Alfa Romeo models have fallen short in one or other of these areas and some in both, the very best have ticked both boxes and continue to be celebrated as true classics. The 1954 Giulietta Sprint, by Bertone, is just such an example: not only did it provide designer-label exotic looks at an everyday price, but it was also great to drive. The Giulia Sprint of the 1960s, the GTVs of the 1970s and 1990s, and the post-2005 Brera coupé all encapsulate just such a philosophy.

Coupés and open-topped Spiders have always been Alfa's forte, providing fertile ground for Italy's car designers to display their couture creations to appreciative audiences. Some of these cars, such as »Zagato's Ferrari-like Giulia TZ or the flamboyant Giulietta Sprint Speciale by Bertone, were manufactured in small quantities. By the time of later coupés, such as the Giugiaro wedge-shaped front-

2009 GIULIETTA

1954 GIULIETTA SPRINT

engined, rear-gearbox GTV of the 1970s, the driving experience had fallen behind that of such competitors as BMW, but the exotic style remained a powerful attraction.

A key moment in Alfa Romeo's history was the launch of the compact Alfasud in 1971. The first car to be styled by Giugiaro as an independent designer, the Alfasud's revvy flat-four engine, racy handling and low price made it an instant hit. Sadly, however, the entire Alfasud family proved to be fragile, unreliable and rust-prone, and few survive today.

Inspirational though the Alfasud was, Alfa Romeo's fortunes began to slide. Its products lost their aesthetic and technical focus, and customers deserted to rival brands, leaving Alfa as a quirky niche choice. The takeover by »Fiat in 1986 put Alfa Romeo on a more secure technical footing, yet, crucially, the company missed a trick in not allowing a strong enough design character to shine through: the feeling among many buyers was that Alfas had become little more than glorified Fiats.

Yet two breakthrough models – the Spider/GTV sports car pairing of 1995 and the 156 saloon of 1997 – showed that advanced design could rebuild Alfa Romeo's equity. The sports models, authored by Pininfarina and with their dramatic concept-car-like wedge profiles, were particularly good ambassadors for the brand, and also brought an up-to-date design language to the long-cherished Spider nameplate. The 156, acclaimed

1952 DISCO VOLANTE SPIDER

1969 GIULIA GTAM

1995 GTV

1910	ALFA founded
1915	ALFA acquired by entrepeneur Nicola Romeo
1923	First of ten Alfa wins in Targa Florio race
1930s	First of eleven Mille Miglia race wins
1933	Taken over by IRI as recession hits
1946	Resumes car production
1950–51	F1 world champion
1960s	Racing successes with Giulia TZ with 33
1968	Establishes plant for new small car
1975	World sports car championships with 33
1986	Ailing company acquired by Fiat

PRINCIPAL MODELS

1931	8C
1950	1900 saloon
1952	Disco Volante Spider
1954	Giulietta Sprint
1955	Giulietta Berlina
1960s	Giulia: saloon, Sprint GT, Spider Duetto, GTV, GTAm and TZ
1969	33 racing car
1971	Alfasud compact car
1972	Alfetta
1977	Giulietta
1974	Alfetta GTV
1983	Alfa 33 replaces Alfasud
1987	164 large saloon
1992	155
1994	145 replaces 33
1995	GTV, Spider
1997	156 medium saloon
2001	147
2003	Alfa GT
2005	159, Brera coupé
2006	Brera Spider
2007	8C Competizione
2008	MiTo replaces 147
2009	Giulietta

2007 8C COMPETIZIONE

1997-GENERATION 156

2005 159

for its looks and driving performance, confirmed Alfa Romeo as a credible brand in the growing sports-premium segment – precisely the type of car the company had invented in 1955 with the original Giulietta Berlina sedan.

The elegant six-headlamp face of the 156's successor, the »159, is a logical development of this theme: this look is at its most successful in the »Brera and post-2006 Brera Spider. Yet by the end of that decade Alfa Romeo had surprised – and even shocked – many with its chunky, confrontational design for the new »MiTo, a small car to compete with the Mini Cooper.

The MiTo incorporates cues from the blatantly retro »8C Competizione (by »Wolfgang Egger, now chief designer at Audi), and aspects of this new look, including the heart-shaped grille set lower, can be seen on Alfa's latest and most commercially significant product: the third incarnation of the »Giulietta. Designed to compete with the Volkswagen Golf and reviving Alfa's most celebrated name, the Giulietta may not be classically pretty in the vein of its forebear, but it achieves a skilful balance between boldness and universal acceptability. As such, it is right in line with Alfa's core values, and worthy of a marque with more standout designs than almost any other.

ALFA ROMEO 8C COMPETIZIONE

2007 | LUXURY SPORTS CAR

2010 8C COMPETIZIONE	
LENGTH	4380 mm (173 in.)
LAYOUT	Front engine, rear-wheel drive
ENGINE	4.7 petrol V8
HORSEPOWER	450
MAX. SPEED	292 km/h (181 mph)
CO_2 EMISSIONS	379 g/km

If good car design is a car that you can fall in love with in an instant, then Alfa Romeo's 8C Competizione exemplifies it. The carmaker's 'halo model', the model that inspires all the others, became an instant icon when it was first seen in concept form at the 2003 Frankfurt motor show.

Entering production four years later in a limited run of 500 specially produced cars, the 8C takes its styling references from classic Alfas from the 1960s, with similar volumes and detailing, although the car has a heritage that can be traced as far back as the 8C-2300 racing car of the 1930s.

The modern 8C, despite having the kind of classic and compact proportions so often dictated by a front-engined, rear-wheel-drive layout, manages to have a really quite soft and flowing form. With so little embellishment, the car is an example of sophisticated design restraint and is the kind of simple and classical sports-car design that hails from an earlier age.

The 8C Competizione and its later Spider derivative have already influenced all Alfas that have followed, and have given a new family face and a continuity of design that Alfa Romeo has not seen in recent years. The shield-shaped grille, frameless side windows, headlamp clusters and sculpted V-shaped hood have all gone on to become vital design cues for the broader Alfa Romeo line-up.

ALFA ROMEO 159

2005 | EXECUTIVE CAR

2010 3.2 V6 JTS	
LENGTH	4660 mm (183 in.)
LAYOUT	Front engine, front-wheel drive
ENGINE	3.2 petrol V6
HORSEPOWER	260
MAX. SPEED	250 km/h (155 mph)
CO$_2$ EMISSIONS	260 g/km

Introduced at the Geneva motor show in 2005, the 159 – a replacement for the successful 156 – was designed by the masterly »Giorgetto Giugiaro, working with Alfa Romeo Centro Stile in Milan. The resulting car is one of the best in its segment for sheer good looks, and Alfa was confident that it had finally produced a car that could more than level with the »BMW 3 Series. Even so, the 159 was launched into a segment that values quality, practicality and reputation above beauty, and nowhere was that more apparent than in the products of the 159's German rivals. For any Italian car it would be an uphill battle.

The 159 shares many visual cues with Alfa's »Brera coupé, although some observers felt it looked a little too similar to the 156 it replaced. The nose features the traditional Alfa Romeo triangular grille and hood, plus a cluster of three cylindrical lights on each side. The high waistline, which widens back to the C-pillar at the rear, ensures some musculature, yet overall the stance manages to convey lightness and precision, making the 159 an attractive alternative to the businesslike models produced by its opponents.

ALFA ROMEO BRERA

2005 | SPORTS CAR

2010 BRERA 2.0 JTDM	
LENGTH	4415 mm (175 in.)
LAYOUT	Front engine, front-wheel drive
ENGINE	2.0 turbo diesel 4-cyl
HORSEPOWER	170
MAX. SPEED	218 km/h (135 mph)
CO$_2$ EMISSIONS	142 g/km

The Brera concept, designed by »Giorgetto Giugiaro, was introduced at the 2002 Geneva motor show, and since its release in 2005 the car has been built by »Pininfarina. Although the initial concept version had a 390 horsepower V8 engine from Maserati, production engines proved disappointing: a 3.2-litre V6 was the most powerful offered, and even with this in place the press judged the Brera not quick enough for a car that is so beautiful and had so much promise.

But on the positive side, in terms of its styling the production version of the Brera had made it through almost unchanged from the concept: it was only just slightly smaller, and would ultimately become the replacement for Alfa's long-serving GTV, itself a Pininfarina design. The just-as-beautiful Brera Spider followed in 2006. It benefited from losing the two rear seats, a consequence of taking in the folding convertible roof; in the coupé the rear perches had in any case been so small as to be of next to no use.

Improvements to the powertrain and chassis settings would later improve the fabulous-looking Brera, but nevertheless it is disappointing that it still lacks the performance and handling it should by rights have had from the outset.

2006 CHEVROLET CAMARO CONCEPT

2007 CHEVROLET VOLT CONCEPT

ASTON MARTIN

GREAT BRITAIN | FOUNDED 1914 | LUXURY SPORTS CARS | ASTONMARTIN.COM

1958 DB4

2003 DB9 AND 1960s DB5

1980 LAGONDA SALOON

Even by the roller-coaster standards of most small British automakers, the long story of Aston Martin makes scary reading. Today, the firm is a globally admired maker of elegant and potent sports cars, on a par with Ferrari for exotic status and successful in international motorsport, but the story could so easily have been completely different. The company could have gone to the wall, as so many other specialist sports-car makers have done, at half a dozen points in its up-and-down history: on three or more occasions Aston Martin had to be rescued from bankruptcy, and at one stage it was even advertised for sale in *The Times* as a 'high class motor business'.

That classified newspaper advert of 1946 proved to be a key turning point for Aston Martin, for it was spotted by tractor magnate David Brown. It was under Brown's tenure in the 1950s that the company scored a succession of racetrack victories, and established the now-famous sports-car design language that would be later revived, when Aston Martin finally found stability and financial security under Ford's ownership in the 1990s, to define the style and the aura of the marque.

It was Brown's personal wealth that allowed Aston Martin to survive and grow

1966 DB6

2005 DBR9 RACING CAR

1990 VIRAGE VOLANTE

33

PRINCIPAL MODELS	
1950	DB2
1953	DB2/4
1958	DB4
1963	DB5
1966	DB6
1967	DBS
1976	Prototype Lagonda saloon, designed by William Towns
1977	V8 Vantage
1980	Lagonda saloon
1986	V8 Zagato
1990	Virage
1994	DB7
2001	V12 Vanquish
2002	DB7 Zagato limited edition
2003	DB9
2005	V8 Vantage
2006	Rapide concept
2007	DBS
2009	V12 Vantage; Lagonda SUV and One-77 concepts
2010	Rapide and One-77 production models
2011	Virage, V12 Zagato

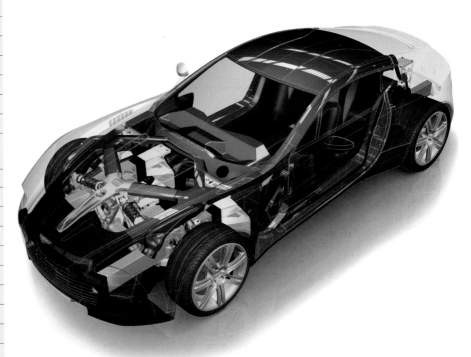

2009 ONE-77 CONCEPT

2009 LAGONDA SUV CONCEPT

in this formative phase without having to make a profit or satisfy shareholders. The crowning glory of this creative period was the fresh and graceful, but also strikingly modern, DB4 of 1958. Styled by Touring of Milan but incorporating the iconic shark-mouth grille shaped much earlier, reputedly by Aston body engineer Frank Feeley, the DB4 was the perfect synthesis of Italianate elegance and upper-class British refinement. The later DB5, essentially similar but with faired-in headlights, found global fame as secret agent James Bond's four-wheeled weapons system in the film *Goldfinger* (1964); this would be the first of seven movies in which an Aston Martin was Bond's vehicle of choice.

The DB6 of 1966 and, especially, the larger DBS of 1967 saw more muscular evolution of what had by now become a classic soft DB style; by the early 1970s, however, Aston's star was waning and its only product was the brutal and brawny V8 development of the DBS, with sharper lines and an aggressive-looking blanked-off grille. Through several changes in ownership over the next decade Aston Martin appeared to focus more on power than on refined style, although a brief flirtation with ultra-modernism in the shape of William Towns's razor-edged Lagonda saloon brought more criticisms than compliments.

Under Ford control in the 1990s Aston Martin was at last able to invest in the modernization of its models and its engineering. Styled by »Ian Callum, later to be Jaguar's head of design, the 1994 DB7 marked an emotional return to the voluptuous elegance and universally recognized grille profile that had characterized the 1950s and 1960s cars. The model was an immediate success and quickly became the brand's best-ever seller. It was followed in 2001 by the much larger V12 Vanquish, also by Callum; this unashamed top model saw Aston Martin square up against the glamorous Ferrari for the first time since the 1960s.

The arrival of ex-BMW designer »Henrik Fisker as chief designer in the same year saw a refinement and a smoothing out of Callum's template to produce the highly cultivated »DB9 and »V8 Vantage. The smooth and flowing shared design cues of these models are what continue to provide the aesthetic language for all Aston Martin models under Fisker's successor, »Marek Reichman. Nowhere is this more clearly visible than in Reichman's »Rapide, in effect a DB9 extended in length to form a four-door luxury saloon. Although this tricky task has been accomplished with much grace and beauty, the price of Aston Martin's new-found global identity is a sometimes disappointing uniformity across its model ranges.

While the occasional (and often highly eccentric) »Zagato-styled versions of Aston Martin models have become highly prized collectors' items, one diversion was less than welcome: the brash and overstated SUV concept presented at the 2009 Geneva show to mark the return of the Aston-owned Lagonda brand to the luxury-car market.

2006 RAPIDE CONCEPT

ASTON MARTIN DB9

2003 | LUXURY SPORTS CAR

2010 DB9	
LENGTH	4710 mm (186 in.)
LAYOUT	Front engine, real-wheel drive
ENGINE	5.9 petrol V12
HORSEPOWER	477
MAX. SPEED	306 km/h (190 mph)
CO_2 EMISSIONS	368 g/km

The DB9, successor to the much-feted DB7 of 1994, was eagerly anticipated before it became available back in the early 2000s. How on earth would Aston Martin improve upon the aesthetics and timelessness of the outgoing DB7, considered to be a modern classic and – at the time – one of the most beautiful Aston Martins ever?

But the more relevant question was, who actually designed the DB9? Who contributed most to its form? Was it »Ian Callum (who had left Aston Martin to lead Jaguar's design operations), or new design director »Henrik Fisker? Only those present at the time have the answer, but in truth both men had an influential hand in it, with Fisker finishing what Callum had begun.

What matters most is that the DB9 emerged with breathtakingly clean and harmonious proportions that built upon the tradition of the archetypal British GT sports car and put the design in contention for the most beautiful sports car of all time. Whoever's pen it came from, Aston's DB9 represents a high-water mark in luxury car design, just as the graceful DB4 did almost half a century earlier.

2005 DBR9 RACING CAR

ASTON MARTIN ONE-77

2010 | EXTREME SPORTS CAR

2011 ONE-77	
LENGTH	–
LAYOUT	Front engine, rear-wheel drive
ENGINE	7.3 petrol V12
HORSEPOWER	750
MAX. SPEED	350 km/h (218 mph)
CO$_2$ EMISSIONS	–

If the »DB9 represents automotive design at its most beautiful, then it is possible that the One-77 may elevate automotive design into an art form for Aston Martin. And as is the case with fine art, it is expensive to collect and hard to obtain.

The car was first revealed at the 2009 Geneva motor show, and went into production just eighteen months later, in 2010. Limited to a production run of only seventy-seven units, the bespoke One-77 is hand-built at Aston Martin's Gaydon HQ in Warwickshire, and has a carbon-fibre chassis and an extruded body tub clothed in handcrafted aluminium bodywork.

The One-77's combination of traditional craft techniques with leading-edge technology is proving to be a seductive proposition – if Aston's order-book figures are to be believed. The £1.2 million price tag (plus taxes) will buy a 750 horsepower, 7.3-litre V12-engined hypercar with a projected weight of just 1500 kilograms (3307 lb); the build process alone is estimated to take 2700 man-hours to complete.

Visually, the One-77 is as extreme as its price tag and is dominated front and side by gill vents that at the front incorporate possibly the most complicated headlamp design ever seen. The rear of the car is a single panel entirely unspoiled by any shut lines, and the wing mirrors appear to be extruded from the car's body, as if still liquid.

ASTON MARTIN RAPIDE
2010 | LUXURY FOUR-DOOR COUPÉ

2010 RAPIDE	
LENGTH	5020 mm (198 in.)
LAYOUT	Front engine, rear-wheel drive
ENGINE	6.0 petrol V12
HORSEPOWER	477
MAX. SPEED	303 km/h (188 mph)
CO_2 EMISSIONS	355 g/km

Many observers would have judged it an impossible endeavour to take the existing curvaceous silhouette of a »DB9, lengthen it to the proportions of a four-seater grand tourer, and still retain so much beauty.

Yet the Aston Martin Rapide may even have managed to trump the DB9 aesthetically. The Rapide is undoubtedly one of the most elegant Aston Martins ever built, and almost certainly the most beautiful four-seater luxury sports car in the world. In all likelihood it will be the car that will remain most closely associated with its designer, Aston Martin design chief »Marek Reichman, who pushed for an elegant design when tasked with creating the four-door, four-seat Aston by CEO Ulrich Bez. The Rapide concept was unveiled at the 2006 Detroit auto show and the response was ecstatic.

In the end, the Rapide production model had grown 25 millimetres (1 in.) taller and 10 millimitres ($^3/_8$ in.) longer than the concept, in order to improve the interior package so that 2 metre-tall (6ft 6in.) Reichman himself could sit in the back – yet all without making the car visually appear taller. With this focus on rear-seat access, that such a very elegant exterior appearance was maintained is testament to the passion, skill and dogged determination of the Rapide's design team.

ASTON MARTIN V8 VANTAGE
2005 | LUXURY SPORTS CAR

2010 4.7 V8	
LENGTH	4385 mm (173 in.)
LAYOUT	Front engine, rear-wheel drive
ENGINE	4.7 petrol V8
HORSEPOWER	426
MAX. SPEED	288 km/h (179 mph)
CO_2 EMISSIONS	328 g/km

Arguably »Henrik Fisker's finest design, the Vantage took the graceful Aston Martin »DB9 form and design cues and reshaped them by adding a raw, muscular energy.

The idea behind the V8 Vantage was to build a smaller car using a shortened DB9 chassis that could compete with the iconic »Porsche 911, and the result is as precocious as any Aston has ever looked. The form of the Vantage, perhaps more than any other car in the current line-up, communicates a singular sense of purpose and is more brutal, even aggressive, compared to the usual Aston Martin elegance.

Introduced at the Geneva motor show in 2005, Aston's smallest and possibly coolest two-seat, two-door sports car has classic sports-car proportions: a long hood and a cabin set far back with a wide stance. Writer and broadcaster Jeremy Clarkson concluded that the Vantage was 'an Aston Martin for gentleman thugs', and there is no doubt that the car lacks some of the grace of other Aston Martins. This has proved to work entirely in the company's favour, as the Vantage is picking up buyers who might otherwise have spent their money with Mercedes-Benz or Porsche.

AUDI

GERMANY | FOUNDED 1909 | PREMIUM CARS AND SUVS | AUDI.COM

No other car company is as closely identified with excellence in design – and the consistent delivery of impeccable design – as Audi. A subsidiary of Volkswagen since the 1960s, Audi has systematically built up what is probably the most powerful design identity in the car business. This is a considerable achievement, considering the rapid expansion of the brand's model range from just sedans and station-wagons in the 1980s to take in compact cars and luxury cars in the 1990s, and SUVs, crossovers, supercars and superminis after the turn of the millennium.

Spanning so many segments, the modern Audi look is all the more powerful as it is founded not on such pasted-on design cues as grille frames and light shapes, but on the smooth execution of the complete design and the pure and elegant manner in which surfaces are handled and details are defined. Whether it is a large SUV, such as the Q7, a supercar such as the »R8 or a Mini Cooper competitor in the shape of the A1, the design cues are different, but it is always clearly an Audi. The Audi quality can be seen running right through the complete design, from the way such key exterior details as precise tyre-to-wheel-arch clearances are handled, to the fit and feel of the switches on the dashboard and the meticulous graphics of the instrumentation.

Yet there is much more to Audi design than the rigid application of a thick brand book and the strict control of form language and surfaces. The company has rarely shocked or startled – although the radically proportioned 1991 Avus quattro concept by »J. Mays and »Martin Smith might be counted an exception. Instead, its products come across as classically modern, still displaying the Bauhaus-style simplicity and purity of surface that characterized the two streams of influence that made up its first designs: the breathtaking modernity of the 1967

1986 80

1980 QUATTRO

HISTORY

1909	August Horch founds Audi in Zwickau
1932	Auto Union formed from Audi, DKW, Horch and Wanderer
1949	Auto Union re-established in Ingolstadt
1959	Daimler Benz takes control
1965	Becomes part of Volkswagen
1969	Combines with NSU to form Audi NSU Auto Union, later Audi AG
1974	Ex-Porsche Ferdinand Piëch becomes technical director
1976	Hartmut Warkuss becomes chief designer
1982	Enters world rally championship with Quattro
1991	Martin Smith becomes chief designer
1994	Peter Schreyer takes over as chief designer
1998	Takes over Lamborghini
2002	Walter de'Silva becomes chief designer
2007	Wolfgang Egger takes over as chief designer
2008	Audi sells more than 1 million units per year for the first time

1967 NSU RO80

1982 100

1987 PIKES PEAK AUDI QUATTRO RACING CAR

2000 A2

NSU Ro80 and the down-to-earth solidity of the Auto Union-derived models.

Audi designs have been profoundly influential within the auto industry for three decades or more, from the 1982 100 that opened up the aerodynamic era, to the 1998 »TT that launched the idea of the boutique sports coupé and the A2 of 2000, the first aluminium-construction small car. In the same year the Steppenwolf concept was the first to propose a tough, high-riding but sensibly compact-sized crossover; by the end of the decade dozens of automakers had this type of vehicle in volume production.

Particularly accomplished was the way Audi upgraded the original TT – by this time universally celebrated as a classic design icon – for its 2006 relaunch: the new version was more muscular and more powerfully planted in its stance, but still conveyed the geometric purity of its forebear.

Since the arrival of »Wolfgang Egger as chief designer in 2007, Audi designs – beginning with the »A5 coupé – have begun to allow slightly more emotion and sensuality into the crafting of their lines. Yet when the company was put to the test in 2010 with the launch of its »A1 rival to the Mini Cooper in the premium small segment, it opted for a classically simple and pure design, in contrast to the Mini's mass of busy, overstated detailing and retro design cues.

Audi's *Vorsprung durch Technik* mission statement ('progress through technology') is no hollow slogan, either. Over the years the company has been responsible for such key innovations as five-cylinder engines, turbocharging, quattro four-wheel drive, direct-injection diesel and petrol engines, galvanized bodies, aluminium structures, dual clutch gearboxes and, most recently, concepts that make high-performance electric cars attractive. Yet it is a measure of the quality of Audi design that the precisely milled, millimetre-perfect execution of its exterior style can always trump the technology that is underneath.

2000 STEPPENWOLF CONCEPT

2002 ROSEMEYER CONCEPT

2003 NUVOLARI QUATTRO CONCEPT

PRINCIPAL MODELS

1967	NSU Ro80
1968	100
1969	100 S coupé
1979	200 Turbo
1980	Quattro
1982	100
1986	80
1988	V8
1991	Cabriolet; Quattro Spyder and Avus quattro concepts
1994	A4, A6, A8
1995	TT concept
1996	A3
1997	A6 (2nd gen); Al2 concept
1998	TT
2000	A2; Steppenwolf concept
2002	A8 (2nd gen); Rosemeyer concept
2003	Le Mans Quattro, Pikes Peak Quattro and Nuvolari Quattro concepts
2004	A6 (3rd gen)
2005	Q7
2006	R8, TT Mk2; Roadjet concept
2007	A5; A1 Metroproject quattro concept
2009	A5 Sportback, A8 (3rd gen); e-tron concept
2010	A1, A7; Quattro concept

2008 Q7 (V12)

2010 QUATTRO CONCEPT

2009 E-TRON CONCEPT

AUDI A1

2010 | COMPACT CAR

2010 1.4 TFSI	
LENGTH	3955 mm (156 in.)
LAYOUT	Front engine, front-wheel drive
ENGINE	1.4 turbo petrol 4-cyl
HORSEPOWER	122
MAX. SPEED	200 km/h (124 mph)
CO_2 EMISSIONS	119 g/km

By the time of the commercial launch of Audi's compact city car it felt as if we'd been looking at it for years. Audi had shown its A1 model in concept form on no fewer than three separate occasions before its official introduction at the 2010 Geneva motor show. Previewed at the 2007 Tokyo motor show as the Audi Metroproject quattro concept car, the A1 was seen again in five-door Sportback form in 2008 before making a further appearance in e-tron electric form.

Audi's smallest car, the A1 has been created to offer all of Audi's virtues in a car less than 4 metres (13 ft) long – and also to steal premium sales in the sub-compact segment from such cars as BMW's »Mini Cooper and the »Alfa Romeo MiTo. Much of any premium car's appeal lies in the brand, not the vehicle. Although almost identical under the skin to the cheaper »Volkswagen Polo and even the SEAT Ibiza, the A1 is clearly a pure Audi in design, precise and predictable, and deliberately avoiding the wild-card factor that draws customers to the Mini and MiTo. Even its defining colour-contrasted roof arch, which dominates the exterior design, is an optional item. Clearly, the A1 is yet another Audi that asks to be differentiated by size, not style.

AUDI A3

2003 | MEDIUM CAR

MODEL HISTORY 1996 A3 1ST GENERATION • 2003 A3 2ND GENERATION

2010 1.8 TFSI	
LENGTH	4240 mm (168 in.)
LAYOUT	Front engine, front-wheel drive
ENGINE	2.0 turbo petrol 4-cyl
HORSEPOWER	160
MAX. SPEED	222 km/h (138 mph)
CO$_2$ EMISSIONS	155g/km

It's difficult to believe now, but when the Audi A3 was introduced into the »Volkswagen Golf segment back in 1996 there was just as much controversy surrounding its arrival as there would be a decade and a half later with the »Audi A1. The question then was whether Audi should be manufacturing such a small car and whether a premium car had any place in the segment at all – particularly when the A3 could potentially steal sales from the VW Golf, the principal cash cow of Audi's parent company. Now, the discussion is just the same, but with the A1 and the »VW Polo substituted for the A3 and the Golf.

Initially the first-generation A3 was sold only as a three-door hatchback in order to differentiate it from the Golf and to ensure a sportier offer to consumers. In silhouette the A3 became flatter towards the rear, suggesting a sporty coupé form. The second-generation A3, designed by »Walter de'Silva, was introduced in 2003, while the roomier five-door Sportback version followed in 2004 with a much more aggressive full-depth grille graphic. Since then, both models have become edgier, with tauter surfaces and more aggressive DRG.

A hint at the third-generation A3 was given by a concept car displayed at the Geneva motor show in 2011. Unlike any previous A3, this was a four-door sedan, large and imposing in its presence and more akin to an »A4.

1996 A3

AUDI A4
2007 | EXECUTIVE CAR

MODEL HISTORY 1994 A4 1ST GENERATION • 2000 A4 2ND GENERATION • 2005 A4 3RD GENERATION • 2007 A4 4TH GENERATION

2010 2.0 TDI	
LENGTH	4700 mm (186 in.)
LAYOUT	Front engine, front-wheel drive
ENGINE	2.0 turbo diesel 4-cyl
HORSEPOWER	120
MAX. SPEED	205 km/h (127 mph)
CO_2 EMISSIONS	134 g/km

The Audi A4 nameplate took over from the Audi 80 (designed by »Martin Smith) as Audi's mainstay medium model in 1994. In common with the »A3, the »TT and especially the short-lived A2, the styling of the first-generation Audi A4 has »Peter Schreyer to thank for its clean, clear body panels with an emphasis on the minimization of shut lines.

Schreyer based the clearly identifiable design language he developed for Audi on the Auto Union racing cars of the 1930s, continuing a process that had begun with »J. Mays's influential Avus quattro concept of 1991. Since then, the clean, clear form of the A4 has been embellished over time and tweaked to add more emotion. The second-generation A4 was first seen at the end of 2000 and was heavily influenced by the »Audi A6, although the continuity with its predecessor was very strong.

By 2004 »Walter de'Silva's influence saw the introduction on the A4 of the full-height, tall trapezoidal front grille – or 'goatee' – first rolled out on the third-generation Audi A6 and still present on current Audi models. A further revision in 2007 saw a sharpening up of details and, for the first time, the appearance of a subtle swage line along the flanks. Some would say the key emotion being expressed here is increased forcefulness, taking the brand towards greater visual drama.

1994 A4

2007-GENERATION A4 ALLROAD

AUDI A5
2007 | LUXURY COUPÉ, CONVERTIBLE

2010 3.0 V6 TDI	
LENGTH	4625 mm (183 in.)
LAYOUT	Front engine, front-wheel drive
ENGINE	3.0 turbo diesel V6
HORSEPOWER	240
MAX. SPEED	250 km/h (155 mph)
CO_2 EMISSIONS	173 g/km

Based on the Nuvolari quattro concept car introduced in 2003, the A5 coupé is, said »Walter de'Silva, head of Volkswagen Group design at the time, 'the most beautiful car I have ever designed'. There is no doubt that the A5 is one of the more striking designs in the current Audi family. It is more handsome and certainly more emotional than other Audi designs – perhaps with the exception of the »A7 sportback – and represents a step forward for the marque as it adds some passion to a brand that was beginning to feel a little devoid of warmth.

The production A5 was introduced in 2007 as the third coupé in Audi's line-up, after the »TT and »R8. It manages to take the elegance of other Audi sedans and yet, by mixing traditional Audi design cues with the aggressive front end and flowing body surfaces, be different enough. Of all Audi's current products, the A5 manages to achieve the ideal balance of emotion and elegant restraint.

A five-door sportback version followed, created by Audi design head »Wolfgang Egger. Although less beautiful than the coupé, it is more practical yet avoids the ordinariness of a regular saloon, and is another example of Audi's niche filling.

AUDI A6, A7

20011 (A6), 2010 (A7) | LARGE EXECUTIVE CAR

MODEL HISTORY 1994 A6 1ST GENERATION • 1997 A6 2ND GENERATION • 2004 A6 3RD GENERATION • 2010 A7 • 2011 A6 4TH GENERATION

2010 A6 2.0 TDI	
LENGTH	4930mm (195 in.)
LAYOUT	Front engine, front-wheel drive
ENGINE	2.0 turbo diesel 4-cyl
HORSEPOWER	136
MAX. SPEED	208 km/h (129 mph)
CO_2 EMISSIONS	139 g/km

2011 A6

2010 A7 SPORTBACK

A replacement for the Audi 100, the first-generation Audi A6 was introduced in 1994 to rival BMW's 5 Series and Mercedes-Benz's E-Class. This initial A6 suffered from a similar identity problem to the »A8 in that it looked too similar to the smaller »A4. To many consumers, the cars were distinguishable only by their physical size and the alphanumeric badges on their trunk lids.

Since then each generation of A6 has added greater tension and dynamism as part of a design development process that began under »Walter de'Silva and has continued across all Audi's products. The sweeping, single-arched roofline introduced in the 1997 model change was a major step forward in premium-car architecture. A more dynamic shoulder line, in combination with a more aggressive face, now suggests greater power and performance. Yet despite such changes, when side-by-side with its siblings the third-generation A6, introduced in 2004, still looks a little stuffy.

A hint of the fourth-generation A6 was provided by the A7 Sportback in 2010, itself previewed by the Sportback concept shown at Detroit the previous year. The production A7, a luxury five-door coupé designed to compete against the Mercedes-Benz CLS and BMW 5 Series Gran Turismo, shares its principal architecture with the A6 sedan. The A7 is slimmer and more athletic, and brings a greater crispness to Audi's design language: the sharp edge to the fastback tailgate references the Audi 100 coupé from the late 1960s. Unusually, the A7 was developed without a formal design brief,

so it represents the uncompromised preferences of the designers. Perhaps for this reason the A7 is exceptionally attractive in the metal.

For its part, the new A6 brings added sophistication into the more restrained format of the four-door sedan, but with a lower and more purposeful frontal stance than the outgoing generation.

AUDI A8

2009 | LUXURY CAR

MODEL HISTORY 1994 A8 1ST GENERATION • 2002 A8 2ND GENERATION • 2009 A8 3RD GENERATION

2010 4.2 V8	
LENGTH	5140 mm (203 in.)
LAYOUT	Front engine, all-wheel drive
ENGINE	4.2 petrol V8
HORSEPOWER	372
MAX. SPEED	250 km/h (155 mph)
CO₂ EMISSIONS	219 g/km

Audi's luxurious A8 sedan was launched in 1994 into a market dominated by BMW and Mercedes-Benz. It was the first series production car to have an aluminium spaceframe structure and bodywork, yet, although it was well received at its launch, there was little to distinguish it from the cheaper »A4 other than its bigger size. This contributed to disappointing sales for the A8. By the time of the 2002 model year restyle, the car had begun to take on a distinct and separate character from its A4 and »A6 siblings, and this process has continued.

In the eyes of the market, the A8 may not yet have quite caught up with the top premium status of the »Mercedes S-Class and »BMW 7 Series, but with its lower stance, more cockpit-like driving position and firmer chassis it could be seen as offering a sportier and more youthful alternative. This trend was confirmed in 2009 with the latest A8, the biggest in the Audi range. Adopting a more graceful look thanks to a more pronounced shoulder line, it has begun to look both classy and very sporty, at a time when its two home-grown rivals may have begun to lose their way.

2002-GENERATION A8

1994-GENERATION A8

AUDI R8

2006 | LUXURY SPORTS CAR

2010 4.2 V8	
LENGTH	4430 mm (175 in.)
LAYOUT	Mid engine, all-wheel drive
ENGINE	4.2 petrol V8
HORSEPOWER	420
MAX. SPEED	301 km/h (187 mph)
CO$_2$ EMISSIONS	349 g/km

When Audi unveiled its production R8 supercar at the 2006 Paris motor show it was something unusual. Not just because it represented a new avenue for the brand and a serious challenge to Porsche but also because, unusually, it added even more drama than the Le Mans concept that had been shown three years earlier. Normally, production cars are toned-down versions of concepts.

As the R8 was the brand's first mid-engined sports car – and a car that would inevitably become a 'halo model' or brand hero for Audi – it was perhaps no surprise that its design was more extreme than had been seen at Audi before. Guided by then head of design »Walter de'Silva, the design of the R8 looks so technical because key functional elements, such as the huge air intakes for cooling at the front, were made fundamental elements of the design rather than added as an afterthought.

The R8 has somehow succeeded in finding a form that combines the muscularity of its sculpture with calm, even elegant surfaces, all driven by the revelation of its technology. Second only to the front vents are the two side blades, which also direct air for cooling. These blades are picked out in a contrast finish to highlight their function.

Interestingly, on the R8 Audi chose to position the four rings of the logo not on the grille but higher up, on the hood. This could be seen as a sign of confidence in how recognizable it would be as an Audi. The R8 also introduced the LED daytime running

lights that not only gave the design so much attitude but also would become an identifiable Audi signature across the entire range.

The R8's launch model, using a 4.2-litre V8 engine, was swiftly followed by a V10 edition, and then a concept with a V12 diesel and a different frontal treatment. The later open-topped Spyder version is aesthetically less pleasing, the loss of the roof and the signature contrast colour side blades changing the visual harmony of the car and leaving it with an unbalanced side profile.

2010 AUDI R8 SPYDER

AUDI TT

2006 | SPORTS CAR

MODEL HISTORY 1998 TT 1ST GENERATION • 2006 TT 2ND GENERATION

2010 3.2 V6	
LENGTH	4180 mm (165 in.)
LAYOUT	Front engine, all-wheel drive
ENGINE	3.2 petrol V6
HORSEPOWER	250
MAX. SPEED	250 km/h (155 mph)
CO$_2$ EMISSIONS	247 g/km

Undoubtedly one of the automotive world's most instantly recognizable designs, the original Audi TT would become a halo car for Audi and revolutionize the brand's image in terms of its design and execution. Exceptionally, such was the resonance of the TT's design that it was quickly recognized outside the normally insular environment of automobiles and took on iconic status in the wider world of architecture and product design.

The TT began life as an extremely well crafted concept car, introduced at the 1995 Los Angeles motor show. With its clean, smooth and unspoiled lines – inspired by the Bauhaus art and design movement – the petite TT coupé resembled the result of an unconstrained product-design exercise more than it did a conventional automotive product. The shape of the original concept is credited to »Peter Schreyer and »Freeman Thomas, with the interior by designer Romulus Rost. As in the case of Alec Issigonis's late-1950s Mini, the original Audi TT is believed to have begun as a casual paper sketch by Thomas in 1994.

In its design the TT clearly referenced Auto Union racing cars of the 1930s, just as the Audi Avus showcar designed by »J. Mays had done, and, again as was the case with the Avus, the TT added much-needed drama to a brand that had for too long been regarded as an unexciting rival to other premium German labels. The first-generation TT made it from concept to production with minimal changes in 1998; the only visible difference was the addition of a rear quarter-window on each side, something that improved the overall balance.

The second generation, in 2006, traded the original TT's perfect roundness, purity and geometric control in favour of a more masculine, more securely planted stance on the road, an update that moved the design in the direction of the market but that also cleverly kept continuity with the original.

1998 AUDI TT

2006 AUDI TT

CHRIS BANGLE

UNITED STATES | BORN 1956 | CAR DESIGNER AND MANAGER

It is a measure of Chris Bangle's impact on the auto industry that he is at the same time one of the most celebrated designers ever to have put pen to paper, and one of the most controversial – and even despised. No other designer has had to endure the indignity of grass-roots online hate campaigns and 'get him out' petitions, yet few have had such a profound influence on automotive design and how designers interact with car-company management.

Bangle's best-known work was with »BMW, where his 2001 »7 Series polarized opinion but created the template for a decade of designs that set the German sports sedan manufacturer apart from its more conservatively orientated arch-rival, Mercedes-Benz. At motor shows and other such events Bangle, who has a deep-seated belief in the car as sculpture and art, could be seen contemplating his designs for long periods, engaged by what he often described as the tension, control and craftsmanship of their lines. Car designers, in common with artists, are in love with their creations, he has been fond of saying.

After graduating from the Art Center College of Design in Pasadena, California, in 1981 (he had earlier toyed with the idea of becoming a priest) Bangle joined »Opel in Germany as an interior designer. In 1984 he moved to Fiat in Italy, where he became head of the exterior design the following year. The design that first flagged him up as a controversial figure in the industry was the 1993 Fiat Coupé, released after he had already left for BMW. The Coupé's rounded contours, its flanks dramatically gashed by deep slanting cuts that clashed with the underlying curves, divided the critics, although most loved the painted-metal dashboard finish and the driving experience. The Fiat Barchetta roadster, launched in 1997, is also attributed to Bangle.

Having gained the confidence of BMW management, Bangle set about convincing them that for the company to advance it would be necessary to break from the strictures of its past, and even from the conventions of the car business. Show concepts such as the Z9 coupé of 1999 gave a foretaste of what Bangle described as flame surfacing – the juxtaposition of convex and concave surfaces and creases to produce a dynamic effect. But the Z9 and the less extreme convertible that followed in 2000 were greeted with bafflement bordering on hostility, few commentators realizing that these would be the blueprints for the big »BMW 6 Series models launched into production in 2003. An asymmetrically bodied study for a high-riding coupé at the 2001 Detroit show caused still further head-scratching.

But it was the 2001 »BMW 7 Series luxury sedan that was the first to stir up the hornet's nest. The polar opposite of the slender, understated and classically restrained third-generation 7 Series from which it took over, the Bangle 7 came across as big, bulky and confrontational; critics rounded especially ferociously on its apparently tacked-on raised trunk line, which soon became known disparagingly as the Bangle butt. *Time* magazine named it one of the fifty worst cars of all time, yet it went on to become commercially successful. Tellingly, Bangle was quoted in a *Business Week* interview as saying 'we aren't copying anyone else's design language, not even our own, and I think that makes some people uncomfortable'.

Bangle's once-divisive boldness was vindicated in the years that followed with a series of well-received designs, notably the 2003 »BMW 5 Series sedan and Z4 sports roadster. These intensified the flame-surfacing theme with concave panels and slanted creases, but the designs worked much better and the heavy, slab-sided look of the 7 was avoided. However, controversy returned in 2004 with the launch of the compact 1 Series, with its long hood and truncated tail, although, as the Bangle 7 had been, the Bangle 1 was commercially successful.

A notable design study displaying Bangle's imagination and desire for fresh approaches was the Gina concept for an open two-seater sports car, revealed in 2008. Fabric rather than sheet metal is used for its exterior surfaces, and its forms can thus be altered in an organic way. For example, the hood is able to part in the middle to reveal the engine, and the slots for the headlights open and shut as if they were eyes.

1999 BMW Z9 CONCEPT

1993 FIAT COUPÉ

2008 BMW GINA CONCEPT

Bangle parted from BMW in 2009, announcing that he wished to work outside the auto industry. An always passionate figure, he divided opinion with his designs like no one else, yet the fact that so many other manufacturers have adopted aspects of his surface techniques is testament to his lasting influence on car design.

2001 BMW 7 SERIES

BENTLEY
GREAT BRITAIN | FOUNDED 1919 | SUPER-LUXURY CARS | BENTLEYMOTORS.COM

HISTORY

1919	Aero engine-maker W.O. Bentley builds his first car engine
1921	Sells first car
1924	First of five Le Mans 24 Hours wins
1931	Taken over by rival Rolls-Royce
1935	W.O. Bentley leaves to join Lagonda
1970	Rolls-Royce group collapses
1980	Rolls-Royce Motors, including Bentley, bought by Vickers
1992	Rolls-Royce sales two-to-one in favour of Bentley
1997	Bentley put up for sale by Vickers
1998	Acquired by Volkswagen
2003	Brand split means BMW takes over rights to Rolls-Royce; Bentley wins Le Mans
2008	Bentley announces CO$_2$ reduction strategy

1952 R-TYPE CONTINENTAL

Given Bentley's current status as one of the world's premier super-luxury carmakers, it is hard to believe that it faced extinction at several points during its ninety-year history.

A string of wins at the prestigious Le Mans 24 Hours in the 1920s made Bentley world-famous, but the company did not have the stamina to survive the business collapse following the 1929 Wall Street Crash and was scooped up by rival Rolls-Royce. Under Rolls-Royce the Bentley identity was steadily squeezed out so that – with the exception of such special models as the R-Type Continental – by the 1960s Bentleys had become no more than clones of the equivalent Rolls, and sales dwindled to a tiny proportion of the Crewe factory's already low hand-built output.

Ownership by Vickers in the 1980s brought a belated realization that Bentley's illustrious heritage could be lucrative commercially, and that muscular performance combined with exquisite

luxury could be an attractive proposition to a rising generation of wealthy individuals. The result was the Mulsanne Turbo, whose surging power and gentlemen's-club interior provided the template for all Bentleys that followed.

After Volkswagen's controversial takeover of Bentley in 1998, further shock was expressed when VW appointed Skoda designer »Dirk van Braeckel to lead Bentley design. It was hard to imagine two companies further apart in customer profile than Skoda and Bentley, but Van Braeckel steered the shaping of a new generation of so-called mid-size Bentleys, spearheaded by the »Continental GT coupé; these lower-priced but still massively powerful models use VW Group engineering elements under the skin but proved tremendously successful during the boom years up to 2008, raising Bentley sales to record highs of more than 10,000 cars a year and allowing the company to record a profit for the first time in decades. Even Queen Elizabeth II played her part in these boom years for Bentley: the State Limousine, delivered in time for the British queen's

Golden Jubilee in 2002, marked the first time the head of state had used anything other than a Rolls-Royce or Daimler for a state occasion.

The Continental GT had arrived after a very emotional return of the Bentley racing team to Le Mans in 2001; victory followed in 2003, using a car derived largely from the previously successful Audi Le Mans racers. The Le Mans return had been hinted at by the presentation in 1999 of the awkwardly titled Hunaudières supercar concept. As with all Bentleys, it took its name from the Le Mans track, yet, styled by VW chief designer »Hartmut Warkuss and assembled from Volkswagen Group components (including a Lamborghini chassis and a mid-mounted VW 8-litre W16 engine), the Hunaudières was seen as a worrying sign of an impending 'Germanization' of Bentley design; some saw it as a 'me-too' supercar that was alien to the Bentley heritage. In the event, the Hunaudières proved a blind alley for Bentley and the engineering layout was taken up for the VW Group's next elite brand, in the shape of the »Bugatti Veyron 16.4.

1930 8-LITRE AND 2009 MULSANNE

Worries that Bentley would lose its aristocratic British exclusivity in the face of rising sales and increasing component sharing with the VW Group gradually evaporated. Van Braeckel skilfully modernized Bentley's design language, making the models sleeker and more firmly grounded and keeping both the traditionalists and the new customers happy. His sure hand has most recently been seen in the last cars based on the old Arnage architecture, the Azure convertible and the particularly accomplished Brooklands coupé, as well as in the elegant, powerfully poised stance of the new »Bentley Mulsanne saloon – all indicating the return of true Bentley individualism in the very highest segment of all.

1995 AZURE

BENTLEY CONTINENTAL GT

2010 | SUPER-LUXURY CAR

MODEL HISTORY 2002 BENTLEY CONTINENTAL 1ST GENERATION • 2010 BENTLEY CONTINENTAL 2ND GENERATION

2010 6.0 W12	
LENGTH	4805 mm (190 in.)
LAYOUT	Front engine, all-wheel drive
ENGINE	6.0 turbo petrol W12
HORSEPOWER	560
MAX. SPEED	318 km/h (197 mph)
CO2 EMISSIONS	396 g/km

Expectations, and also apprehensions, ran high in the run-up to the launch of the so-called MSB (medium-size Bentley) just after the turn of the millennium. In the wake of the Volkswagen takeover there was excitement at the prospect of new investment and an all-new, more accessible Bentley line, but this was tempered by worries that it would be built on the platform of the VW Phaeton and thus would be little more than a gentrified Volkswagen.

In the event, concerns were swiftly allayed when »Dirk van Braeckel's powerful, solidly planted shape for the Continental GT coupé was revealed. Its size and flowing curves were a big departure for Bentley, but a broad spectrum of enthusiasts immediately rushed to own this massively powerful piece of Anglo-German engineering. An attractive convertible and the less elegantly proportioned Flying Spur sedan followed, each later gaining an even more performance-focused Speed derivative.

The latest chapter in the Continental saga is the second-generation GT coupé, released in 2010. Although it was billed as a full model change, little seems to have changed externally apart from large, »Mulsanne-like headlights and a raising in the line of the trunk – to the detriment of the overall proportions.

2002 CONTINENTAL GT

BENTLEY MULSANNE

2009 | SUPER-LUXURY CAR

DATA 2010	
LENGTH	5575 mm (220 in.)
LAYOUT	Front engine, rear-wheel drive
ENGINE	6.8 turbo petrol V8
HORSEPOWER	512
MAX. SPEED	296 km/h (184 mph)
CO_2 EMISSIONS	393 g/km

It certainly felt as if the successor to Bentley's ageing Arnage limousine had been a long time coming when it was introduced at the 2009 Pebble Beach Concours d'Elegance in California. The Mulsanne was the first flagship Bentley in almost eighty years to have been designed independently of its former parent, Rolls-Royce, yet when it arrived the response was not universally positive.

The automotive world had changed, such that for the first time in its history Bentley was creating a car that would go up against a Rolls-Royce. The smaller »Rolls-Royce Ghost is an all-too-capable rival for the Mulsanne.

Taller and 150 millimetres (5⅞ in.) longer than the Arnage it replaces, the Mulsanne has a huge on-road presence thanks to its sheer size alone. With a long V-shaped hood and locomotive-style shoulders influenced by the earlier Brooklands coupé, the Mulsanne has a short front overhang and a long rear one, suggesting power and movement. Although it succeeds in fusing Bentley sportiness and upper-class elegance, the design may be a little too muscular for some (particularly in its haunches), making the Mulsanne less graceful than its predecessor. The result is a flagship Bentley that is perhaps a little too imposing, if such a thing is possible.

BERTONE

ITALY | FOUNDED 1912 | DESIGN, COACHBUILDING AND MANUFACTURE | BERTONE.IT

The real genius behind Carrozzeria Bertone was Nuccio Bertone, who in 1933 joined the coachbuilding business his father, Giovanni Bertone, had founded in 1912. Armed with a training in business, Nuccio realized that the market for luxurious one-off special cars for wealthy individual customers was dwindling and that the future lay in the styling – and, later, manufacture – of cars for automotive companies. Paradoxically, however, it was an overcommitment to industrial manufacture that would eventually bring Bertone to its knees in 2007, a decade after the death of its inspirational leader.

Nuccio Bertone took over the running of the company in 1952, and he was soon approached by a troubled »Alfa Romeo, which needed a morale-boosting appetiser for its delayed Giulietta sedan. The resultant Giulietta Sprint coupé, penned by Bertone chief designer Franco Scaglione, became an instant and astonishing success, stayed in production for thirteen years and is now universally acknowledged as a design classic. The Sprint's fabulous good looks, sparkling performance and affordable price brought a flood of orders and forced Bertone to transform its craft-scale production system into a modern industrial manufacturing operation.

The late 1950s and the following two decades were to prove Bertone's heyday, with a succession of groundbreaking designs that are today recognized as important milestones in vehicle design. Among these are the series of flamboyantly aerodynamic BAT concept cars in the 1950s, the Alfa Romeo Giulietta Sprint Speciale, designed in 1957 but not built until two years later, and the elegant NSU Sport Prinz coupé of 1959.

There was a change of tone as the new decade dawned and »Giorgetto Giugiaro replaced Scaglione as chief designer. Giugiaro's designs, exemplified by BMW's 3200 CS of 1961, the Alfa Romeo

Giulia GT in 1963 and the Chevrolet Corvair-based Testudo showcar of the same year, were calmer, simpler and more restrained, with a greater emphasis on proportion and surface.

Even greater heights were to come as Bertone linked up with a very young »Lamborghini company that was determined to challenge Ferrari (which was at the very top of the sports-car market and had a near-exclusive deal with Bertone's rival »Pininfarina for design). The Lamborghini Miura, which caused one of the biggest sensations the automobile world has ever known, appeared in 1966, just after Giugiaro had left Bertone to be replaced by Marcello Gandini, a twenty-seven-year-old with no previous experience in car design. The Miura presented a dramatically new proportion – low, flat and wide – and intriguing detailing, such as the 'eyelashes' above the pop-up headlamps and sinister-looking slats covering the near-horizontal rear window. Images of the Miura soon adorned every magazine cover and every teenage boy's bedroom wall, and the term 'supercar' was born.

Gandini went on to pen a series of epoch-defining designs for Lamborghini, including the Marzal concept, which introduced glazing in the doors below the waistline, the Espada and the Uracco. But the design community was stopped in its tracks in 1971 with the unveiling of the Countach, successor to the legendary Miura. There had been hints in the 1968 Carabo showcar, which introduced the wedge shape into design vocabulary, and the more extreme Lancia Stratos Zero concept of 1970, but the Countach's brutal shape, composed of a series of skewed planes and sharp intersections, challenged the classical concept of curvaceous and elegant beauty. A new and alien aesthetic was in place, one that again set car design on a new course.

While the Stratos concept metamorphosed into the Lancia Stratos HF rally car of 1974,

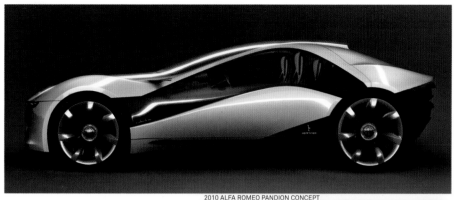

2010 ALFA ROMEO PANDION CONCEPT

Bertone was enjoying a spectacular run with »Fiat's lightweight X1/9 sports car, echoing its success with earlier Fiat roadsters. Yet when Fiat pulled the plug on the X1/9 manufacturing contract in 1981, prompting Nuccio Bertone to market the model under his own brand, the Bertone star began to fade. Few truly memorable designs emerged in the next decade, with only Citroën as a volume-car customer. Nuccio Bertone's death in 1997 appeared to hasten the decline, with only the 2003 Alfa Romeo GT and the 2005 Villa concept as highlights. Although BMW's cancellation of the C1 motorcycle-manufacturing contract in 2002 was followed by a limited-edition build of special »Mini Coopers until 2007, no new contracts followed and Bertone's manufacturing arm declared bankruptcy. A period of undignified family squabbling over the rights to the Bertone name appeared to signal the end of the company as a credible entity, until a solution – as a full-service design company – emerged in 2009.

The Alfa Romeo Pandion concept shown by the recast Bertone at the Geneva motor show in 2010 has done little to convince critics that a Bertone revival is under way. It is likely that the Italian design house will be best remembered for its defining designs of the 1950s, 1960s and 1970s, and for its role in nurturing some of the best designers the industry has ever seen.

KEY DESIGNS	
1954	Alfa Romeo Giulietta Sprint; Fiat 1100
1959	NSU Sport Prinz
1961	BMW 3200 CS; Maserati 5000 GT
1963	Alfa Romeo Giulia GT
1966	Lamborghini Miura
1967	Alfa Romeo Montreal; Lamborghini Marzal concept
1968	Lamborghini Espada
1969	Fiat Dino coupé
1970	Lancia Stratos Zero concept
1971	Lamborghini Countach
1972	BMW 520; Fiat X1/9
1974	Lancia Stratos HF; Audi 50 (becomes 1975 Volkswagen Polo)
1982	Citroën BX
2003	Alfa Romeo GT
2005	Villa concept
2010	Alfa Romeo Pandion concept

1974 LANCIA STRATOS HF

1967 LAMBORGHINI MARZAL CONCEPT

2000 BMW C1

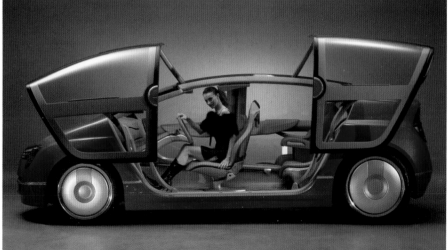

2005 VILLA CONCEPT

BMW

GERMANY | FOUNDED 1916 | PREMIUM CARS AND MOTORCYCLES | BMWGROUP.COM

If there is a single carmaker that best defines the rise of the premium brand phenomenon, it is BMW. Prior to the ascent of BMW from its shaky restart in the early 1960s to its twenty-first-century status as the world's premier producer of blue-chip vehicles, cars were either volume-market or luxury. Just a few brands – Rover, Lancia, Saab, perhaps – saw themselves as a cut above the rest, but they never pretended to be near the likes of such luxury marques as Mercedes-Benz, Jaguar or Daimler. What BMW has done in the intervening years, partly through design but largely through quality of engineering and manufacture, is to make premium design values accessible in every segment of the market, from »Mini Cooper upward; no longer is a small car necessarily a cheap car. Thanks to the snowballing success of BMW and its imitators, everyone now wants to cash in on the premium act.

Today, although the BMW range covers a huge spectrum of segments (from sensible sedans to hotshot near-racers, chunky SUVs and family-centric gran turismo wagons), they all share sufficient common traits from the BMW gene pool to ensure their identity can instantly be seen. And as in the case of any aspirational brand, the individual models within each segment – sedans, for instance – are very similar in their shape and their proportions; models are differentiated by size, not style. This strategy, as with »Audi's homogeneous design language and »Mercedes-Benz's distinctive star, is a powerful builder of brand identity.

While BMW's double-kidney grille can be traced back to the 1933 303, the real template for today's BMWs came with the 'Neue Klasse' 1500 sedan of 1962, its calm and elegant lines (inspired by the Michelotti Italian design house) emphasizing the horizontal to make the tall design look longer and wider. The 1500 introduced the full-width grille with the double kidneys,

1936 328

1956 507

now shorter and wider, superimposed in the centre. But it was the shortened two-door 02 series derived from this design that really put BMW on the map as a maker of sporty cars, and by 1972, with the launch of the first 5 Series and the Turbo concept (shaped by Paul Bracq, who also designed France's TGV train), the BMW identity was set. It has evolved in a linear manner across the broadening line-up until the big break just after the turn of the millennium.

American »Chris Bangle had taken over as chief designer in 1992, but it was only

1955 ISETTA

HISTORY

1916	Bayerische Flugzeug Werke founded
1917	BMW GmbH formed from aero engine-maker Bayerische Flugzeug Werke
1923	First boxer motorcycle
1927	Production of Dixi, Austin Seven under licence
1934	Aero engine division becomes separated
1945	Company rebuilt from scratch
1949	First post-war motorcycles
1959	Quandt family takes control
1967	Takes over Glas
1970	Eberhard von Kuenheim becomes chairman
1983	Nelson Piquet becomes F1 champion with BMW power
1985	BMW Technik established as technology think tank
1990	FIZ R&D centre opens
1992	US plant announced for construction of Z3 sports car. BMW V12 engine in McLaren F1 supercar, wins Le Mans 24 Hours in 1995. Chris Bangle becomes head of design
1993	Von Kuenheim retires
1994	Purchase of Rover group
1998	Acquires right to sell Rolls-Royce cars from 2003
1999	Enters SUV market with X5. BMW-Williams car wins Le Mans
2000	Land Rover sold to Ford. Mini retained, Rover sold for £10
2001	Mini relaunched
2004	BMW global sales pass 1 million a year
2005	BMW sells more cars globally than Mercedes-Benz
2006	BMW Hydrogen 7 is world's first production hydrogen car
2008	Forms Project i to develop low-emission Megacity vehicles
2009	Bangle leaves and is replaced by Adrian van Hooydonk as head of group design

1973 2002 TURBO

1978 M1

1988 Z1

2001 7 SERIES

2002 X-ACTIVITY CONCEPT

2005 H2R CONCEPT

2000 Z8

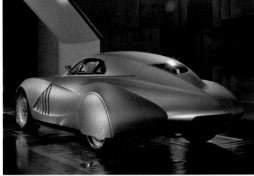
2006 MILLE MIGLIA CONCEPT

towards the end of that decade that his influence became clear to see. The two Z9 showcars, although shaped by »Adrian van Hooydonk (who would later take over as design head), were the first to incorporate Bangle's technique of flame surfacing – complex combinations of convex and concave surfaces that created light, shade and reflections. While the concepts were met with bafflement, the production E65 7 Series of 2001 generated hostility bordering on hysteria: Bangle was accused of treason and the wilful abandonment of BMW's long heritage, but the car sold well.

Two models mark the design high points of what became known as the Bangle era: the E60 5 Series and the »Z4 sports car, both launched in 2003 and both featuring intricate and fascinating sculpting of their exterior surfaces. Before long the furore had died down, showing that Bangle had succeeded in his desire to move the BMW design identity on to something more fluid and expressive. Soon, other designers were busy trying to copy him.

A clear post-Bangle identity for BMW products has yet to emerge, but early evidence – such as the 2008 »7 Series, the 2009 »5 Series and the X1 SUV – suggests that the themes are becoming plainer and less overtly sculptural, but with exaggerated design cues that include larger grilles. While this might indicate a slight cooling off of BMW's desire to inflict disruptive change in mainstream model lines, the intricate and multi-layered Vision EfficientDynamics concept of 2009 provides a thrilling insight into how a future BMW sports car might look.

PRINCIPAL MODELS

1933	303 is first BMW with 6 cylinders and double-kidney grille
1936	328 sports car
1952	501 'Baroque Angel' V8 sedan
1955	Isetta bubble car
1956	507 roadster, by Albrecht Goertz
1962	'Neue Klasse' 1500 sports sedan
1967	First 02 compact
1972	First 5 Series. BMW Turbo concept for 1972 Munich Olympics
1973	2002 Turbo
1975	First 3 Series
1977	First 6 Series
1978	First 7 Series; M1 supercar, by Giorgetto Giugiaro
1988	Z1 roadster
1992	First M3 sports sedan
1995	Z3 roadster, built in United States
1999	X5 is first BMW SUV; Z9 concept is first Bangle-era design
2000	Z8 luxury roadster
2001	7 Series (E65) (4th gen), Mini Cooper; X-Coupé concept
2002	X-Activity concept
2003	Z4, Rolls-Royce Phantom
2004	1 Series, 3 Series (5th gen)
2005	H2R concept
2006	X5 (2nd gen); Mille Miglia concept
2007	CS four-door coupé concept
2008	X6, 7 Series (5th gen)
2009	5 Series (6th gen), Z4 (2nd gen); Vision EfficientDynamics concept
2011	6 Series (3rd gen)

2007 CS CONCEPT

2009 VISION EFFICIENTDYNAMICS CONCEPT

2001 X-COUPÉ CONCEPT

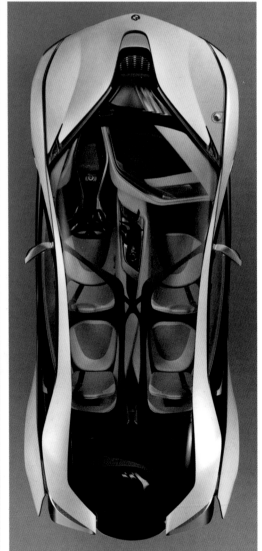

BMW 3 SERIES

2004 | EXECUTIVE CAR

MODEL HISTORY 1975 3 SERIES 1ST GENERATION • 1982 3 SERIES 2ND GENERATION • 1990 3 SERIES 3RD GENERATION • 1998 3 SERIES 4TH GENERATION • 2004 3 SERIES 5TH GENERATION

2010 320D	
LENGTH	4530 mm (178 in.)
LAYOUT	Front engine, rear-wheel drive
ENGINE	2.0 turbo diesel 4-cyl
HORSEPOWER	184
MAX. SPEED	235 km/h (146 mph)
CO_2 EMISSIONS	125 g/km

The 3 Series is the model that, more than any other, helped BMW to grow from a German-based producer of enthusiast-appeal sporty cars in the late 1960s to a global organization selling premium cars at all levels of the market in the twenty-first century. Taking its visual cues from the successful »5 Series of 1972, the 1975 two-door 3 Series was smaller, handier and sportier. It soon found friends beyond BMW's traditional constituency and among those who admired clean, quality design, classy interiors and the fast-growing prestige of the BMW badge.

With the second-generation 3 Series fine-tuning the sober style and adding a four-door, a compact station-wagon and a super-successful, image-building convertible, BMW became a badge for the ambitious and upwardly mobile, and sales soared. The race-inspired M3 sports version, launched in 1985, became an instant hit among enthusiasts and sired a line that, a quarter-century later, has developed into someting of a legend. By the time of the 3 Series' third generation (E36) in 1990, the company-car market had cottoned on that premium cars were good for value retention as well as employee feel-good factor, thus extending the BMW experience to an even broader base of drivers.

This model followed the generation pattern established with the 5 Series in 1989, alternating a major design shift with a more limited refresh. Thus the 1990 E36 3 Series debuted a more fluid, low-nose and high-tail style, and was the first BMW to have its signature quad headlamps shielded behind smooth glass covers. For the first time, a coupé was among the derivatives, as was the shorter hatchback compact, taking BMW to the level of the »Volkswagen Golf GTi in the market for the first time.

The follow-on E46 3 Series in 1998 smoothed up the style once more, restoring the interior quality that had been lost in 1990; by now diesels were in full swing and the five body-shape variants had become mass-appeal vehicles selling in greater quantities than such familiar favourites as the »Ford Mondeo and Renault Laguna. The 3 Series was the last BMW to embrace the Bangle-era styling revolution, in 2004. For the 3 this was a major change, even if »Chris Bangle's controversial design cues were now presented in a watered-down format. This toning down was more acceptable to the big-numbers sales game that this once-individual model had come to contest.

1998 3 SERIES

1975 3 SERIES

2008 M3

2004-GENERATION 3 SERIES

BMW 5 SERIES
2009 | LARGE EXECUTIVE CAR

MODEL HISTORY 1972 5 SERIES 1ST GENERATION • 1982 5 SERIES 2ND GENERATION • 1989 5 SERIES (E34) 3RD GENERATION • 1996 5 SERIES 4TH GENERATION • 2003 5 SERIES 5TH GENERATION • 2009 5 SERIES 6TH GENERATION

2010 530D	
LENGTH	4900 mm (193 in.)
LAYOUT	Front engine, rear-wheel drive
ENGINE	3.0 turbo diesel 6-cyl
HORSEPOWER	245
MAX. SPEED	250 km/h (155 mph)
CO$_2$ EMISSIONS	166 g/km

To the 5 Series goes the honour of being the first truly modern BMW, the model that launched the Series hierarchy around which other carmakers now structure their products, and the first to combine the qualities of a sports sedan with the creature comforts of a luxury saloon.

The car that appeared in 1972 had a fresh and glassy four-door body by Frenchman Paul Bracq, a four-cylinder, 2-litre engine and a revolutionary interior, with the instruments and controls grouped around the driver. The 5 Series was an outstanding success, and soon six-cylinder versions appeared, introducing business drivers to the new world of smoothness and mechanical sophistication that was to become a BMW trademark for the next thirty years.

The follow-up 5 Series in 1982 was criticized for being very conservative in its evolution of the design theme. This did not deter three-quarters of a million buyers, who had been tempted by ever more powerful engines and, for the first time on a BMW, a diesel engine. The jump to the next generation was a big one, the 1989 car replacing its predecessor's straight-line formality with soft curves and a sporty stance. These were the design cues of the late-1980s 7 Series, and the formula worked wonders: with the addition of the Touring station-wagon and the hotshot M5 into the mix, the E34 was the first big BMW to sell more than a million units over the course of its production run.

After this big change the next step for the 5 Series, in 1996, was once again an evolutionary one, and it, too, was highly successful. There was some trepidation prior to the announcement of the fifth generation in 2003, in the light of the divisive shape »Chris Bangle had chosen for the new »7 Series two years earlier. In the event, however, the model proved to be perhaps the best resolved of all the Bangle-era designs: intricately sculpted, but with great proportions and a sporty stance on the road, especially as a station-wagon.

For its sixth incarnation the 5 Series played it safe with what for some was a disappointingly cautious evolution, although the interior was much improved. Next, all eyes will be on the seventh generation to see how new design director »Adrian van Hooydonk reinterprets this classically successful formula.

1996 5 SERIES

5 SERIES TOURING

BMW 6 SERIES

2011 | LUXURY SPORTS CAR

MODEL HISTORY 1977 6 SERIES 1ST GENERATION • 2003 6 SERIES 2ND GENERATION • 2011 6 SERIES 3RD GENERATION

2010 650I	
LENGTH	4895 mm (193 in.)
LAYOUT	Front engine, rear-wheel drive
ENGINE	4.4 petrol V8
HORSEPOWER	407
MAX. SPEED	250 km/h (155 mph)
CO₂ EMISSIONS	243 g/km

The elegant 6 Series coupé of the 1970s, with its clean flanks, slim pillars and classically balanced proportions, was one of the most admired of all BMWs, encapsulating all the marque's coupé heritage to date – including that of the famous 507 and the ferocious CSL of the previous decades.

So there was some anxiety in 2003, with the furore over the 2001 »7 Series still fresh in the collective memory, as to what designer »Chris Bangle would do for the new 6 Series coupé. Would it overturn traditions of elegance and impose an unaesthetic shape that would once again divide the critics? In the event, the shape that emerged was a familiar one; most of it had been previewed a few years earlier by the Z9 showcars. Once the hysteria surrounding the awkward trunk-lid profile had settled down, the new 6 came to be seen as a fine GT car. The later convertible version showed very classy proportions indeed.

The next phase in the 6 Series history was previewed by a concept model in 2010 prior to the presentation of the production convertible and coupé the following spring. The new model marks a return to the classical elegance of the first generation of the 1970s: there is no longer anything in the design to shock or offend, and in terms of proportion and surface language it owes much to the smaller »3 Series coupé. It may have sacrificed the controversial streak of the 2003 model, but as a result it has become more acceptable to a wealthy conservative clientele.

2003 6 SERIES CONVERTIBLE

BMW 7 SERIES

2008 | LUXURY CAR

MODEL HISTORY 1978 7 SERIES 1ST GENERATION • 1986 7 SERIES 2ND GENERATION • 1994 7 SERIES 3RD GENERATION •
2001 7 SERIES 4TH GENERATION • 2008 7 SERIES 5TH GENERATION

2010 730D	
LENGTH	5070 mm (200 in.)
LAYOUT	Front engine, rear-wheel drive
ENGINE	3.0 turbo diesel 6-cyl
HORSEPOWER	231
MAX. SPEED	245 km/h (152 mph)
CO₂ EMISSIONS	178 g/km

When, towards the end of the 1990s, BMW design director »Chris Bangle and his team were putting the finishing touches to the fourth-generation 7 Series, they could have had little idea of the furore their design would unleash after its unveiling in 2001. The hostility from the press and other commentators was palpable and frequently personal, and at times the debate degenerated into bitterness and talk of betrayal of cherished BMW values. Bangle is even said to have received hate mail.

A decade on, it is hard to see what all the fuss was about. The 7 Series's shape (actually penned by »Adrian van Hooydonk, although Bangle took all the flak) is calm and measured, if somewhat slab-sided; the only aspect that still jars is the raised trunk area, and this was softened somewhat in a later facelift. Yet at the time its shock value was enormous, for it did indeed represent a move away from BMW's then-current philosophy of gradual, evolutionary change; with hindsight, buyers and commentators had clearly felt threatened by the possible loss of the BMW they knew and to which they felt loyal.

Bangle's intention with the 7 Series had been to move the game on, but he got more than even he had bargained for. Yet the fact that the car's shape is now widely accepted is proof that the designer's plan has worked; the 7 was a watershed in the normally conservative, slow-moving world of luxury-segment design. Bangle was right to provoke: the previous-generation 7 Series had been an extremely anodyne upgrade of the earlier, more progressive 1986 model, itself a big step from the first 7 dating back to 1978.

The current, fifth generation has seen further refinement; bigger grilles proclaim the BMW identity more loudly, but subtler and more fluid surface language does more to disguise the design's substantial bulk. And, in contrast to the Bangle-era uproar, few have complained — or even noticed.

2001 7 SERIES

1994 7 SERIES

BMW X5, X6

2006 (X5), 2008 (X6) | LUXURY 4x4

MODEL HISTORY 1999 X5 1ST GENERATION • 2006 X5 2ND GENERATION • 2008 X6

2010 X5 30D	
LENGTH	4855 mm (191 in.)
LAYOUT	Front engine, all-wheel drive
ENGINE	3.0 turbo diesel 6-cyl
HORSEPOWER	245
MAX. SPEED	222 km/h (138 mph)
CO$_2$ EMISSIONS	195 g/km

Known for its fast and fine-handling premium sedans and station-wagons, BMW had to think carefully when considering a possible entry into the temptingly booming market for SUVs in the mid-1990s. The brand could not afford to compromise its reputation for dynamism with a clunky off-roader in the mould of Land Rover or Jeep.

Therefore the design of the X5 – by »Frank Stephenson, later to be credited with the »Mini Cooper – deliberately avoided the aggressiveness of the mainstream players, taking only the raised ride height and chunky tyres as SUV signifiers. The 1999 model was an immediate hit, both aesthetically and dynamically, and cleverly bridged the gap between a friendly, conventional station-wagon and the intimidating aura of a full SUV.

The follow-up X5 in 2006 was equally sophisticated. It needed to be significantly bigger, so as to make space for the cheaper X3; BMW cleverly disguised the X5's extra bulk through subtle surfacing and by enlarging such familiar features as the grilles and lights.

The oddball X6 that was later spun off may come to be seen as an aberration, its proportions altered from benign to aggressive by the simple expedient of chopping height off the roof and sloping the rear window like that of a coupé.

2008 X6

2006 X5

2006 AND 1999 X5

BMW Z4

2009 | SPORTS CAR

MODEL HISTORY 2003 Z4 1ST GENERATION • 2009 Z4 2ND GENERATION

2010 23I	
LENGTH	4240 mm (167 in.)
LAYOUT	Front engine, rear-wheel drive
ENGINE	2.5 petrol 6-cyl
HORSEPOWER	204
MAX. SPEED	242 km/h (150 mph)
CO_2 EMISSIONS	199 g/km

In the mid-1990s, expectations ran high for the new BMW sports car, which was to be built in the United States: the car, aimed at America's lucrative sports-car market, would be BMW's first roadster since the legendary 507 of the 1950s, promised the company.

The 507 influence was indeed clearly visible in the Z3 unveiled in 1995: the long and flowing hood fronted by the twin BMW kidney grilles, the rear-set cockpit and, most obviously of all, slotted air vents on the front fenders incorporating the BMW roundel. Stylistically, the Z3 was a romantic throwback to an earlier age of curvaceous roadsters that expressed their power through proportion and stance. It was an immediate success, even though the driving experience remained disappointing until larger engines were fitted.

The Z4, which relieved the by-now fading Z3 in 2003, was a much more modern design, although equally emotional in its aura and painstakingly sculpted in »Chris Bangle's flame-surfacing idiom. This and a pretty but short-lived coupé were replaced in 2009 by a new design from an all-female team led by thirty-two-year-old Juliane Blasi; the emotion is still strong, but the classical balance of the roadster has returned.

2003-GENERATION Z4

BRILLIANCE

CHINA | FOUNDED 1992 | VANS AND LICENCE-BUILD OF BMW CARS | ZHONGHUACAR.COM

HISTORY AND PRINCIPAL MODELS	
1992	Manufactures minibuses and Toyota Hiace
1999	Listed on New York stock exchange
2001	Receives technical assistance from BMW
2002	Launches Zhonghua sedan (BS6) with design by Giorgetto Giugiaro
2003	Joint venture with BMW begins building 3 and 5 Series in China
2005	New 3 Series BMW launched
2006	Brilliance BS4 launched in China. Long-wheelbase BMW 5 Series. BS6 imported into Europe in small numbers, gets 1 star out of 5 in European crash test
2007	Brilliance BS4 launched in Europe; BS6 and BS4 withdrawn from Europe
2009	Brilliance sells loss-making Zhonghua sedan business
2010	Opens second factory to build BMW models

2006 BS4

Originally a producer of small commercial vans – the Toyota Hiace made from knocked-down kits, and its own domestically designed eleven-seater model – Shenyang Automotive entered into a series of deals with other automakers in the 1990s once its cooperation agreement with Toyota had come to an end. Armed with locally made Mitsubishi engines and a sedan body styled by the Italian maestro »Giorgetto Giugiaro, the company (which was soon to be known as Brilliance China) began preparing to manufacture the new model, dubbed Zhonghua (BS6).

Even though Brilliance had entered into a technical agreement with BMW to help it to manufacture the Zhonghua series efficiently, the programme was fraught with problems, and initial sales following the launch were judged disappointing. By this time discussions were well under way on

a much more profitable venture: the manufacture of BMW models, first from imported kits and later using a higher percentage of parts sourced locally in China.

By late 2003 both the 3 and the 5 Series were being turned out and snapped up by customers hungry for premium German brands. Based on the kudos and implied quality of being BMW's chosen production partner in China, Brilliance felt confident it could sell its own models in Europe and the United States. The venture was to prove deeply damaging, however, after a BS6 was submitted for a crash test by Germany's ADAC organization in 2006. Scoring just one star out of a possible five, the BS6 was labelled dangerous by the testers. Chinese cars got a bad name, and Brilliance retreated to redesign its structures.

Despite boasting the superficial cachet of such Italian designer names as Giugiaro

and »Pininfarina (for the smaller M2 model), as well as the involvement of Porsche and Lotus in chassis development, Brilliance's models still have some way to go before they become genuinely competitive with Western designs. Perhaps recognizing this, in 2009 Brilliance sold off its still loss-making Zhonghua sedan operation in order to concentrate on the manufacture of premium-segment BMWs and the ever-popular multi-seater minibuses.

BRISTOL

GREAT BRITAIN | FOUNDED 1946 | HAND-BUILT LUXURY CARS | BRISTOLCARS.CO.UK

HISTORY AND PRINCIPAL MODELS

1945	Bristol Aeroplane Company creates a car division
1946	400, developed using BMW components
1949	401
1961	407 first with Chrysler V8
1969	411
1975	412, body by Zagato
1976	603
1980	Beaufighter Turbo
1993	Blenheim
2002	Fighter V10
2003	Speedster
2011	Bristol declared bankrupt. Assets acquired by Kamkorp Autokraft, part of Frazer-Nash group

Even by the individualistic standards of Britain's specialized car companies, Bristol is a complete eccentric. Founded just after the Second World War when the directors of the Bristol Aeroplane Company realized they would need something to replace military aircraft production, Bristol Cars' early designs were carbon copies of BMWs that had been seized by the Allied armies as they pushed into Germany. Yet as aeronautical engineers, Bristol's designers were able to apply such aircraft techniques as lightweight aluminium construction and streamlining to the BMW template – in this case, the already aerodynamic pre-war 328 – and the hand-built construction process made it simpler to incorporate running improvements.

Bristol continued with the same basic design, using the BMW-derived six-cylinder engine in a narrow aluminium chassis and smooth, streamlined body, until the early 1960s, when the need for more power brought American Chrysler V8 engines and automatic transmission. Along with the bigger engines came a heavier, more solid look and the loss of the aerodynamic elegance of the

1946 400

1969 411

1976 603

1993 BLENHEIM

earlier models; by 1975 the 412, with its body shaped by »Zagato, had become rectilinear and brutal in its contours. The later 603 and subsequent models – many named after famous Bristol aircraft – saw a softening up of the style, although Bristol has never relaxed its belief that a long and narrow car is best for modern traffic conditions. It has also always insisted on mounting the spare tyre upright within the bodywork just behind the front wheel arch, something that forces a tall proportion on the car's side view.

These are only a few of the eccentricities of a carmaker that crafts just a few hundred cars in a good year (it refuses to release sales data), that never advertises, has no dealers and sells from a single showroom in central London's Kensington area to a loyal clientele of aficionados. The clients value the single-minded approach and the refusal to follow fashion that have been Bristol hallmarks since the 1960s.

Few were prepared for the shock that came in 2002. Bristol had to all intents and purposes appeared to be a dormant company, yet behind the scenes it had developed the Fighter: this forbiddingly potent coupé was powered by the Dodge Viper's 8-litre V10 engine and clad in a slim, aerodynamic body – still in hand-shaped aluminium – with gullwing doors and more than a hint of style to its long sweeping roofline and narrowing tail. More recently still, an even more muscular Turbo version with more than 1000 horsepower and 1400 Nm torque has been announced. Anachronistic but also ahead of its time, the secretive Bristol Car Company is a uniquely British enigma.

2003 SPEEDSTER

2002 FIGHTER

BUGATTI

FRANCE | FOUNDED 1909 | EXTREME SPORTS CARS | BUGATTI.COM

HISTORY

1909	Racing driver Ettore Bugatti establishes atelier in Molsheim, Alsace
1911	Ettore designs Bébé small car for Peugeot
1920	First Grand Prix victory
1927	Dancer Isadora Duncan strangled when scarf is caught in Bugatti wheel
1929	Type 35B wins first Monaco GP
1931	Ettore's son Jean designs first open Royale
1933	Production of railcars helps Bugatti to survive slump
1937	Le Mans 24 Hours win
1939	Jean Bugatti dies in testing crash
1940	War forces sale of plant
1947	Ettore Bugatti dies
1956	All production ceases
1963	Sold to Hispano Suiza
1977	Schlumpf Textile works closes, revealing large collection of Bugattis
1987	Romano Artioli acquires Bugatti name
1991	EB 110 introduced on anniversary of Ettore Bugatti's hundred-and-tenth birthday
1993	Bugatti buys Lotus
1995	Bugatti bankrupt
1998	Wolkswagen buys rights to Bugatti name
2001	VW decides to manufacture Veyron
2003	Veyron spins off Laguna Seca track during public launch
2004	Bugatti Atelier complete

PRINCIPAL MODELS

1910	Type 13
1924	Type 35 racing car
1926	Type 41 Royale
1935	Type 57 SC Atlantic prototype, designed by Jean Bugatti
1991	EB 110, by Marcello Gandini
1993	EB 112 four-door sedan concept, by Italdesign
1998	EB 118 two-door coupé concept, by Giorgetto Giugiaro for VW
1999	EB 218 four-door sedan concept and Chiron 18.3 concept, both by Giugiaro; Veyron 18.4 concept, by Hartmut Warkuss
2005	Veyron 16.4 enters production
2009	Galibier four-door sedan concept
2010	Veyron Super Sport with 1200 hp

As in the case of Ferrari, Bugatti is the stuff of legends – all of them romantic, all of them very expensive and very beautiful, and most of them with a happy ending. The difference between the two firms is that at Bugatti there have been a lot more tears along the way. During the bumpy ride of its century-long history Bugatti has been bankrupt and left for dead on several occasions, yet each time an incurable romantic with very deep pockets has ridden to its rescue and set it back on its wheels to roll once more.

The company was founded by Ettore Bugatti. Born in Milan into a family of artists, he was racing cars before the turn of the nineteenth century; he set up his own atelier in Molsheim, Alsace, where he built exquisitely shaped and finely engineered racing cars that would dominate competition and secure his reputation. While others relied on huge engines and brute force for their speed, Bugattis were light, lithe and agile – the most exotic cars of their day.

Ettore Bugatti came unstuck when he responded to taunts that his customers had to look elsewhere for a true luxury car. He commissioned the gigantic and sumptuously finished 12.7-litre Royale, whose hood alone was the length of a small car; sadly, the Royale's arrival coincided with that of the inter-war economic slump and only six were ever made. But while the racetrack successes continued until 1939, Bugatti's business never recovered from the upheavals of the Second World War. Ettore Bugatti died in 1947 and the firm closed in 1956.

Three decades later Italian entrepreneur Romano Artioli announced that he had acquired the rights to the Bugatti name; by 1991, in time for what would have been Ettore Bugatti's hundred-and-tenth birthday, the reconstituted Bugatti had launched the quad-turbo, V12-engined EB 110 from its ultra-modern factory in northern Italy. Aesthetically, the car was a disappointment, despite having been shaped by Lamborghini architect Marcello Gandini. With its slab sides and tiny, tokenistic Bugatti horseshoe grille, the EB 110 looked too much like a me-too supercar to appeal to the truly wealthy. Sales were slow, and in 1995, after just 135 cars had been sold, Bugatti was again declared bankrupt.

This would have been the end of the Bugatti story but for the relentless ambition of Volkswagen Group boss Ferdinand Piëch. Not content with having absorbed both Lamborghini and Bentley into the VW stable, Piëch saw an opportunity for Bugatti at the very pinnacle of the luxury market, where the French marque could give true expression to Ettore Bugatti's maxim that 'nothing is too beautiful; nothing is too expensive'. There followed a series of three concept cars, all by »Giorgetto Giugiaro, exploring different formats for a future production Bugatti; each featured an eighteen-cylinder engine formed out of six triple-cylinder units. Eventually, however,

it was a fourth design, by VW's style head »Hartmut Warkuss, that was given the go-ahead for development.

There was a stunned silence when Piëch announced to reporters at the 2000 Geneva motor show that the »Bugatti Veyron 16.4 would boast 1001 horsepower and would be 'the most advanced and the most exciting car of our time'. Such power figures were beyond the domain of Formula One cars and, with a centrally mounted sixteen-cylinder engine, four-wheel drive and a world's fastest top speed of over 400 km/h (250 mph), it would be a formidable technical challenge. But this was to be no track-day roadburner, commanded the VW chief: the Veyron would also represent the ultimate in comfort, luxury and convenience. It would be a car to take to the opera as well as the race circuit.

The finished item pays homage to its ancestors with a two-tone paint scheme, liberal use of the EB logo, and a beautifully milled metal dashboard inside the sumptuous two-person cabin. Although beyond those details there is little to link the squat and rounded exterior shape of the Veyron to the simple purity of Bugatti's pre-war classics, the design does deliberately avoid the raw sensationalism characteristic of many supercars. In that sense, it does convey a classier, more refined air – but whether it looks like a million euros' worth of motor car is another matter.

When the five-year, 300-unit Veyron production run neared completion, Bugatti's VW controllers began considering alternatives for a follow-up model. A somewhat anodyne four-door concept sedan was presented in 2009 as a possible option. Named Galibier in honour of a special version of the pre-war Type 57 Atlantic, the new design carefully avoids reviving the historic Royale badge. This is a sign, perhaps, that VW's senior management is anxious to avoid any associations with the grandiose commercial folly the 1926 project symbolized.

BUGATTI VEYRON 16.4

2005 | EXTREME SPORTS CAR

MODEL HISTORY 2005 VEYRON 16.4 • 2010 VEYRON SUPER SPORT

2010 8.0 W16	
LENGTH	4460 mm (176 in.)
LAYOUT	Mid engine, all-wheel drive
ENGINE	8.0 petrol W16
HORSEPOWER	1001
MAX. SPEED	407 km/h (253 mph)
CO₂ EMISSIONS	574 g/km

Mere superlatives were hopelessly inadequate when it came to describing the astonishing performance of this million-euro supercar when it finally made its debut in 2005. Packing a sensational 1001 horsepower into a footprint little larger than that of a »Ford Focus required an extraordinary engineering investment, and resulted in Formula One levels of acceleration and a top speed of over 400 km/h (250 mph).

In that sense the born-again Bugatti had certainly equalled, if not exceeded, the allure of its illustrious GP-winning forebears of the 1920s and 1930s. But the bigger challenge had been how to reinterpret those famously pure and graceful classical designs on an aesthetic level and for a modern audience.

»Hartmut Warkuss's squat, geometrically rounded profile for the Veyron favoured simplicity and understatement when the norm — if such is the word — for ultra-high-performance cars is huge wheels, extravagant contours and complex aerodynamic devices. Rather than sensation, Warkuss chose decoration: the Bugatti horseshoe grille, two-tone paintwork and a plush, although not suffocatingly luxurious, cockpit. The Veyron's aura is thus a technical rather than emotional one — and it will have to be for history to decide how this efficient Germanic approach sits within Bugatti's catalogue of outstanding aesthetic creations.

BUICK

UNITED STATES | FOUNDED 1903 | CARS AND SUVS | BUICK.COM

HISTORY

1903	Buick incorporated in Flint, Michigan
1904	David Dunbar Buick sells out
1908	Buick overtakes Cadillac and Ford. Becomes founding company in General Motors
1909	Buick wins inaugural race at Indianapolis
1925	6-cyl engines replace 4-cyl
1949	Portholes design feature appears
1995	Joint venture signed for production in China
1999	Buick Regal production in China
2001	Buick Sail produced in China

1936 ROADMASTER

1963 RIVIERA

1953 WILDCAT CONCEPT

When as a child David Dunbar Buick, who later invented the overhead valve, sailed from his native Scotland to Detroit in the 1850s, he could have had little idea that the company he would found in 1903 would become the foundation stone for »General Motors. Regrettably for him, however, Buick the man had sold out before these developments and could not share in the corporate glory that surrounded Buick the carmaker for the next hundred-plus years.

Buick has always prided itself on producing the most American of American cars; more premium in their presentation than run-of-the-mill Chevrolets, but still deferring to top-level Cadillac in the overall hierarchy. In its early decades Buick gained a reputation for toughness and solidity, but the differences became less noticeable as GM began to share more parts across models and brands.

The company scored several firsts worthy of note: Harley Earl's Y-Job, of 1938, is widely credited as being the world's first concept car, while in 1948 Buick brought DynaFlow, the world's first torque converter automatic transmission. The following year saw the first appearance of portholes on the front fenders – a Buick design cue that came and went over the following years – and the 1953 Super Riviera Coupé introduced another Buick signature, the waterfall grille. Further high points were the 1963 Riviera, one of GM design head Bill Mitchell's very best, as well as the 1971 boat-tailed Riviera.

As Buick's style was beginning to go stale in the 1990s, and the brand had gained a well-justified image as 'the car your dad drives', an unexpected new avenue opened up: China. Soon the conservative Regal was in hot demand in China, significant concept cars (such as the 2004 Velite, 2007 Riviera and 2008 Invicta) had re-energized the brand, and Buick had been spared in GM's drastic pruning of its brand portfolio. By 2010, smart new designs such as the Enclave crossover and the »Buick LaCrosse sedan had finally shaken off the golf-club-retiree stereotype.

PRINCIPAL MODELS

1904	Model B
1925	First 6-cyl models
1931	Series 50 is first 8-cyl Buick
1936	Roadmaster, by Harley Earl
1938	Y-Job, by Harley Earl, is world's first concept car
1953	Super Riviera coupé; Wildcat concept
1959	Electra 225
1961	Invicta is first sporty Buick
1963	Riviera, by Bill Mitchell
1971	Boat-tail Riviera
1988	Reatta sports coupé
1992	Roadmaster nameplate returns
2001	Rendezvous is first Buick SUV
2004	LaCrosse (1st gen); Velite concept
2007	Riviera concept
2008	Enclave; Invicta concept
2010	LaCrosse (2nd gen)

2008 INVICTA CONCEPT

2008 ENCLAVE

2004 VELITE CONCEPT

BUICK LACROSSE
2010 | EXECUTIVE CAR

MODEL HISTORY 2004 LACROSSE 1ST GENERATION • 2010 LACROSSE 2ND GENERATION

DATA 2010 3.0 DI	
LENGTH	5005 mm (197 in.)
LAYOUT	Front engine, front-wheel drive
ENGINE	3.0 petrol 6-cyl
HORSEPOWER	258
MAX. SPEED	200 km/h (124 mph)
CO$_2$ EMISSIONS	–

On the wane in its homeland in the 1990s, Buick was spared in »General Motors' post-bankruptcy brand-culling exercise thanks to its substantial – and initially surprising – success in what is now the biggest car market in the world, China. The marque's Asian renaissance enabled investment in new designs, several of them originating from GM's China studios, to feed back into the American market and help to overturn the perception of the brand as one aimed at retirees and older buyers.

The well-received 2007 Riviera concept was designed and engineered in China; so too was the Invicta study, from which the production LaCrosse is directly derived. It is built on a platform drawing on the same pool of components as the »Opel/Vauxhall Insignia in Europe, but comes across as a larger, more imposing design; here, the thrusting waterfall grille – a longstanding Buick signature – and a crisply defined undulating bone line along the front and rear fenders make for an eye-catching interplay of light and shade, while a shallower arched DLO bordered by a prominent brightwork strip give the rear a more »Lexus-like aspect. The LaCrosse is thus representative of the new Buick: not sensational, but at least distinguished enough not to pass unnoticed.

BYD AUTO

BYD was a little-known maker of Toyota-like Chinese cars until 2008, when it hit the headlines for a reason that made everyone sit up and take notice: American billionaire financier Warren Buffet, well known for being ahead of the game in his investments, had taken a 10 per cent stake for almost $230 million. By this stage BYD (the initials stand for Build Your Dreams) had been in the car business for less than five years; what had attracted Buffet was not its fledgling range of cars but the parent company's expertise in lithium batteries and its bullish plans for applying those batteries to electric vehicles.

BYD insisted that with the launch of its F3, F6 and F7 it was learning the ropes of carmaking with conventional vehicles in anticipation of hybrid and all-electric models later; sure enough, BYD was first to market anywhere in the world with a plug-in hybrid, in the shape of the 2008 Chinese-market F3 DM. The auto establishment was further impressed – or, in the case of Western competitors, given a stark wake-up call – at the 2009 Detroit auto show when BYD exhibited the e6, a clean and smart-looking battery-powered family minivan claiming a remarkable 400-kilometre (248-mile) range. Along with the convincing design came the promise of production that same year and exports to the United States the next.

Soon afterwards Volkswagen concluded a cooperation deal with BYD, and in 2010 Daimler, parent company of Mercedes-Benz, announced that it would form a partnership with BYD to build electric vehicles for the Chinese market under a new brand. Since then, BYD has backtracked slightly on some of the technical claims for its lithium-iron phosphate battery technology and delayed the public launch of the e6. Nevertheless, with unparalleled experience in batteries and a doubling of its sales each year since 2004, BYD is unquestionably a company to watch.

HISTORY AND PRINCIPAL MODELS

1995	BYD Company formed, with twenty employees
2000	First to supply Motorola with lithium-ion batteries
2002	First to supply Nokia
2003	Purchases Tsinchuan Automobile Company to form BYD Auto
2005	First F3 compact car off line
2006	F3e demonstrates new battery technology
2007	F7 business sedan
2008	Warren Buffet takes stake in BYD. F0 small car; F6 mid-size car; F3 DM dual-mode hybrid
2009	e6 electric crossover
2010	Enters partnership with Daimler to develop new electric brand for China

2009 E6

2008 F6

2008 F6

CADILLAC

UNITED STATES | FOUNDED 1902 | PREMIUM CARS AND SUVS | CADILLAC.COM

HISTORY

1902	Founded by Henry Leland
1909	Bought by GM for $4.75m
1912	Pioneers electric starter
1914	First V8 engine
1915	Pioneers dipping headlights
1924	Confirmed as luxury brand in Alfred Sloan's GM strategy
1928	Introduces 'crashless' synchromesh gearbox
1929	Chrome plating becomes standard
1948	Cadillac is first to introduce fins
1959	Eldorado Biarritz has tallest and longest-ever fins
1960	Cadillac begins reducing fin size
1977	Downsized models appear
1979	First diesel engines prove disastrous
1982	Compact Cimarron is upscale Cavalier
1985	Further downsizing and front drive
2001	CTS introduces 'Art and Science' design theme
2002	Letter designations replace model names

1959 ELDORADO BIARRITZ

2003 SIXTEEN CONCEPT

Named after the French explorer who founded Detroit in the early eighteenth century, Cadillac was drawn into the »General Motors fold in 1909; GM's founder, William Durant, had been impressed by Cadillac's precision engineering and build quality, and was determined to give the brand the role of innovator and prestige flagship within his growing group of companies.

Engineering developments flowed thick and fast: electric start, the first V8 engine, dipping headlights, safety glass, synchromesh gears and, by 1930, a V16 engine. In terms of style Cadillac was a pace-setter, too: to the 1927 La Salle goes

the honour of being the world's first fully styled production automobile. This model was penned by Harley Earl, the legendary head of GM's Art and Color Section, the first automaker design studio. The studio itself was the embodiment of GM president Alfred P. Sloan's vision of a spectrum of brands, each one carefully designed and targeted at a particular customer group.

In this strategy, which was remarkably advanced for its time, Cadillac was to be the undisputed luxury and style leader. A stream of designs would prove the point: the Aerodynamic V16 concept sedan built for the 1933 World's Fair in Chicago; the

fastback rear of the 1940 Cadillac Sixty; the wraparound windshield; and, of course, the beginning of the whole aircraft-inspired era of the 1950s.

This is seen by many as the golden age of American car design, and nothing symbolizes it better than Cadillac and the 'fin wars'. First introduced by Cadillac in 1948, fins grew spectacularly in height, complexity and aggressiveness over the next decade, reaching their ultimate expression in the 1959 Eldorado Biarritz and Cadillac's rocket-like 1959 concept, the Cyclone.

From that point on, however, Cadillac began to adopt a steadily more sober attitude to style, shrinking its fins year by year until by 1965 they had disappeared; outrageous flamboyance had given way to calmer, simpler basic shapes, still immensely long and wide but with complex detailing front and rear. With the exception of the 1967 Eldorado, which used the novel front-wheel-drive V8 powertrain of sister brand Oldsmobile's Toronado coupé, the next decades were lean years for Cadillac design as GM's attention stayed focused on the high-powered muscle cars that followed in the wake of the »Ford Mustang. Cadillac had little to contribute and, along with its clientele, its products slipped into middle age.

Things got tougher still with the advent of the 1970s fuel crisis and downsized vehicles; shortened and simplified Cadillacs really did not work, the reluctantly adopted diesel engines were disastrous, and, in 1982, Cadillac was ridiculed for its Cimarron – an attempt by GM to make a luxury car out of the small sedan that was also sold as the Chevrolet Cavalier and, in Europe, as the Opel Ascona.

The Cimarron episode had shown Cadillac for what it had become: little more than fancy trimmings on a volume-car base, with few unique technical or aesthetic qualities of its own. GM appeared powerless to reactivate Cadillac until the late 1990s, when design vice president »Wayne Cherry commissioned a series of concept cars from UK-based designer Simon Cox to establish an entirely fresh design language for the brand. Under the new slogan of 'Art and Science', Cox gave Cadillac crisply chiselled lines, coarse mesh grilles, pointed lights and razor-sharp details. The style was brash and aggressive in a way that was entirely appropriate for an American brand, yet it also conveyed the precision of the technology underneath and, most vitally, it proved very distinctive in a market dominated by the smooth and efficient German premium products.

Perhaps fittingly, the outrageous Sixteen concept of 2003 evoked the glories of its 1930 forebear. Although economic pressures mean that the Sixteen will never be produced in volume, the new look translates well into smaller formats, such as the CTS coupé and the SRX crossover, which many believe will be where Cadillac's future lies.

1999 ESCALADE LINE

PRINCIPAL MODELS	
1906	Model H, with enclosed cabin
1927	La Salle is first car entirely styled by a designer (Harley Earl)
1930	V16 is first 16-cyl car
1940	Cadillac Sixty introduces fastback style
1952	Eldorado convertible introduces wraparound windshield
1953	Orleans dream car with fighter-jet fins
1959	Eldorado Biarritz; Cyclone concept car
1967	Eldorado is first front-drive Cadillac
1975	Seville is first smaller Cadillac
1984	DeVille and Fleetwood shortened by 60 cm (over 23 in.)
1987	Allante is shipped in from Pininfarina in Italy
1988	Voyage concept has four-wheel drive, navigation, phone
1992	4th-gen Seville adopts European flavour
1999	Escalade is first Cadillac SUV; Evoq luxury sports car concept
2000	Imaj luxury sedan concept
2001	CTS introduces razor-edge style
2002	Cien supercar concept
2003	XLR sports car aimed at Mercedes SL; Sixteen super-luxury sedan concept
2008	CTS coupé concept
2009	Converj concept: range-extended electric coupé
2010	CTS sport wagon

1999 EVOQ CONCEPT

2004 SRX

2010 CTS SPORT WAGON

IAN CALLUM

SCOTLAND | BORN 1955 | CAR DESIGNER

2001 JAGUAR R-COUPÉ CONCEPT

2005 JAGUAR ALC CONCEPT

2009 JAGUAR XJ

1994 ASTON MARTIN DB7

Although Ian Callum spent the early part of his career designing cars for Ford of Europe, for the Ford-owned Ghia studio in Turin, and for the TWR design consultancy in the UK, he will always be most closely associated with »Jaguar.

As a young boy growing up in Scotland in the 1960s, Callum was so moved by the allure of the fabulous Jaguar E-Type sports car and the 1968 XJ sedan that he vowed to one day become a car designer, and to design Jaguars.

After completing his master's in product design at the Royal College of Art in London, Callum joined Ford of Europe and later moved to Ghia in Turin as design manager. In 1990 he accepted the challenge of opening a brand-new design studio for industry consultancy TWR. There he shot to international recognition for his work on the Aston Martin DB7, the first of a series of modern Aston Martins.

When Jaguar design director Geoff Lawson died suddenly in 1999 Callum was the natural choice to succeed him. Frustrated by the old-fashioned image of the then-current Jaguars and unable to influence models already in the pipeline, Callum set about planning a new generation of Jaguars that reflected where the brand would have been had the momentous advance of the 1968 XJ been followed up. Positive reaction to such concepts as the R-Coupé and RD-6, and to the »Jaguar XK coupé, helped to gain the confidence of Jaguar managers for the really big strides of the 2008 »XF and 2009 »XJ sedans.

Callum's greatest achievement to date has been to take Jaguar out of its downward retro spiral and reconnect it with its roots as a manufacturer with passion, style and head-turning good looks. The challenge in the years to come will be to reinterpret this emotional design language for smaller cars, an area where mistakes made by Callum's predecessor hurt the company badly.

2007 JAGUAR C-XF CONCEPT

MORAY CALLUM

SCOTLAND | BORN 1958 | CAR DESIGNER

CV	
1980	Degree in industrial design, Napier University, Edinburgh
1982	Master's in vehicle design, Royal College of Art, London. Joins Chrysler Corporation UK, taken over by PSA Peugeot Citroën
1988	Ghia studios, Turin, consultant designer
1995	Ford North America
2001	Head of worldwide design, Mazda
2006	Director of car and crossover design, Ford North America
2009	Executive director, Ford Americas Design

2005 MAZDA MX-5

1993 ASTON MARTIN LAGONDA VIGNALE CONCEPT

Younger brother of Jaguar design director »Ian Callum, Moray was initially tempted by a career in architecture before deciding to follow in his brother's footsteps – including a postgraduate degree at the prestigious Royal College of Art in London.

Callum's career in the auto industry began with an appointment to Chrysler Europe's respected studio in the UK. When Chrysler's European operations were then taken over by PSA Peugeot Citroën, Callum worked on a series of Peugeot and Citroën passenger-car and light commercial vehicle projects. A spell at Ford's Ghia studios in Turin saw him work on such successful designs as the futuristic Via concept of 1989. But it was with the elegant Aston Martin Lagonda Vignale concept of 1993 that Callum first came to prominence: the finely detailed design, although never turned into a production model, was one of the first to suggest that super-luxury cars could once again become of serious interest to automakers.

From Ghia, Callum was lured across the Atlantic to Ford's studio in Dearborn, near Detroit, where he created the 1998 Super Duty truck and 2000 Taurus before being promoted to head of worldwide design for Mazda, which Ford controlled and which was suffering in the market because of a bland product range.

Callum succeeded in revitalizing Mazda's design and image, creating a strong range of cars with a consistent and clear identity. In particular, he relaunched the iconic »Mazda MX-5 sports car in a larger and more powerful format. By 2006 Callum had once again been recalled to Detroit, supervising a line of key products before being given overall responsibility for all of Ford's North American design, including the Lincoln and Mercury brands.

2004 CORVETTE

1962 CORVETTE STINGRAY

Big Three (Chrysler, Ford and General Motors) have to a genuine sports car.

No discussion of Chevrolet design could be complete without mention of the Corvair. This 1959 compact was highly influential on many levels. In terms of style, its fresh and clean body surfaces, with a prominent high waist that ran symmetrically round the whole vehicle, represented a welcome relief from a decade of increasingly absurd fins and excess decorations; this style influenced »Fiat in Italy, Hillman in Britain, NSU in Germany and Simca in France.

On an engineering level, the Corvair was astonishingly brave for an auto establishment more concerned with fashion than technical innovation: with an air-cooled flat-six engine mounted in the rear, it was totally different from familiar Detroit iron. Unfortunately for Chevrolet, this novelty backfired as the Corvair's handling was tricky. A spate of crashes helped to prompt Ralph Nader's 'Unsafe at Any Speed' campaign, and the Corvair had been dropped completely by 1969.

Skilful use of rebranded small cars from such Asian makers as »Isuzu, »Suzuki, »Toyota and »Daewoo helped Chevrolet to navigate the many crises of the 1970s, 1980s and 1990s with marginally less damage than the other majors; the boom in light trucks in the 1990s helped to mask the dismal state of Chevrolet's car design during that period, and it was only with the arrival of product tsar Bob Lutz in the early 2000s that some momentum returned. It was Lutz's energy in cutting through GM's highly bureaucratic processes that helped to keep Chevrolet on track, paving the way for a new generation of small cars originating from Korea and a significant reshaping of American tastes. Much, too, is vested in the landmark range-extended electric »Volt, on which the brand's post-bankruptcy and post-rescue credibility rests.

2008 STINGRAY CONCEPT

PRINCIPAL MODELS

1915	Model 490 selling at $490
1929	First 6-cyl trucks
1935	Suburban is first people-carrier
1950	Bel Air
1953	Corvette
1958	Impala
1959	Corvair, El Camino car-derived pickup
1962	Corvette Stingray; Corvair Monza GT concept
1963	Malibu
1967	Camaro
1969	Blazer SUV
1976	Chevette sub-compact
1983	Nova is version of Toyota Corolla
1999	Silverado
2004	Corvette (6th gen); Nomad concept
2005	HHR; Sequel hydrogen fuel-cell concept
2006	Camaro concept
2007	Aveo; Volt range-extended EV concept; Beat, Groove and Trax small-car concepts
2008	Malibu; Stingray concept
2009	Camaro (5th gen), Spark, Cruze
2010	Volt plug-in hybrid, Orlando

2010 VOLT

2010 ORLANDO

2009 CRUZE

CHEVROLET CAMARO

2009 | COUPÉ

MODEL HISTORY 1967 CAMARO 1ST GENERATION • 1970 CAMARO 2ND GENERATION • 1982 CAMARO 3RD GENERATION • 1993–2002 CAMARO 4TH GENERATION • 2009 CAMARO 5TH GENERATION

2010 6.2 V8	
LENGTH	4835 mm (190 in.)
LAYOUT	Front engine, rear-wheel drive
ENGINE	6.2 petrol V8
HORSEPOWER	432
MAX. SPEED	250 km/h (124 mph)
CO_2 EMISSIONS	–

Three icons now define the Chevrolet brand as it is perceived by the global audience: the »Corvette, an unbroken line of models since the 1950s; the ultra-modern plug-in hybrid »Volt that made its debut in 2010; and the Camaro.

The Camaro archetype remains remarkably strong, considering that the muscle-car original had its heyday in the late 1960s and that later generations became ever feebler until the nameplate was allowed to fade out in 2002. Yet the sentiment remained strong, as was demonstrated by the rapturous reception given to the new Camaro concept shown in 2006. General Motors had little option but to bow to pony-car enthusiasts' wishes and put the car into volume production.

The 2009 Camaro remains remarkably true to the 2006 concept, itself a faithful re-evocation of the late-1960s model with its curvy Coke-bottle theme, its high rear deckline, and even its twin-pod instruments and deep-dished steering wheel. Yet with the new model comes a much more modern surface treatment to go with the familiar proportions, and an altogether more sinister look; this has been heightened by the bird-of-prey stare of the slender but wide grille, and the brooding presence of the now much shallower greenhouse and the heavy top rail to the windshield. Mission accomplished.

CHEVROLET CORVETTE

2004 | LUXURY SPORTS CAR

MODEL HISTORY 1953 CORVETTE 1ST GENERATION • 1963 CORVETTE 2ND GENERATION • 1968 CORVETTE 3RD GENERATION • 1984 CORVETTE 4TH GENERATION • 1997 CORVETTE 5TH GENERATION • 2004 CORVETTE 6TH GENERATION

2010 6.2 V8	
LENGTH	4435 mm (175 in.)
LAYOUT	Front engine, rear-wheel drive
ENGINE	6.2 petrol 8-cyl
HORSEPOWER	436
MAX. SPEED	306 km/h (190 mph)
CO_2 EMISSIONS	316 g/km

Dating back six generations and as many decades, the Corvette is in equal measure a sports car, an American cultural icon and a litmus test of contemporary automobile fashion. The first generation, in 1953, reflected a simple, free and easy approach to sports-car driving and came as a revelation to a generation of drivers used to stodgy, heavy sedans with slow reflexes. An update in 1958 brought quad lights, a broader grille and scooped-out flanks, but the feel was still open and simple.

Dramatic change came in 1963 with the second-generation Corvette, subtitled Stingray because of its aggressive shark-like form language and the distinctive raked rear window of the coupé model. It remains a classic to this day, as does the 1968 third generation that succeeded in combining still stronger shark influences with the 1960s Coke-bottle look to spectacular effect.

Things calmed down from then on, with the fourth-, fifth- and sixth-generation Corvettes gradually becoming softer and less distinctive in their tone and tending to rely on the four-light tail panel for their identity. Clearly, the time is ripe for a fresh iteration, to reinvent the Corvette for a new generation of drivers who look for brain as well as brawn.

1968-GENERATION CORVETTE

CHEVROLET SPARK

2009 | CITY CAR

MODEL HISTORY 1998 DAEWOO MATIZ • 2009 CHEVROLET SPARK

2010 1.2	
LENGTH	3640 mm (143 in.)
LAYOUT	Front engine, front-wheel drive
ENGINE	1.3 petrol 4-cyl
HORSEPOWER	81
MAX. SPEED	164 km/h (102 mph)
CO_2 EMISSIONS	119 g/km

In large swathes of Asia, Europe and South America, the Spark is the most visible face of Chevrolet. A greater contrast between this handy 3.6-metre (less than 12 ft) hatchback and the 6-metre (nearly 20 ft) monsters of Chevrolet legend is hard to imagine, but the simple fact is that Chevrolet has been reinvented as »General Motors' global entry-level brand, and the Spark, made by Daewoo in Korea as well as numerous other GM-controlled locations around the world, is the lead model in many markets – China and Europe among them.

The replacement for Daewoo's Matiz, the Spark had an unusually democratic genesis: at the 2007 New York motor show GM aired three alternative small-car concepts and asked the public to vote online for their favourite. The clear winner was the sharply chiselled Beat, smaller and more city-car-like than the Groove or Trax, and the production model (now expanded to five doors) retains that energetic theme. Oversized headlights, grille and tail lights all make exaggerated statements on the complex surfaces of the tall and narrow body, and the distinctive wedge profile of the DLO is reinforced by a heavy black mask running back from the A-pillar. In a market segment where the first battle is to get noticed, the hectic Spark certainly succeeds.

CHEVROLET VOLT

2010 | HYBRID ELECTRIC MEDIUM CAR

2010 EV	
LENGTH	4400 mm (173 in.)
LAYOUT	Front engine, front-wheel drive
ENGINE	Plug-in hybrid electric plus petrol range extender
HORSEPOWER	150
MAX. SPEED	160 km/h (99 mph)
CO_2 EMISSIONS	109g/km (US test cycle)

The Chevrolet Volt made its first appearance – as a provocative technology-based concept car – at the 2007 Detroit motor show, its mission to prove to the world that parent company »General Motors was up to speed on environmental technologies, and that alternative drive systems, such as its series hybrid powertrains, were under active consideration. Hence the Volt label, to signify the batteries that are permanently connected to the drive motor and the compact combustion engine tasked with keeping those batteries topped up.

The Volt's design deliberately avoided being over-futuristic because GM wanted people to be aware that its technology was within reach; it was given a warm reception. Yet in the three years that followed that show, a combination of external events conspired to give the Volt far more importance than even GM may have expected. First, fuel price spikes and the belated tightening of North American emissions standards highlighted the company's need for an electric or part-electric vehicle; secondly, the escalating economic crisis, plunging sales and GM's own bankruptcy meant that the company desperately needed to have a big hit – both for its morale and for its bottom line.

The stakes were thus raised tenfold: the Volt was hailed as a crucial 'make or break' model for GM by the American media and became prime-time news – especially when President Obama drove the first production example off the line in 2010. GM has been careful to distance the model from existing

hybrids, highlighting the uniqueness of the Volt's ability to run some 65 kilometres (40 miles) emission-free on its batteries before the gasoline engine kicks in.

In design terms, Chevrolet has taken care to ensure that the Volt does not intimidate customers who might be apprehensive about its new technology. It thus grafts a familiar Chevrolet face on to a body that is wider and significantly taller than on the concept, but retains the same feel. The European Opel/Vauxhall Ampera version is different in badging only.

Initial production numbers may be low, but for GM, a battered and bruised company rarely at the forefront of innovation, the Volt is a major roll of the dice on every level.

CHRYSLER

UNITED STATES | FOUNDED 1929 | CARS AND LIGHT TRUCKS | CHRYSLER.COM

1955 C300

Although there are many parallels with the other major American carmakers, the story of Chrysler is significantly different, sometimes dramatically so. Where caution and careful cost-counting characterized most of the decisions taken by »Ford and »General Motors, Chrysler and its sub-brands tended to be more adventurous, to take more risks and to push the boundaries a lot further – and nowhere more so than in the area of design.

Chrysler is the company that stunned the establishment in 1934 with the streamlined, locomotive-like Airflow sedan; in 1940 it was the smooth low-rider Newport Phaeton and Thunderbolt, and in 1961 the space-age Turboflite concept. More recently, Chrysler's prodigious output of concept cars has borne witness to a huge reservoir of imagination and ideas; some of these, such as the Viper, have gone on to become successful, brand-enhancing production models.

Yet Chrysler's innovation has backfired as often as it has succeeded, and the company has had a bumpy ride as a result. Its history is a drama-laden story of booms and near-busts, last-minute rescue deals and miracle recoveries, until the group finally hit the buffers in the wake of the global financial crisis of 2008 and had to submit to the control of Fiat.

Hailed by today's critics as visionary and ahead of its time, the 1934 Airflow was

1984 PLYMOUTH VOYAGER

2004 300C

2005 FIREPOWER CONCEPT

2004 ME 4-12 CONCEPT

2006 IMPERIAL CONCEPT

firmly rejected by buyers at the time and had to be restyled by designer Raymond Dietrich to make it less aerodynamic. No such problems befell the 1955 C300 series designed by his successor, Virgil Exner: influenced by Chrysler's continued collaboration with Italy's Ghia on a series of elegant concept vehicles, the C300 had a sense of harmony and clean simplicity that contrasted with the worst excesses of the rest of Detroit's fin culture.

Chrysler was the first American carmaker to move away from the traditional separate chassis to the lighter and safer unitary structure, and in the muscle-car boom of the late 1960s it produced the most extreme design of all: the 1970 Plymouth Road Runner Superbird, complete with a dramatic tailplane spoiler. The group's fascination with power and speed saw it unprepared for the oil shocks of the 1970s. To provide customers with economical vehicles, it had to import European and later Japanese models, leading to a life-saving alliance with »Mitsubishi.

Chrysler's survival through the 1980s is down to one design: the 1984 Voyager. The boxy multi-seater vehicle was an instant hit,

inventing the family minivan segment and setting the company's profits soaring once more. In typical Chrysler fashion, in 1987 the carmaker then proceeded to rescue the ailing American Motors Corporation (and with it the Jeep brand) and buy Italy's Lamborghini. During the next decade, with Chrysler's innovative cab-forward models a big hit among buyers, the group's new-found momentum attracted the attention of »Mercedes-Benz in Germany: in 1998 the DaimlerChrysler alliance was formed.

It is testament to the enormous creative energy in Chrysler's design department (under »Trevor Creed) that its output of imaginative and often sensational concept cars continued unabated throughout the nine years of turmoil that marked the DaimlerChrysler period; highlights include the 1995 Atlantic concept, the 2004 ME 4-12 supercar concept and the Aston Martin-like 2005 Firepower coupé concept. The number of concepts making it into production (such as the PT Cruiser, the TT-like »Crossfire, the 'American sedan' »300C and the Magnum muscle wagon) is also impressive. Not all were successful, though: buyers did not

take to the 2003 Pacifica, an imaginative cross between a minivan and an SUV, and it lasted only four years in the range.

Starved of investment cash after Daimler pulled out in 2007, Chrysler failed to develop the economical cars demanded by buyers. Its sales slid precariously until the inevitable collapse and another rescue, this time by Fiat. The Italian carmaker had bold plans to build small, modern cars in the United States and for engineer collaboration between the Chrysler and »Lancia brands. As always with Chrysler, it is a daring idea, and it might just pay off.

PRINCIPAL MODELS

1924	Six
1934	Airflow
1940	Newport Phaeton showcar; Thunderbolt showcar
1950	Plymouth XX-500 concept, by Ghia
1955	C300
1961	Turboflite concept
1970	Plymouth Road Runner Superbird
1984	Plymouth Voyager
1988	Chrysler/Lamborghini Portofino concept
1994	LH, New Yorker
1995	Atlantic concept
2001	PT Cruiser
2002	Crossfire
2003	Pacifica; 300C concept
2004	300C production; ME 4-12 concept
2005	Firepower concept
2006	Imperial concept
2007	200C EV
2008	Ecovoyager concept
2011	300C (2nd gen)

2007 200C EV

2008 ECOVOYAGER CONCEPT

CHRYSLER 300C

2011 | EXECUTIVE CAR

MODEL HISTORY 2004 300C 1ST GENERATION • 2011 300C 2ND GENERATION

HEMI 5.7 V8	
LENGTH	5000 mm (197 in.)
LAYOUT	Front engine, rear-wheel drive
ENGINE	5.7 petrol V8
HORSEPOWER	365
MAX. SPEED	250 km/h (155 mph)
CO$_2$ EMISSIONS	295 g/km

As the American auto industry bowed to industrial rationalization and switched over to front-wheel drive platforms in the 1990s, one company – Chrysler – was able to reverse the trend. Thanks to its fusion with »Mercedes-Benz to form DaimlerChrysler in 1998, it had a handy catalogue of decent-quality chassis components from which to develop a modern rear-drive car. Chrysler's bosses were able to translate into sheet metal their dream of reviving what they called the 'great American sedan': high-powered, rear-wheel-driven, and with an unmistakable stateside style.

The 300C concept that design director »Ralph Gilles presented in 2003 was an immediate hit with American critics. Its combination of straight lines, deep flat flanks and a low-rider glasshouse with narrow windows gave it the mean and menacing air of a customized special – and that is precisely how it remained when the 300C entered production in 2004, propelled by Chrysler's potent reborn Hemi V8 engine. A station-wagon, just as sharply styled as the sedan, soon followed, and with the addition of a diesel, too, the 300C became a hit beyond the United States with business buyers intent on making a big impression.

The latest chapter in the 300C's story is the 2011 version, reshaped for more maturity and less aggression, but retaining the subtle mean streak that has given the 300C its strong character.

2004-GENERATION 300C

CHRYSLER CROSSFIRE

2002–2007 | SPORTS CAR

2007 3.2	
LENGTH	4060 mm (160 in.)
LAYOUT	Front engine, rear-wheel drive
ENGINE	3.2 petrol V6 18V
HORSEPOWER	218
MAX. SPEED	250 km/h (155 mph)
CO_2 EMISSIONS	–

The work of designer Eric Stoddard, the Chrysler Crossfire concept was the sensation of the 2001 Detroit motor show. Compact, powerful and highly distinctive with its chiselled central spine running up the windshield and over the roof to form a divided rear screen, it seemed as if it could be the American answer to the universally lauded »Audi TT.

So euphoric was the TT's reception that Chrysler decided to put it into production, but with an unusual twist: it would use a platform and engines from partner »Mercedes-Benz and would be built by respected German coachbuilder Karmann. This would be a rare blend of American style and trusted German engineering, and made in Germany.

Yet this seemingly irresistible combination proved disappointing in practice. The production TT had softer contours and had lost the centre spine, and on the road it was evident that the previous-generation Mercedes componentry did not give the required dynamic finesse. What should have been a »Mercedes-Benz SLK in an American suit turned out to be less than the sum of its parts, and although a convertible and a more powerful SRT version followed, sales remained sluggish. Big discounts were rife, and production of what should have been an image-builder for Chrysler was halted at the end of 2007.

CITROËN

FRANCE | FOUNDED 1919 | VOLUME CARS | CITROEN.COM

When it comes to innovation, original thinking and sheer inspiration in design, there is only one name among today's surviving carmakers that springs to mind: Citroën. One or two firms may have been more outlandish in their imaginations or even more bizarre in their styling, but they have long since fallen by the wayside. Citroën has not – although it has repeatedly come close, a penalty of investing heavily in technical innovation with scant regard for conventional financial disciplines.

Twice Citroën has stunned the world with cars that represented quantum leaps in design: the Traction Avant in 1934, which pioneered front-wheel drive, all-steel unitary construction and hydraulic brakes; and the DS, astonishingly futuristic in 1955 with its streamlined shape, hydropneumatic suspension and fully hydraulic steering, brakes and clutch.

Twice, too, Citroën has been bankrupt: first in the run-up to the launch of the Traction Avant in the early 930s, when a rescue by tyremaker Michelin was engineered by the French government; and secondly in 1973, when Citroën was overstretched, having developed in quick succession the highly sophisticated GS small car, the complex and costly SM supercar, and the equally elaborate CX, replacement for the still-strong DS. Small wonder that cautious investors tended to equate innovation with insolvency.

The second half of Citroën's ninety-year history has been dominated by the way in which its rescuer, the arch-conservative »Peugeot, has judged the precarious trade-off between the need for Citroën to make money, and the requirement for it to please its customers by offering challenging and innovative design and engineering. While early models were unhappy emergency revamps of Peugeot models, a stronger Citroën character began to emerge with the BX of 1982 and the 1989 XM, the first car to have Citroën's Hydractive suspension (a development of the 1950s hydropneumatic

1934 TRACTION AVANT

suspension); both were styled by Marcello Gandini, the great Lamborghini architect from »Bertone. Citroën's individuality was cast aside during the 1990s as such dull designs as the ZX and Xsara trawled the middle market in search of quick profits. Only occasional flashes of inspiration, such as the 1994 Xanae concept for a Renault Scénic rival and the advanced C6 Lignage large car of 1999, kept hopes alive that Citroën had not forgotten its core constituency of drivers who like to be daring and different.

Sensing that Citroën was losing its identity, PSA Peugeot Citroën hired »Jean-Pierre Ploué to lead the brand's design. With experience at Renault, Volkswagen and Ford, Ploué knew all about quality, creativity and mass production, and a series

1979 2CV

1989 XM

A RANGE OF DS MODELS

1994 XANAE CONCEPT

of inspirational concept cars followed. With a clever new double-chevron logo incorporated into the grille profile, these concepts had the important psychological effect of reassociating the brand with daring design. They paved the way for such production models as the first »C4, which, with its innovative glass roof style and unorthodox fixed-centre steering wheel, made Citroëns visibly different to other Volkswagen Golf-segment models. The luxury »C6, although expensive and sold only in small numbers, was seen as a conspicuous return to the individualistic Citroën values, too.

Four designs from the Ploué period stand out: the oddball C-Cactus concept of 2007, which effectively deconstructed the automobile to explore low-cost, eco-friendly solutions, and the 2008 Hypnos concept, with its outstanding interior. Among the production models the funky »C3 Picasso is a perfect family-friendly people-carrier, and the Mini Cooper-sized »DS3 is the first of a series of smart semi-premium urban designs that seek to recapture some of the allure of Citroën's overarching brand icon, the 1955 DS.

The big challenge remaining for Citroën is to create a replacement for the brand's other, diametrically opposed, icon, the 2CV, a replacement that is true to the 2CV's core appeal of bohemian minimalist chic. With the debate currently revolving around simple and original urban electric runabouts, this could be the best chance yet for a 2CV comeback.

2008 HYPNOS CONCEPT

CITROËN C3 PICASSO

2008 | COMPACT MINIVAN

2010 1.6 HDI	
LENGTH	4080 mm (161 in.)
LAYOUT	Front engine, front-wheel drive
ENGINE	1.6 turbo diesel 4-cyl
HORSEPOWER	90
MAX. SPEED	173 km/h (108 mph)
CO_2 EMISSIONS	119 g/km

Speed, sportiness and aggression do not get a look-in on the Citroën C3 Picasso. Instead, this small five-seater minivan majors on the things that matter to its family-centric clientele: spacious and flexible accommodation for people and luggage; comfort and safety; visibility; and – as is evident from its upright, almost toy-like profile – a strong sense of fun.

Launched in 2008 but preceded by a concept version the previous year, the C3 Picasso is quirky and different, advertising its role clearly. Deep, upright doors, near-vertical side glass and the unusual three-piece windshield proclaim generous interior space. The gentle curves of the nose project a friendly face, and the horizontal section of hood in front of the windshield immediately marks it out from the mass of one-box people-carriers that dominate the family market. A kick-up in the subtle waistline just behind the rear door handles serves to enclose the passenger compartment, and a central instrument pod helps to keep the dashboard uncluttered and family-friendly.

Confident enough not to follow the general trend, the C3 Picasso is an excellent design that is perfectly in sync with the priorities of its target market.

CITROËN C4, DS4

2010 | MEDIUM CAR, MINIVAN

MODEL HISTORY 2004 C4 1ST GENERATION • 2006 C4 PICASSO • 2010 C4 2ND GENERATION, DS4

2010 1.6 HDI	
LENGTH	4329 mm (170 in.)
LAYOUT	Front engine, front-wheel drive
ENGINE	1.6 turbo diesel 4-cyl
HORSEPOWER	90
MAX. SPEED	180 km/h (112 mph)
CO_2 EMISSIONS	110 g/km

2010 DS4

2010 C4

The C4 will come to be seen as a very significant model in Citroën's evolution in the early twenty-first century. The original hatchback version, launched in 2004, marked the end of the era of dull design at Citroën, while the classy C4 Picasso minivan at last wrested the people-carrier initiative from »Renault, the company that had pioneered the genre with the »Scénic more than a decade earlier. And to bring the story up to date, a fresh C4 and its accompanying premium DS4 derivative appeared in 2010, cementing Citroën's twin-track approach to the major market segments.

In the 1990s, with a CEO intent on rationalization and producing models that generated quick cash rather than commendations from design critics, Citroën was not a happy place. Its cars were losing their individuality and the marque had lost touch with its inventive, imaginative roots. In the early years of the twenty-first century incoming design director »Jean-Pierre Ploué was determined to reverse this spiral, and he set about restoring morale with a series of brand-enhancing concepts. Two of these, the C-Airdream and the C-Sportlounge, strongly influenced the shape of the production C4.

On its debut in 2004 the C4 was something unusual in the Volkswagen Golf class. The front was the first to feature Citroën's striking new grille signature, and the two versions differed markedly in their silhouettes: the coupé-like three-door featured a dramatically arched roofline finishing high up above the rear bumper,

with the rear window set into the vertical tailgate, while the five-door had an uninterrupted sweep from the windshield header rail to the back bumper. There was innovation inside, too, with a novel fixed-hub steering wheel.

Next it was the turn of the C4 Picasso to present a clean, fresh and modern alternative to the Scénic people-carrier; again the five- and seven-seater versions were differentiated visually through different tail-end treatments and, on the smaller model, an upward kink in the beltline.

Compared with its predecessor, however, the 2010 C4 seems disappointingly plain and featureless, while its premium DS4 counterpart, with its curved creases and sharp detailing, tries too hard to turn the same basic shape into a pseudo crossover for smart city types.

2004 C4

CITROËN C6

2005 | LARGE EXECUTIVE CAR

2.2 HDI	
LENGTH	4910 mm (193 in.)
LAYOUT	Front engine, front-wheel drive
ENGINE	2.2 turbo diesel 4-cyl
HORSEPOWER	173
MAX. SPEED	210 km/h (131 mph)
CO_2 EMISSIONS	199 g/km

As a high-cost, high-complexity luxury car selling mere thousands, the Citroën C6 looks like an endangered species in the mass-production model mix of PSA Peugeot Citroën, Europe's second-biggest automaker. The fact that this sumptuous techno-fest of a limousine still merits a place in the Citroën portfolio has everything to do with pride and prestige, and little to do with hard-nosed business logic.

French president Nicolas Sarkozy often travels in a C6, as do French ambassadors and French business leaders; most of all, however, the car is proudly symbolic of Citroën's own heritage, the ultimate expression of what this famous marque stands for. Thus, alone among Citroën's dozen model lines, the C6 has an extravagantly long and aerodynamic fuselage, a sweeping arched glasshouse terminating in a concave rear window, and astonishing fin-like rear lights that wrap round the rear fender corners. Inside, a host of extraordinary details are integrated without apparent regard to cost. And, most emblematically for this *grande routière*, the suspension is an advanced Hydractive system like no other.

For those accustomed to straight-down-the-line German business sedans, this is all too strange. But for Citroën loyalists it's everything they believe in, wrapped in a single sensational shape.

CITROËN DS3

2009 | COMPACT CAR

2010 1.6 TURBO	
LENGTH	3950 mm (156 in.)
LAYOUT	Front engine, front-wheel drive
ENGINE	1.6 turbo petrol 4-cyl
HORSEPOWER	156
MAX. SPEED	214 km/h (133 mph)
CO_2 EMISSIONS	155 g/km

With its tall stance and 2CV-like domed cabin profile, the Citroën C3, predecessor to the DS3, stood out among supermini hatchbacks; the longer and roomier DS3 is more mainstream in its proportions and thus less distinctive alongside its immediate competitors. Yet, surprisingly, this is intentional, for it is part of Citroën's grand plan to produce both mainstream, big-selling hatchbacks and pricier, premium-appeal models under the new DS branding in the same segment.

That is why the launch of the DS3 and the DS sub-brand is a significant development, in terms of both design and marketing. The company is asking buyers to pay more money for less car but a lot more style: the DS3 is very »Mini Cooper-like with its contrast roof, chunky chrome detailing and huge list of personalization options. The distinctive shark's-fin half-height B-pillar is purely Citroën, however, as are the smart lacquers in its interior and the aggressive front, with its vertically stacked LED identity lights.

The DS3 is original and energetic, and might just catch on. The only thing the DS3 has in common with the signature Citroën of the 1950s is that it, too, promises to take Citroën on a brand adventure of a very different kind.

DONATO COCO

ITALY/FRANCE | BORN 1954 | CAR AND PRODUCT DESIGNER

CV	
1970s	Studies architecture in Besançon, France
1981	MA in vehicle design, Royal College of Art, London
1983	Wins design competition for position at Citroën
1984	Joins Citroën
1998	Chief designer, small cars, Citroën
2005	Director of design and development, Ferrari
2010	Director of design, Lotus

KEY DESIGNS	
1998	Citroën Xsara Picasso
2002	Citroën C2, C3
2003	Citroën C3 Pluriel
2005	Citroën C1
2007	Ferrari F430 Scuderia
2009	Ferrari California, 458 Italia
2010	Lotus Elite, Elan, Elise, Esprit and Eterne concepts

2003 CITROËN C3 PLURIEL

2005 CITROËN C1

Appointed to the new role of director of design at »Lotus in 2010, Donato Coco is charged with stepping up the British specialist sports-car maker's design activities, especially those relating to the company's expanding portfolio of outside customers. As the former director of design at Ferrari, Coco is one of a growing number of ex-Ferrari executives at Lotus to have been recruited since Dany Bahar, former vice president for brand management at the Italian supercar maker, was hired as Group Lotus CEO in 2009. In September 2010 Coco astonished the design establishment by rolling out no fewer than five new Lotus concept cars, just nine months after he had joined the company.

During his five-year tenure at »Ferrari, Coco oversaw the development of a host of exotic models, ranging from the F430 Scuderia and its successor, the »458 Italia, to the more mainstream »Ferrari California – aimed at the luxury GT market – and the 599XX evolution of the top-line front-engined GT model. At Ferrari he had to manage the sometimes tricky relationship between an in-house design team and the company's longstanding design partner, »Pininfarina, whose signature always appears on production models.

Coco, an Italian whose family moved to France when he was a young boy, came to Ferrari from »Citroën, where he had risen to become head of small-car design.

He was responsible for the 2002 C3 hatchback, which pioneered a more rounded architecture as a sentimental echo of the classic 2CV, as well as the C2 and the novel 2003 C3 Pluriel, where the roof and side rails could be removed to create a cabriolet effect. Coco's biggest success at Citroën, however, had been the earlier Xsara Picasso, a compact minivan launched to counter the runaway success of the Renault Scénic.

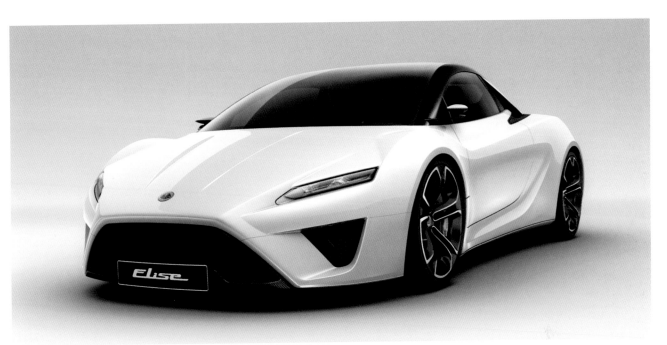

2010 LOTUS ELISE CONCEPT

2010 LOTUS ELAN CONCEPT

TREVOR CREED

GREAT BRITAIN | BORN 1946 | CAR DESIGNER AND MANAGER

CV	
1966	Graduates from University of West Midlands, Birmingham, UK. Joins Ford UK
1973	Design executive for truck exterior studio, Ford UK
1976	Exterior design executive, Ford Germany
1979	Chief designer for interior design, Ford of Europe, UK
1982	Design director for interior design, Ford North America
1985	Director of interior design, colour and trim, Chrysler
1998	Director of advanced design, Jeep
1999	Vice president, Chrysler brand design
2000	Senior vice president of design, Chrysler
2008	Retires from Chrysler

KEY DESIGNS	
1986	Ford Taurus (interior)
1992	Dodge Viper
1994	Dodge Ram, Stratus; Chrysler Cirrus
1995	Chrysler Atlantic concept
1996	New-generation Chrysler, Plymouth and Dodge minivans
1997	Plymouth Prowler
1998	Chrysler Chronos concept
1999	Jeep Grand Cherokee
2003	Dodge Tomahawk concept
2004	Chrysler 300C; Chrysler ME 4-12 concept
2005	Jeep Hurricane concept
2008	Dodge Challenger

Trevor Creed was born and educated in the industrial heartland of Britain, and spent sixteen years designing cars and trucks for Britain's leading automaker, Ford. But, as in the case of many other British industry executives, he crossed the Atlantic to further his career in an even bigger theatre of carmaking – that around Detroit – working first for Ford and then, for an uninterrupted stretch of twenty-three years, Chrysler. And it was at »Chrysler that Creed rose to become one of the major industry figures in catalyzing innovative car and truck design, establishing Chrysler design as one of the world's leading centres for dramatic concept cars that took risks and pushed the creative boundaries.

As in the case of his opposite numbers at General Motors and, to a lesser extent, Ford, Creed oversaw a design operation with a prolific output of concept vehicles and a strong track record in production-car innovation. A quick count reveals a dozen or more significant concept models under Creed's watch for both Chrysler and Jeep, with the Dodge tally closer to twenty. Highlights include the dual Hemi-powered 2005 Jeep Hurricane concept, which could steer all four wheels and spin round in its own length; the Chrysler Chronos concept (a passable stab at an Italianate luxury sedan); and the gangster-like »Chrysler 300C, which went on to become another turnaround production car for the group. Dodge shows the most varied portfolio of all, its concepts under Creed ranging from the spectacular V10-engined Tomahawk motorcycle to the technically advanced Intrepid ESX hybrid of 1977 and the 2005 Slingshot, a petite two-seater coupé derived from the Smart Roadster.

Creed's achievement in liberating all this talent is all the more impressive when one considers the constantly shifting managerial background, as Chrysler was first absorbed by and then abandoned by Germany's Daimler.

2003 DODGE TOMAHAWK CONCEPT

1997 PLYMOUTH PROWLER

1992 DODGE VIPER

1999 JEEP GRAND CHEROKEE

DACIA
ROMANIA | FOUNDED 1968 | ENTRY-LEVEL CARS | DACIACARS.COM

HISTORY AND PRINCIPAL MODELS

1966	Renault cooperation opens under communist regime
1968	Dacia 1100 (based on Renault 8)
1969	Dacia 1300 (based on Renault 12)
1981	Dacia 2000 (based on Renault 20)
1995	Dacia Nova, first in-house design
1999	Renault acquires 51% stake and begins modernization programme
2000	SuperNova launched as interim model
2002	Renault CEO announces programme for €5000 car
2004	Dacia/Renault Logan launched in Eastern Europe
2006	Logan Steppe concept previews wagon model
2007	Logan van
2008	Logan pickup, Sandero hatchback
2009	Sandero Stepway urban crossover; Duster concept
2010	Duster production SUV

2004 LOGAN

2009 DUSTER CONCEPT

2010 DUSTER SUV

The story of Dacia falls conveniently into two very different phases: the three decades under the Romanian communist regime, when it built outdated Renault models under licence for purely domestic consumption; and the period after its takeover by Renault in 1999, when it developed the apparatus of a modern car company, began to export cars all over the world and embarked on manufacture in other countries, too.

The contrast could not be greater. Dacia's low-budget versions of the cast-off Renault 8, 12 and 20 in the 1970s and 1980s did not need to be good: production was fed into controlled markets where cars were scarce and any vehicle was regarded by its owner as a bonus. By 1996, however, Dacia had

developed and launched its own small car, the Nova, using Renault mechanicals, and it was this model and its sister, the Solenza, that Renault upgraded as an interim measure when it took control in 1999.

Few believed Renault CEO Louis Schweitzer when he announced in 2002 that he planned to turn Dacia into an international low-cost entry brand for the Renault group, with a family car priced at under €5000. Yet the design for the Logan revealed in 2004 defied expectations. It was decidedly unstylish, but it was simple, roomy and solid, and was clever in the way that it included components from other Renault models – even the Trafic van – to save costs.

The Logan was an immediate hit in Europe and internationally, and soon also appeared as a van, pickup and station-wagon (the MCV). In 2008 the smaller Sandero hatchback showed evidence of greater styling flair. Yet the big surprise came at the following year's Geneva motor show, when Dacia displayed a genuinely stylish concept, the Duster SUV, complete with mountain bike alongside the passenger's seat. The production Duster that followed in 2010, although lacking any affinity with the concept, looks strong and credible alongside such pricier competitors as the »Toyota RAV4. This is something that augurs well for the next-generation Logan.

DAEWOO

KOREA | FOUNDED 1978 | CARS AND SUVS | DAEWOO.COM

HISTORY AND PRINCIPAL MODELS

1978	Daewoo industrial group purchases Saehan Motor
1983	Daewoo name first used
1984	Agreement with General Motors to build 'world car'
1986	Sets up 50/50 joint venture with GM
1992	Splits with GM
1994	Establishes technical centres in UK and Germany
1995	Becomes first foreign automaker in India
1997	Takes over SUV maker Ssangyong. Launches Lanos, its first in-house design
1998	Asian financial crisis. Daewoo bids for Kia. Matiz small car, styled by Giorgetto Giugiaro
1999	Daewoo is bankrupt, chairman Kim Woo Choong goes into hiding
2000	Group split up; Ford is preferred bidder
2002	GM buys brand and selected plants; establishes GM Daewoo Auto & Technology. Kalos
2004	Daewoos branded as Chevrolets in most export markets. Lacetti
2005	Daewoo models rebranded Chevrolet in export markets. Avro, Epical
2006	Captiva SUV
2008	Cruze
2009	Spark
2011	Chevrolet branding replaces Daewoo worldwide

Small and mid-size cars built by Daewoo in Korea are selling in large numbers across all continents, but few consumers are familiar with the brand name. That's because »General Motors, which took full control of Daewoo in 2002, decided in 2004 that it would use the Chevrolet brand for its value models worldwide, and most of these principally compact cars come from Daewoo.

Highly effective though Daewoo might now be as a world-class designer and builder of small cars, the company did not arrive at this privileged position without a good deal of pain and turbulence, and many ruptures in its relationship with GM. The American giant first used Daewoo in the 1980s to build the Pontiac LeMans – a rebadged Opel Kadett – but split in 1992 over the wish to build a Japanese-based smaller car, too. Freed of its GM constraints, Daewoo embarked on a policy of massive expansion at home and abroad, building factories and technical centres, hiring such top-level engineers as Ulrich Bez (ex-Porsche), and boasting about how it would become a global top-five automaker.

Snapping up SUV maker »Ssangyong in 1997 and bidding for »Kia the following year, Daewoo chairman Kim Woo Choong appeared to be oblivious to the mounting Asian economic crisis. By 1999 it was too late: Daewoo Motors collapsed under a mountain of debt and was broken up, with DaimlerChrysler, Ford and GM fighting over the pieces.

By 2002 GM had got the deal it wanted: Daewoo's most modern and efficient factories but few of its liabilities. Capitalizing on the good reputation of the compact Matiz (styled by Giorgetto »Giugiaro), which had found a worldwide audience, Daewoo has become a vital piece of the global small-car puzzle. It is playing an increasingly important role in helping GM to downsize its operations in the United States to suit the post-crisis auto industry climate.

2004 DAEWOO RANGE

2006 DAEWOO/CHEVROLET CAPTIVA

2008-GENERATION DAEWOO/CHEVROLET CRUZE

2009 DAEWOO/CHEVROLET SPARK

DAIHATSU

JAPAN | FOUNDED 1907 | SMALL CARS AND SUVS | DAIHATSU.COM

HISTORY AND PRINCIPAL MODELS

1907	Hatsodoki Seizo Co. begins making engines
1930	500cc petrol engine
1937	FA small car
1951	Company renamed Daihatsu
1958	Vesta mini-truck
1963	Compagno
1970	Electric vehicles for World Expo
1974	Taft small 4x4 SUV
1977	Charade small car
1980	Mira/Cuore
1984	Rocky 4x4
1992	Opti
1995	Toyota takes 33% stake. Move
1997	Terios compact 4x4
1998	Toyota takes controlling stake
2000	YRV compact car
2002	Copen mini sports car
2003	EFE-II concept car
2004	Sirion small car
2006	Materia medium car, new Terios
2007	Trevis
2009	Basket concept

1963 COMPAGNO

1995 MOVE

2006 MATERIA

Now fully integrated into the »Toyota empire, Daihatsu is best known for its small – and very small – cars and its rugged four-wheel-drive models, many of which are sold worldwide. The company, which had its origins in the early twentieth century as an engine maker, began building small cars, many of them midget three-wheelers, in the 1950s. Graduating to four-wheelers, including several attractive variations on the compact Compagno, Daihatsu developed considerable know-how in the 'kei-class' minicars that have always figured strongly in Japanese sales.

This expertise was an incentive for market leader Toyota to build up its stake

2003 UFE-II CONCEPT CAR

in Daihatsu: Daihatsu-developed small-capacity engines began appearing in Toyota models in the late 1990s, and by 2004 the two companies were launching parallel models with only slight differences in bodywork.

Today, Daihatsu is in effect the small-car division of Toyota, but it still has a parallel existence as an independent-minded producer of mini vehicles of often quite radical style. Its history is peppered with unusual designs and – to the amusement of Western observers – such curious model names as D-Bone, Naked Turbo, Be>Go and the more recent Basket and DecaDeca concepts.

On a more serious note, Daihatsu's sequence of UFE ('ultimate fuel economy') concepts from 2001 onward shows that large efficiencies can be gained from ultra-lightweight aerodynamic three-seater minicar configurations.

The first production models that brought attention to Daihatsu outside Japan were the Charade small car of the late 1970s and the Rocky compact 4x4 of the mid-1980s. Known as Feroza or Fortran in certain markets, the Rocky was influential in creating a new market sector: that of the light and affordable leisure 4x4.

More recent production-car highlights include the YRV minicar (2000), the tiny but authentic Copen open two-seater sports car (2002), and the distinctive Materia (2006), a radical take on a practical compact family minivan in the »Renault Scénic class.

2006-GENERATION TERIOS

2002-GENERATION COPEN

WALTER DE'SILVA

ITALY | BORN 1951 | CAR DESIGNER AND MANAGER

Walter de'Silva has risen to become a figure of major influence within the automotive industry, overseeing the visual identities of the nine major brands that constitute Europe's largest carmaker, »Volkswagen. His advance to one of the most responsible roles in the automotive design world comes after a long career, in which he has shown himself adept at revitalizing troubled or failing brands by building a consistent new corporate image, and sustaining this throughout the model range.

No brand demonstrates this more powerfully than »Audi, where de'Silva took charge in 2002. Audi design was already strong in its core sedan segments, but de'Silva was able successfully to apply and adapt this precise design language across such new segments as large SUVs (Q7, 2005) and supercars (R8, 2006). De'Silva's reworking of the iconic »Audi TT sports car in 2006 is a textbook example of adding power and presence to a much-loved design while preserving its original appeal. More recent Audi designs, including his »A5 (2007), have begun to allow slightly more emotion into their surface treatment.

De'Silva took responsibility for all the group's brands in 2007. He turned his attention to the muddled image presented by Volkswagen under »Murat Günak and rolled out a series of designs showing a fresh and above all consistent brand identity. The Up! concepts of 2007 are classics of Bauhaus-style clarity, simplicity and proportion.

Where de'Silva has been less successful in his turnaround mission is with Spanish brand »SEAT: well-received concepts failed to translate into successful showroom models. This is in sharp contrast to de'Silva's work at »Alfa Romeo, the first brand he controlled, where the stylish 156 sedan triggered a much-awaited return to form for the Italian carmaker.

1997-GENERATION ALFA ROMEO 156

2003 AUDI NUVOLARI CONCEPT

2006 AUDI TT

2007 VOLKSWAGEN UP! CONCEPT

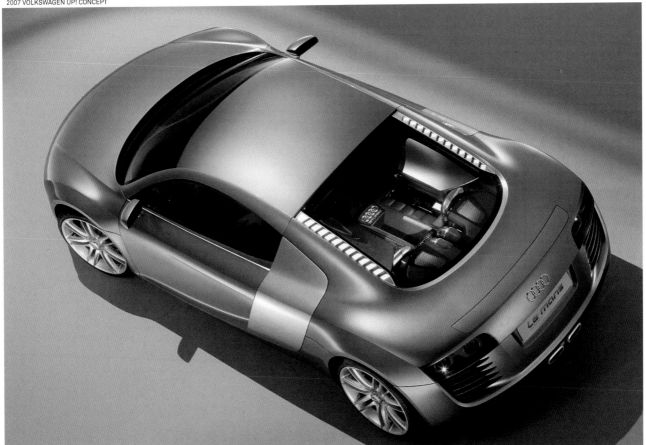

2003 AUDI LE MANS CONCEPT

DODGE

UNITED STATES | FOUNDED 1914 | CARS AND LIGHT TRUCKS | DODGE.COM

The last American brand to join the »Chrysler Group – it was lured in as an already successful automaker in 1928 – Dodge was originally positioned as middle-market nameplate in Chrysler's portfolio, its mission being to compete with General Motors' smart but not premium »Buick. Yet after eight decades and countless generations of models, the erstwhile rivals could hardly be further apart in their standing: while Buick is known for being staid and sensible, Dodge has made a name for itself by being brash, rash and provocative, and generally pushing things to the extreme.

Dodge's two signature products of the early twenty-first century say it all: the mighty Viper sports car with its thundering 8-litre V10; and the oversized and intimidating »Ram series of pickups, whose classification as light trucks seems entirely inadequate. These high-profile designs seem to overshadow almost everything else that Dodge does. This would include the Charger and »Challenger, high-powered revivals of legendary 1960s muscle cars; the Caravan minivan, which has been quietly keeping the company afloat since 1984; and the smaller Journey (2007), which has been an unsung success in the middle market.

The same extremely polarized approach is seen in the rich back catalogue of Dodge-branded concept cars, where Chrysler's always inventive designers are frequently at their wild and way-out best. Who would think of mounting a massive V10 engine in a motorcycle, for instance? Dodge did, in the 2003 Tomahawk. A 6-litre V8 Hemi-powered muscle car that's also a family station-wagon? That will be the Dodge – in this case the Magnum (2003), a production car.

With so many disparate ideas fighting for attention, it is hard to find any shared 'DNA', apart from Dodge's cross-hair grille and ram's-head mascot. Yet that broad-brush approach very much represents the Dodge of the past, the pre-bankruptcy era when

HORACE AND JOHN DODGE

1969 CHARGER DAYTONA

anything that caused a sensation was seen as good for business. Following its rescue by Fiat in 2009, Dodge is already having to focus more selectively: the Viper is gone, Ram is to become a separate brand and the charismatic muscle cars are threatened by upcoming fuel-efficiency standards.

Dodge's designers will need to redouble their ingenuity, if they are to reshape this larger-than-life brand in a way that both acknowledges its past excesses and translates them into a format fit for a very different future.

1992 VIPER

2004 SLINGSHOT CONCEPT

2008 ZEO ELECTRIC CONCEPT

2007 DEMON CONCEPT

DODGE CHALLENGER

2008 | COUPÉ

MODEL HISTORY 1969–74 CHALLENGER 1ST GENERATION • 1978–83 CHALLENGER 2ND GENERATION • 2008 CHALLENGER 3RD GENERATION

2010 6.1 SRT8 V8

LENGTH	5025 mm (198 in.)
LAYOUT	Front engine, rear-wheel drive
ENGINE	6.1 petrol V8
HORSEPOWER	431
MAX. SPEED	270 km/h (168 mph)
CO_2 EMISSIONS	–

To Jeff Gale of Chrysler's Pacifica studio fell the onerous responsibility of reinterpreting one of Dodge's most venerated brand heroes, the Challenger, for the twenty-first century. The 1969 Challenger had been late to join the muscle-car party, but made up for this by being even more extreme than its »Ford Mustang and »Chevrolet Camaro rivals. Low and wide, and with long overhangs front and rear, race-style chrome gas cap and a huge air scoop on the hood, it ticked all the boxes, became a huge success, and passed into automotive mythology.

The born-again Challenger was well received as a concept in 2006 and, two years later, the production car remained absolutely faithful to the concept's design. Substantially longer than the 1969 original, it sported huge 20-inch wheels to keep the relative proportions the same; Gale even extended the front overhang for better balance. The shape is just as evocative as it was in 1969, with the short, low DLO kicking up sharply over the muscular rear wheel arches, and the flat rear deck and full-width tail lights gives it real authenticity.

As a footnote, the late-1970s second-generation Challenger is best forgotten. It was a rebadged Mitsubishi Sapporo hardtop.

DODGE RAM
2008 | PICKUP

MODEL HISTORY 1981 RAM 1ST GENERATION • 1994 RAM 2ND GENERATION • 2002 RAM 3RD GENERATION • 2008 RAM 4TH GENERATION

5.7 V8 HEMI	
LENGTH	5816 mm (229 in.)
LAYOUT	Front engine, rear-wheel drive
ENGINE	5.7 petrol V8
HORSEPOWER	390
MAX. SPEED	–
CO$_2$ EMISSIONS	–

Big pickup trucks are an exclusively American phenomenon, and among them the Dodge Ram is by common consent king. Since Dodge pickup trucks took on the Ram label back in 1981, successive generations have seen a steady escalation in the model's power, proportions and sheer intimidation factor.

The biggest step came with the second-generation Ram, in the 1990s, when the flat hood and perpendicular front (adorned with a weighty, heavily chromed full-width grille) were replaced by a lofty domed hood, tapering towards the equally monumental radiator, complete with the Dodge 'cross-hairs' brand identifier rendered in heavy chrome. The impact of this thrust-forward grille was enhanced by the big step down to the front fenders and the headlights.

Ram generations three and four have continued the trend, further exaggerating the height and forcefulness of the grille. By the 2008 edition the Ram looked as if it could swallow a compact hatchback in a single gulp. Along with size, weight and engine power – an 8-litre V10 related to that in the Viper sports car – the luxury has increased, too; this rugged vehicle even has in-floor storage for ten beverage cans and ice.

LUC DONCKERWOLKE

PERU/BELGIUM | BORN 1965 | CAR DESIGNER

The son of Belgian diplomats, Luc Donckerwolke was born in Peru and travelled widely throughout South America and Africa before returning to Brussels to study industrial engineering. He then moved to Vevey, in Switzerland, to complete his studies in vehicle design. Donckerwolke is a fluent speaker of at least six languages, and his cosmopolitan upbringing is echoed in a career that has taken in the diverse cultures of French, German, Czech, Italian and Spanish car brands. In particular, he was well placed within the »Volkswagen Group in the early 2000s, when there was much cross-fertilization between brands at the design centre belonging to the sportier Audi group taking in SEAT and Lamborghini.

Having begun his design career at »Peugeot in France, Donckerwolke was quick to accept an opportunity at »Audi; soon, he transferred to »Skoda in the Czech Republic, where he was instrumental in the design of the Skoda Octavia. This was a key model, with a mission to establish Skoda as a credible quality brand, and its style and presentation had to be perfectly judged. The subsequent rise of Skoda as a respected brand shows the success of the Octavia design and the later Fabia.

After another short spell at Audi, Donckerwolke moved to »Lamborghini in Italy upon its acquisition by Audi in 1998: his »Murciélago successfully floated a sharp, progressive style that was dramatically distinct from that of arch-rival »Ferrari. Moved to what is often seen as the VW Group's problem brand, »SEAT, in 2005, Donckerwolke responded with an image overhaul and a series of concepts showing a stronger face and more dynamic body proportions. The 2008 Ibiza and 2010 IBE concept are the first examples of this new style.

2010 SEAT IBE CONCEPT

2003 LAMBORGHINI GALLARDO

2008 SEAT IBIZA

2007 SEAT TRIBU CONCEPT

DONKERVOORT

THE NETHERLANDS | FOUNDED 1978 | LIGHTWEIGHT SPORTS CARS | DONKERVOORT.NL

HISTORY AND PRINCIPAL MODELS	
1978	S7
1985	S8
1994	D8 with Cosworth engine
1999	D8 with Audi engine
2000	Moves to modern factory in Lelystad
2008	D8 GT coupé

1999 D8

Not many years after »Lotus founder Colin Chapman had sold the rights to the legendary Seven back-to-basics sports car to »Caterham in 1973, on the other side of the Channel another enthusiast for lightweight sports cars had a similar idea. Joop Donkervoort, working from his home in Tienhoven in the centre of The Netherlands, began designing and building his open two-seater sports cars in 1978, and by the early 1980s word was spreading in sporting circles that his self-titled designs were at least as good as the original Lotus or, indeed, as Caterham's official version of the Lotus.

What worried Caterham at the time was that the Dutch car, with its fuselage-like body, its open scoop of a cockpit and its exposed front wheels, looked almost indistinguishable from the Seven it was building. Whether or not the Donkervoort was too close a copy of the Caterham is now immaterial: both have evolved into much more sophisticated designs, and both are highly successful in circuit racing. Each has its own fanatical bunch of owners devoted to pushing the envelope of extreme driving thrills, with little thought for comfort or convenience.

Yet, of the two, it is Donkervoort that has made the greatest effort to update the aesthetic design, as opposed to the engineering, of this stark and minimalist machine. The major changes that came with the D8 in the late 1990s saw a tidying up of the body and its exposed suspension, and separate lights.

The most radical move of all has been the closed-coupé D8 GT, which debuted in 2008. Incorporating experience from the racing car that snatched the Nürburgring production-car lap record from »Porsche, the GT has a carbon-fibre glasshouse and rear bodywork; tail lights are neatly integrated below each side spoiler; and at the front the narrow slit headlight housings and lower air dam give a sense of single-seater racing-car style. Rather as in the case of »Morgan's Eva GT, Donkervoort's D8 GT coupé is a highly purposeful and more modern take on a classical theme, and is all the more intriguing for it.

1999 D8

1978 S7

2008 D8 GT

WOLFGANG EGGER

GERMANY | BORN 1963 | CAR DESIGNER

2007 ALFA ROMEO 8C COMPETIZIONE

1999 SEAT IBIZA

Although he grew up in Germany (albeit in its most southerly town), even from a young age Wolfgang Egger appeared to have a fascination with all things Italian. This led him to choose design capital Milan for his studies in product design. He then joined »Alfa Romeo, becoming the marque's chief designer four years later and contributing to such key models as the 145, 146 and 156 under the influential »Walter de'Silva.

Egger also had a hand in the 1996 Nuvola concept for a front-engined sports coupé built on an aluminium spaceframe. The voluptuous lines of this design could be seen as an early indication of the very emotional design language he would use on the »Alfa Romeo 8C Competizione, the car that would come to be seen as his masterpiece.

As chief designer at »SEAT, Egger was tasked with building greater respect and a stronger identity for the brand; he sharpened the image of such core products as the Ibiza, but proved less successful with larger models. Returning to his Alfa Romeo roots (after a short spell at Lancia), Egger brought in the sharp new frontal identity, including six headlamps and a slender grille, for the emotionally important Spider, »Brera and »159 models. Yet it was the unashamedly retro 8C that really put him into the who's who of designers.

Egger was headhunted by his former boss, de'Silva, to take charge of »Audi design in the Volkswagen Group brand reorganizations after Martin Winterkorn became CEO in 2007. His more emotional approach can be seen in the voluptuous »Audi A5 coupé and, especially, its five-door Sportback derivative launched in 2009.

1996 ALFA ROMEO NUVOLA CONCEPT

2009 AUDI SPORTBACK CONCEPT

FERRARI

ITALY | FOUNDED 1947 | LUXURY AND EXTREME SPORTS CARS | FERRARI.COM

HISTORY

1919	Enzo Ferrari makes debut as racing driver
1921	Works as driver for Alfa Romeo
1929	Founds Scuderia Ferrari to race Alfa Romeos
1938	Becomes head of Alfa Corse in Milan
1939	Leaves Alfa Romeo
1945	Starts designing V12 engine
1947	First car is 125S
1951	Ferrari driver Alberto Ascari is first F1 world champion
1963	Ford tries to buy Ferrari
1969	Sells 50% stake to Fiat
1971	Builds Fiorano circuit, Maranello
1987	F40 is last car under Enzo's stewardship
1988	Enzo Ferrari dies
2006	Fiat owns 86% of Ferrari

1964 250 GTO

2003 612 SCAGLIETTI

Legends do not come much more powerful or more passion-filled than Ferrari. The only company to have contested every Grand Prix season since Formula One started in 1951, Ferrari was first and foremost a racing-car maker; Enzo Ferrari's first road car, the 1.5-litre V12 125S of 1947, was a racing car at heart and needed only bodywork revisions to take to the track. Later single-seater Formula One cars became more specialized, but Ferrari's sports-racing models continued to retain strong links with the road-car ranges and, in some cases, to be derived from designs that customers could buy from Ferrari showrooms.

The 1950s and 1960s were without question a golden age for Ferrari – and Italian – design. Stylists and *carrozzerie* vied with each other to produce the most elegant and exotic shapes and materials, and there was a certain blurring of boundaries as to which were official Ferrari

1987 F40

PRINCIPAL MODELS	
1948	166 Inter
1956	250 GT Berlinetta
1962	250 GTO
1968	365 GTB/4 Daytona
1969	Dino 246 GT
1975	308 GTB
1987	F40
1992	456 GT
1995	F50
1996	550 Maranello
1999	360 Modena
2002	Enzo
2003	612 Scaglietti
2004	F430
2006	599 GTB Fiorano
2007	F430 Scuderia; FXX concept
2009	California, 458 Italia
2011	FF four-seater, four-wheel drive

2011 FF

2011 FF

2007 F430 SCUDERIA

2007 FXX CONCEPT

designs and which were interpretations built by others. Nevertheless, designs that stand out particularly strongly are the 1957 250 GT Cabriolet by »Pininfarina; the semi-racing 250 GTO, by designer/coachwork maker Scaglietti, of 1962; and Ferrari's first mid-engined road car, the pretty and petite Dino 206 GT of 1967, again penned by Pininfarina.

The late-1960s Dino was the first Ferrari to be assembled on a production line, as opposed to being built by hand. This development, along with the advent of unitary construction as opposed to spaceframe chassis, would have a profound effect on Ferrari design and the company's relationship with the coachbuilding firms. No longer could even Ferrari afford the extravagance of limited production runs of different styles by different designers on the same basic car. Instead, just one interpretation of each model was produced, which meant that only one designer could be chosen. That choice, to no one's surprise, fell on Pininfarina, and with only one exception (the 308 GT4 by »Bertone) all Ferraris since 1973 have borne Pininfarina's signature. The symbiotic relationship

between Ferrari and Pininfarina has been a major influence in shaping the design of today's elite high-performance luxury sports cars.

Three parallel lines of evolution can be identified in Pininfarina's work for Ferrari. The large high-performance GT cars, generally front-engined, have a stronger focus on comfort and show a fairly linear development from the 456 GT of 1992 to today's »599 and 612. The more lithe and agile mid-engined sports models have grown steadily in power, size and complexity, from the elegant template of the 1975 308 GTB to the elaborate 4.5-litre »458 Italia launched in 2009. The third strand, that of the hardline extreme-performance Ferrari, is epitomized by the brutal but beautiful F40 of 1987, the last Ferrari to be built under Enzo's stewardship; it found subsequent expression in the somewhat disappointing F50 of 1995 and the Formula One-shaped »Enzo of 2002. There has as yet been no real follow-up to the Enzo, although the GTO version of the front-engined 599, developed to an extreme-performance brief, goes some way towards filling that gap.

An important new direction was opened up in 2009 with the launch of the »California. As the first Ferrari in several generations to be aimed at a broader and less conspicuously wealthy customer base, the California majors on comfort and convenience. In order to allow it to compete with such luxury-orientated designs as the »Mercedes-Benz SL, the California includes automatic dual-clutch transmission and a rigid folding hardtop. Yet the proportions of the rear body section, imposed by the fixed size of the folding roof, are an issue that even master-designer Pininfarina has not fully resolved, and Ferrari enthusiasts contend that truly pleasing lines can be achieved only by having separate berlinetta and spider versions.

FERRARI 458 ITALIA

2009 | LUXURY SPORTS CAR

2010 4.5 V8	
LENGTH	4525 mm (179 in.)
LAYOUT	Mid engine, rear-wheel drive
ENGINE	4.5 petrol V8
HORSEPOWER	570
MAX. SPEED	325 km/h (202 mph)
CO₂ EMISSIONS	307 g/km

Since the advent of the 308 in 1975, the V8-powered, mid-engined berlinetta has always been the most visible and most widely recognized model in the Ferrari range. »Pininfarina's designs spanning the 308, 328, 348, 355, 360 Modena and F430 through to the 458 Italia, provide a fascinating sequence of shapes illustrating the stylistic evolution of the supercar template through nearly four decades of engineering advance, new materials and changing fashions.

Compared with the elegant and well resolved »F430 that went before it, the 458 Italia is busier, more complex and more extreme. Although its function – to provide extreme performance and the ultimate in handling and agility for two people – is unchanged, its proportions and the balance of its masses have altered. The 458 Italia is very cab-forward in its stance, looking much lighter and more nimble. Immediately noticeable are the slimmer pillars and the greater area of glass in relation to body mass. This is the result of two things: the beltline diving steeply towards the front, and the deliberate slimming of the flanks by the drawing in of the rocker panel below the doors. The contrast with the heavier look of the F430, with its outwardly flared rockers, is striking. On the 458 Italia, the visual mass is also reduced by the placing of the engine air intakes under the car, allowing smooth sides undistorted by slots or ducts.

The 458 Italia's long and narrow black-highlighted headlamp assemblies are stretched far back along the edges of the hood. At the back, the complex surfacing of the fenders twists inwards as it moves towards the rear, forming the angled edges of the rear screen. Bullet-shaped rear lights straddle the rear fenders and rear panel at each end of the spoiler lip.

The 458 Italia's complex rear, which houses an intricate diffuser, triple exhaust outlets and twin lateral grilles, is more imposing than the slender, almost delicate front would lead one to expect. The short flat rear deck between the trailing edge of the rear screen and the spoiler provokes a deliberate imbalance to create a feeling of tension and propulsive force, making this an overtly dynamic, rather than classically beautiful, member of the Ferrari line of succession.

FERRARI 599 GTB FIORANO

2006 | LUXURY SPORTS CAR

2010 6.0 V12	
LENGTH	4665 mm (184 in.)
LAYOUT	Front engine, rear-wheel drive
ENGINE	6.0 petrol V12
HORSEPOWER	620
MAX. SPEED	330 km/h (205 mph)
CO$_2$ EMISSIONS	415 g/km

The 599 GTB Fiorano is the latest in the long lineage of Ferrari grand tourers with front-mounted V12 engines, picking up the mantle from such greats as the 250 GT, 365 GTB/4 Daytona, and, in the 1990s, the 456 GT. Coming after the disappointing 575 Maranello and running in parallel with the unloved larger 2+2 seater 612 Scaglietti, the 599 had the important mission of restoring the traditional greatness to the front-engined Ferrari. This it has done with considerable aplomb.

The 599 GTB Fiorano's design, by »Pininfarina as always, celebrates the front-engined layout with a long hood, a cockpit stretched front and rear by steeply raked screens, and an elegant sweep of the beltline up and over the rear wheel arches to meet a forward-slanting tail panel in the idiom of the 456 GT. The proportions are more thrusting and forward-leaning than in other recent Ferraris, placing the centre of the visual mass just ahead of the rear wheels. Two additional versions of the 599 – the even higher-performance GTO and the limited-edition SA Aperta convertible, both from 2010 – are visually very successful, too, marking a real return to form for this most classic of Ferrari formats.

FERRARI CALIFORNIA

2009 | LUXURY SPORTS CAR

2010 4.3 V8	
LENGTH	4565 mm (180 in.)
LAYOUT	Front engine, rear-wheel drive
ENGINE	4.3 petrol V8
HORSEPOWER	460
MAX. SPEED	310 km/h (192 mph)
CO_2 EMISSIONS	306 g/km

Launched in 2009, the California signalled the addition of a new and very different direction for Ferrari. In providing a softer and more accessible design that is easy to drive and practical in everyday use, the Italian supercar maker is addressing a broader, more general clientele: drivers for whom the hardline, mid-engined sports cars are too extreme and the big front-engined V12 models are unnecessarily powerful and intimidating. The target market is Mercedes-Benz SL-owners who value comfort, convenience and easy performance, but want to graduate to an exotic brand without having the hassle of driving anything too fragile or temperamental.

The new car, which takes its name from the California of the 1950s (itself also a more mainstream design that played well in the American market), bears »Pininfarina's signature. Yet, in contrast to most Pininfarina offerings, it failed to win instant praise. In particular, the need to incorporate the fixed dimensions of a rigid folding metal hardtop imposed unbalanced proportions on the car's exterior, especially around the rear, where the high deckline and bluff tail gave an uncomfortable feeling of excess visual mass at the back of the car. Viewed from the rear, roof up or down, the California does indeed present a bulky visual mass, the bullet-like tail lights, quadruple exhausts and full-width blacked-out strip doing little to relieve the large vertical tail surface.

While the conventional nose and faired-in headlights provide pleasant echoes of the original California, extra detailing (such as

the recessed slots around the lights, the scooped channels along the bodysides and the deepening slots in the rocker panels) serve to complicate the design, stripping it of the purity that a front-engined convertible can traditionally enjoy.

In the interior, however, there have been dividends in one of the California's mainstream innovations: the seven-speed automated dual clutch transmission. Freed of the traditional Ferrari open gearlever gate, the centre console and instrument panel are now simpler and more elegant, as well as being immaculately crafted. Yet in the absence of the exotic grace and raw excitement that even a Ferrari-lite is expected to exhibit, the California fails to gel as a harmonious design.

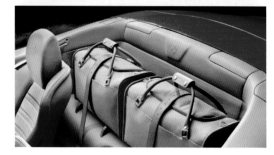

FERRARI ENZO

2002–2004 | EXTREME SPORTS CAR

2004	
LENGTH	4702 mm (186 in.)
LAYOUT	Mid engine, rear-wheel drive
ENGINE	6.0 petrol V12
HORSEPOWER	660
MAX. SPEED	363 km/h (225 mph)
CO_2 EMISSIONS	545 g/km

With its run of less than four hundred all pre-sold to Ferrari customers who had already bought an F40 or an F50, the Enzo is in the finest tradition of Ferrari's most extreme sports cars, a line that began in 1962 with the 250 GTO. Where the Enzo differs from its predecessors is that it is much closer to a pure racing car in its configuration and construction, and that this pursuit of absolute performance has come at the expense of a conventional, easily understood aesthetic.

The Enzo's design is best seen as that of a Formula One car with the gaps filled in between the front and rear wheels. Three principal volumes make up its shape: the sharply pointed F1-style nose that broadens out to take in the narrow passenger cell and engine cover; the fairings that cover the front wheels; and the broad, flat rear deck and muscular rear fender assembly that provide the car's visual propulsive force.

Certain details hark back to the 1987 F40, while others, such as the relationship of the rear fenders, rear deck and bullet-shaped rear lights, look ahead to the 2009 »458 Italia. Overall, however, while the F40 was both beautiful and brutal, the complex Enzo tends more towards the latter.

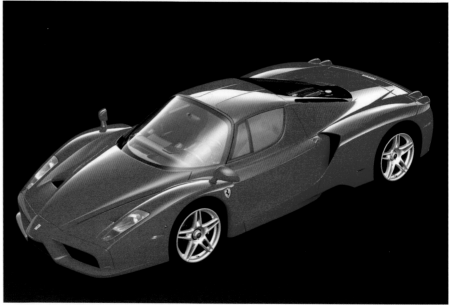

FERRARI F430

2004–2010 | LUXURY SPORTS CAR

2010 3.6 V8	
LENGTH	4510 mm (187 in.)
LAYOUT	Mid engine, rear-wheel drive
ENGINE	3.6 petrol V8
HORSEPOWER	490
MAX. SPEED	315 km/h (195 mph)
CO_2 EMISSIONS	420 g/km

As the follow-up to the successful Ferrari 360 Modena and facing a resurgent »Lamborghini, the 2004 F430 needed to move the exotic-car game on, both dynamically and in terms of style. Aluminium spaceframe construction, an electronic differential and novel vehicle dynamic control took care of the former, while »Pininfarina achieved a remarkable enhancement of the car's image – all the more remarkable when one considers that the front hood, doors and roof were carried over from the 360.

Switching the F430's headlamps to run rearward and upwards rather than across the car, and at the same time bringing the air intakes to the centre, helped to re-create the famous shark-nose look of the 1960s Formula One cars, and to improve the overall proportion to one not quite so wide. Deep channels in the doors feed the lower rear air intakes and relieve the visual mass of the flanks, while larger intakes set higher on the rear fenders add to the muscular feeling of the rear.

Rear on, the F430 takes elements of the »Enzo's rear-window and deck treatment but turns them into something of grace and style, as well as efficiency. Aside from the over-use of the Ferrari emblem (it appears eight times on the exterior), the F430 is one of Ferrari's very best.

FIAT

ITALY | FOUNDED 1899 | VOLUME CARS | FIAT.COM

HISTORY

1899	Giovanni Agnelli invests in Fabbrica Italiana Automobili Torino (Fiat)
1900	First factory, 150 workers
1916	Construction of modern Lingotto factory
1945	Giovanni Agnelli dies
1966	Grandson Gianni Agnelli becomes president
1969	Takes over Lancia and Ferrari
1978	Ritmo is first robot-built car
1979	Auto sector operations grouped in holding company Fiat Auto
1986	Acquires Alfa Romeo
1993	Acquires Maserati
1996	Gianni Agnelli becomes honorary president
2000	Joint venture agreed with General Motors
2003	Gianni Agnelli dies
2004	Sergio Marchionne becomes CEO
2006	GM joint venture dissolved
2009	Strategic alliance with Chrysler
2010	New business plan envisages 6 million vehicles per year by 2014. Car division separates from group

1953 1100

1969 128

2009 500C AND 1957 NUOVA 500

When it comes to design, Fiat leads the world in many respects. It has taken more European Car of the Year awards than any other automaker, it is much more willing to employ outside design agencies and bold ideas in its creative processes and, perhaps as a consequence, it has suffered periodic crises more frequently and more intensely than its competitors. Yet, as a further consequence, it has also been able to conjure up a remarkable series of bounce-back models that through the sheer brilliance of their design have changed the

2003 PANDA

1980 PANDA

rules of the game, brought buyers back to the brand and restored it to health just as it appeared close to collapse.

Among Fiat's most celebrated rescue models is the 1983 Uno, when Fiat effectively bet the company on a daring new tall-format hatchback designed by »Giorgetto Giugiaro. The Punto a decade later provided a further much-needed energy boost, and in 2005 the streamlined »Grande Punto, again by Giugiaro, reversed what had appeared to be a dangerous decline in Fiat's fortunes. It could also be argued that the spectacularly successful 2007 reinterpretation of the classic »500 minicar helped Fiat to survive the 2008–2010 financial downturn with much less trauma than competitors with larger and less characterful designs.

In the sector below that of the Uno and Punto, Fiat has again benefited from inspirational Giugiaro designs, such as the ingeniously simple 1980 »Panda, which lasted two decades in production, and its 2003 successor. But while Fiat's small-car judgement tends to be spot on, in the medium and larger sectors the track record is less good, and the company's bigger bets have often turned embarrassingly sour. The very boxy style of the 124 and 128 that had served Fiat so well in the 1960s and early 1970s was beginning to look very stale by the time the »Volkswagen Golf arrived in 1974. »Bertone's oddball Ritmo of 1978 – famous also for being the first robot-built car – was regarded as too weird and failed badly. Its successors, the Tipo (the first production car designed by the »I.DE.A institute), the Bravo/Brava and finally the 2001 Stilo all missed the mark. It was only

1993 COUPÉ

1998 MULTIPLA

in 2007, with the new Bravo, a Giugiaro-penned enlargement of the successful Grande Punto, that Fiat finally struck gold in the medium sector.

As well as needing to sell in significant numbers, any new Fiat has a formidable heritage to live up to; most notably, the legacy left by the company's legendary designer and engineer Dante Giacosa (1905–1996), architect of many generations of Fiats that marked major steps forward in design. Examples include the Topolino of 1936 and the Nuova 500 of 1957, both of which helped to promote the mass mobilization of the Italian nation. Mainstream Fiat models in the post-Giacosa era have helped to trigger broader design trends, too: the boxy 'non-design' look of the 124 in the mid-1960s, the tall architecture pioneered by the Uno in 1983, and the sports-car-like noses of the Grande Punto and Bravo in 2005 and 2007.

Yet not all of Fiat's new directions find followers. Designer »Roberto Giolito's highly original 1998 Multipla seated six in two rows and, although extremely practical, looked too bizarre to appeal to the volume market. The same applied to the 1993 Fiat Coupé by »Chris Bangle, in which the bug eyes and dramatic angled slashes in the bodysides were rejected by buyers looking for classical coupé beauty.

It has been the same story with Fiat's often imaginative showcar concepts, such as the 1993 Downtown city car, which proposed the three-seater layout later used by McLaren designer Gordon Murray, and the 2000 Ecobasic. Most of these concepts did not get the attention they deserved, because of their perceived ugliness. Where Fiat design has, perhaps paradoxically, cashed in in a big way is with the 2007 reinterpretation of the classic 1957 Nuova 500: authentic in profile, tone and detail, the Giolito/»Frank Stephenson remake is affectionate and appealing, and avoids the overstated retro of BMW's more recent »Mini Cooper.

2000 ECOBASIC CONCEPT

1983 UNO

FIAT PANDA

2003 | CITY CAR

MODEL HISTORY 1980 PANDA 1ST GENERATION • 2003 PANDA 2ND GENERATION

2010 100 HP	
LENGTH	3540 mm (140 in.)
LAYOUT	Front engine, front-wheel drive
ENGINE	1.4 petrol 4-cyl
HORSEPOWER	100
MAX. SPEED	185 km/h (115 mph)
CO$_2$ EMISSIONS	154 g/km

With just two generations – both of them by »Giorgetto Giugiaro at »Italdesign – spanning more than thirty years on the market, the Fiat Panda is a classic of minimalist small-car design. The original, launched in 1980, lasted a remarkable twenty-three years in the showrooms, sustained by a shape that would today be described as bohemian chic, but which in its day came across as a highly rational blend of style, simplicity and sensible practicality. This shone through not only in the flat-panelled exterior and flat glass all round but also in the interior, with its thin but comfortable seats, full-width dashboard shelf and such clever details as an ashtray that could be positioned anywhere along this shelf.

Having been started from a clean sheet of paper, the second-generation Panda reflects the changing mood of the market by being more luxurious and more sophisticated, but the basic concept of practical simplicity is preserved. The exterior has some of the compact, upright proportion of the Ecobasic concept of 2000 but little of its quirky, Fisher-Price toy-like design language. Instead, there is a classy charm to its shape and, specifically, its cant-rail drop over the C-pillar, something later exaggerated by »Mini for its Countryman wagon.

FIRST AUTO WORKS

CHINA | FOUNDED 1958 | CARS, TRUCKS AND BUSES | FAW.COM

2006 HONGQI HQ3

By far the oldest of China's carmakers, First Auto Works produced its first vehicles in the late 1950s using technology from the Soviet Union; Chairman Mao Zedong was known to have praised its Hongqi ('red flag') state limousines on several occasions, and the organization built a special model for American president Richard Nixon's historic visit to China in 1972. In more recent times, since the opening up of China to foreign joint ventures after 1980, First Auto Works (FAW) has been one of the leading players in linking up with Western automakers in order to bring modern vehicle designs to the huge Chinese market – now the largest in the world.

FAW began by building the Audi 100 in 1988, and this soon became established as the main official vehicle in the country. Now the company builds a dozen different Volkswagen–Audi models, including designs specially tailored for the Chinese buyer. Cooperation with Toyota began in 2002, and with Mazda the following year; the Mazda6 forms the basis for FAW's new Besturn sports premium brand, with the Besturn 50 sports sedan launched in 2009.

Although it is state owned, FAW has a keen commercial approach to its branding strategies, and it will soon launch a new small car under the Hongqi Vita label. It is also seeking to develop a higher profile for

the 'Red Flag' official limousine side of the business. The HQD concept displayed at the Shanghai motor show in 2005 did FAW no favours: brash, brutal and laden with chrome, it came across as a gaudy pastiche of a Rolls-Royce, but without the substance or heritage. A large concept SUV that followed in 2008 was equally imposing, but styled with more balance and restraint. This perhaps showed the hand of the external design consultants that have helped so many Chinese carmakers to throw off their copycat image.

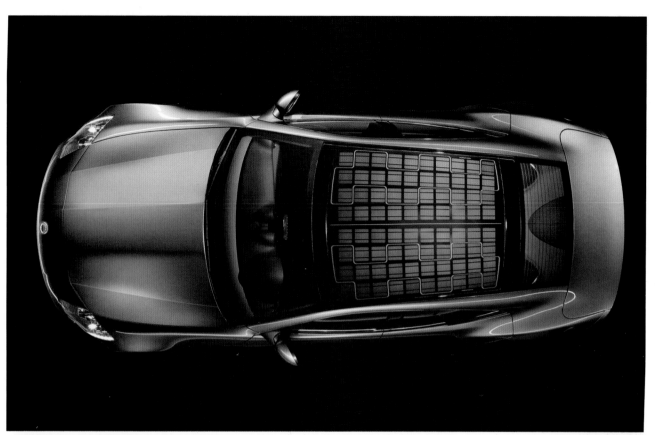

FORD

UNITED STATES | FOUNDED 1903 | CARS AND LIGHT TRUCKS | FORD.COM

For the first seventy-five of its hundred-and-ten-year history the Ford Motor Company was much more famous for its mass-production system and the huge impact of its products on society than for the engineering of the products themselves. Indeed, it was only in the 1950s that Ford began to employ design to promote sales actively, and buyers had to wait until the 1970s for Ford to relax its inbuilt resistance to such technical advances as front-wheel drive.

For Ford, the major aesthetic landmarks historically always came about as a result of marketing requirements, rather than as opportunities presented by engineering advances or new technologies. The 1954 Thunderbird, 1963 Cortina and 1964 Mustang all repackaged ordinary mechanical elements in a form that caught the mood of the moment. The same can be said of the 1996 »Ka minicar and the 2008 »Fiesta. Today, thanks to its dalliance with European premium marques in the early years of the new millennium and its impressively staffed global design departments, Ford is one of the most design-conscious of the major automakers.

Farmer's son Henry Ford became a worldwide celebrity thanks to the whirlwind success of the Model T (1908) and his pioneering of the moving assembly line that cut production time from twelve hours to ninety-three minutes. This, along with his doubling of workers' wages to $5 a day, transformed the car from a rich person's luxury item to something within the reach of every worker, including those who built the cars. Ford's fame brought him friendship with presidents and statesmen, and even tea at Buckingham Palace with the British King and Queen. But Ford was reluctant to subscribe to the value of styling or design, until some changes implemented by his son Edsel gave the Model T a sales boost late in its life.

Under Edsel Ford's management, the company laid the foundations for its long-familiar brand structure, buying the luxury »Lincoln nameplate in 1922 and launching »Mercury to catch image-aware middle-class buyers in 1938. Edsel died in 1943; two years later his son Henry became chairman, aged just twenty-eight, and, after having rejected internal designs, he turned to outside stylist George Walker to shape Ford's post-war range. The investment was worthwhile: the 1949 Fords were strong and confident, and ideally placed to profit from the new sense of prosperity. European Fords were soon developing a sense of style, too, with such models as the Consul and the Taunus sharing many of the design cues of their American counterparts. This continued through several model generations until the big break represented by the compact Fiesta in 1976, the first European Ford (apart from the troublesome V4 Taunus in Germany in the 1960s) to switch to front-wheel drive.

When the 1980 Escort also made the switch to front drive, its crisp lines showed Ford in a new, sharper light, but few were prepared for the shock of the 1982 Sierra, despite the early warning signalled by the previous year's aerodynamic Probe III concept car. Designed by then-chief designer Uwe Bahnsen with some involvement from »Patrick le Quément (who would later

1963-GENERATION CORTINA

1954 THUNDERBIRD

1964 MUSTANG

1969-GENERATION CAPRI

HISTORY

1896	Henry Ford demonstrates his Quadricycle
1903	Ford Motor Company incorporated; first car sold
1913	Begins mass-production on a moving assembly line
1922	Buys Lincoln
1924	First to make 1 million cars in a year
1927	Model T production ends
1938	Mercury upper-medium brand launched
1947	Henry Ford dies
1956	Ford floated as public company
1973	Takes stake in Ghia of Turin
1987	Buys 75% of Aston Martin
1989	Buys Jaguar for £1.6 billion
1993	Alex Trotman is first non-US chairman
1995	F-series pickup overtakes Volkswagen Beetle as biggest-selling vehicle
1996	Takes effective control of Mazda
1998	William Clay Ford Jr, great-grandson of Henry Ford, becomes chairman
1999	Buys Volvo for $6.45 billion
2000	Buys Land Rover from BMW
2002	Revitalization project begins
2004	Martin Smith becomes director of design
2006	Alan Mulally from Boeing becomes CEO. Downsizing plan begins
2007	Sells Aston Martin to Prodrive consortium
2008	Refuses US government bailout. Sells Jaguar Land Rover to Tata Motors
2010	Completes sale of Volvo to Geely of China

1968 ESCORT

1985 SIERRA COSWORTH RS

1996 KA

175

revolutionize Renault design), the Sierra was smooth and rounded and very different from most buyers' expectations of a Ford; public response was negative, and over the years Ford steadily tinkered with details to make it look more mainstream. From that point on, Ford managers appeared to be again opposed to bold design, and it was not until the advent of the so-called New Edge styling theme in the 1996 Ka minicar that the brand re-embraced progressive looks. The 1998 Focus is perhaps the high point of this style, yet it was followed in 2004 by a very toned-down update.

Ford's American design had in the meantime been going through a strong period, with plentiful investment and an array of interesting concepts. These included the 2005 Shelby GR1 (by »Henrik Fisker), the contrasting 2006 Reflex and F250 Super Chief concepts, and the 2007 Airstream concept minivan. Several back-to-basic designs were never followed up (product designer Marc Newson's unusual 021C, the 24/7 of 2000 and the later Model U), and the template for a modernized Explorer SUV, the 2008 Explorer America concept, fell victim to the downsizing plans implemented by Ford's ex-Boeing turnaround CEO, Alan Mulally. The fresh 2006 »Edge crossover and Range Rover-like 2008 »Flex minivan survived.

The end of the decade witnessed the wheel turning full circle, as European Ford designs, notably the accomplished 2008 Fiesta and 2010 »Focus penned under design chief »Martin Smith, became mainstream models in a North American market that is now very concerned with fuel economy and CO_2 emissions.

2009 IOSIS MAX CONCEPT

PRINCIPAL MODELS

1903	Model A
1908	Model T
1928	New Model A
1932	Model Y, first to be designed for Europe
1948	F- series truck is first new post-war design
1949	'49 Ford, designed by George Walker
1954	Thunderbird
1959	Anglia 105E (UK)
1963	Cortina
1964	Mustang; GT40 prototype
1965	Transit
1968	Escort, Torino
1969	Capri
1976	Fiesta, first front-wheel-drive Ford
1981	Probe III concept
1982	Sierra
1985	Sierra Cosworth RS
1986	Taurus
1990	Explorer
1992	Ghia Focus concept
1993	Mondeo
1996	Ka
1998	Focus
1999	021C concept, by Marc Newson
2005	GT; Shelby GR1 and Iosis concepts
2006	Edge; Reflex and F250 Super Chief concepts
2007	Mondeo (3rd gen)
2008	Flex, Fiesta (6th gen), Ka (2nd gen)
2009	F-150 (F-series 12th gen), Mustang (6th gen), Taurus (6th gen); Iosis Max concept
2010	Focus (3rd gen)

2003 MODEL U CONCEPT

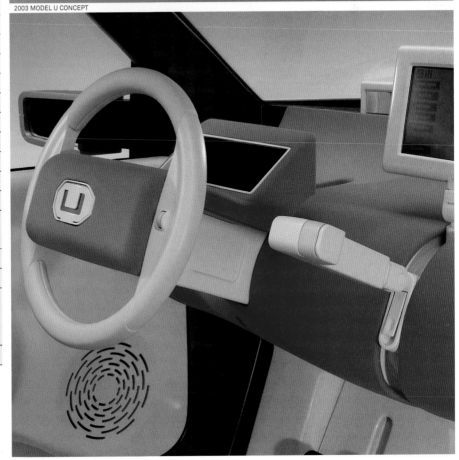

FORD EDGE

2006 | CROSSOVER SUV

2010 3.7 V6	
LENGTH	4720 mm (187 in.)
LAYOUT	Front engine, front-wheel drive
ENGINE	3.7 petrol V6
HORSEPOWER	309
MAX. SPEED	180 km/h (112 mph)
CO$_2$ EMISSIONS	–

The Edge was conceived in an era when heavyweight SUVs were approaching their peak in North America and company planners were anticipating a backlash against their excesses. The Ford Edge, a crossover built on a car platform rather than a crude truck chassis, is one such response. When it appeared in 2006 the Edge's strikingly clean lines and fresh, smooth look made a poignant contrast to the complex and domineering full-size 4x4s of the era.

And for good reason: Ford deliberately shaped the Edge's stance and its detailing so as to distance it from the conventional SUV. The smooth, non-confrontational front features Ford's three-bar grille, gently sloping back and blending with the simple headlights and the rounded corners of the hood; a straight-through waistline runs the length of the sides, and the wheel-arch flares are understated. But the biggest clincher for the friendly look is the glasshouse: with its front and rear pillars raked strongly, stretching the screens front and rear, the silhouette became more that of a stylish minivan than a brutish 4x4.

The fact that the Edge's 2010 facelift was so minor – just a revision of the grille and front apron – bears witness to the clarity and balance of the original design.

FORD F-150

2009 | PICKUP

5.4 V8	
LENGTH	5362mm (211 in.)
LAYOUT	Front engine, rear-wheel drive
ENGINE	5.4 V8
HORSEPOWER	310
MAX. SPEED	–
CO$_2$ EMISSIONS	–

With a history spanning six decades and twelve model generations, Ford's F- series of pickup trucks is an American institution to rival that of its long-time sparring partner, Chrysler's »Dodge-branded Ram. The F- series has been one of the world's biggest-selling vehicles of any kind, regularly topping the American charts and outselling the most popular cars for several million-unit years. For Ford these were highly profitable units, given the truck's simple chassis-frame construction.

The raised hood and separate fenders of the original F- series, launched in 1948, are familiar from old movies; successive generations saw the gradual integration of hood and fenders, leading to a tall, square front where detailing tended to follow the fashions of the day. Big steps came in 1961, with a more car-like look, and with the tenth generation in 1997, when the increasingly big and brutal look was scrapped and a more rounded, car-like nose appeared.

Generations eleven and twelve reversed that move, with the current model displaying a bold, heavily chromed grille that stands much taller than the headlights. Clearly, the F-150 is hoping to muscle in on the super-duty truck market, where the Dodge Ram calls itself king.

1997-GENERATION F- SERIES

179

FORD FIESTA

2008 | COMPACT CAR

MODEL HISTORY 1976 FIESTA 1ST GENERATION • 1983 FIESTA 2ND GENERATION • 1989 FIESTA 3RD GENERATION • 1995 FIESTA 4TH GENERATION • 2002 FIESTA 5TH GENERATION • 2008 FIESTA 6TH GENERATION

2010 1.6 TDCI ECONETIC	
LENGTH	3950 mm (156 in.)
LAYOUT	Front engine, front-wheel drive
ENGINE	1.6 turbo diesel 4-cyl
HORSEPOWER	90
MAX. SPEED	175 km/h (109 mph)
CO_2 EMISSIONS	110 g/km

Small, square-edged and skinny-tyred, the first-generation Fiesta looks dated now, but in 1976 it represented the cutting edge of innovative design for Ford, if not for the rest of the auto industry. For American-owned Ford it marked the major technical step of moving into front-wheel drive – an arrangement Europeans had been employing for more than a decade – as well as a shift into the small-car segment.

The Fiesta would also be Ford's first hatchback, signalling a further break with tradition for what was then an ultra-conservative company. Fittingly, these important cultural shifts were accompanied by a fresh and unaffected design language. The Fiesta's crisp and clean lines, its glassy (if tight) cabin and its agile handling soon endeared themselves to buyers. The follow-up second generation of 1983 was similar in feel but more rounded in its contours and less spartan inside. This was the model that saw the first XR2 derivative, a sports version that was a successful junior partner to the popular Escort XR3.

The theme was refined further for the slightly larger third-generation Fiesta in 1989, the first to offer the option of five doors. The swage line had now gone, rendering the design even more anonymous. Even on launch this came across as a dated car – such direct competitors as the Peugeot 205 and Fiat Uno had raised the game dramatically several years earlier – yet it had a long production run, staggering on from one facelift to the next. The reworked fourth generation of 1995 was

much better but still looked dull, and further disappointment greeted the all-new 2002 design, a timid effort despite the clean-sheet opportunity it represented.

The big and much needed step forward came in 2007 when, under new design director »Martin Smith, the Verve hatchback concept was unveiled. It was vividly coloured and dramatically shaped, with sharply plunging belt and side feature lines, a high tail and diamond-shaped rear lights set high up. Little altered, this became the 2008 Fiesta, once again at the top of its game and now with an additional role to play as Ford's low-emission model for North America.

1983 FIESTA

2007 VERVE HATCHBACK CONCEPT, BECAME 2008 FIESTA

FORD FLEX

2008 | CROSSOVER

2010 3.5 T	
LENGTH	5120 mm (202 in.)
LAYOUT	Front engine, front-wheel drive
ENGINE	3.5 petrol turbo V6
HORSEPOWER	360
MAX. SPEED	180 km/h (112 mph)
CO$_2$ EMISSIONS	–

The early years of the twenty-first century were boom years for Ford design, with new brands, new studios and the recruitment of scores of top designers from all around the world. The result was an intensely creative climate and rush of new ideas, a large number of which appeared as crowd-pleasing show concepts. Many of these went on to pass through the numerous organizational hoops to become production models.

One such example is the Flex, a seven-seater people-carrier dramatically different in tone from the traditional American 'soccer mom' minivan, and derived from the 2005 Fairlane concept model. The Fairlane impressed onlookers with the fresh, clean-sided look to its long, station-wagon-style body; even more striking was the elegant 'floating' roof, picked out in white and supported on blacked-out pillars. This was precisely the technique used by Land Rover, which Ford owned at the time, to imbue its high-class »Range Rover with the requisite aristocratic air – and it did the same trick with the Fairlane.

Relabelled Flex, the Fairlane concept appeared as a production car for the 2008 model year, looking just as smart but minus the concept's differentiated three-row seating and side-hinged tailgate.

FORD FOCUS

2010 | MEDIUM CAR

MODEL HISTORY 1998 FOCUS 1ST GENERATION • 2004 FOCUS 2ND GENERATION • 2010 FOCUS 3RD GENERATION

2010 FOCUS 1.6 TDCI	
LENGTH	4337 mm (171 in.)
LAYOUT	Front engine, front-wheel drive
ENGINE	1.6 turbo-diesel 4-cyl
HORSEPOWER	109
MAX. SPEED	188 km/h (117 mph)
CO_2 EMISSIONS	115 g/km

As the replacement for the unloved and utterly outmoded Ford Escort, the 1998 Focus could hardly have failed. Yet it did much more than supersede the Escort in the Ford portfolio: the spectacular new design by Ford veteran Claude Lobo broke fresh ground on many levels, sold rapidly and widely, and continued strongly in a very competitive market. It was replaced in 2004 by a new model that, paradoxically, seemed less modern than the original.

What made the original 1998 Focus such a breakthrough was the way it used sophisticated design tricks to disguise the high build proportions forced by the requirement to offer segment-leading passenger accommodation. The exciting – but also divisive – 'New Edge' surface language first seen on the »Ka minicar two years before provided the visual distraction to minimize the apparent height of the roof. Angled cuts and graceful curves, intersecting in sharp points around lights and pillars, made the Focus distinctive and attractive on the road, even if its interior, designed on similarly pointy lines, was less well received.

Much less imagination was evident in the 2004 second-generation Focus: it seemed as if Ford had designed a conventional family hatchback and simply tacked on a couple of trademark Focus details, such as the rear lights set into the C-pillar, to provide token continuity. A convertible, bearing the badge of Ford-owned coachbuilder/design house Vignale, suffered awkward proportions. But an intelligent facelift brought more class

and more presence to the whole line-up in 2007 to tie it in with the new Kinetic design language being rolled out with the »Mondeo and S-Max.

Significantly, Ford chose the 2010 Detroit auto show to unveil the next-generation Focus and its expanded mission as the company's global medium car. Designed in Europe under the direction of »Martin Smith, the Focus 3 takes the feel of the sporty, wedge-shaped »Fiesta and scales it up to suit the larger category. The result is a design with even better proportions and much greater dynamism, particularly from the rear three quarters, where the distinctive arrowhead tail lights combine with the tapering DLO and the clever C-pillar treatment to excellent effect. Even the sedan and station-wagon versions, which are frequently mere afterthoughts in the design stakes, look good.

2004 FOCUS

1998 FOCUS

2010 FOCUS RS500 (RALLY SPORT)

185

FORD GT

2005–2006 | EXTREME SPORTS CAR

MODEL HISTORY 1964 GT40 RACING CAR • 2005 GT

2006	
LENGTH	4645 mm (184 in.)
LAYOUT	Mid engine, rear-wheel drive
ENGINE	5.4 petrol V8 32V
HORSEPOWER	558
MAX. SPEED	330 km/h (205 mph)
CO₂ EMISSIONS	–

Strictly speaking, there is no direct link between Ford's 1960s GT40 and its post-millennium namesake. But the emotional bonds are clear, and in terms of design the pair initially appear to be exact twins, right down to the colour schemes, the lamp shapes, the distinctive doors that take in part of the roof, and the upturned lip spoiler on the engine cover. Only a tape measure will reveal one big difference, that of dimensions: the new car is a sizeable 45 centimetres (17¾ in.) longer and 10 centimetres (nearly 4 in.) taller than the original.

While the original GT40 was a highly successful Le Mans-winning racing car, with just a handful having been adapted for road use, the GT40 concept built to commemorate those victories for Ford's centenary in 2003 had a very different purpose. As a limited-edition high-performance road car, it had to be not only street-legal but also practical enough to sell to the wealthy individual enthusiasts Ford hoped would queue up to buy it.

Trademark rights prevented Ford using the racing car's GT40 label (originally, the height of the car in inches) on the production model, but in other respects the $150,000 GT came across as highly authentic, and it sold well after build began in 2005. Yet while the 500-horsepower supercar may be a meticulously accurate re-creation of the historic racer, it did not develop that design in any way. As in the case of »Lamborghini's Miura concept of 2006, the GT paid faithful tribute rather than seeking to move the game on.

1964 FORD GT40 RACING CAR

2005 FORD GT

FORD KA

2008 | CITY CAR

2010 1.3 TDCI	
LENGTH	3620 mm (143 in.)
LAYOUT	Front engine, front-wheel drive
ENGINE	1.3 turbo diesel 4-cyl
HORSEPOWER	75
MAX. SPEED	161 km/h (100 mph)
CO$_2$ EMISSIONS	112 g/km

Two concepts, both by Ghia, Ford's captive studio and design hothouse in Turin, brought about the small-car shock that was the 1996 Ford Ka. The first, a 1994 concept already bearing the name, was a softly sculpted minicar with a gaping oval grille mouth and the cuddly overall shape of the eventual production Ka. It was the superimposition of the much sharper style of the 1996 Ghia Saetta roadster concept that would add the acute angles, pointed corners and distinctive plastic front and rear bumpers that gave the final car such a dramatically different look from everything else on the road.

Tall, rounded and without a sharp edge in sight, Ford designer Chris Svensson's Ka design exploited the intersections of curves and surfaces to provide strong graphic elements and visual drama. This clever design appealed to aesthetic types as well as to fans of the cute and cuddly. The design lasted a remarkable twelve years in production, despite facelifts that ruined the original's balance.

The 2008 successor is now based on the »Fiat 500's platform and attempts to mix the familiar Ka proportion with the busy design language of the »Ford Fiesta. The result is a hyperactive small car – a far cry from the calm clarity of that 1997 original.

1996-GENERATION KA

FORD MONDEO

2007 | EXECUTIVE CAR

MODEL HISTORY 1993 MONDEO 1ST GENERATION • 2000 MONDEO 2ND GENERATION • 2007 MONDEO 3RD GENERATION

2010 2.0	
LENGTH	4840 mm (191 in.)
LAYOUT	Front engine, front-wheel drive
ENGINE	2.0 petrol 4-cyl
HORSEPOWER	145
MAX. SPEED	210 km/h (130 mph)
CO_2 EMISSIONS	189 g/km

Having learned the hard way with the 1982 Sierra that big steps in design don't always pay off at the upper end of the family-car segment, Ford played it very safe with the 1993 Mondeo that ended the Sierra era. Instead of eye-catching styling, the Mondeo had impressive engineering. A facelift brought a less anonymous nose. The second generation, in 2000, had the tough task of countering the »Volkswagen Passat, the solidity and quality of which had astonished the whole industry. The 2000 Mondeo design had a very strong Passat flavour to it, especially in its dramatically better interior.

By the middle of the decade, incoming design director »Martin Smith was previewing a new design language with the 2005 Iosis concept. 'Kinetic design' marked a major shift in tone, with an expressive nose, a grippy stance on the road and a dynamic overall feel. Three Fords drew their inspiration from the Iosis: the good-looking S-Max and Galaxy minivans, and the 2007 third-generation Mondeo. This car is clearly more dynamic than the Passat, and cleverly disguises its considerable size with a lot of plan shape at the front and a tight swage line reducing the visual mass of the flanks.

2000 MONDEO

1993 MONDEO

189

FORD MUSTANG

2009 | SPORTS COUPÉ

MODEL HISTORY 1964 MUSTANG 1ST GENERATION • 1974 MUSTANG 2ND GENERATION • 1979 MUSTANG 3RD GENERATION • 1994 MUSTANG 4TH GENERATION • 2004 MUSTANG 5TH GENERATION • 2009 MUSTANG 6TH GENERATION

2010 5.4 V8	
LENGTH	4780 mm (189 in.)
LAYOUT	Front engine, rear-wheel drive
ENGINE	5.4 petrol V8
HORSEPOWER	548
MAX. SPEED	270 km/h (167 mph)
CO$_2$ EMISSIONS	–

In common with its longstanding adversaries from »General Motors (the »Chevrolet Camaro and Pontiac Firebird) and »Chrysler (the »Dodge Challenger and Charger), the Ford Mustang is the stuff of legend. Yet the Mustang trumps them all, having invented the pony-car genre in 1964 and having boasted Steve McQueen among its brand ambassadors.

The wildfire success of the 1960s Mustangs has been well documented. So, too, have the miseries of the interim generations and how these dragged the model's reputation into the gutter. It was only with the design boom at the start of the new millennium and »J. Mays's passion for 'retrofuturism' that the Mustang was at last allowed to reconnect with the pony-car ethos of its youth. Designer Doug Gaffka's 2004 'living legend' reincarnation brought back many of the sacred design cues, such as the crowned hood, the outer headlights set back from the grille, and the triangular rear quarter-lights. There was plenty of muscle again, too, and it sold well.

The current generation – the sixth – adds to the 2004 Mustang's authenticity with a more pronounced upkick to the beltline at the B-pillar, echoing the original, and a smoother, yet more substantial grille treatment. The Mustang is the real thing once more.

Surprisingly, »Italdesign volunteered a Mustang tribute concept car in 2006; this did little apart from confirming the frontal design identity and the characteristic beltline kick.

1964-GENERATION MUSTANG: 1968

1964-GENERATION MUSTANG: 1970

FORD TAURUS

2009 | EXECUTIVE CAR

MODEL HISTORY 1986 TAURUS 1ST GENERATION • 1992 TAURUS 2ND GENERATION • 1996 TAURUS 3RD GENERATION • 2000 TAURUS 4TH GENERATION • 2004 FIVE HUNDRED REPLACES TAURUS • 2008 REBRANDED TAURUS • 2009 TAURUS 6TH GENERATION

2010 3.5 V6	
LENGTH	5155 mm (204 in.)
LAYOUT	Front engine, front-wheel drive
ENGINE	3.5 petrol V6
HORSEPOWER	267
MAX. SPEED	190 km/h (118 mph)
CO$_2$ EMISSIONS	–

The Ford Taurus is one of the few models that is as familiar to readers of business textbooks as it is to car fans flipping the pages of auto magazines. When it launched in 1986, the first-generation Taurus was something of a milestone in the American mainstream market: it was decently made, it was front-driven, and it had smooth, grille-less aerodynamic bodywork reflecting the style of European Fords. For many years it was America's bestselling car, but the soggy, oval-themed 1996 edition was less popular and allowed the Toyota Camry to take top spot.

It was the beginning of a long slide as Ford, preoccupied with producing SUVs to cash in on the 4x4 boom, took its eye off the sedan ball and allowed the Taurus to stagnate. A new and more conservative, Mondeo-like Taurus in 2000 did little to shore up sales, yet it still came as a shock when Ford announced that it would drop the Taurus nameplate and replace it with a new model. When the dull Five Hundred failed, new Ford CEO Alan Mulally ordered a swift rebranding. The new Taurus was set in metal with a 2008 facelift and was confirmed at the 2009 Detroit motor show with a strong new model, which again borrowed cues from the European »Mondeo.

2008-GENERATION TAURUS

GAZ

RUSSIA | FOUNDED 1929 | CARS, VANS, TRUCKS AND ENGINES | ENG.GAZGROUP.RU

The GAZ Group is Russia's largest automotive enterprise, with eighteen plants in ten regions of the vast country, yet the name GAZ does not appear on the grille of any car in Russia. Almost all of GAZ's output is for domestic consumption, and the bulk of this is what its many constituent companies have produced for seventy-five years or more: heavy trucks, earth-moving equipment, engines and components. However, two of GAZ's brand names have some recognition outside Russia: »Volga, the car used by Russian officials and dignitaries since way back in the Soviet era; and GAZelle light vans and minibuses. GAZ also produced the large Chaika government limousines. The group briefly hit the headlines in Britain when it took over struggling vanmaker LDV in 2006.

The origins of the GAZ company go back to 1929, when Ford reached a deal with the Soviet authorities to set up a factory to build the Model A at Nizhny Novgorod. Soon GAZ's engineers had built up enough expertise to develop their own designs. These gradually evolved into the Volga sedans and station-wagons that were Russia's staple mid-size vehicles for forty years or more. As in many Russian organizations, however, investment was scarce and the model ranges became increasingly out of date.

After the reorganization of vast numbers of factories in 2005, GAZ struck a deal for the supply of 2.4-litre Chrysler engines from Mexico. Later, it bought the entire production line for the Dodge Stratus from Chrysler and re-established it at Nizhny Novgorod to build the car under licence, with only minor design changes, as the Volga Siber.

GAZ was also involved in the failed 2009 bid by Austro-Canadian parts supplier Magna to buy General Motors' European operations.

1962 VOLGA

HISTORY AND PRINCIPAL MODELS

1929	Deal with Ford to establish new factory
1956	First Volga model (GAZ 21)
1959	First Chaika limousine
1988	Chaika production ends
1998	Cooperation agreed with Fiat; later falls through
2005	Reorganization
2006	Volga cars begin using Chrysler engine. Secures licence to build Dodge Stratus as Volga Siber in Russia. Takes over UK vanmaker LDV
2007	Invests in diesel engine plant. Siber car revealed at Moscow motor show
2008	Siber production starts. Layoffs as market collapses and production slows
2009	LDV collapses. Ex-General Motors head of purchasing Bo Andersson becomes CEO. Magna/GAZ bid for Opel fails
2010	Discussions with Volkswagen

GEELY

CHINA | FOUNDED 1986 | VOLUME CARS | GEELY.COM

HISTORY AND PRINCIPAL MODELS

1986	Geely founded in Zhejiang
1997	Starts producing cars
2002	CK (formerly Ulion) sedan and coupé
2006	Agreement to built TX4 London Taxi in China. MK (formerly King Kong) medium hatchback
2007	Takes 23% stake in London taxi maker Manganese Bronze. FC (formerly Vision) medium-large sedan
2008	Presents twenty-three new cars at Beijing motor show, including LC Panda minicar
2009	Announces twenty-two new cars for Shanghai show, including iG city car and GE concepts. Named preferred bidder for Volvo. Tiger GT
2010	Presents six new and ten upgraded models at Beijing show, including six 'new-energy' vehicles. Says iG to cost only $1500 plus power unit. Acquires 100% of Volvo

One of the most aggressively expansionist of China's four large independent carmakers, Geely came to the notice of commentators outside the People's Republic only in 2006, when it began talks with the British company that builds the iconic London taxi. Three years later, Geely was building the TX4 taxi and shot back into the news as it signalled its intention to bid for Swedish carmaker »Volvo, which the parent Ford group had put up for sale. The acquisition of Volvo was a move that would make Geely a significant player in the global auto business as well as in China's internal market, now the largest in the world.

Unlike its major competitors in China, Geely has not benefited from technology transfer from a Western partner; instead, it has been a largely independent operator and has developed most of its own intellectual property. Its early models from 1997 were

1998 GEELY HQ (ABOVE AND BELOW)

unremarkable, but a decade later much stronger designs were emerging. The 2008 Panda minicar – nothing to do with the Fiat of the same name – is round and friendly, and its large rounded grille and headlights resemble the mouth and eyes of a panda.

Successive auto shows have seen Geely with an almost unstoppable momentum of new products and sub-brands. Notable among the concept designs is the 2009 GE, which shocked onlookers with its borrowed Rolls-Royce looks, and the intriguing iG city car. Appearing in revised form in 2010, the 2+2-seater iG has twin gullwing doors, solar panels on its roof and hood and will, says Geely, sell for $1500 plus the cost of whatever powertrain (electric, hybrid or gasoline) the buyer chooses.

Other noteworthy designs are the long and sinuous Tiger GT coupé which, aside from its exaggerated grille style, could well find export customers, and the related Gleagle GS – which is well detailed but also suffers a brash frontal treatment. With designs such as these, as well as a rash of small cars and considerable momentum in 'new-energy' models, Geely's target to hit 2 million annual sales (from 400,000 in 2010) seems realistic.

GENERAL MOTORS

UNITED STATES | FOUNDED 1908 | CARS AND LIGHT TRUCKS | GM.COM

HISTORY

1908	Buick is founding marque of General Motors. GM buys Oldsmobile
1909	Buys Cadillac and Oakland
1918	Chevrolet merges with GM
1925	Buys Vauxhall
1929	Buys Opel
1931	Buys Holden. Oakland becomes Pontiac
1985	Launches Saturn as new brand
1986	Buys Lotus
1990	Buys 50% of Saab
1993	Sells Lotus
1999	Deal with Hummer. Divests Delphi parts business
2000	Buys remainder of Saab. Cross-shareholding with Fiat. Announces Oldsmobile phase-out
2001	Project Olympia for restructuring Europe
2002	Takes over Daewoo
2003	Sells defence interests
2005	Loses $10.6 billion. Deal to cut capacity by 1 million units each year
2006	Sells finance company. Refuses deal with Renault
2008	Puts Hummer up for sale. Saturn may close
2009	GM files for Chapter 11 bankruptcy. Puts Opel/Vauxhall up for sale; decides to retain them after talks collapse. Pontiac closes. Saab files for bankruptcy after talks fail
2010	Saab bought by Spyker. Hummer and Saturn close after talks fail

2005 SEQUEL CONCEPT

PRINCIPAL MODELS	
1990	Impact electric concept
1996	EV-1
2002	Autonomy concept
2003	Hy-Wire concept
2005	Sequel and Graphyte concepts
2007	Volt concept

Although it did not produce a car under its own name until 1996, and its run of inter-war engineering innovations fizzled out in the 1950s as it began to get fat and extravagant on its profits, General Motors has unquestionably been the most influential organization in the 120-year history of the automobile.

GM's influence was not so much on the technical side, however, as in the popularizing, marketing and selling of cars. GM taught the industry the art and science of salesmanship: everything from creating and cultivating the right brands for each segment of the market, to the science of market research and the art of styling and positioning each model. And it was astonishingly adept at generating interest in its models through the annual GM Motorama roadshow that swept through major cities in the United States in the 1950s, leaving customers gasping with excitement about the futuristic styles on offer.

However, by the late 1950s GM's cosy segmentation of the market had begun to break down in the face of imports, first from »Volkswagen and then by the Japanese. By the 1970s GM was on the defensive, juggling brands, models, alliances, factories and personnel in the vain hope of stemming the tide. Its steady retrenchment in successive decades has been well documented, as has its divestment of brands, the halving of its workforce and the final bottoming out in 2009 with Chapter 11 bankruptcy and government bailouts.

Yet none of this happened without a fight. As the biggest automaker in the world until overtaken by Toyota in 2009, GM commanded a sizeable R&D and design budget, spending that yielded a series of important concept vehicles under the GM brand – and, of course, the still-debated 1996 EV-1 electric car, the only publicly available model (it was leased, not sold) with a GM badge on its hood.

2003 HY-WIRE CONCEPT

2005 GRAPHYTE CONCEPT

2002 AUTONOMY CONCEPT

199

RALPH GILLES

UNITED STATES | BORN 1970 | CAR DESIGNER AND BUSINESS LEADER

CV

1992	Degree in fine arts, College for Creative Studies, Detroit. Joins Chrysler design office
1998	Design manager, Jeep interiors
2001	Director, Chrysler Group large-car family vehicles studio
2002	MBA, Michigan State University
2005	Director, Jeep/Dodge truck design studio
2006	Vice president, Jeep colour and trim, speciality vehicles
2009	Senior vice president, Chrysler Group design. President and CEO, Dodge car brand

KEY DESIGNS

2002	Jeep Liberty (interior)
2003	Dodge Viper (interior), Magnum; Chrysler 300C concept
2007	Chrysler and Dodge minivans
2008	Dodge Ram

A Haitian-American star-struck by glamorous cars from an early age, Ralph Gilles has followed a fast-track path within »Chrysler to take charge of the group's entire design output before the age of forty and, more unusually still, to assume full responsibility, including profit-and-loss accountability, for one of its key brands, »Dodge. Among Gilles's calling cards along the way have been the Dodge Magnum, which reintroduced that American folk favourite, the muscle car, in 2003, and the perfectly pitched »Chrysler 300C, which, as so many group models before it, caught on just in time to save the company from one of its regular downward spirals.

Reflecting his passion for motor racing in all its forms, Gilles's designs have always

2003 CHRYSLER 300C

2008 DODGE RAM

showed a powerful edginess and a desire to push boundaries. It was Gilles who pressed for the revival of the station-wagon, just when it seemed to have been rendered extinct by the minivan. He realized that a station-wagon would need to appeal to male buyers, so he recast it in the shape of the Dodge Magnum, a potent rear-wheel-drive muscle wagon. An equal passion resulted in the Chrysler 300C, also rear-wheel drive: the gangsterish, low-rider stance of this four-door sedan (and, later, wagon) proved an instant hit: as with other Chrysler designs, it had the allure of a custom hot rod straight out of the showroom.

With Chrysler now controlled by Italy's Fiat, Gilles's unusual move into senior business management as CEO of Dodge gives him financial accountability for this most American of the group's brands. This is in addition to his responsibility for all group design, including the key small cars to be derived from Fiat architectures.

ROBERTO GIOLITO

ITALY | BORN 1962 | CAR DESIGNER AND MANAGER

CV	
1985	Degree in industrial design, Istituto Superiore per le Industrie Artistiche, Rome. Freelance furniture and computer graphic design
1989	Hired by Fiat to join Chris Bangle's team
2001	Head of newly formed Fiat advanced design team
2007	Head of design, Fiat

KEY DESIGNS	
1993	Fiat Downtown concept
1994	Fiat ZIC concept
1996	Fiat Multipla concept
1998	Fiat Multipla minivan
2000	Fiat EcoBasic concept
2004	Fiat Trepiuno concept
2007	Fiat 500

2007 FIAT 500

2000 FIAT ECOBASIC CONCEPT

1998 FIAT MULTIPLA

When, as a recently graduated freelance furniture and computer interface designer, the twenty-seven-year old Roberto Giolito responded to an advertisement looking for computer-literate car designers, he could have had little idea that he would go on to design some of Europe's most popular small cars, including the celebrated reinterpretation of the »Fiat 500, one of Italy's sacred auto texts. Giolito's 500 was declared World Car Design of the Year at the 2009 New York motor show.

Joining Fiat under the controversial »Chris Bangle in 1989, Giolito soon found his niche in advanced design, where his unconventional thinking clearly chimed with the confident, risk-taking ambience of the time. His first publicly acknowledged input was on the tiny Downtown electric concept of 1993, and this was followed by a second-generation electric concept, the ZIC (Zero Impact Car) of the following year. But it was with the 1998 Multipla six-seater medium minivan that Giolito really hit the headlines. The design's 3+3 seating was extremely space-efficient, but the double-decker body style was mocked by all except the design community, who celebrated its boldness and practicality. More designer plaudits followed the equally radical EcoBasic concept of 2000: almost toy-like in its bulbousness, it paved the way for the later second-generation »Fiat Panda.

With the brilliant Trepiuno ('three plus one') concept of 2004, Giolito scored the bullseye hit that would see him elevated to international recognition. This small car was an affectionate tribute to the classic Fiat Nuova 500 of the 1950s, yet it avoided the retro feel of the BMW »Mini Cooper. Slightly enlarged, and minus the novel 3+1 seating layout of the concept, the production 500 of 2007 was a worldwide hit for the Fiat brand.

GIORGETTO GIUGIARO

ITALY | BORN 1938 | CAR AND PRODUCT DESIGNER AND CONSULTANT

CV	
1952	Studies art and design in Turin
1955	Joins Fiat styling centre under Dante Giacosa
1959	Moves to Bertone
1965	Joins Carrozzeria Ghia
1968	Establishes Italdesign with Aldo Mantovani
1999	Elected Car Designer of the Century by international panel
2010	Volkswagen buys Italdesign

Individual designers may differ widely in their styles, the way they interpret tradition, or their approach to proportion, stance and detail. But few, if any, would dispute the assertion that the greatest designer the car world has yet seen is Giorgetto Giugiaro. For everyone, he is the maestro.

Born in 1938 and still contributing to the output of the company he founded in the late 1960s, Italdesign, Giugiaro has designed more than two hundred production cars and one hundred concepts during his career so far, as well as a wide variety of other products: cameras, watches, sewing machines, furniture and even pasta shapes. In the automotive field, among his most familiar products are the original Volkswagen Golf and Fiat Uno, the Fiat Panda and the Lancia Delta, and his frequently seminal show concepts are credited with having sparked off major trends in car design and consumer preference.

Perhaps the most striking example of Giugiaro's visionary design is the 1978 Lancia Megagamma concept, which first proposed the high-build, practical and space-efficient configuration that went on to become the family minivan or people-carrier. These and many other achievements led him to be voted Designer of the Century in a 1999 poll of automotive writers.

Giugiaro grew up in northern Italy just after the Second World War, and moved to Turin to study art and technical design. Remarkably, he was spotted by the legendary Fiat designer and engineer Dante Giacosa (1905–1996) and joined the company's advanced styling department, under Giacosa's wing, at the age of seventeen. Giacosa's influence as a brilliant designer of small and space-efficient cars would shine through later as Giugiaro's work broadened from the normal designer fare of extravagant and powerful supercars towards compact and affordable – yet at the same time stylish – family cars built in large numbers. These cars democratized good design in a way no other designer had until then managed.

At »Bertone, a renowned nurturer of design talent, Giugiaro's elegant 3200 CS for BMW already showed how his technique of starting from a technical specification rather than a clean sheet of paper was able to produce beautiful cars. His designs were always calmer and simpler, and had a better understanding of form, than those of his contemporaries, and this trait has continued to the present day.

Already celebrated for his design for Alfa Romeo's 1963 GT, successor to the legendary Giulietta Sprint, Giugiaro broke away from the Italian *carrozzerie* establishment in 1968 to form »Italdesign, a consultancy that would soon challenge »Pininfarina for top billing among Italian design houses. A sequence of milestone designs followed, including the »Lotus Esprit (1975), which introduced the wedge shape and 'folded paper' design language to the world; the »Volkswagen Golf; and perhaps one of the most perfect examples of Giugiaro's art, the 1979 »Lancia Delta. Giugiaro moved the game on further (and higher, for greater interior space) with the low-cost but stylish »Fiat Panda in 1980 and the Fiat Uno in 1983. Having established a worldwide reputation in car design, he

1971 ALFA ROMEO ALFASUD

1974 VOLKSWAGEN GOLF

1979 LANCIA DELTA

1980 FIAT PANDA

1978 BMW M1

GIORGETTO GIUGIARO

KEY DESIGNS

1961	BMW 3200 CS
1962	Ferrari 250 GT
1963	Alfa Romeo Giulia GT; Corvair Testudo concept
1964	Alfa Romeo Canguro concept
1966	De Tomaso Mangusta, Maserati Ghibli
1971	Alfa Romeo Alfasud
1974	Volkswagen Golf
1978	Audi 80, BMW M1; Lancia Megagamma concept
1979	Lancia Delta
1980	Fiat Panda
1983	Fiat Uno
1984	Saab 9000 Turbo; SEAT Ibiza
1988	Renault 19
1991	Toyota Aristo, became 1993 Lexus GS 300
1993	Fiat Punto
1998	Maserati 3200 GT
2003	Lamborghini Gallardo initial proposal
2004	Fiat Croma
2005	Fiat Grande Punto; Alfa Romeo Brera

2005 ALFA ROMEO BRERA

2005 FIAT GRANDE PUNTO

was able to expand into other fields, such as motorcycles (for Ducati) and cameras (for Nikon).

Many of Giugiaro's best and most successful designs have been small cars. Indeed, his designs have saved Fiat three times: the 1983 Uno, the 1993 Punto and the 2005 »Grande Punto all came at moments of great crisis for the Italian company, but their instant success brought the operation back to health.

In 1996 Giugiaro was joined by his son Fabrizio, himself a talented designer, on the board of Italdesign; the two now share the role of chairman. In 2010, however, the Volkswagen Group took a controlling interest in Italdesign.

1998 MASERATI 3200 GT

GREAT WALL

CHINA | FOUNDED 1976 | CARS, SUVS AND PICKUPS | GWM.COM.CN/EN

2004 HOVER H3

HISTORY AND PRINCIPAL MODELS

1976	Truck manufacture
1997	First exports
2002	'Safe' SUV
2004	Hover H3 SUV
2006	Wingle pickup; Coolbear concept
2007	Cowry large minivan, Peri small car
2008	Florid compact hatchback
2009	Company launches in Australia. Four models gain approval for EU. Coolbear compact minivan, Phenom compact hatchback
2010	Voleex 30 and Tengyi C70 sedans, Hawal SC60 SUV

Great Wall, which began as a maker of light trucks before Chinese businesses were opened up to the external market in 1980, is today a significant manufacturer of small and medium cars and is best known – or perhaps most notorious – for the similarity of its designs to well-known Western or Japanese models.

Fiat protested noisily when Great Wall released its Peri hatchback in 2007: the model bore a striking resemblance to the Italian carmaker's »Panda, especially in profile. Fiat was powerless to prevent the Peri's production, although it did claim breach of copyright and stopped the Peri from being exhibited in Europe.

Other Great Wall models that have caused a copycat stir in recent years are the highly distinctive and boxy Coolbear compact minivan, which comes across as a direct clone of Toyota's Scion xB and the related

Daihatsu Materia; and the smaller Florid hatchback, a dead ringer for the »Toyota Yaris (when seen from the front) and the Scion xA (from the sides and rear). Great Wall's classy-looking Phenom, another small hatchback, has something of the allure of the »Lancia Delta with its dramatic vertical grille, but from the sides and rear it apes the Yaris. The Phenom is a good-looking car, but many question its legitimacy, and it could be tricky to sell outside China.

Commentators have been very tough on Great Wall, complaining that the company's models serve to perpetuate the myth that the Chinese prefer to steal designs from others rather than create their own. Perhaps stung by these criticisms, Great Wall is embarking on a new generation of original designs, of which the Hawal SC60 hybrid SUV and the Tengyi C70 sedan stand out.

MURAT GÜNAK

TURKEY | BORN 1958 | CAR AND ENVIRONMENTAL VEHICLE DESIGNER

Although born in Turkey, Murat Günak was quick to gravitate to Germany, where he studied theatre design in Kassel. After a spell working at Mercedes-Benz in the late 1970s, he completed the postgraduate car-design course at the Royal College of Art in London. After three years in Ford's Cologne studio he returned to »Mercedes-Benz, where he contributed to the design of the revolutionary »A-Class small car and »SLK sports car.

Günak first came to general attention when he was recruited by »Peugeot in 1994. There, he was under considerable pressure to produce an emotional replacement for the much-loved 205, which had been penned by »Pininfarina. Günak's 206 evoked some of the feel of the 205 and was a success in the market, although many felt its busy detailing prevented it achieving the clear elegance of the 205.

Returning to Mercedes-Benz in 1998, Günak created some of his best work, including the neat A-Class-based SLA roadster concept and the voluptuous CLS sedan, based on the E-Class. The CLS hit the zeitgeist perfectly, and Günak was able to repeat the exercise after his recruitment to »Volkswagen in 2003, with the CC version of the »Passat.

At Volkswagen Günak set about giving individual models what he called a segment-related identity, rather than an overall corporate identity. This led to complication and confusion. In the 2007 reshuffle initiated when Martin Winterkorn took charge of the VW Group and installed »Walter de'Silva as overall head of design, Günak's policy was swiftly overturned after he left VW abruptly.

Günak went on to design the highly imaginative Commuter hybrid car for Mindset, the Swiss-based eco-car company he founded after leaving VW.

1998 PEUGEOT 206

2004 MERCEDES-BENZ CLS

2003 VOLKSWAGEN CONCEPT R

2008 MINDSET COMMUTER HYBRID CONCEPT

KARIM HABIB

LEBANON/CANADA | BORN 1971 | CAR DESIGNER AND ENGINEER

2008-GENERATION BMW 7 SERIES

Identified as a rising star by BMW while he was still completing his car-design studies at Art Center College of Design in Pasadena, California, Beirut-born Karim Habib joined the German automaker's advanced design studio directly after graduation.

Habib first appeared on the radar of the design community in 2007, when »BMW unveiled its CS concept for a large, sporty coupé-sedan at the Shanghai show in China. The CS, which prior to the financial crisis of 2008–2009 BMW had fully expected to put into production, was to have been the company's response to what seemed an accelerating trend towards large luxurious four-door coupés, exemplified by the Mercedes-Benz CLS, »Aston Martin Rapide and »Porsche Panamera. The CS's design was of particular interest, as it represented the first BMW design since the departure of »Chris Bangle from front-line design work. In the event, Habib's exterior design both surprised and shocked, with its great width and flat proportion, its large upright grilles and its angry stare.

The CS production model was cancelled in 2008, but a similar design language characterized the new »BMW 7 Series, which debuted that autumn. Again credited

to Habib, the design's proportions were less extreme but its detailing – such as the big grilles and the pronounced bone line running the length of the bodyside – is still bold.

Fresh from the success of the 7 Series, Habib was expected to rise fast at BMW. But he surprised the industry with a move to Mercedes-Benz advanced design in 2009. The expectation is that he will add more style to the brand's typically engineering-driven F-series of research cars.

2003 BMW 5 SERIES INTERIOR

2007 BMW CS CONCEPT

GERT HILDEBRAND

GERMANY | BORN1953 | CAR DESIGNER

Gert Hildebrand is best known as the designer who has taken a single iconic model – the born-again »Mini Cooper, as developed by »BMW – and turned it into a range of models serving a wide variety of customers. From that single model basis there are now convertibles, station-wagons and crossover SUVs, with a range of coupés and two-seater speedster convertibles in the pipeline, too.

When Hildebrand arrived at BMW in 2001 to work for his one-time colleague »Chris Bangle, with whom he had worked at Opel on the influential Tech 1 and Junior concepts, the design of the Mini Cooper under »Frank Stephenson was complete. After Stephenson's departure in 2002 Hildebrand began work on extending the Mini line-up, with a series of concepts in 2005 exploring themes for a station-wagon derivative. These were packed with brilliant and entertaining ideas for communications and leisure equipment, but did little to develop the Mini design language that Stephenson had derived from the original 1959 Mini.

The second-generation Mini Cooper under BMW, launched in 2006, was greeted with disappointment by many observers: it had exaggerated the design features of the 2001 car, already a caricature of the 1959 original, rather than seeking new ideas. The subsequent Clubman wagon, with its complicated door arrangement, took this caricature further still.

Hildebrand was often quoted as saying that he did not want dramatic changes to the Mini, preferring it to evolve seamlessly, as the »Porsche 911 had done. This was confirmed in 2010 with the presentation of the four-door Mini Countryman crossover: despite this model's much greater size, it has stuck resolutely to the design cues that made the 2001 model such a worldwide hit.

2009 MINI COUPÉ CONCEPT

2010 MINI COUNTRYMAN

2007 MINI CLUBMAN

HINDUSTAN

INDIA | FOUNDED 1942 | CARS AND SUVS | HINDMOTOR.COM

Although it has been in business since 1942, Hindustan has only one model of its own, the Ambassador, and that model has remained substantially unchanged since its launch in 1954. Only recently has Hindustan linked up with Mitsubishi of Japan to offer a greater variety of vehicles; it now also markets the Mitsubishi Pajero SUV as well as the previous-generation »Mitsubishi Lancer sedan and the newer Cedia hatchback.

Yet anyone who travels to India will immediately see why the Hindustan Ambassador is such an important product. Despite its near-historic status as a cast-off Morris Oxford of 1954 vintage, the Ambassador is one of India's most popular cars, beloved by government officials and taxi drivers, and by drivers who prefer to do their own servicing and repairs (it is very simple to maintain). Of course, much of the Ambassador's popularity was built up before the Indian economy was opened up to foreign competition in 1980, when it shared a totally protected market with its great rival, the Premier Padmini (itself a throwback to the early-1950s Fiat 1100). And yes, the Ambassador is technically obsolete, and every single automotive fad of the past half century has completely passed it by. Some details, such as the grille and the headlights, have been tweaked, but the sheet metal remains as Morris designed it.

And that, as Hindustan Motors has begun to realize, is precisely what gives the Ambassador such a lasting appeal. For many years press reports have been predicting the demise of Hindustan, its ancient car and its chronically inefficient Uttarpara factory, but it seems to survive regardless. A million Ambassadors are still on India's roads, and with a re-engineered model (still retaining the retro look) set for production in 2011, that total will continue to creep up, just as it has done for almost six decades.

HISTORY AND PRINCIPAL MODELS

1942	Hindustan Motors incorporated in Gujarat
1948	Moves to Uttarpara, West Bengal, to build cars and trucks
1954	Begins production of Ambassador
1971	Sets up earthmoving equipment division
1985	Sets up power products division
1986	Sets up commercial vehicles division
1987	Produces engines with Isuzu
1998	Cooperation with Mitsubishi begins
2001	Sells earthmoving equipment division to Caterpillar
2002	Grille is restyled
2004	Front disc brakes
2008	Diesel engine, 5-speed gearbox, CNG (compressed natural gas) options

AMBASSADOR

WAHEI HIRAI

JAPAN | BORN 1949 | CAR DESIGNER AND MANAGER

1989 LEXUS LS400

1998-GENERATION TOYOTA YARIS

Because Toyota is so vast and has such a firmly entrenched management structure, Wahei Hirai's achievement in bringing design to its current level of prominence within the organization is considerable. Shortly after being made global design director in 2004, Hirai was named as a managing officer, the highest grade in the Toyota hierarchy below director level. This was the first time a designer had risen so high in the company's ranks.

Major waypoints during Hirai's career-long Toyota service (he retired in 2009) include the launching of the »Lexus premium brand in 1989 and the developing of a hybrid sub-brand around the »Toyota Prius in the 2000s.

Having worked in Japan, Europe and the United States on such key Toyota designs as the 1985 Celica and 1987 »Corolla, Hirai was acutely aware of the corporate culture, which regarded design as simply clothing for a package that had been conceived by marketing and assembled by engineering. He helped to implement a system that was more model- and market-orientated, rather than engineering-centric.

As president of Toyota's ED2, the European design centre he helped to set up in 2000, Hirai was instrumental in establishing true competition between the carmaker's many global studios. With such designs as the »Toyota Yaris in 1998, it became clear that European design had a wide international appeal.

Hirai has long maintained that, with more than ninety body types in its portfolio, Toyota is too large to have a uniform design theme around the world. Yet towards the end of this century's first decade the Lexus brand was beginning to develop a clearer identity, and the radical »iQ had brought genuine originality to the city-car sector. Most mainstream Toyota models now have more spark than they ever had before.

2001 TOYOTA COROLLA

2003 TOYOTA CS&S CONCEPT

2007 TOYOTA FT-HS COUPÉ CONCEPT

HOLDEN

AUSTRALIA | FOUNDED 1856 | CARS AND PICKUPS | HOLDEN.COM.AU

HISTORY AND PRINCIPAL MODELS

1856	Founded as saddlery maker
1914	Begins making auto bodies
1931	Bought by General Motors
1948	Holden sedan is first Australian-designed car
1953	FJ
1968	Monaro
1969	Torana LC
1978	Commodore VB
1997	Commodore VT
1998	Monaro concept
2001	Monaro
2002	SSX crossover concept
2003	Global V6 engine plant exports worldwide
2004	Restyled Monaro becomes Pontiac GTO for USA. Torana TT36 concept
2005	EFIJY concept, by Richard Ferlazzo
2006	Commodore VE, Statesman, Caprice
2008	Commodore shipped to USA as Pontiac G8. Coupé 60 concept
2010	GM EN-V Xiao concept for Shanghai motor show. Caprice shipped to USA as Chevrolet police car

2001 MONARO

1997 COMMODORE

Holden has been part of »General Motors since the 1930s, initially building adapted North American designs under licence but progressing to the construction of the first Australian-designed car – known simply as the Holden – in 1948. This four-door sedan was followed by a utility pickup, helping to kick-start what would eventually become a huge market for 'utes', and by the 1953 FJ, which went on to become a major success.

Holden has trodden an often uneasy path in its model policies, switching at GM's behest between developing its own models tailored for Australian conditions and building North American models locally.

An added dimension over the years has been the series of deals bringing in Holden-branded versions of small cars from Japanese manufacturers.

What makes Australia unique in the automotive world is its strong requirement for large cars that are not just roomy but also very rugged and powerful. Even in a modern context, that means rear-wheel drive and large V6 or, preferably, V8 engines. It is by specializing in this type of vehicle that Holden has also been able to export two variants of its staple Commodore platform to the United States as sporty »Pontiacs – the Monaro as the GTO in 2004 and the G8 in 2008. Even Britain took a version as the Vauxhall VXR8 in the late 2000s.

Holden's design studio in Australia is the third biggest in the GM universe, and in addition to developing models for the local market it has also been responsible for a run of concept cars. Prominent among these is chief designer Richard Ferlazzo's 2005 EFIJY; this warm tribute to the 1953 FJ, which gave Holden its identity, had some interesting fresh design features, especially in its exaggerated fastback tail.

A sign of the times for Holden is that it will be building the Korean-designed Chevrolet Cruze from 2011, yet with the demise of the Pontiac brand it has lost an export avenue for which even regular orders from the American police – who like the rugged rear-drive format of the Commodore and Caprice – will not be able to compensate.

2008 COUPÉ 60 CONCEPT

1953 FJ

2005 EFIJY CONCEPT

HONDA

JAPAN | FOUNDED 1948 | CARS, MOTORCYCLES AND POWER PRODUCTS | WORLD.HONDA.COM

Honda was the world's most prolific builder of motorcycles when it decided in the early 1960s that it would enter the car business, too. Right from the start its four-wheeled products were very different from those of its competitors in Japan and abroad: the 1963 S500 sports car was a miniature masterpiece engineered like a racing motorcycle, and even the tiny TN delivery van had a mid-mounted underfloor engine for optimum weight distribution. Honda's first few cars were air-cooled and front-wheel-drive, which was unusual even in the small-car segment at that time.

Honda continued to savour that difference for many years, lavishing attention on engines and transmissions but making less effort when it came to design of chassis and, in particular, body. The company's styling back catalogue is in consequence extremely varied: a mix of original production-car designs and inspirational concepts interspersed with routine models of surprising blandness and Japanese show models of baffling eccentricity.

The company's current design strategy continues to reflect that scattergun approach. Hondas can be very brave and radical – as with the bold 2005 »Civic hatchback and 2009 »CR-Z hybrid sports coupé – or they can play things disappointingly safe, as most often seen in products aimed at the conservative North American markets, such as the 2004 Legend luxury sedan and the medium-sized Accord.

Even within a model series the change of pace can be surprising. The Prelude coupé, for instance, began as an oddball hardtop design in the late 1970s and went through two further very bland generations until 1992, when a much sportier, more progressive format appeared. In 1997 it was back to bland again. The Civic, especially in its European forms, has followed a similarly zigzag path.

It is often in the more niche areas that Honda has produced its most memorable designs. The tiny but sporty CR-X 2+2 coupé

1972 CIVIC

1990 NSX

1999 S2000

1999 INSIGHT

2004 FRV

2005 CIVIC CONCEPT

of the 1980s created a strong following, as did the Integra Type R, another racy coupé. In marked contrast, the miniature mid-engined Beat roadster of 1991 arrived a matter of months after perhaps the most seminal Honda of all – the 1990 all-aluminium NSX supercar that frightened Ferrari with its new levels of dynamics, integrity and ease of use. Around the turn of the millennium Honda explored two different types of six-seater people-carriers – the novel FR-V which, in the manner of Fiat's Multipla, had two rows of three seats each – and the Stream, a smooth and elongated derivative of the then-current Civic with three rows of seats. The 1999 S2000 sports roadster, with its high-revving engine and taut handling, is already seen as a classic and, at the opposite end of the performance spectrum, the boxy, back-to-basics »Honda Element van was a big hit not just with West Coast surfers, but also with design critics.

Yet it is with major technical firsts that Honda cars are most closely associated. The 1972 Civic was a breakthrough in more than just style and format: it was the first car to comply with the Clean Air Act that was due to be passed in 1975 in the United States, and came to market so far ahead of the deadline that the slow-moving American automakers had the implementation delayed. The 1999 »Insight not only was the first-ever production hybrid, but also sported a compact and highly aerodynamic two-seater aluminium body. In 2005 the »FCX Clarity concept presented a template for the first publicly available fuel-cell-powered passenger car (it was leased to selected customers) and went on sale in 2008. And, true to its promise to popularize hybrids, Honda launched the new Insight as a mainstream hatchback – looking very much like the fuel-cell FCX – in 2009 and wrapped the world's first hybrid sports coupé, the CR-Z, in a dramatic wedge-shaped body in 2009.

Progressive production models, such as the CR-Z, are often preceded by a concept version, yet Honda is also prolific in its output of pure design studies that are not linked to an upcoming showroom model. The best of these, such as the 2008 FC Sport, the 2007 Remix coupé and the 2000 Spocket, explore worthwhile design avenues. Others, such as the severe 2003 Kiwami and the 2007 Puyo – typical of many bizarre Tokyo motor show specials – are harder to fathom.

PRINCIPAL MODELS

1963	S500 sports car and T360 light commercial vehicle
1967	N360 small car
1968	Honda 1300 air-cooled medium car
1972	Civic is first car to comply with US Clean Air Act
1976	Accord
1983	CR-X
1989	Integra Type R
1990	NSX
1991	Beat
1992	Prelude
1995	Argento Vivo concept, by Pininfarina
1998	HR-V
1999	Insight, first hybrid production car, and S2000
2000	Spocket concept
2002	Element
2003	Kiwami concept
2004	FRV
2005	Civic (8th gen); FCX Clarity concept
2007	Remix, CR-Z and Puyo concepts
2008	FCX Clarity production; OSM roadster concept
2009	Insight hatchback, CR-Z production; Skydeck concept
2010	3RC concept

2008 FC SPORT CONCEPT

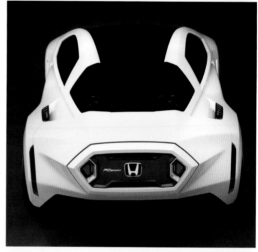

2005 FCX CLARITY CONCEPT

HONDA CIVIC

2005 | MEDIUM CAR

MODEL HISTORY 1972 CIVIC 1ST GENERATION • 1979 CIVIC 2ND GENERATION • 1983 CIVIC 3RD GENERATION • 1987 CIVIC 4TH GENERATION • 1991 CIVIC 5TH GENERATION • 1995 CIVIC 6TH GENERATION (W220) • 2000 CIVIC 7TH GENERATION • 2005 CIVIC 8TH GENERATION

2010 2.2 CTDI	
LENGTH	4245 mm (168 in.)
LAYOUT	Front engine, front-wheel drive
ENGINE	2.2 turbo diesel 4-cyl
HORSEPOWER	140
MAX. SPEED	205 km/h (127 mph)
CO₂ EMISSIONS	141 g/km

The story of the Civic is really the story of the whole of Honda, so important has this core model been to the brand, especially in the 1970s and 1980s. It was from this innocent-looking little hatchback from 1972, which caught on in a big way in North America, that the Civic phenomenon expanded. That hatchback has multiplied to become a complete dynasty of models tailored in shape, size and temperament to different regional tastes, and manufactured in dozens of locations around the globe.

In common with all long-running model lines – the »Toyota Corolla is a close parallel – the Civic started small and went on to steadily greater things, growing in stature and power along with expectations of the market and the rising fortunes of its clientele. In contrast to the Corolla, however, the Civic was always at the forefront of engineering developments and, as an early advocate of front-wheel drive, was always fun to drive and responsive in its handling.

The short and rounded first-generation Civic was the first car to comply with the American Clean Air Act; since the second, slightly larger, generation, changes have been made every four to five years. This, along with an increasing profusion of hatchback, sedan, wagon, coupé and crossover derivatives, has led to an immense back catalogue of designs, all badged Civic.

Highlights from this varied collection include the sporty, low-slung third-generation Civic hatchbacks from 1983; the move to a much more strait-laced five-door

CIVIC GENERATIONS ONE TO SEVEN

SEVENTH-GENERATION AND FIRST-GENERATION CIVIC

HONDA INSIGHT

2009 | HYBRID ELECTRIC MEDIUM CAR

MODEL HISTORY 1999 INSIGHT COUPÉ • 2009 INSIGHT HATCHBACK

2010 1.3 HYBRID	
LENGTH	4375 mm (173 in.)
LAYOUT	Front engine, front-wheel drive
ENGINE	1.3 petrol-electric hybrid 4-cyl
HORSEPOWER	98
MAX. SPEED	186 km/h (115 mph)
CO₂ EMISSIONS	101 g/km

Two completely different Honda cars have used the Insight nameplate; both, however, share the distinction of being pioneers in the field of hybrid power. The original 1999 Insight, a lightweight and highly aerodynamic two-seater coupé, was the world's first production hybrid, and thus the ambassador for what might become the dominant vehicle type in the early twenty-first century. With an electric motor sandwiched between its tiny three-cylinder engine and the gearbox, it was intriguing to drive but also astonishingly economical. Its weird teardrop-shaped body and narrow, faired-in rear wheels give it the appearance of a strange vision of the future.

Taking up the Insight name a decade later is Honda's biggest bet so far in pushing its hybrid agenda: with five seats, four doors and a hatchback tailgate, the new Insight is aimed at the volume market rather than at an obscure clique of eco pioneers. This Insight is not as clearly futuristic as its namesake was, although the smooth nose, clean sides and high, cut-off tail are clearly aerodynamic. The influence of the »FCX Clarity is clear, too. But, with large volumes of buyers as its target, the Insight is lower in cost and less lavish in its detailing, to the detriment of its futuristic feel.

PETER HORBURY

GREAT BRITAIN | BORN 1950 | CAR DESIGNER AND MANAGER

CV

1972	Degree in industrial design, Newcastle College of Art and Industrial Design (now Northumbria University)
1974	Master's in vehicle design from Royal College of Art, London, sponsored by Chrysler. Works at Chrysler and Ford UK
1979	Consultant designer at Volvo, The Netherlands
1986	Director of styling and design, MGA Developments, UK
1991	Returns to Volvo as design director
2002	Executive director of design, Ford Premier Automotive Group
2004	Executive director of design, Ford Motor Co., Dearborn, Michigan
2009	Returns to Volvo as vice president of design

KEY DESIGNS

1992	Volvo ECC environmental concept car
1995	Volvo S40, V40
1996	Volvo C70 Coupé
1997	Volvo ACC adventure concept car
1998	Volvo S80
2001	Volvo SCC safety concept car
2002	Volvo XC90 SUV
2006	Volvo C30
2007	Lincoln MKR
2008	Ford Flex
2009	Lincoln C concept

Few in the car-design world can be identified with a single brand more closely than Peter Horbury is with »Volvo. As design director in the 1990s, Horbury made the really bold moves that would change Volvo's image for ever and turn it into the innovative, style-conscious brand we know today.

Ever since the 240 series of the 1970s, Volvo's image had been that of extreme safety, exemplified by the boxy sedan and cavernous, rectilinear wagon. Horbury's triumph was to roll out a new style that was smooth, softer and less confrontational, helping to break the association in some customers' minds that only big, blocky cars can be safe. The process was kicked off by the dramatic Environmental Concept Car in 1992: this introduced the low, rounded nose and pronounced rear shoulders that would characterize such later production designs as the S80.

For Volvo these were big steps, but buyers liked the new look and it was successfully rolled out across an expanding line-up of medium and large models; the 'friendly' XC90 large SUV was a particular success.

Following Ford's acquisition of Volvo in 1999 Horbury took overall charge of design at Aston Martin, Jaguar and Land Rover too, only to be moved to Ford's headquarters in Dearborn, near Detroit, in 2004 to head all Ford, Lincoln and Mercury design for North America. Under his watch many key designs emerged, notably a new »Ford Mustang, the Range Rover-like »Ford Flex and the imaginative six-seater Lincoln C compact-car concept.

In 2009 Horbury returned to the company he had always regarded as home, Volvo, promising to make even bigger steps than he had done in the 1990s.

1992 VOLVO ECC CONCEPT

1998 VOLVO S80

2002 VOLVO XC90

2008 FORD FLEX

2007 LINCOLN MKR

2009 LINCOLN C CONCEPT

HUMMER

UNITED STATES | FOUNDED 1983/1999–2010 | EXTREME SUVS | HUMMER.COM

HUMMER®

HISTORY AND PRINCIPAL MODELS

1983	US military awards AM General contract for HMMWVs (High-Mobility Multipurpose Wheeled Vehicles, or Humvees)
1992	AM General launches civilian version, later known as H1
1999	General Motors buys rights to Hummer brand
2002	GM develops H2, a more civilized version
2003	H2T pickup concept
2005	H1 Alpha
2006	H3 on GM truck platform
2007	H3X. H1 discontinued
2008	H3 Alpha. Rumours of smaller H4 model for 2010 release. GM strategic review to explore options for Hummer
2009	South Africa plant stops H3 production. GM says sale deal finalized with Tengzhong. H3T
2010	Tengzhong pulls out of deal. Last H3 built as GM winds brand down

HUMMER H1, H2 AND H3

Heroic though the military Humvee's accomplishments may have been on the battlefields of the Persian Gulf War of 1990–91, the Hummer's history as a civilian vehicle is short and much less distinguished. Indeed, Hummer ranks as one of the shortest-lived and most disastrous of »General Motors' brand acquisitions.

GM was initially drawn to the high-profile celebrity clientele – notably Arnold Schwarzenegger – who had seen the military Humvee in action in news reports and had persuaded its manufacturer, AM General, to build a more civilized version suitable for ordinary users. The American giant struck a deal in 1999 giving it the right to make civilian versions of the Hummer, while AM General would continue to supply the army.

At the time, sales of large and luxurious SUVs were booming in North America, so GM set about designing a fresh Hummer, the H2, that would be plusher and more user-friendly than its military-derived H1 counterpart. An absolute priority in the design was total authenticity: the H2 needed to look just as vast, tough and intimidating as the real thing, and it had to perform convincingly off and on road, too.

Eager customers lined up for the H2 when it launched in 2002; GM gave it the full brand treatment, with truck derivatives and even special editions. Despite its vast size and prodigious thirst, the H2 became a must-have fashion accessory among the wealthy, and sales boomed. Seeking to broaden Hummer's market, GM developed the smaller H3 model on an existing truck

platform; again, the design was authentic and intimidating, but by now it was too late. The craze had peaked and, despite the lure of the still-smaller HX concept, sales nosedived and GM put the Hummer division up for sale in June 2008.

Many names were mentioned as potential buyers, but in the end only one Chinese company came forward. Yet after months of nervous waiting for confirmation came the news that the bid had not materialized. With no one else interested in what was seen as a flashy macho status symbol totally at odds with the post-crisis spirit of understatement, GM quickly announced it would wind down the brand. The last H3 came off the production line in April 2010. It was a quiet end to a turbulent interlude that GM would prefer to forget.

HUMMER H2
2002–2010 | EXTREME SUV

2010 6.0 V8	
LENGTH	5170 mm (204 in.)
LAYOUT	Front engine, all-wheel drive
ENGINE	6.0 petrol V8
HORSEPOWER	330
MAX. SPEED	160 km/h (99 mph)
CO$_2$ EMISSIONS	412 g/km

The Hummer H2 was the American auto industry's fall guy, the vehicle that took the flak for the worst excesses of the fixation for monster SUVs. Fittingly, perhaps, the whole Hummer brand provided the ritual sacrifice for all this extravagance when the only company interested in buying the name pulled out and the factory closed its doors for good in 2010. Few mourned the Hummer's passing.

Yet whatever one's views on the morality of such big and brutish vehicles, there are aspects of the H2's design that deserve examination. Hummer's designers succeeded brilliantly in their brief to use a civilian SUV platform to build a super-SUV that was just as dominating as the military-derived H1, but more civilized, roomier and more fit for on-road use.

The H2's machismo comes from more than just its vast bulk. Large square shapes, tough flat body panels and screens, straight sides, sharp edges and right-angled corners all signal strength and indestructibility. The huge tyres, great ground clearance and short, slanting front overhang give the impression that the three-ton H2 can bulldoze away any obstacles in its path. This is just what its designers intended, and precisely what its buyers, bored with such mere playthings as the Cadillac Escalade, wanted to buy into.

HYUNDAI

KOREA | FOUNDED 1967 | CARS AND SUVS | WORLDWIDE.HYUNDAI.COM

HISTORY

1946	Chung Ju-Yong establishes first Hyundai companies
1967	Hyundai Motor company established in Seoul
1968	Builds Cortina in cooperation with Ford
1974	Pony is Hyundai's first design
1983	Cumulative production passes 3 million
1984	Establishes Hyundai Motor America
1987	Moves into trucks
1997	Establishes plant in Turkey
1998	Takes over Kia Motors
2002	First Elantra built in China
2005	First US assembly plant, in Alabama
2006	Becomes 6th largest automaker
2007	Work begins on Czech Republic plant
2008	Launches Genesis luxury sub-brand

If a prodigious output of concept cars and styling studies can be seen as a sign of a fertile design department, then Hyundai must be one of the most creative companies in the global auto industry. With design studios in Korea, California and Germany all competing with one another to produce the brightest and bravest ideas, Hyundai has brought two dozen or more concept models to international auto shows since the new millennium. And that's not counting those studies that are lightly disguised production models being given an early airing just prior to release, or those serving as demonstrators for alternative powertrain technologies.

Some may take the view that such a flow of new shapes and formats is a sign that Hyundai is struggling to find a direction for its future model policy. But it is much more an indication of an immense number of ideas in development, of a powerful bow-wave of potential new models waiting for the right moment to hit the market.

Fascinating though concept cars unquestionably are, they are less successful in shifting the needle of public opinion if they are too far removed from the other cars on the show stand, if they are so implausibly sophisticated compared with the standard showroom fare that the buyer fails to make the connection. This used to be the case with Hyundai, when the far-fetched claims made for such 1990s concepts as the HCD-1 and HCD-III appeared irrelevant to the mundane Accent and Elantra that people could actually buy. Now, however, such production models as the i30, iX35 and, especially, the premium Genesis show how far Hyundai has come in a few short years, and the creative showcars no longer seem so fanciful.

Among the concepts first to alert the international community to the new-found inventiveness of Hyundai design were the 2002 HCD-7 flagship sedan concept, complete with elegant tail and Bentley-like rear fenders, and the HCD-8 and 9 concepts of 2004 and 2006. The latter, subtitled Talus, was a development of the earlier low-riding coupé but with chunky wheels, a raised ride height and a much more macho stance. Two years later BMW brought just such a sports SUV to market, arguably less well resolved, in the shape of the »BMW X6.

By 2007 Hyundai was enjoying the respect of the design community. It continued to up its game with such key concepts as the i-Blue fuel-cell crossover and the Veloster coupé, which has been tipped as a possible replacement for the production Coupé (itself one of the showroom models that put Hyundai on the map for more performance-orientated buyers). Later concept designs, in particular the sleek i-Mode and the large Blue Will crossover, show complex and sophisticated surfacing and the beginning of a gradually more fluid and flowing design language – something that may have reached its natural limit in the edgier and even more elaborate 2010 i-Flow, a concept

2002 HCD-7 CONCEPT

2006 HCD-9 TALUS CONCEPT

2011 VELOSTER

2007 i-BLUE FUEL-CELL CONCEPT

PRINCIPAL MODELS	
1974	Pony
1984	Excel
1988	Sonata, by Giorgetto Giugiaro
1992	HCD-1 concept
1994	Accent
1996	Coupé
1997	Atos
2000	Neos roadster concept
2002	HCD-7 flagship sedan concept
2003	NEOS-2
2004	Tucson SUV; E3 and HCD-8 coupé concepts
2005	HED-1; Portico concept
2006	HCD-9 Talus concept
2007	i30; Qarmaq, Genus, Veloster and i-Blue fuel-cell car concepts
2008	i20 and Genesis premium sedan; i-Mode concept
2009	iX Metro, Nuvis small-car and Blue Will crossover concepts
2010	i40/new Sonata; i-Flow concept
2011	Veloster

2010 i40 / NEW SONATA

2007 i30

2008 i-MODE CONCEPT

233

2009 BLUE WILL CONCEPT

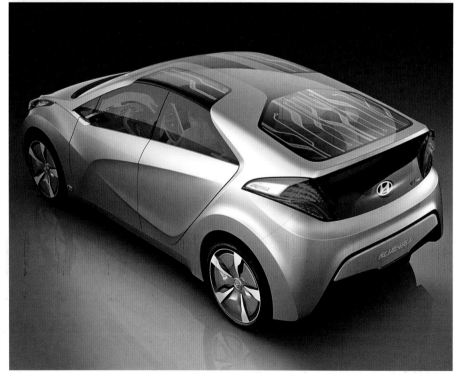

for a premium upper-medium sedan. Borrowing some of its wave-like external forms and interior details from »Mazda's Nagare (also meaning 'flow') series, the i-Flow has interesting proportions and complex, sculptural shapes that interlock and overlap; nevertheless, as a production car it would be a polarizing design.

In parallel with these concepts of increasing sophistication, Hyundai's production offerings have become steadily smarter and better resolved. Such models as the 2010 Sonata/i40 and iX35 are showing a more distinct sense of style. It is hard to believe that these products stem from an organization that just two generations ago switched from building Ford Cortinas under licence to making their own first-ever car, inspired by George Turnbull, the man behind the 1970s Morris Marina.

HYUNDAI GENESIS

2008 | LARGE EXECUTIVE CAR

DATA 2010 3.8 COUPÉ	
LENGTH	4630 mm (182 in.)
LAYOUT	Front engine, rear-wheel drive
ENGINE	3.3 petrol V6
HORSEPOWER	303
MAX. SPEED	240 km/h (149 mph)
CO_2 EMISSIONS	235 g/km

Although Genesis is still officially no more than a pair of models (a sedan, from 2008, and a coupé introduced in 2009) within the Hyundai portfolio, the Korean company's ambitions are huge. Toyota and its luxury division, »Lexus, are its role model, and Genesis has all the makings of a future semi-independent premium brand to challenge not only Lexus but also Mercedes-Benz, Cadillac and the entire luxury establishment.

The parallels with Toyota and Lexus are unavoidable. As in the case of its Japanese rival, Genesis opened its campaign with a large but conservative design, aiming to impress with quality and dignified restraint rather than artistic flair. The 5-metre-long (16 ft) sedan is an intelligent synthesis of design cues from BMW and Mercedes-Benz, and will not offend anyone – or be recognized in a crowd.

The Genesis coupé is a more emotional design, with a strong stance on the road and an eagerness signalled by its forward-leaning profile and, especially, the intriguing surfacing of its sides; this is derived from the blending of the rear fender feature line sweeping forward to overlap below a second crease diving forward from the B-pillar. Unusually, too, the beltline drops down for the rear quarter-light. This could be a hint, perhaps, of more unusual design to come from this aspiring premium-league player.

I.DE.A INSTITUTE

ITALY | FOUNDED 1978 | DESIGN AND ENGINEERING | IDEA.INSTITUTE.IT

High ideals marked the launch of the I.DE.A institute (an acronym for Institute of Development in Automotive Engineering) in Turin in 1978. This was hardly surprising, since its founders included entrepreneur Franco Mantegazza and the renowned architect Renzo Piano. The aim of I.DE.A was to take a 360-degree view of the product, looking at everything from materials choice to manufacturing and distribution.

It helped, of course, that Piano was already in the midst of a comprehensive re-examination of every aspect of carmaking in conjunction with »Fiat; indeed, the Institute's work was largely defined by this ambitious programme, which resulted in the Fiat VSS concept car in 1981. The point of the VSS was not to show aesthetic design, but rather to demonstrate how a modular construction, with a standardized substructure but differentiated external plastic body panels, could save weight and cost and boost safety. Some of the ideas and the manufacturing flexibility came through in the 1988 Fiat Tipo, but Fiat bosses took fright at the high cost of shifting the company's whole model palette to the VSS system.

The versatility of the Tipo structure proved to be an important industry milestone. It was soon providing the underpinnings for a host of other models from Fiat, Alfa Romeo and Lancia, in effect launching the era of platform sharing that Volkswagen was later to use to such devastating effect.

Other successes of I.DE.A include the four-model Fiat Palio family of world cars, the Lancia Kappa luxury car and several models for Chinese and Indian companies. Yet I.DE.A's fortunes began to fade in the late 1990s, and it was with only two concepts – the ERA sports roadster of 2009 and the Sofia hybrid sedan of 2010 – that it signalled an end to a decade-long creative drought.

1994 LANCIA KAPPA RANGE

1988 FIAT TIPO

2005 TATA XOVER CONCEPT

2009 I.DE.A ERA CONCEPT

2010 I.DE.A SOFIA CONCEPT

INFINITI

JAPAN | FOUNDED 1989 | PREMIUM CARS | INFINITI.COM

As in the case of other Japanese automakers who had been successful in the United States in the 1970s and 1980s, Nissan began wondering how it could begin to tap the booming market for premium cars in North America, with its smart dealerships and fatter profit margins. And, as in the case of Toyota, Honda and Mazda, Nissan concluded that only by developing a fresh brand with a premium identity could it seek to compete with its targets of Cadillac, Mercedes-Benz, BMW and Jaguar.

Under the project code-name of Horizon Task Force, Nissan began studying organizations well known for their customer service, such as Four Seasons Hotels and Nordstrom department stores. By July 1987 the name Infiniti had been chosen and the customer-centric philosophy established. The brand launched in 1989 with the Q45 large performance sedan, which, true to Infiniti's promise, was not a rebadged Nissan at a higher price but a completely fresh design.

Yet while the rival LS400 from Toyota's »Lexus, which launched at around the same time, was a deeply conservative design reminiscent of a previous-generation Mercedes-Benz S-Class, the Q45 was much more elegant and Jaguar-like. This did not play well with the cautious American premium customer and sales were slow. Successive updates made the Q45 and the smaller models that followed ever more mainstream; at one point Infiniti even imported rebadged UK-made Nissan Primeras as the G20 sports sedan.

Although Infiniti was one of the first in the United States to offer a luxury SUV, its generally bland products were losing momentum in the late 1990s. With Nissan itself in trouble, the premium brand looked vulnerable. But after the declaration of the Renault-Nissan Alliance in 1999, Nissan's new CEO, Carlos Ghosn, began investing in a fresh look and a new suite of products for Infiniti, promising also to bring greater awareness of the brand by launching in other markets outside North America.

The G35 sedan and coupé that followed immediately set a sportier and more progressive tone, while the 2003 FX established a new niche in the luxury-car market: that for a sporty crossover wagon with four doors but a coupé-like glasshouse. Together these models provided the template for Infiniti's expansion into other world markets in the first decade of this century – and the FX formula has appeared in competitors' showrooms in the shape of the »BMW X6, Cadillac SRX and Audi Q5 and Q7.

Launching into Europe in 2008 in the midst of an economic crisis and a rush towards low-emission cars, Infiniti faced an uphill battle as it had no diesels or hybrids to offer. These gaps were eventually filled, yet despite a profusion of sophisticated technology and standard equipment Infiniti's vehicles are not truly distinctive and the brand has yet to make a big impact in Europe.

Perhaps aware of this shortcoming, Infiniti designers wheeled out the striking Essence concept car in time for the 2009 Geneva motor show. This sleek, polished-metal luxury coupé with the voluptuous allure of an Aston Martin or Maserati displayed several novel design features, such as negative (concave) surfacing, a ridged roof and a slide-out trunk fitted with customized Louis Vuitton travel cases. The Essence was criticized by some for being over-complex in its body language and detailing, but – taken with with a just-released sketch for a 2013 electric luxury car – it does give a hint of the more progressive design set to distinguish next-generation Infinitis.

2008 FX

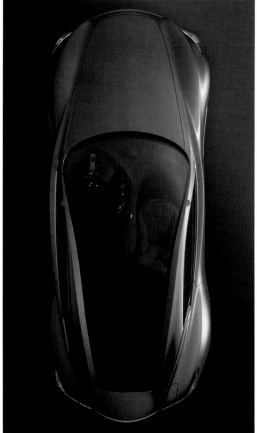

2009 ESSENCE CONCEPT

HISTORY AND PRINCIPAL MODELS

1989	Infiniti division of Nissan opens first showrooms. Q45 performance sedan. M30 luxury coupé
1991	G20 compact sedan
1993	J30 luxury medium sedan
1999	Sales reach 75,000 units a year
2002	G35 sedan, coupé
2003	Passes 100,000 units a year in USA. FX crossover
2004	Enters Middle East market. QX56 luxury SUV
2005	Enters Korean market. M-series performance sedan
2006	Enters Russian market
2007	Enters Chinese market
2008	Enters European market. EX coupé crossover, FX (2nd gen)
2009	Essence concept
2010	First diesel and hybrid. IPL cabriolet
2011	Etherea hybrid concept

2008 EX COUPÉ

2009 ESSENCE CONCEPT

241

ISUZU

JAPAN | FOUNDED 1949 | LIGHT TRUCKS | ISUZU.CO.JP

HISTORY AND PRINCIPAL MODELS

1949	Tokyo Automobile Industries splits into Hino and Isuzu
1953	Isuzu begins building Hillman cars
1959	TL compact truck
1961	Bellel passenger car
1968	117 coupé, by Giorgetto Giugiaro at Ghia
1971	Signs capital agreement with General Motors
1974	Gemini small car built for GM
1981	Piazza coupé, by Giugiaro at Italdesign; Rodeo Bighorn
1987	Coa III concept
1989	Mu/Amigo recreational vehicle; 4200 R concept
1990	Production starts in USA
1991	Trooper
1992	Abandons car production in favour of SUVs
1993	Amigo built in UK as Opel/Vauxhall Frontera. Vehicross concept, by Simon Cox
1997	Vehicross
1998	VX2 concept
2001	Axiom, upscale version of Rodeo; Zen concept
2002	Moves focus to commercial trucks
2003	Agreement with GM on diesel engines
2006	GM sells stake
2009	Withdraws from US market

Isuzu is today known as a maker of commercial trucks and vans, yet in the 1980s it was an important force in the popularization of SUVs among mainstream buyers – and prior to that it was feted as a builder of very pretty Italian-designed coupés alongside its work as a contract producer of small cars for General Motors' American operations.

The story began, as with so many Japanese automakers, with the manufacture of British cars under licence; Isuzu's first own design, the Bellel sedan of 1961, bore a distinct likeness to BMC's Farina models. »Giorgetto Giugiaro designed the pretty 1968 117 Coupé during his brief spell at Ghia: the front recalls the elegant Fiat Dino coupé he had earlier completed at Bertone.

For the 117's replacement Isuzu again went to Giugiaro, who was by now fully established in his own »Italdesign organization, and gave the designer a free hand to clothe the Gemini 1800 platform with a new coupé shape. The result was the 1979 Ace of Clubs concept, a sleek and glassy wedge-shaped coupé of such breathtaking purity that it caused a sensation in the design world. So impressed were Isuzu's managers that the prototype was shipped directly back to Japan to be prepared for production as the 1981 Piazza.

Already, however, Isuzu was beginning to focus on the chunky SUVs that would ensure its reputation, and by the early 1990s it had decided to quit car production in favour of 4x4s. Occasional flashes of brilliance, including the sporty 1997 Vehicross leisure SUV and the striking Zen concept of 2001, punctuated the company's catalogue of clunky 4x4s such as the Amigo, built in Britain as the Opel/Vauxhall Frontera. Yet in the face of mounting losses Isuzu failed to invest in new product, and the company saw its crude American-market 4x4s wiped out by smoother and more effective crossovers from mainstream automakers, ending its spell as a maker of passenger cars.

2001 ZEN CONCEPT

2001 ZEN CONCEPT

1998 VX2 CONCEPT

243

ITALDESIGN

ITALY | FOUNDED 1968 | DESIGN AND ENGINEERING | ITALDESIGN.IT

HISTORY

1968	Founded by Giorgetto Giugiaro and Aldo Mantovani
1969	Research laboratory opens
1970s	Relationships begin with Volkswagen, BMW, Hyundai
1975	Begins working with Lancia, part of Fiat group
1980s	Customers include SEAT, Renault, Chrysler, Ford, Toyota
1997	Dario Trucco joins Italdesign as general manager, later becomes CEO
2008	Commissioned to design Delle Alpi stadium for Juventus football club
2010	Volkswagen Group buys 90.1% of Italdesign

KEY DESIGNS

1968	Bizzarrini Manta showcar
1971	Alfa Romeo Alfasud
1974	Volkswagen Golf, Hyundai Pony
1977	New York Taxi concept
1978	Lancia Megagamma concept
1980	Fiat Panda
1983	Fiat Uno
1984	Saab 9000 Turbo, Lancia Thema, Fiat Croma
1993	Bugatti EB112
2002	Aston Martin Twenty Twenty
2003	Lamborghini Gallardo
2006	Fiat Sedici/Suzuki SX4; Vadho concept
2007	Quaranta concepts
2009	Frazer Nash Namir concept
2010	Proton EMAS small-car concept

Italdesign is without question the most influential independent design agency ever to have operated within the auto industry. The company has done more than any other to apply design excellence across a wide spectrum of products, affordable to motorists and consumers at all levels of society. Such design themes as the 'folded paper' wedge profile, the people-carrier and the chic minimalist small car, first proposed by Italdesign, have gone on to become major trends in global car design. The agency's influence spreads far beyond the automotive sector: Italdesign has also designed consumer goods, trains and even cameras.

Founded in 1968 by ex-»Bertone designer »Giorgetto Giugiaro and Aldo Mantovani, a senior engineer from Fiat, Italdesign melded two important influences: those of the artist and those of the seasoned industrial planner. Right from the start, Italdesign differentiated itself from the then-dominant Italian houses by offering a full engineering service; indeed, the agency's first project, the Alfa Romeo Alfasud, even included the design of the manufacturing plant.

Such broad competence soon attracted the attention of Volkswagen, desperate to draw itself out of the Beetle era in the late 1960s. The resultant Scirocco and »VW Golf were huge hits and rewrote the rules of small-car design, and a succession of groundbreaking models followed. Notable among these were the low-cost »Fiat Panda and Uno, and the Lancia Megagamma concept, which anticipated the trend towards high-rise people-carriers.

The turn of the millennium saw Giugiaro's son Fabrizio playing an increasingly important role in design, with the VW W12, »Lamborghini Gallardo and Chevrolet Corvette Moray concept among his credits. In 2010, however, came the surprise announcement that Volkswagen was taking control of Italdesign, putting an end to its forty-year reign as the world's most celebrated independent design studio.

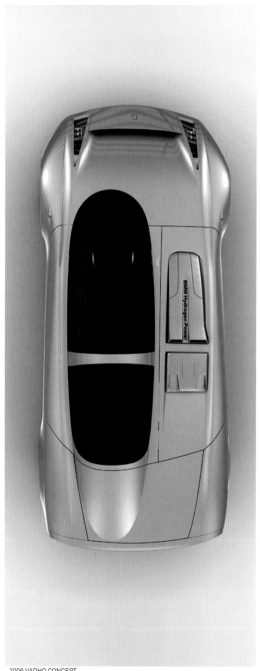

2006 VADHO CONCEPT

2009 FRAZER NASH NAMIR CONCEPT

2007 QUARANTA CONCEPT

JAGUAR

GREAT BRITAIN | FOUNDED 1935 | SPORTS AND LUXURY CARS | JAGUAR.COM

HISTORY

1935	William Lyons adopts Jaguar name for SS Cars models
1943	Engineers design XK engine at night while on wartime fire watch
1951	C-Type wins Le Mans 24 Hours
1952	Company moves to Browns Lane, Coventry
1957	Fire destroys Jaguar factory. D-Types take top four places at Le Mans
1960	Jaguar acquires Daimler
1966	Jaguar merges with BMC
1968	Jaguar/BMC merge into British Leyland
1975	BL becomes state-owned
1980	John Egan becomes CEO
1984	Egan takes Jaguar private
1985	Sir William Lyons dies
1988	Jaguar wins Le Mans and world sports-car championship
1989	Jaguar bought by Ford for £1.6 billion
1992	Nick Scheele becomes CEO
2000	Ian Callum becomes design director. Jaguar enters Formula One
2008	Jaguar sold to Tata Motors

To anyone growing up in 1950s and 1960s Britain, there was nothing more exciting or more glamorous than a Jaguar. Jaguar's designs were lithe, sensual and suggestive, a splash of shapely colour in a dull, monochrome world. Proprietor Sir William Lyons had such a fine eye for proportion and style that his designs always hit the spot, and it helped, of course, that the D-Type racing car – arguably the first truly aerodynamic modern-era car – had notched up a string of victories at the Le Mans 24 Hours.

Yet nothing, not even the exemplary D-Type, could have prepared the public for the absolute sensation that was the 1961 E-Type. Slimming and stretching the curvaceous D-Type into a voluptuous grand-touring coupé, Lyons and his aerodynamicist, Malcolm Sayer, created the finest piece of automobile sculpture ever seen, a smoothly honed shape that was at the same time evocative and seductive, elegant and irresistibly exciting. The fact that it was extremely fast and eminently affordable served to boost its charisma still further. The E-Type became an instant icon, and the world of car design was never the same again.

The same could also be said about the 1968 XJ, the last Jaguar to show the direct hand of Lyons. This large and wide executive saloon, with its low waistline, big wheels and slim pillars giving a generous glass area, immediately changed the proportions of a big car from staid and sedate to slender and athletic. Again the aesthetic had been redrawn for all, and Jaguar was at its unchallenged peak.

The reasons for the slide that would take hold over the next two decades are many and complex, and centre on changes of management and ownership, shortage of investment and the unwillingness of successive generations of managers to modernize a formula that had been so successful in the past. The XJS coupé of 1975 failed to carry over the animal magnetism of the E-Type it replaced, and cautious, cash-strapped updates to the XJ – the last of them by »Pininfarina – had left it looking old-fashioned and poorly packaged. Ford, taking charge in 1989, found the cupboard bare. It quickly embarked on a renovation programme that saw a facelifted XJ – now looking much more like the original model – in 1994 and, two years later, the XK new sports car, which felt modern but also recalled some of the emotion of the E-Type.

Seeking to turn Jaguar into a competitor for BMW and Mercedes at all levels of the premium class, Ford bet heavily on a doubling and a subsequent redoubling of

1949 XK 120

1954 D-TYPE

1959 MARK II

2001 X-TYPE

1968-GENERATION XJ: 1976

2000 F-TYPE CONCEPT

1988 XJ 220

1961 E-TYPE

2001 R-COUPÉ CONCEPT

2001 AND 2003 XJ

PRINCIPAL MODELS	
1931	SS1 fixed-head coupé
1938	SS Jaguar 100
1949	XK 120
1950	Mark VII
1954	D-Type, XK 140
1957	XKSS, XK 150
1959	Mark II
1961	E-Type, Mark X
1963	S-Type
1966	XJ 13 race prototype
1968	XJ, the last car designed by Lyons
1975	XJS replaces E-Type
1986	XJ 40 replaces XJ6
1988	XJ 220 prototype
1994	XJ6 (X300)
1996	XJS replaced by XK V8
1998	S-Type; XK 180 concept
2000	F-Type concept
2001	X-Type executive sedan; R-Coupé concept
2003	New XJ has aluminium body; R-D6 concept
2005	2nd-gen XK is aluminium
2007	XF (replaces S-Type); C-XF concept
2009	XJ (4th gen)
2010	C-X75 concept

Jaguar volumes to produce new models aimed at the BMW 5 and 3 Series. The strategy was logical enough, but the implementation was faulty. The mid-size S-Type of 1998 was sentimentally retro in its style and compromised in its dynamics by the need to share a platform with an American Lincoln; the smaller X-Type, meanwhile, caused humiliation when it was revealed it was built on the same platform as the mass-appeal Ford Mondeo. Worse, with its exterior styled like a miniature XJ, it looked outdated right from launch, and Jaguar soon found itself labelled a nostalgia brand.

Behind the scenes, Jaguar had been working on advanced lightweight aluminium architectures that would give its new cars class-leading performance and efficiency, but once again the company scored a disastrous own goal with the all-new 2003 XJ. Sophisticated underneath but clothed in a body that looked no different from its already old-fashioned predecessor, the XJ was a major missed opportunity and it did badly in the market, despite its advanced engineering.

By now, new design director »Ian Callum, who had taken over in 2000 but had been powerless to change the XJ, was putting the finishing touches to a new »XK. This was

2009 XJ

2003 RD-6 CONCEPT

2010 C-X75 CONCEPT

the first of a series of dramatic new designs intended to bring Jaguar style into the modern era and to catch up the ground lost since the company's identity had effectively frozen around the look of its 1968 XJ icon.

The C-XF concept of 2007 was arguably the biggest single step ever taken by Jaguar design: few cues could be traced back to the once ever-present XJ, and the production »XF that followed was an immediate hit, despite the economic downturn at the time. Extending his thinking to the larger 2009 »XJ, Callum pushed the theme still harder to redefine luxury-car proportions once more, especially at the rear and in the elegant interior.

India's Tata, owners of Jaguar since 2008, have freed Jaguar from the focus-group orthodoxy that stifled the company during its tenure with Ford. There is genuine belief that groundbreaking design will once again come to the fore. There are active plans to provide an emotional successor to the E-Type (perhaps fulfilling the promise of the cancelled 2000 F-Type concept), as well as an inspirational new-technology beacon in the shape of the 2010 C-X75 concept and its polished new supercar aesthetic.

JAGUAR XF

2007 | LARGE EXECUTIVE CAR

2010 5.0 XF-R V8	
LENGTH	4960 mm (196 in.)
LAYOUT	Front engine, rear-wheel drive
ENGINE	5.0 petrol V8 supercharged
HORSEPOWER	510
MAX. SPEED	250 km/h (155 mph)
CO_2 EMISSIONS	292 g/km

At its launch in 2007 the XF was a car with a double mission. Not only did it have to appeal directly to business-class buyers who had been loyal to BMW, Mercedes-Benz or Audi for decades, but it also had to make up for almost forty years of stagnation in Jaguar design and to fast-forward the British brand's image into the twenty-first century. So great was this stride, reasoned design director »Ian Callum, that an advanced concept car would be required to prepare public opinion for the shift.

In 2007 Callum pulled the wraps off the C-XF concept. The future face of Jaguar was smooth, dynamic and dramatic, with a long hood and a fastback rear; thrust forward between twin narrow slits of rearward-sweeping lights was a recessed mesh grille resembling the air intake of a jet fighter.

The reaction was positive, but the production car later that year scored a bullseye. The XF's coupé-like profile was moderated only slightly, with a higher roofline; the rear panel was tidied up; and a calm and elegant interior took the place of the showcar's flashy techno-fest. The XF takes getting used to as a Jaguar, but as a reawakening of a once world-class design benchmark it is an outstanding success.

JAGUAR XJ

2009 | LUXURY CAR

MODEL HISTORY 1968 XJ6 1ST GENERATION, SERIES I–III • 1986 XJ6 2ND GENERATION (XJ40, X300) • 2003 XJ 3RD GENERATION (X350) • 2009 XJ 4TH GENERATION

2010 3.0D V6	
LENGTH	5120 mm (202 in.)
LAYOUT	Front engine, rear-wheel drive
ENGINE	3.0 turbo diesel V6
HORSEPOWER	275
MAX SPEED	250 km/h (155 mph)
CO$_2$ EMISSIONS	184 g/km

Fresh from the critical success of the »XF and its catapulting of Jaguar's image into the twenty-first century, design director »Ian Callum faced the even more daunting task of bringing a contemporary dimension to the crown jewels of the Jaguar marque, the iconic XJ sedan. So firmly had the XJ's style been frozen around the image of the 1968 XJ, the last car in which Jaguar founder William Lyons had a hand, that Jaguar had shut its eyes to visual progress and had become a heritage brand.

This was especially paradoxical in the case of the flagship XJ, for although all generations since 1968 had shared the same unchanging design cues, the 2003 iteration had been highly advanced mechanically, with a lightweight aluminium structure and state-of-the-art diesel engine.

Acknowledging the 1968 XJ as a landmark design that had revolutionized the aesthetic of the luxury car, Callum set about replicating the impact and the ethos of the original in a modern context, but without transplanting direct design cues. One of the most striking aspects of the new design is the extended window graphic, sweeping back and stretched right out to the rear wheel, highlighted with brightwork so as to lengthen visually the passenger compartment. The nose is an evolution of the XF's, but the tail is where Callum really stirred up debate. The trunk lid is a pure unadorned surface, flanked by elegantly striated tail lights that stretch upward to roll over into the rear deck just aft of the steeply raked rear screen, itself visually widened by taking the glazing over the rear pillars.

This is an unusual example of polarizing design in the luxury segment, and ensures the XJ is instantly recognized. The car's outstanding interior also rewrites the rules, with a low-set dashboard separated from the windshield by a shallow hoop of wood that arcs round to meet the upper door panels; this visually extends the interior for the passengers and provides a greater sense of space. Callum set out to make an impact with this new XJ, and he has certainly done that.

2003 XJ

253

JAGUAR XK

2005 | LUXURY SPORTS CAR

MODEL HISTORY 1996 XK 1ST GENERATION • 2005 XK 2ND GENERATION

2010 5.0 V8	
LENGTH	4790 mm (189 in.)
LAYOUT	Front engine, rear-wheel drive
ENGINE	5.0 petrol V8
HORSEPOWER	385
MAX SPEED	250 km/h (155 mph)
CO$_2$ EMISSIONS	264 g/km

Even though the legendary E-Type had become a gross caricature of its lithe and sculptural 1961 self, its supplanting by the heavyweight XJS in 1975 was greeted with regret rather than anticipation. The new car, configured around a massive V12 engine and stringent US safety regulations, had none of the E's animal intensity or athletic poise.

Jaguar enthusiasts would have to wait a further twenty years for a car that in any way revisited the emotional values of that brand hero. Although the 1996 XK V8 was much more of a luxury GT than a hardline sports car, it sent out all the right messages: from the open oval frontal air intake, the front fenders flowed voluptuously into the narrower centre section before rising again over the rear wheels. The tail may have been truncated rather than tapered, but a hint of that old magic was back.

The second-generation XK in 2005 amplified those sentiments, preserving a similar overall form but employing much crisper surface language and more sharply resolved details. The interior was thoroughly revised along contemporary lines, too, confirming the classy XK as the first fresh design of Jaguar's new era.

1996 XK

255

JEEP

UNITED STATES | FOUNDED 1945 | UTILITY 4x4S AND SUVS | JEEP.COM

HISTORY

1941	Willys Overland produces general-purpose vehicle for US army
1950	Jeep registered as international trademark
1953	Willys Overland sold to Henry J. Kaiser
1963	Company renamed Kaiser Jeep
1970	American Motors Corporation buys Kaiser Jeep
1983	Renault takes control of AMC
1987	Chrysler buys AMC
1994	Grand Cherokee production begins in Austria
1998	Chrysler merges with Daimler
2007	Daimler sells Chrysler Group
2009	Bankruptcy. Fiat takes control

1941 WILLYS MA

1945 CJ2A

1962 WAGONEER

1984 CHEROKEE

As with the iPod MP3 player, the Hoover vacuum cleaner and the Biro ballpen, the Jeep name is so familiar that it has become a generic term in everyday language for a tough and agile vehicle that is as at home on rough, boulder-strewn terrain as on open highways or city streets. Yet it was not until 1950 – nine years after Willys Overland had begun building the first 'General Purpose' MA models for the American army – that the company sought to protect the name as a trademarked brand. Half a century later, and having suffered six changes of ownership and several close encounters with bankruptcy, the Jeep brand was perhaps the strongest within the Chrysler Group.

The archetypal Jeep, now known as the »Wrangler, is very clearly a direct descendant of the wartime transport of GIs and generals, and is still the main brand anchor seventy years after it first saw action. Everything is now larger and more sophisticated, but Jeep's designers have cleverly developed the basic straightforwardness of the concept into a powerful sales magnet over the years, using its starkness and simplicity as positives rather than drawbacks. The result is instant recognizability and identification with a rugged, adventurous outdoor lifestyle, and an ability to dismiss the creature comforts of more civilized vehicles.

Jeep's second brand anchor, perhaps more interesting from a design point of view, is the station-wagon. Originally no more than a wood-adorned wagon rear end tacked on to the familiar front of a CJ civilian Jeep, the concept evolved into the Wagoneer in 1962. As the first-ever sport utility vehicle, the Wagoneer was something of a breakthrough product, and it was the precursor of a whole generation of lifestyle 4x4s triggered in Europe by the Range Rover and in Japan by the Toyota Land Cruiser. The original Wagoneer was skilfully designed to minimize the visual impact of its bulk and height, with a low waistline, slim pillars and large glass areas. Fascinatingly, designers a generation later, at the height of the American macho SUV boom, would reverse this thinking to make their products look even tougher and more intimidating.

The Wagoneer was a technical pioneer, too, as the first 4x4 with independent front suspension and the option of automatic transmission. The Wagoneer evolved into successive generations of Cherokees and Grand Cherokees, restyled at regular intervals to keep pace with customer demands for ever-increasing levels of luxury and safety. Yet apart from the seven-space grille, symbolically punched out of sheet metal or stamped in chrome, few visual clues link the large Jeeps to their smaller siblings.

Where Jeep designers have been at their most active and most ingenious is in devising variations on the archetypal theme of the basic Jeep. One of the most intriguing is the 1998 Jeepster concept for a cut-down sports roadster Jeep that provides roadster thrills on tarmac as well as off-road climbing ability (sufficient to complete the daunting Rubicon Trail near Lake Tahoe in California, for many years a technical requirement for all production Jeeps). The 2005 Hurricane concept was astonishing for very different reasons: with 335-horsepower Hemi V8s front and rear and steering on all four wheels, it could spin round in its own

2006 COMPASS

2005 HURRICANE CONCEPT

2007 TRAILHAWK CONCEPT

length and must rate as one of the most agile high-mobility vehicles ever devised.

Where Jeep can with hindsight be seen to have gone wrong is when it sought to broaden its appeal to a non-enthusiast audience by making family-orientated models on car platforms. Despite familiar Jeep styling cues, the blocky Patriot and the softer, more crossover-like Compass came across as cheap fakes, almost as if a low-budget competitor had tried its hand at copying a Jeep. Roundly rejected by Jeep loyalists, these examples show how a brand can be damaged if it is diluted or applied to unsuitable products.

Jeep is one of the world's most recognized and most valuable brands, yet, as in the case of »Land Rover in Britain, it needs to evolve in a fresh direction in order to compete in the new climate-change-conscious world. This will be the responsibility of Fiat, which now controls Jeep parent Chrysler. One thing is certain, though: the Jeep brand will never again be sold on the cheap, as it was in 1987 when Chrysler rescued American Motors Corporation from its period of Renault ownership.

PRINCIPAL MODELS

1941	Military MA, MB vehicles
1945	CJ2A is first civilian Jeep
1946	Jeep station-wagon is first all-new post-war car in US
1949	Station-wagon offered with four-wheel drive
1955	CJ5, continues in production to 1984
1962	Wagoneer is first SUV
1976	CJ7
1984	Cherokee
1987	YJ Wrangler
1992	Grand Cherokee
1997	TJ Wrangler
1998	Jeepster concept
2002	Treo concept
2005	Hurricane concept
2006	Wrangler (4th gen), Compass and Patriot crossovers, Commander
2007	Trailhawk concept
2009	Renegade electric Jeep concept

2009 RENEGADE ELECTRIC CONCEPT

POST-2006 PATRIOT ELECTRIC CONCEPT

JEEP WRANGLER

2006 | MEDIUM 4x4

MODEL HISTORY 1945 CJ 1ST GENERATION • 1987 YJ WRANGLER 2ND GENERATION • 1997 TJ WRANGLER 3RD GENERATION • 2006 JK WRANGLER 4TH GENERATION

2010 2.8 CRD	
LENGTH	4225 mm (167 in.)
LAYOUT	Front engine, all-wheel drive
ENGINE	2.8 turbo diesel 4-cyl
HORSEPOWER	177
MAX.SPEED	180 km/h (111 mph)
CO_2 EMISSIONS	255 g/km

The type of 4x4 vehicle typified by the Jeep is blessed with unrivalled longevity of design, for the simple reason that, as a device built purely for utility, its design is entirely functional and therefore immune to the influences of external fashion. Thus there is no reason for the design to change – unless, as became the case with the original Jeep CJ of 1945, the design itself becomes fashionable, and thus vulnerable to distortion.

The 1945 CJ (for 'civilian Jeep') was little more than the wartime military vehicle with a few concessions to everyday practicality. Successive generations added more power, more space and, in response to consumer demand, more equipment and refinement, although chassis comfort and on-road dynamic qualities were never high on the agenda.

Jeep remained faithful to its founding ethos of uninhibited off-road trail performance. The Wrangler in its series of incarnations has steadily gained in length, girth, weight and complexity. Yet, even with clumsy fashion-dictated wide tyres and fully rigid bodywork, the clarity of purpose was still there and new generations visibly shared the same genes as the original. The result is the highest possible accolade for brand identity: 'Jeep' becoming the generic word for '4x4'.

KIA

KOREA | FOUNDED 1944 | CARS AND SUVS | KIA-MOTORS.COM

HISTORY AND PRINCIPAL MODELS

1944	Kyungsung Precision Industries begins producing bicycle parts
1970	Kia builds Fiat 124 and Mazda Titan truck
1973	First Korean company to build own engines
1976	Buys truckmaker Asia Motors
1983	Mazda takes 8% stake
1986	Kia Pride is version of Mazda 121. Ford takes 10% stake
1992	Sephia is Kia's first own design
1993	Sportage compact SUV
1997	Buys rights to build Lotus Elan
1998	Asian crisis puts Kia into receivership; rescued by Hyundai. Carnival/Sedona minivan
2002	Sorento SUV
2003	Picanto compact car
2006	Peter Schreyer becomes chief design officer. Zilina plant in Slovakia begins production. Cee'd medium hatchback; Soul concept
2008	Soul production
2009	Venga, Cerato, Cerato Koop, Sorento
2010	Sportage medium SUV; Pop 3-seater electric concept

The auto world was quick to express its astonishment in 2006 when renowned Volkswagen and Audi designer »Peter Schreyer, one of the select group credited with the iconic »Audi TT, announced he was to become the chief design officer for Kia worldwide. On one level, the surprise was a natural reaction: Kia was an almost invisible brand in design terms, hailing from Korea and competing against other nondescript models at the value end of the market. Many of its models owed their origins to »Mazda products, and its only nameplates to have achieved significant recognition in the market were the Picanto compact car and the Sorento SUV, the latter because it cleverly capitalized on the look of the then-fashionable Mercedes-Benz ML class to attract image-conscious buyers unable to afford the genuine article.

Yet Schreyer was enthusiastic about the Kia appointment, openly excited at the prospect of the blank canvas of a brand with no real heritage, a canvas on which he could build a completely fresh identity, free of any historical constraints. The fresh start under Schreyer's direction was given added credibility by the opening of a factory in Slovakia to build the first cars identified with his style, the Golf-class Cee'd hatchback and its coupé and wagon derivatives.

These were well received by European consumers, as was Kia's Venga compact minivan in 2009, but it was the funky urban »Soul, with its boxy body and tough attitude, that really captured the imagination. More recently, the new Sportage SUV has won praise, and the 2010 Pop concept for a three-seater urban electric vehicle, with its dramatic side-window graphic and imaginative interior, has placed Kia design just where Schreyer wanted it to be: at the leading edge of fresh and practical thinking in the industry.

2010 SPORTAGE

2002 SORENTO

2003 PICANTO

2010 POP ELECTRIC CONCEPT

KIA SOUL

2008 | COMPACT MINIVAN

2010 1.6	
LENGTH	4105 mm (162 in.)
LAYOUT	Front engine, front-wheel drive
ENGINE	1.6 petrol 4-cyl
HORSEPOWER	126
MAX. SPEED	177 km/h (110 mph)
CO$_2$ EMISSIONS	153 g/km

Any notion that Asian automakers, especially those relatively new to the car scene, are timid designers was comprehensively shattered by the Kia Soul. First displayed as a concept in 2006, this chunky urban-cool crossover immediately caused a stir: its edgy, solid-hewn lines, by Kia Design America chief designer Tom Kearns, gave it a heavyweight feel, despite its small-car overall footprint, and the dramatic open-mouth shape of its window graphic projected both the protective signature of a full-face crash helmet and a hunger for off-road adventure.

Two years later, and displayed as near-production concepts at the Geneva show, the Soul had morphed in its role, not its shape; the three studies, differing only in trim, colour and equipment, presented alternative visions for fashionable, youthful and luxury-orientated buyer groups. Most importantly, the design was carried over undiminished: with the exception of the rear-hinged back doors (expensive to engineer), all its key points were retained, even the architecture of the interior.

And that is precisely how the Soul entered Kia showrooms in 2008: as an aggressively radical take on a practical five-door hatchback, at home in the urban jungle and more than a match for the familiar family favourites boasting big-brand names rather than the Soul's strong attitude.

2006 SOUL CONCEPT

KOENIGSEGG

SWEDEN | FOUNDED 1994 | EXTREME SPORTS CARS | KOENIGSEGG.SE

2007 CCXR

As an ambitious and enterprising young man born into an affluent Swedish family, Christian von Koenigsegg became impatient when companies rejected two of his innovative ideas for new products. Disappointed, he decided to go back to a childhood inspiration that had been triggered by a Norwegian film about a bicycle repair man who builds a racing car, and at the age of twenty-two he set up the Koenigsegg company dedicated to building the ultimate car. At Koenigsegg, he promised, no technical solution would be deemed too difficult.

It has been to Koenigsegg's immense credit that just a decade after the roll-out of the first prototype, the CC, the company's line-up of extreme sports cars is ranked among the very best in the world by the people who should know – the millionaire enthusiasts who can afford to buy them, and the specialist magazines who drive them to their limits and compare them with top offerings from such long-established names as Ferrari and Lamborghini and comparative newcomers McLaren, Noble and Pagani.

Operating out of a disused jet-fighter base in southern Sweden, with a handy 1.7-kilometre (1 mile) runway for testing the cars, Koenigsegg's company hand-builds its range of ferociously powerful mid-engined supercars, which are often tailor-made to the requirements of individual customers. The cars' dramatically cab-forward proportion emphasizes the length of the engine bay behind the driver, and, uncluttered by extraneous details such as air scoops and large spoilers, the body language is cleaner and smoother than that of many of its competitors.

While a small and elite clientele is fiercely loyal to the company, Koenigsegg came close to a dramatic expansion of its customer base in 2009 when, but for a last-minute hitch, it would have bought »Saab from General Motors; a measure, perhaps, of the scale of its ambition. Significantly, the eventual buyer turned out to be another enthusiast builder of extreme supercars, The Netherlands' »Spyker.

KOENIGSEGG AGERA

2010 | EXTREME SPORTS CAR

2010 AGERA	
LENGTH	4295 mm (170 in.)
LAYOUT	Mid engine, rear-wheel drive
ENGINE	5.0 petrol supercharged V8
HORSEPOWER	850
MAX. SPEED	390+ km/h (242+ mph)
CO_2 EMISSIONS	–

The magazines describe it as inspirational, insane and the most exciting supercar on Earth, bar none; even traditionally modest Koenigsegg itself calls its cars individual pieces of art, an environment for adventure. The Agera (the name means 'to act' in Swedish) is the latest in a fifteen-year sequence of ever more extreme supercars developed by Swedish entrepreneur and car fanatic Christian von Koenigsegg at his converted airbase in the south of the country.

In common with its predecessors the CC, CCR and CCXR, the Agera builds on the prototype's mid-engined, two-seater configuration. Although front and rear detailing has been upgraded over the years, the very distinctive screen and side-window graphic has been retained, with the blacked-out A-pillars giving the unusually cab-forward passenger compartment the look of a racing helmet and visor. A long, flat rear deck behind the twin head fairings adds to the dramatic racing-car proportions.

New on the Agera are electronic instruments, minor controls illuminated at night by microfibres implanted in the aluminium surfaces, and a lateral cornering force g-meter reading up to 1.6 g – just the accessory for the elite customer for whom Ferrari, Lamborghini and McLaren are too ordinary.

KTM

AUSTRIA | FOUNDED 1934 | MOTORCYCLES AND LIGHTWEIGHT SPORTS CARS | KTM-X-BOW.COM

HISTORY AND PRINCIPAL MODELS

1934	Hans Trunkenpolz opens workshop in Mattighofen, Austria
1951	First KTM-designed motorcycle
1954	First racing successes
1970	First KTM engines
1970s	First world championships
1991	Bankruptcy; company split up
2007	KTM X-Bow concept at Geneva show
2008	X-Bow production car on sale

2008 X-BOW

Very highly regarded in the motorcycle world for its motocross, enduro, adventure and, more recently, powerful street bikes, Austria's KTM dipped its toes into the car business in 2007 when it unveiled its X-Bow sports-car concept at the Geneva auto show. The enthusiast community's response was electrifying: KTM's stand was besieged by press, media and excited drivers impatient to get behind the wheel and experience the thrills promised by this most outrageous of machines. Shortly afterwards, and to no one's surprise, the Austrian company announced that it would explore options for the production of what had been just a concept.

The wildly enthusiastic reception given to the KTM was entirely understandable. This was one of the most original and outlandish designs on the show circuit for many years, a crazy blend of exposed engineering elements, visible racing-style carbon-fibre chassis tub, twin open cockpits and elaborate bright orange bolted-on body panels that appeared to float above the main black chassis structure. It was as if a four-wheeled motorcycle had been superimposed on a Formula One car: every component was functional, highly technical and packed with the promise of an intense driving experience.

In design terms, KTM had succeeded in producing a highly focused track car that was thoroughly modern and in complete contrast

to the stark and old-fashioned minimalism of the many Lotus Seven-inspired hardline sports cars that had dominated the extreme lightweight sports-car scene for so many years. With the X-Bow the minimalism is a calculated design choice rather than a historical accident.

Yet, even with a relatively inexpensive 2-litre Audi engine in the rear, the X-Bow costs almost as much as a »Porsche 911, and the fragility of the market was revealed in 2009 when sales slumped as the economic crisis struck. KTM's response has been to chase export markets and promote interest in its X-Bow racing series, giving credence to its 'Ready to Race' tagline across both bike and car sectors. And Fiat's performance brand, »Abarth, is believed to be eyeing up the chassis to underpin a new sports car it is planning.

LADA

RUSSIA | FOUNDED 1970 | CARS AND SUVS

When it opened in 1970, Avtovaz's factory at the newly created city of Togliattigrad on the banks of the Volga was the biggest car plant not just in the Soviet Union, but also the whole world. It had been the brainchild of Soviet leaders in search of a simple and rugged domestically produced people's car, and of Italy's Fiat, which had been keen to supply the manufacturing expertise and adapt its already aged 124 sedan.

An integral part of the plan had been to earn foreign currency by also selling the car abroad, where it was named Lada. But as exports began to trickle into Western markets it soon became clear that the Lada, although it retained the Fiat's boxy lines, was badly made, heavy on fuel and clumsy to drive. Before long, unreliability and depreciation were added to that list. For some it represented a lot of car for the money, but for the majority it came to be seen as symptomatic of the incompetence of Soviet industry.

Relatively early in Avtovaz's history came its most distinctive product, one that predated currently fashionable light SUV models, such as the Toyota RAV-4. The 1977 Lada Niva, a neatly styled compact 4x4, was well priced and performed well off-road, although its on-road behaviour was still unrefined. It is still in production, having survived the meltdown of the Russian auto industry following the break-up of the Soviet Union and the tense partnership with GM that saw it labelled the Chevrolet Niva. Astonishingly, there has even been speculation that »Pininfarina may build an updated version at its plant in Turin.

Symbolizing much of what was worst about the Soviet era, Lada's bland, underfunded and shoddily made products will soon give way to shiny new Renault and Dacia designs as the French carmaker seeks to make the most of its controlling stake in Avtovaz. Few but a handful of loyal Niva fans will be sad to see them go.

1970 1200

1977 NIVA

1984 SAMARA

2007 C CONCEPT

2008 C-CROSS CONCEPT

LAMBORGHINI

ITALY | FOUNDED 1963 | EXTREME SPORTS CARS | LAMBORGHINI.COM

HISTORY

1963	Tractor magnate Ferruccio Lamborghini decides to build 'flawless GT car'
1965	Miura chassis displayed at Turin show
1970	Expands factory for Urraco production
1972	Ferruccio Lamborghini pulls out
1976	Contract to design and build M1 for BMW
1978	Receivership and bankruptcy
1981	Reformed by Mimran brothers
1987	Taken over by Chrysler
1994	Chrysler sells company to Indonesians
1997	Turns to Audi for V8 engine
1998	Full takeover by Audi. Luc Donckerwolke becomes head of design

1966 MIURA

It's not often that a bare chassis can change the direction of car design, but that's precisely what happened at the Turin motor show in 1965 when, just two years after the formation of his company, Ferruccio Lamborghini displayed an extraordinarily neat and compact platform with a potent V12 engine tucked in transversely, directly behind the hollows for the driver and passenger. No components stuck out ahead of the front wheels or behind those at the rear, and it was clear that this ingeniously packaged layout offered the potential for a radically different configuration in high-performance car design, a complete break from the existing formula of a big V12 engine under a long hood ahead of the driver.

Legendary design manager Nuccio »Bertone, who until then had not worked for Lamborghini, immediately saw the possibilities and had done a deal with Lamborghini before the show closed. Bertone put Marcello Gandini, a promising twenty-seven-year-old, on to the job. The result, just a few months later, was the Lamborghini Miura, a landmark car that exploded on to the design scene, ripped up the rulebook and launched a new breed of car: the supercar.

1974 COUNTACH

Gandini's design changed for ever the proportions of the world's most powerful cars. The Miura was able to package tremendous potency within a remarkably smooth, low and compact silhouette. It established an arresting new design language for a genre that until then had been confined to the racetrack, and such details as the headlamp 'eyebrows' and slatted rear window were swiftly copied across the industry.

The Miura catapulted Lamborghini ahead of the once-unchallenged Ferrari as the true innovator in extreme sports-car design. It was several years before Ferrari responded, but by then Lamborghini had struck another blow: in 1971 Gandini had sensationalized the design world yet again with the Countach prototype. Its humped wedge silhouette was formed from twisted planar surfaces and crisp intersections, and – for the first time – the windshield dipped down to the nose of the car without a change of angle. If the Miura was beautiful, the Countach was aggressive and confrontational, especially in its later versions when, on the suggestion of Canadian motor-racing entrepreneur Walter Wolf, it was bedecked with wide wheels, extended arches, gaping air scoops and a large but superfluous rear wing. After this, the die was cast and each supercar had to be more dramatic, more dangerous and more macho than the one that went before.

As for Lamborghini design, the golden era of the 1960s and early 1970s turned into a bleak period of uncertain management and control by the remote Chrysler, until, in the late 1990s, takeover by a well-organized and well-resourced parent, Audi, at last brought security and stability.

Its confidence and that of its customers restored, Lamborghini rebounded in 2001 with the »Murciélago, by »Luc Donckerwolke, which established a smoother and more contemporary aesthetic for the brand, while retaining all the drama of Countach-style proportions and stance. Best of all, the cars were well made and sold in what for Lamborghini were unprecedented numbers. The smaller, neater V10 »Gallardo of 2003 marked a further step-up in volumes.

Yet, having slipped into a comfortable new identity for the marque, Lamborghini cannot afford to stand still; innovation and provocation are deep in its corporate DNA, and, to stay true to its mission, it needs to

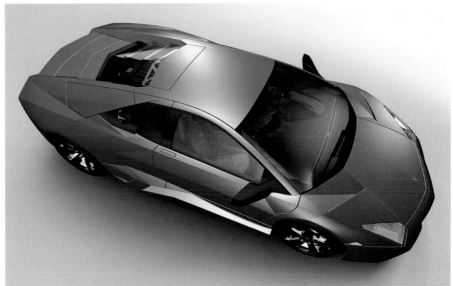

2007 REVENTON

2006 MIURA CONCEPT

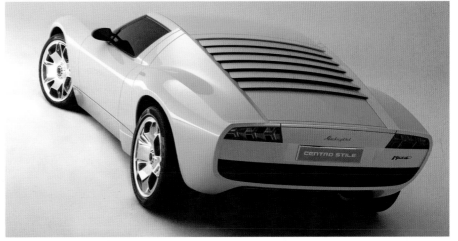

PRINCIPAL MODELS	
1963	350 GTV, by Franco Scaglione
1964	350 GT, rebodied by Touring
1966	Miura, by Marcello Gandini
1967	Marzal
1968	Espada
1971	Countach prototype, by Gandini
1974	Countach enters production
1976	Silhouette
1980	Athon concept, by Bertone
1986	LM extreme SUV
1988	Genesis concept, by Bertone
1990	Diablo
1995	Calà concept, by Giorgetto Giugiaro
2001	Murciélago
2003	Gallardo
2005	Concept S
2006	Miura concept
2007	Reventon
2008	Estoque concept
2010	Sesto Elemento concept
2011	Aventador

2008 ESTOQUE CONCEPT

shake up the establishment once more. Projects such as the Concept S and Reventon were no more than spin-offs, and the 2008 Estoque concept – Lamborghini's first four-door sedan – was poorly received. The attempt to re-create the Miura in 2006 was an embarrassingly untypical and unwanted step into retro.

With the 2010 Sesto Elemento (for the sixth element, carbon), design director Manfred Fitzgerald has sharpened up the surfacing to create a more edgy and complex crystalline look, but the balance of volumes and masses remains unchanged. Despite the reappearance of such past Lamborghini themes as the hexagons of the 1960s and the Miura's opening front and rear sections, this advanced technology concept is still not quite the shock of the new, the outrageous game changer that the world expects from a company of Lamborghini's revolutionary record.

LAMBORGHINI GALLARDO

2003 | EXTREME SPORTS CAR

2010 LP560	
LENGTH	4345 mm (172 in.)
LAYOUT	Mid engine, all-wheel drive
ENGINE	5.2 petrol V10
HORSEPOWER	560
MAX. SPEED	325 km/h (202 mph)
CO_2 EMISSIONS	351 g/km

The mighty V12-engined »Murciélago may be the Lamborghini that grabs all the headlines, but it is the slightly smaller, slightly more restrained Gallardo, with its more modest ten cylinders and 560 horsepower, that has been the real engine of Lamborghini's revival under the aegis of its owner, Audi.

With the factory turning out three Murciélagos and ten Gallardos on a typical day at the height of Lamborghini's renaissance, it has been the smaller car that has been a hit with buyers: the Gallardo is the one that gets spotted on the street and seen at race meetings. As a design, it started off as a proposal from »Giorgetto Giugiaro, which was then fine-tuned by »Luc Donckerwolke. It may never be known how much of Giugiaro's input remains, but the Gallardo's final design, while certainly very close to the Murciélago in its design language and detailing, is softer and smoother in its contours, and, being shorter but also slightly taller, it has a less aggressively supercar profile. Such power-signifying features as air scoops and aerodynamic devices are more restrained, too.

As in the case of its bigger brother, a series of power upgrades as well as a glamorous open-topped Spyder and performance-focused lightweight Superleggera have helped to keep the Gallardo in the headlines, if not at the top of the sales charts.

GALLARDO SPYDER

GALLARDO SUPERLEGGERA

LAMBORGHINI MURCIÉLAGO

2001–2010 | EXTREME SPORTS CAR

2010 6.5 V12	
LENGTH	4610 mm (182 in.)
LAYOUT	Mid engine, all-wheel drive
ENGINE	6.5 petrol V12
HORSEPOWER	640
MAX. SPEED	340 km/h (211 mph)
CO_2 EMISSIONS	500 g/km

Ever since the pivotal Countach of the 1970s Lamborghini has traded on its image of being more extreme, more daring than its more classically aesthetic arch-rival Ferrari. Whereas Ferrari would astonish or amaze, Lamborghini would set out to startle and shock, and it was with this clear-cut difference in mind that Audi set about rebuilding the Lamborghini mystique following its takeover of the marque in 1998.

»Luc Donckerwolke's 2001 Murciélago hit the spot perfectly. Its mixture of large-radius curves, sharp cuts and crisp details immediately identified it as a Lamborghini, as did its squat low profile, powerful rear and forward-hinging doors. Yet the overarching neatness of the design – at least on the earliest versions – toned down the intimidation factor to a level that brought in a wider circle of customers than would have gone for an overtly wild design.

That wildness soon came, most notably with the Murciélago roadster, where the long rear deck exaggerated the extreme cab-forward proportion still more, and the extreme Reventon special edition, which shocked more because of its wanton extremism than because of any new design direction. This new direction has been mapped out by the successor to the Murciélago: the Aventador, which was unveiled at the 2011 Geneva motor show, is sharper, edgier and more angular in its style. It is narrower but no less imposing in its presence, yet, to the disappointment of some, it lacks the outrage factor many expect of a new Lamborghini.

LANCIA

ITALY | FOUNDED 1906 | VOLUME CARS | LANCIA.IT

1960 FLAMINIA GT

Of all the innovators who have advanced the cause of car design over its 120-year history, Lancia is the company that has done most to combine engineering inventiveness with original thinking in style and aesthetics. Lancia was the first to build a car that did away with that antiquated horse-and-cart legacy, the separate chassis, with the Lambda in 1922; it pioneered V-engines for small cars in the 1930s, transaxles for sporty cars in the 1950s and lightweight coupés in the 1960s; and it has been responsible for some of the most beautiful cars ever built, notably the 1950s Aurelia GT, the 1960 Flaminia GT coupé and the Fulvia coupé of 1965, by »Zagato. Even the 1979 Delta, penned by »Giorgetto Giugiaro, deserves a place on the list, although it owes its aesthetics (as do its ancestors prior to the takeover by Fiat in 1969) to an outside design house rather than an in-house operation.

The Fiat takeover proved to be an abrupt turning point in Lancia's fortunes: the end of free-spending on eccentric engineering and multiple product variants, and the beginning of cost control, component sharing and corporate branding objectives. That said, Lancia's centre of gravity has oscillated wildly for most of its time under Fiat, ranging from such stylish coupés as the Beta HPE and mid-engined Monte Carlo to the elegant Gamma coupé (by »Pininfarina)

and the astonishingly compact but potent extreme-wedge 1970 Stratos rally car by Marcello Gandini (who designed the Lamborghini Countach).

The Stratos began a long run of rally triumphs for Lancia, the focus moving to the Delta in 1987 and helping to centre the brand image around motorsport. Yet with the replacement of the original Delta – surely one of Giugiaro's most accomplished creations – by a very dull design in 1993, Lancia's momentum expired and the brand appeared to have lost its way. It was only at the end of the decade, with the presentation of the Dialogos showcar in 1998, that a coherent new design language emerged.

Fronted by an elegant shield-shaped interpretation of Lancia's upright grille of the 1950s, the soft and sinuous Dialogos marked Lancia out as classy and distinguished, a more sophisticated and cultivated alternative to volume models sharing the same mechanical underpinnings. At the rear, narrow strip tail lights rolled smoothly from the vertical rear panel to the tops of the rear fenders, much as on today's »Jaguar XJ. The production Thesis of 2001 closely followed the feel and proportions of the Dialogos, and since that date the classy Lancia treatment, even on such small, mundane models as the Ypsilon and Musa, has been successful

1953 AURELIA GT

1987 DELTA INTEGRALE

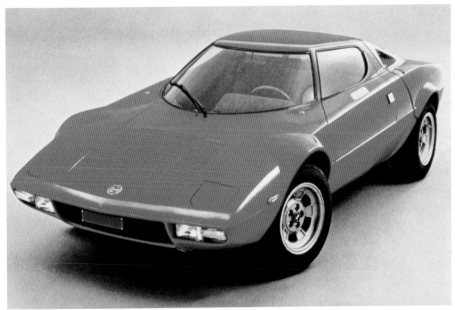

1970 STRATOS

1973 BETA MONTE CARLO

in setting its products apart from the equivalent Fiat.

With the filling of the yawning gap in the centre of the Lancia line-up with the new »Delta in 2008, Fiat appeared to have finally settled on Lancia's brand positioning as a refined and elegant marque, distinctive in its design and detailing but staying away from the sportier inclinations of Alfa Romeo. Representing the return of a very emotional name to the Lancia range, the new Delta is nevertheless very different from its forebear. It is smooth and extravagant in its fastback wagon styling, rather than finely chiselled, as was Giugiaro's compact original; it is especially distinctive at the rear, where its floating roof sweeps down

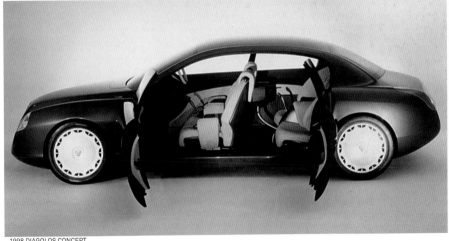

1998 DIAGOLOS CONCEPT

2003 FULVIA CONCEPT

to meet triangular C-pillars drawn upward from the rounded rear flanks and their inset light strips.

Luxurious though Lancia's intended image has come to be, the brand still finds it hard to resist the call of the sporty icons from its past: the 2003 Fulvia Coupé concept was a totally faithful recasting of the 1973 original, and ideas for a latter-day Stratos are bubbling not too far below the surface. But the biggest upset of all could come from an unexpected and, for Lancia, totally alien direction: the United States. Under Fiat group CEO Sergio Marchionne's deal to rescue the Chrysler corporation, Lancia is to pair up with the Chrysler brand to bring Chrysler-branded Lancias to American buyers and Lancia-branded Chryslers to customers in Europe. It is an audacious strategy that could succeed, but it will take all of Lancia's legendary ingenuity to pull it off.

2003 YPSILON

LANCIA DELTA

2008 | MEDIUM CAR

MODEL HISTORY 1979 DELTA 1ST GENERATION • 1993–99 DELTA 2ND GENERATION • 2008 DELTA 3RD GENERATION

2010 1.9 JTD TWIN TURBO

LENGTH	4520 mm (179 in.)
LAYOUT	Front engine, front-wheel drive
ENGINE	1.9 turbo diesel 4-cyl
HORSEPOWER	190
MAX. SPEED	222 km/h (138 mph)
CO$_2$ EMISSIONS	149 g/km

The 1979 Delta marked a high point for Lancia: crisp, charming and beautifully proportioned, it was one of »Giorgetto Giugiaro's very best designs and brought astonishing success to the often-troubled Lancia brand. It stayed in production for a remarkable fourteen years, yet its replacement – a dull car reminiscent of the »Opel/Vauxhall Astra of the day – was a complete let-down, and goodwill for the Delta vanished overnight.

The Delta nameplate disappeared until 2006, when it was revived in concept form as the Delta HPE, recalling a much-admired sports-hatch version of the 1970s Beta coupé. True to Lancia's new role as a classy, luxurious brand, the 2008 production Delta stays faithful to the concept: smart and stylish but in no way sporty. It takes the proportions of a »Ford Focus, but adds dramatic graphics to turn the design into something much more special. The shield-like grille thrusts forward, the tapering DLO kicks up sharply at the rear to form a triangular C-pillar and, most characteristically of all, elegant rear lights roll down from the rear shoulders into the tail panel on either side of the darkened-glass tailgate. All these cues combine to make a car that's classy and clearly different – something to which the rest of the Lancia range must now aspire.

LAND ROVER

GREAT BRITAIN | FOUNDED 1948 | 4x4 VEHICLES | LANDROVER.COM

Legend has it that the shape of the original Land Rover was sketched not on paper but in sand on a beach in Wales. It was just after the Second World War, materials and energy were in short supply; Rover's technical director, Maurice Wilks, was using a »Jeep on his farm in Anglesey when he realized that there could be a gap in the market for a similarly simple cross-country vehicle. Initial development of what would come to be called the Land Rover was carried out using a Jeep chassis modified to accommodate a Rover engine. Initial production models would use light alloy panels and a chassis fabricated from steel offcuts.

The prototype Land Rover, which was ready in time for the 1948 Amsterdam motor show, had the steering wheel in the centre but no doors or roof, and was aimed mainly at farmers. Yet the first big order for production models came from the British Army, and soon the vehicle became an international success and was taken up by all sorts of different groups, from emergency services to off-road enthusiasts.

Remarkably, there were no real changes in Land Rover's offering for two decades, and then it made a significant development: the »Range Rover of 1970. Rover's managers felt there might be a market for something smarter than a Land Rover, something just as capable of crossing ploughed fields and scaling slippery slopes, but more comfortable and able to be driven to a restaurant or the theatre in the evening, once the day's business on the farm was done. The phenomenal success of the Range Rover was due in no small part to longstanding Rover designer David Bache's classy and perfectly proportioned design. Soon waiting lists stretched into years, and a new market – which would come to be labelled the luxury sport utility segment – was born.

Yet Land Rover, by then merged into the amorphous British Leyland conglomerate, was slow to respond to criticisms that the

1948 SERIES 1

Range Rover was heavy to drive and had a clunky manual gearbox and only two doors. Especially in overseas markets, such competitors as Jeep and Toyota were quick to exploit these gaps before Land Rover came out with automatic and four-door versions. The company struck lucky again in 1989 with the »Discovery, a reworking of the Range Rover formula but aimed at a leisure rather than luxury market. With an interior designed by the Conran Design Group, the model was another instant success, but before long the poor reliability of this hastily developed derivative became a major issue.

This unreliability was symptomatic of chronically inadequate investment in Land Rover product development, something that was remedied only when BMW bought Rover in 1994. The German company poured

1990s DEFENDER

HISTORY

1948	First Land Rover debuts at Amsterdam motor show
1949	British Army orders first Land Rovers
1967	Parent Rover company merges with Leyland Triumph
1968	Merges with BMC to become British Leyland
1975	British Leyland comes under state control
1978	Land Rover gains independent management
1988	Rover group sold to British Aerospace
1994	Rover group sold to BMW
2000	Land Rover sold to Ford
2007	Ford puts Jaguar Land Rover up for sale
2008	Tata Motors buys JLR

1970 TO 1993 RANGE ROVERS

2004 RANGE STORMER CONCEPT

2008 LRX CONCEPT

2002-GENERATION RANGE ROVER: 2010

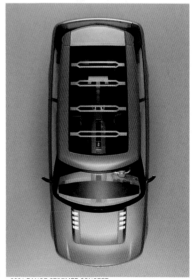

2004 RANGE STORMER CONCEPT

LAND ROVER

2006 FREELANDER

1997 FREELANDER

£1 billion into the development of a much-needed all-new Range Rover, complete with unitary construction – for refinement – and independent suspension to raise ride and handling up to world-class standards. The exterior, by Phil Simmons and »Geoff Upex, and, especially, Gavin Hartley's interior, established new high points in luxury SUV design, yet also clearly projected the classy clarity of the 1970 original.

The presentation of the Range Stormer concept – Land Rover's first concept – at the 2004 Detroit show marked the start of a major expansion; this proposal, for a racy, cut-down Range Rover for buyers who wanted the adventurous image but not necessarily the go-everywhere capability, was the first under new advanced-design director »Gerry McGovern and was rapturously received. This public endorsement translated directly into the 2005 »Range Rover Sport, which, despite its name, was based on the freshly engineered third-generation Discovery, an elegantly clean and pure design that crowned Geoff Upex's long career at Rover and Land Rover.

Yet the mushrooming success of all these large and extravagant products was to present Land Rover with an existential problem. With CO_2 rules tightening and a financial crisis just round the corner, ostentatious gas-guzzlers abruptly fell out of fashion, and Land Rover had to respond fast with a dramatically different concept promising family-car levels of economy. The 2008 LRX was an exciting, wedge-profiled three-door, still classy with its Land Rover cues and clamshell hood, but with youth and vigour in its make-up. Substantially unchanged, the LRX was launched as the »Range Rover Evoque in 2010, premium in its pricing and specification but, as proof of how even Range Rover can change, fashionably minimalist in its emissions.

LAND ROVER DISCOVERY

2009 | LUXURY 4x4

MODEL HISTORY 1989 DISCOVERY 1ST GENERATION • 1998 DISCOVERY 2ND GENERATION • 2004 DISCOVERY 3RD GENERATION • 2009 DISCOVERY 4TH GENERATION

2010 5.0 V8	
LENGTH	4830 mm (191 in.)
LAYOUT	Front engine, all-wheel drive
ENGINE	5.0 petrol V8
HORSEPOWER	375
MAX. SPEED	195 km/h (121 mph)
CO₂ EMISSIONS	328 g/km

The original Discovery hardly deserved to succeed. Conceived in haste, it was in effect a simplified »Range Rover, rethought for family use: super-practical – if plasticky – interior, and glass panels set into the cant rails above the side windows to offer occupants a glimpse of mountain tops. Yet despite the crudity of its details it contrived a superior, adventurous air thanks to its large glass areas and lofty, top-heavy stance.

Eager customers signed up by the thousands, despite the Discovery's poor reliability. A decade later, it was time for a change, but Land Rover's feeble second generation failed to deliver it. Fatally, it was impossible to tell the difference at a glance, apart from some extra overhang at the rear that gave a very unbalanced proportion. Response was lukewarm.

All was forgiven in 2004 with »Geoff Upex's masterly third generation (LR3 in North America). Gone were the dusty old details, and in came a new elegance founded on clean, smooth surfaces and a far more balanced stance on the road. The clamshell hood references the Range Rover more clearly, the stepped roof remains and the asymmetric rear window is distinctive. A facelift in 2009 brought the Discovery 4 label in Europe and LR4 in the United States but did little other than smarten the grille, confirming the intrinsic quality of the design.

2004 DISCOVERY

1989 DISCOVERY

PATRICK LE QUÉMENT

FRANCE | BORN 1945 | CAR DESIGNER AND MANAGER

It is a measure of Patrick le Quément's vision and confidence that when he was headhunted to lead Renault design in 1987 he was able to stipulate his own terms and conditions. Among his demands – revolutionary at the time, especially for a monolithic volume car manufacturer – was that the design department should report directly to the chief executive, bypassing the usual barriers of engineering and planning. Determined to bring design out of the studio and into the boardroom, Patrick le Quément succeeded in making design a strategic element in corporate policy rather than just an awkward afterthought.

Such a design-led approach seems perfectly natural now, but at the heavily loss-making and directionless Renault of the late 1980s it seemed extravagant. Yet CEO Raymond Lévy's faith in le Quément was justified: soon Renault had turned out a series of imaginative designs, such as the Twingo and Scénic, that positioned the brand as a style leader rather than follower, improving its public perception and its sales.

Le Quément has always been a strong believer in the role of concept cars in inspiring both designers and buyers, and Renault has been confirmed as a real thought leader in the auto industry with such landmark concepts as the Argos (1994), Initiale (1995), Ellypse (2002), Koleos (2000) and, most recently, the electric Zoe ZE and Twizy (both 2009). Credit for this continuing creative momentum must go to le Quément and his near quarter-century of inspirational leadership. He retired from Renault in 2009.

Born in France but educated in the UK, le Quément always believed in strong, decisive design that was just a shade ahead of public taste. This worked well with smaller cars, but he admitted defeat when his bid to challenge BMW and Mercedes-Benz, the strikingly styled Vel Satis luxury car, was shunned by buyers.

1992 RENAULT TWINGO

2000 RENAULT KOLEOS CONCEPT

1998 RENAULT VEL SATIS CONCEPT

2004 RENAULT MODUS

2002 RENAULT ELLYPSE CONCEPT

2008 ONDELIOS CONCEPT

LEXUS

JAPAN | FOUNDED 1989 | PREMIUM CARS | LEXUS.COM

1989 LS 400

When, in the early 1980s, word leaked out that Toyota was thinking of contesting the luxury-car market and challenging the likes of Mercedes-Benz and even Rolls-Royce, the only people to take the rumours seriously were the financial analysts. They knew that the Japanese company, although associated in the public mind with uninspiring cars for people not really interested in cars or driving, was highly ambitious, financially rock solid and extremely thorough. Toyota did indeed throw huge resources at the project, codenamed F1 or Flagship One, interviewing thousands of potential customers, stripping down every luxury car, and even replicating several kilometres of Autobahn on its test track in Japan so that the prototypes could be evaluated in German conditions.

The car that emerged from chief exterior designer Kunihiro Uchida's design team in 1989 to launch the Lexus brand caused something of a surprise. The LS 400 was intensely conservative, strongly reminiscent of the previous generation »Mercedes S-Class in its stance, proportions and detailing. Europeans dismissed it, despite an interior that was better designed and more finely finished than anything BMW or Mercedes-Benz could offer, but Americans took to it instantly, wowed by customer service that made them feel special. Lexus had judged the mood just right: within three years it had become America's leading imported premium brand, and soon it would lead the whole luxury market.

But while the bland but super-refined LS 400 sold well in the United States, it found the going much tougher in highly brand-conscious Europe. The Lexus brand had no identity, and its sole product had no clear identity either. Even the smaller 1993 GS, shaped by »Giorgetto Giugiaro some years earlier as the Toyota Aristo, missed the mark, and it was only with the arrival of the more distinctive RX crossover SUV that Lexus began to gain traction in Europe.

2006 LS 460

2009 RX 450H

LINCOLN

1936 ZEPYHR

Were it not for the stretched Continental convertible in which American president John F. Kennedy was assassinated during his fateful tour of Dallas in 1963, Lincoln, Ford's premium brand for North America, would be virtually unknown outside its home market. Internationally, only the smooth and streamlined 1936 Zephyr and the 1956 and 1961 Continentals are recognized as memorable designs.

Although the mission statement 'Large and elegant, but not brash' was coined for the 1956 revival of the Continental nameplate, it is the 1961 model, by designer/stylist Elwood Engel, that best defines the Lincoln brand. Rejecting the huge fins and grandiose chrome ornaments that were the fashion at the time, Engel's Continental was large but also elegant and simple, with its smooth, slab sides, restrained detailing and balanced proportions. The rear doors were hinged at the back, earning the design its 'clap-door' nickname.

Successive generations lost that simplicity, and by the 1990s Lincoln had lost its way, with the Town Car now the flagship. In Ford's big brand-acquisition spree around 2000, when Lincoln was slotted into the

1940 CONTINENTAL

1961 'CLAP-DOOR' CONTINENTAL

2003 NAVICROSS CONCEPT

HISTORY AND PRINCIPAL MODELS

1917	Founded by Henry Leland
1920	L series
1922	Ford buys Lincoln
1936	Zephyr is first streamlined car
1940	Continental
1956	Continental Mark II
1961	'Clap-door' Continental
1981	Town Car
1998	Becomes part of Ford's Premier Automotive Group. Headquarters moves to Irvine, California. Navigator is first luxury SUV
1999	Gerry McGovern becomes design director. Lincoln LS
2002	Continental concept, by Gerry McGovern
2003	Navigator (2nd gen); Navicross concept
2004	MKZ; Aviator concept
2006	MKX
2007	MKR concept
2009	MKT; C concept

2004 AVIATOR CONCEPT

2002 CONTINENTAL CONCEPT

2003-GENERATION NAVIGATOR

Premier Automotive Group, the new design team chose the Continental as the model that would symbolize the renewal of interest in Lincoln. »Gerry McGovern's 2002 Continental concept was an elegant reinterpretation of the 1961 classic and even boasted a V12 engine, as the original model of 1940 had done.

Such further concepts as the Navicross sport sedan and Aviator crossover SUV appeared to promise a full-scale design-led revival for Lincoln. Yet, as so often in the brand's history, the cash was abruptly cut and only the Aviator appeared, followed in 2006 by the significantly smaller and more car-like MKX. Of potentially much greater long-term significance was the complete turnaround in values represented by the California-designed 2009 C concept – a small luxury car based on the European »Ford Focus platform, short but wide with 3+3 seating, an elegant interior, and of course Lincoln's signature clap doors.

2009 C CONCEPT

2007 MKR CONCEPT

LINCOLN MKT

2009 | CROSSOVER STATION-WAGON

2010 3.7 V6	
LENGTH	5275 mm (208 in.)
LAYOUT	Front engine, front-wheel drive
ENGINE	3.7 petrol V6
HORSEPOWER	274
MAX. SPEED	190 km/h (118 mph)
CO₂ EMISSIONS	–

The 2008 Lincoln MKT concept was genuinely just that: a proposal for an entirely different class of automobile, a premium product that would take the best elements of all the key genres – sports coupés, luxury limousines, crossover utilities – and fuse them into a new sort of vehicle. Executive design director »Peter Horbury described it emotively as a Learjet for the road.

The concept did indeed impress, seating four VIPs in first-class comfort within a striking exterior shape that was more sports wagon than crossover in its proportions. As with other Lincolns, the production design remained close to the concept. Dominated from almost any angle by the leering grin of the dramatic double-wing grille and its huge vertical 'teeth', the MKT is also characterized by a crisply chamfered beltline that kicks up into pronounced haunches over the rear wheels, imparting a sedan-like energy to the wagon-style rear. That rear is unique, dominated by a full-width tail-light band, below which is a broad expanse of sheer metal.

With its more rounded corners and edges, the production MKT – now seating six in three rows – loses some of the crispness of the concept, yet it is still one of the most elaborately distinctive designs currently in the Ford group's production repertoire.

ANTHONY LO

HONG KONG | BORN 1964 | CAR DESIGNER

2002 SAAB 9-3X CONCEPT

2006 SAAB AERO-X CONCEPT

2008 SAAB 9-X BIOHYBRID CONCEPT

Prior to his surprise move to Renault in 2010, Anthony Lo had been best known for his work for Saab (then owned by General Motors), most notably on the spectacular Saab Aero-X concept in 2006. With the Aero-X Lo enjoyed what he described as a 'pure vision showcar, not one we intend to build'. Of course the Aero-X incorporated many eye-catching and attention-grabbing features, in particular its fighter-jet-like one-piece windshield canopy and door module that pivoted upward and forward for easy cabin access. Yet it was also a clear statement of where Saab could ultimately go.

The Aero-X, one of many Saab concepts overseen by Lo, came during a period of intense activity when he was given responsibility for Opel/Vauxhall cars, trucks and commercial vehicles in addition to his workload at Saab. Despite the pressure, the advanced-design team was able to map out the future look of GM Europe products with such concepts as the Opel/Vauxhall GTC, Flextreme and Flextreme GTE.

Lo was seen as a high-flyer right from the start, being offered his first job at Lotus by course tutor »Peter Stevens, who also worked at the sports-car maker. At Lotus, Lo worked alongside Simon Cox and Julian Thomson on such projects as the Isuzu 4200 R concept. Next, »Martin Smith drew Lo to Audi, following which Lo moved to Yokohama in Japan to help Olivier Boulay set up a new Mercedes-Benz studio. Then it was back to Europe with Saab and GM. Yet it could be in the highly creative atmosphere of Renault that Lo finally shows what he is truly capable of.

LOTUS

GREAT BRITAIN | FOUNDED 1948 | SPORTS CARS | LOTUSCARS.COM

Future historians are likely to divide the story of Lotus into three distinct parts. The flavour of the first three decades is clear: the engineering genius of founder Colin Chapman, which made Lotus such a leader on the racetrack, translated directly into such brilliantly innovative and accessible road cars as the original Elite and the still-iconic Elan. In contrast, on-track rival Ferrari, with a much less direct link to racing, reserved its road cars for millionaires.

Lotus's second phase, after Chapman's sudden death in 1982, is characterized by boom and bust, multiple changes of ownership – from Toyota to Proton via General Motors and Bugatti – and general uncertainty over policy and products. Two landmark cars were already in full swing: the 1974 Elite, the first Lotus aimed at business buyers; and »Giorgetto Giugiaro's famous 1975 Esprit, the car that launched wedge design into the market. But the cars were troublesome, sales were patchy and momentum drained away until the mid-1990s when the neat, mid-engined Elise (named after then-owner Bugatti CEO Romano Artioli's granddaughter) marked a long-awaited return to form.

With its clever and versatile lightweight aluminium chassis architecture and fibreglass bodywork by Julian Thomson (now at Jaguar), the 1995 Elise was a rare gem; its design celebrated Lotus's trademark lightness at every level, and its interior was a minimalist delight, with the majority of its components left as pure and unadorned aluminium extrusions.

Offshoots of the Elise architecture include the hardcore Exige coupé and race-focused 2-Eleven track-day cars, as well as the Speedster for Opel/Vauxhall and the fashionable Roadster for California electric-vehicle start-up »Tesla. The later Europa, an attempt to provide greater comfort and status, looked awkward and flopped badly, but the »Lotus Evora, which ambitiously packaged 2+2 seating into the silhouette

1958 ELITE

1962 ELAN

1975 ESPRIT

HISTORY

1948	Colin Chapman builds first modified car
1952	Founds Lotus Engineering with £50 loan
1958	Team Lotus enters F1 racing
1961	Stirling Moss gives Lotus first F1 win
1963	Lotus driver Jim Clark is F1 champion
1965	Lotus wins Indy 500 at record speed
1966	Lotus relocates to Hethel, Norfolk
1968	Jim Clark dies: Lotus cars get black badge
1977	Lotus develops DMC-12 for DeLorean
1982	Colin Chapman dies
1983	Toyota takes 17% stake, later 21%
1986	General Motors buys Lotus outright
1992	Lotus bicycle wins at Barcelona Olympics
1993	Bugatti takes ownership
1996	Proton of Malaysia becomes majority shareholder
1999	Lotus builds Speedster for Opel/Vauxhall
2005	Agreement with Tesla to develop electric sports car
2008	Production of Roadster for Tesla
2009	Dany Bahar, ex-Ferrari, becomes CEO
2010	Lotus returns to F1

1966 EUROPA

2002 ELISE SERIES 2

of a compact mid-engined sports car, was well received when first presented in 2008, as much for its exemplary handling as for its distinctive style, penned by designers Russell Carr and Steven Crijns.

Unveiling the Evora at the 2008 London motor show, Lotus managing director Mike Kimberley remarked that it was the first all-new Lotus since the Elise in 1995. That observation bore witness to how disjointed Lotus's product planning had become, leading indirectly to what historians may come to see as the third and potentially most challenging era in the Lotus saga: the reinvention of Lotus as a powerful high-performance marque to rival not just Jaguar and Aston Martin but also even Ferrari.

Taking the Lotus CEO seat in 2009 after a career at Ferrari, Dany Bahar quickly hired

LOTUS

2006 EUROPA S

»Donato Coco, architect of numerous Ferraris, as chief designer, and persuaded several other prestige brand heavyweights to join, too. At the Paris auto show in 2010 came dramatic visible evidence of how Bahar planned to power Lotus into a completely new and much higher-profile position within the luxury-car market. To the astonishment of all present, Bahar presented no fewer than five all-new designs; these new-generation models were set to deliver his plan to propel Lotus from its current specialist status into the top tier of exclusive luxury performance manufacturers by 2015.

The roll-call of Coco's designs was impressive. The new »Lotus Esprit, to be launched in 2013 with a supercharged V8 engine of 550 horsepower, will be the performance flagship and will launch the new design language. The new Elan, also due to appear in 2013, is reinterpreted as a mid-engined 2+2 sports coupé to rival the »Porsche 911; the following year's Elite, a front V8-engined gran turismo, will seat four and feature a retractable hard-top and a Lexus hybrid powertrain; the closely

2010 ETERNE CONCEPT

2010 ELAN CONCEPT

related Eterne, a full four-seater, will be aimed at the »Porsche Panamera and »Aston Martin Rapide. The new Elise, now mutated into a 300-plus horsepower mid-engined coupé of »Porsche Cayman proportions – although with a much sharper style – will be out in 2015.

The plan marks a radical shift away from Chapman's founding dictum of low weight, small engines and high efficiency. Totally missing is anything akin to the small and agile formula of today's much-loved Elise, and Lotus aficionados are sure to berate Bahar for this. Bahar's transformational plan is highly ambitious and represents a completely new beginning for Lotus, with only its name and its aura carried over into the new era. However, questions remain about exactly how the plan can be achieved, and whether it is appropriate for the climate-change-conscious decades that lie ahead.

2007 2-ELEVEN TRACK DAY CAR

LOTUS ESPRIT

2013 | EXTREME SPORTS CAR

DUE 2013	
LENGTH	–
LAYOUT	Mid engine, rear-wheel drive
ENGINE	5.0 turbo V8 hybrid
HORSEPOWER	620
MAX. SPEED	–
CO₂ EMISSIONS	250 g/km (claimed)

When Lotus, as scheduled, pulled the wraps off the new-generation Elite at the 2010 Paris salon, no one expected there to be another significant new-car announcement, let alone four further model reveals. Yet that is precisely the show of strength Lotus decided to put on, and it was a genuine surprise.

A new management team, recruited from Ferrari and other leading automakers, is reinventing Lotus as a luxury sports-car brand to compete with Ferrari and Aston Martin. It was important to make a major impact by presenting a manifesto for the marque's line-up to 2015: the Esprit, Elan, Elise, Elite and Eterne.

Although the Elite luxury coupé-convertible was the model initially flagged up for launch, it will be the Esprit, reborn as an extreme-performance V8 supercar, that will launch the new wave in 2013. The Esprit's aggressive front face, with a bold truncated-pyramid lower grille graphic, wide side intakes and tense, slanting slits for lights, will also appear on the new Elan (also to be released in 2013 and to be V8-powered). The final mid-engined design, the Elise replacement set for 2015, is smaller but has a similarly aggressive stance that is a far cry from the delicate compactness of today's car.

The two front-engined models – the Elite for 2014 and the Eterne, the related four-door coupé, for 2015 – share a design theme in the same way as the »Aston Martin DB9 and »Rapide do. Their noses are less aggressive and their headlamps sweep

rearward over the fenders, while the coupé-like rear of the Eterne sedan is neater than that of the folding-roof Elite. What all five models share is a sharply diving swage line running forward from the rear shoulder; this line runs under the descending line drawn rearward from the front fender, creating an awkward area below the A-pillar on some of the designs.

These are five designs executed in less than a year following »Donato Coco's start as Lotus's chief designer in 2010. Inevitably there will be revisions, and many will question the wisdom of Lotus moving upmarket so conclusively. More regrettably, this complete rewriting of the Lotus script in favour of power and prestige appears to wipe out the entire Lotus heritage of lightweight, agile design.

LOTUS EVORA

2009 | MEDIUM SPORTS CAR

2010	
LENGTH	4340 mm (172 in.)
LAYOUT	Mid engine, rear-wheel drive
ENGINE	3.5 petrol V6
HORSEPOWER	280
MAX. SPEED	261 km/h (162 mph)
CO_2 EMISSIONS	205 g/km

With Lotus having scored a direct hit with the 1995 Elise, the lightweight two-seater roadster that immediately became a worldwide benchmark for handling and agility, the perennially cash-strapped company quite logically began to expand on the design to create a family of closely related models.

Only by the mid-2000s could Lotus afford to invest in an all-new model. Aimed at a more affluent clientele than Lotus's traditional hardline enthusiast customer base, the 2009 Evora was a surprise on many counts. Most notably, it managed to seat four not only within the confines of a mid-engined sports-car package but also in Lotus's exceptionally compact interpretation of that package.

The Evora's proportions are familiar Lotus, but with more sophisticated surfacing, such as the pinched-in flanks, making the cabin section visually much narrower than the front or rear. The stark taper of the beetle-browed DLO towards the rear is distinctive, as is the clever cooling air path on to the rear spoiler. Yet despite the cleverness of its packaging, the Evora lacks the drama many expect from a mid-engined sports car, and its eventual replacement in the new-look Lotus line-up is sure to lack its elegantly understated approach.

LTI

GREAT BRITAIN | FOUNDED 1919 | TAXIS | LTI.CO.UK

2006 TX4

HISTORY AND PRINCIPAL MODELS

1919	Carbodies founded as coachmaker
1948	FX1 taxi built under Austin label
1959	FX4
1973	Carbodies sold to Manganese Bronze Holdings
1982	Manganese takes over rights to FX4 from British Leyland, owner of Austin. London Taxis International formed
1991	TX1
2006	TX4. Agreement with Geely to build TX4 in China
2008	First China-built TX4s
2009	Tanfield begins developing electric TX4

LTI and its parent company, Manganese Bronze, barely show up on the radar of even the most astute industry observer, but LTI's one product is a global icon. The sturdy and dignified silhouette of the London taxi enjoys instant recognition around the world, and serves as an emblem of the British capital on goods ranging from tourist leaflets and album covers to mouse mats and T-shirts.

This is a level of brand awareness for which major automakers would have to invest billions of pounds to achieve, yet the taxi, which began life under the Austin brand name in 1948, has been produced only in very small numbers each year. The secret to its familiarity lies in the very gradual evolution of its design, from the old-fashioned severity of the post-war model to the much smoother and more fluid surface language of the post-1991 TX series. Throughout, however, the taxi's proportions and stance have remained unaltered, and it can be instantly spotted, even in thick traffic, thanks to the unusual height of its glasshouse and the uprightness of the square grille at the front.

Although LTI had enjoyed a virtual monopoly of the London market, by the turn of the millennium it had begun to look further afield in search of sales volume and economies of scale. In 2006 it concluded a deal with China's »Geely – which would later acquire Volvo – to produce the TX4 in much larger numbers at a joint-venture plant in Shanghai. The following year a TX4 graced Geely's stand at the Shanghai motor show and by 2008 the taxi was in production.

With the advantage of lower build costs, Geely has been able to offer the TX4 much more widely, finding a ready market in the Middle East as well as South-East Asia for the model as a prestige shuttle transport for exclusive hotels and clubs. The taxi's appeal among the world's most affluent is paradoxical, considering its crude mechanical make-up. A measure of explanation could lie in the comforting familiarity of its rounded shape and the sense of security that comes from its high-set seating position and, thanks to pull-down seats, the passengers being able to face one another.

MP4-12C PROTOTYPE

MAHINDRA

INDIA | FOUNDED 1945 | CARS, UTILITY VEHICLES AND TRUCKS | MAHINDRA.COM

It is the world's third largest manufacturer of tractors, a globally significant builder of trucks of all sizes, and a major player in many other industry sectors. Yet Mahindra's profile in the car world is relatively low, despite its Scorpio SUV being widely exported, and despite the fact that the company builds large numbers of Fiestas and Fords under licence in India and will soon begin to make Renault Logans under its own badge.

Most recently, Mahindra hit the headlines when it took control of Reva, the Indian manufacturer of battery-electric cars sold in the UK under the G-Wiz label and in other markets under other nameplates. At the Delhi motor show in 2010 Mahindra displayed a wide range of eco technologies, including stop-start, hybrids, electric vehicles and even hydrogen power, in a bid to position itself as a builder of advanced vehicles and to provide a publicly visible flip side to its main business as a truck and agricultural vehicle maker.

Having begun life as a licence-builder of »Jeeps in 1949, Mahindra was able to develop products only slowly in the sealed-off domestic market that prevailed until the 1990s. Anticipating the opening up of India, however, it began developing what would become the Scorpio medium-large SUV with a view to exporting it around the world. While such companion models as the Commander and Bolero have chosen to stay close to their Jeep origins, the newer Xylo SUV/minivan is more modern in its style. The most unusual design, however, is that of the 2009 Gio compact delivery truck; tall and narrow, it is a distinctive competitor to Japanese-style microvans.

2010 MAXXIMO

2009 GIO

2000 BOLERO

HISTORY AND PRINCIPAL MODELS

1945	Mahindra and Mohammed founded
1948	Renamed Mahindra and Mahindra
1949	Begins building Jeeps
1963	Joint venture with International Harvester
1965	Begins building light commercial vehicles
1979	Licence manufacture of Peugeot diesel engines
1996	Mahindra Ford established to make Escort and Fiesta
2000	Bolero SUV
2002	Scorpio SUV launched
2005	Joint venture with Renault; Ford deal cancelled
2007	Renault Logan
2009	Takes majority stake in electric-car maker Reva. Xylo SUV/minivan, Gio light truck
2010	Buys out Renault stake in joint venture. Maxximo light truck

MAYBACH

GERMANY | FOUNDED 1922/REVIVED 2002 | SUPER-LUXURY CARS | MAYBACH-MANUFAKTUR.COM

HISTORY AND PRINCIPAL MODELS

1889	Wilhelm Maybach and Gottlieb Daimler show 'wire wheel' car at Paris Exhibition
1900	35 hp Mercedes, the first modern car
1907	Wilhelm Maybach leaves Daimler to build airship engines
1922	Maybach Manufaktur begins building cars; son Karl takes over
1929	Wilhelm Maybach dies. Type 12 V12 Zeppelin.
1960	Daimler-Benz acquires Maybach
1997	Mercedes-Benz Maybach concept
2002	Maybach 57 and 62
2005	57S; Exelero concept
2007	62S
2009	Zeppelin

1929 TYPE 12 AND 2002 62

When Daimler Benz was outbid by the Volkswagen Group in the race to acquire the struggling Rolls-Royce/Bentley combine in the late 1990s, it knew that its »Mercedes-Benz nameplate would not be prestigious enough to compete with the aristocratic British marques in the exclusive market for super-luxury limousines. Rather than invent a fresh brand, as Toyota had done with »Lexus, Daimler Benz decided to revive a name from its past and, in 1997, it presented the Mercedes-Benz Maybach concept at the Tokyo motor show.

In the 1920s and 1930s Maybach was a prominent competitor to Mercedes-Benz in large and opulent luxury cars. It later moved into industrial engines, then was absorbed by its former adversary in 1960. The 1997 concept, a long and low adaptation of the »Mercedes-Benz S-Class, finished in two-tone paint and with a luxuriously equipped cabin, was indifferently received, yet it proved to be very close to the model that was finally launched as a standalone marque in 2002. The new Maybach, available in either

5.7- or 6.2-metre lengths (19 or 20 ft), still projected the questionable impression of a stretched S-Class; many commentators doubted that customers would regard it as a true super-luxury marque.

Nevertheless, although the front half of the lengthy passenger compartment was a direct S-Class transplant, the rear was truly special: the two seats reclined and stretched in every possible direction, just as in a first-class airline cabin; chilled champagne in silver goblets was always on tap, and occupants could check airspeed, outside temperature and time on dials set into the interior roof.

Despite the meticulous workmanship and the bi-turbo V12 recalling Maybach's glory days, the formula failed to catch on and production was never more than a trickle. Later, even more powerful versions, including the 640 horsepower Zeppelin, still failed to ignite interest, and an embarrassment en route was the gargantuan 7-metre-long (23 ft) Exelero coupé concept commissioned in 2005 by the tyre maker Fulda.

2005 57S

2005 EXELERO CONCEPT

J. MAYS

UNITED STATES | BORN 1954 | CAR DESIGNER AND MANAGER

The fact that J. Mays chose the title 'Retrofuturism' for an exhibition of his work at the Geffen Contemporary at the Museum of Contemporary Art in Los Angeles in 2002 says a lot about the thinking behind his designs at that point in his career. He had been at Ford for five years, yet, apart from the low-rider Forty Nine concept and his contribution to the 2002 Thunderbird, his influence on the brand was hard to spot; that's why the exhibition majored on his Volkswagen New Beetle, the »Audi TT and the Audi Avus quattro concept. What all these designs share is a geometric simplicity that taps into the emotions of past products; the Audi TT's brilliant marriage of Bauhaus-style purity with sports-car energy was already recognized as a design classic.

The high point of Ford's design offensive was around 2005. The group had seven brands, Mays had recently established the innovative Ingeni design studio in London to provide fresh design stimulus, and in the United States overtly retro concepts such as the 2003 Mustang had been well received. Indeed, apart from the Range Rover-like 2005 Fairlane concept (which later became the »Ford Flex), most of the American designs still harked back to the past. Mays was quoted as saying that the designer must 'bend metal in a way that it touches people's heartstrings'.

Midway through the decade, when Mays's products began to come through in quantity, the appetite for retro appeared to be fading, the Thunderbird had been dropped and the »Volkswagen Passat-like Five Hundred had been criticized for squandering the momentum of its predecessor, the Taurus. Bigger changes were to come as the economic crisis struck towards the end of the decade. Mays's response was the elegant and ingenious Lincoln C concept, seating six in a European-sized footprint.

1991 AUDI AVUS QUATTRO CONCEPT

1998 AUDI TT

1994 VOLKSWAGEN CONCEPT 1 NEW BEETLE

2001 FORD FORTY NINE CONCEPT

2002 FORD THUNDERBIRD

MAZDA

JAPAN | FOUNDED 1920 | VOLUME CARS | MAZDA.COM

HISTORY

1920	Toyo Cork Kogyo Co. founded in Japan
1931–32	Mazda's first motor vehicle
1960s	Begins development of the Wankel rotary engine
1967	Introduces production Wankel rotary engine on Cosmo Sport (110S)
1970	Mazda enters US market
1974	Mazda introduces Rotary Pickup (REPU)
1984	Company is renamed Mazda Motor Corporation
1987	Begins vehicle production in the USA
1993	Mazda and Ford strengthen long-term strategic relationship
2002	Introduces 'Zoom-Zoom' brand message
2006	Introduces Nagare concept car at Los Angeles auto show
2010	Ford ends joint vehicle development with Mazda

PRINCIPAL MODELS

1931–32	Mazdago (TCS)
1960	R360 coupé
1961	B-series 1500, its first compact pickup
1962	Carol
1967	Cosmo Sport 110S
1978	RX-7, Bongo minivan
1989	MX-5
1996	121/Demio compact car
2003	RX-8 sports car
2005	MX-5 (3rd gen) convertible sports car
2007	Mazda6
2010	Mazda5 minivan

322

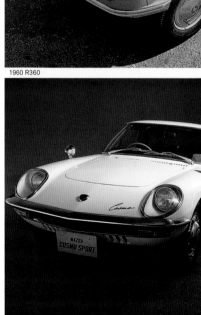

1960 R360

1967 COSMO SPORT 110S

Mazda was a cork-flooring firm until its founder, Jujiro Matsuda, turned the company into a global car manufacturer. The process began in the early 1930s, with the building of three-wheeled trucks for the Chinese market, but it came of age with the introduction of the company's first four-wheel passenger car, the Mazda R360 coupé in 1960.

The R360 captured much of the lightweight kei-class minicar market in Japan, a success cemented by the introduction of the four-seat Mazda Carol in 1962. A convertible Carol followed in 1964; by then more than a million had been built.

Mazda really took flight as an automaker in the 1960s, when it progressed from manufacturing small kei cars for local

1978 RX-7

markets to producing cars for overseas territories. Its first rotary-engined vehicle – the Mazda Cosmo (110S) was to have a significant impact on the American market and become the company's 'halo car'. The 1970s were also something of a boom time for Mazda: its rotary engine regularly outperformed the conventional engines of its rivals, and Mazda put it in almost all its products, including the first-generation RX-7 in 1978. So influential was Mazda that *Ward's Automotive Yearbook* declared that 'Practically every major automaker in the world including General Motors, Ford and Mercedes is trying to develop cars like the Mazda', and predicted that 'by 1980, rotary engines will power 85 per cent of all cars produced in the USA.'

Despite such success, financial problems led to Ford taking a 25 per cent stake in the company; the 1980s saw Mazda becoming more closely integrated into Ford's global empire. The 323 and 626 of this era were big successes, and the introduction of the groundbreaking »Mazda MX-5 sports car (to the American market first) would electrify the global car industry by rediscovering a segment long since considered to be dead. The car was an instant hit.

The 1990s saw mixed fortunes for Mazda's products, and it was not until the early 2000s that the revitalization of Mazda cars would begin. From a design point of view, the period around 2005 was one of intense interest in Mazda, as the company initiated a new design language called Nagare. This was successfully displayed on a succession of concept cars, and added a whole new identity to production vehicles, beginning with the 2010 Mazda5 minivan.

1989 MX-5

2007 MAZDA6

MAZDA MX-5

2005 | COMPACT SPORTS CAR

MODEL HISTORY 1989 MX-5 1ST GENERATION • 1998 MX-5 2ND GENERATION • 2005 MX-5 3RD GENERATION

2010 1.8	
LENGTH	4020 mm (159 in.)
LAYOUT	Font engine, rear-wheel drive
ENGINE	1.8 petrol 4-cyl
HORSEPOWER	126
MAX. SPEED	194 km/h (120 mph)
CO₂ EMISSIONS	167 g/km

The compact open sports car seemed to be an endangered species in the late 1970s as the United States implemented tough rollover safety rules, yet Mazda – at that time little more than a builder of formulaic Japanese family hatchbacks – thought differently. It set up a special team to develop an all-new two-seater that would revive the cult of the roadster and, after having studied such iconic models as the Alfa Romeo Spider, Lotus Elan and MG MGB, came up with the MX-5 in 1989.

It was a huge gamble for Mazda, but the MX-5 was a sensational success. Neatly shaped and reminiscent of the 1960s Lotus Elan, it had agile rear-drive handling yet was also cheap to buy and run. The second generation a decade later was very subtly expanded in power, performance and size, yet still successfully carried across the original's engaging character, and continuity was assured.

A larger challenge came in 2005 with the third-generation MX-5, shaped by »Moray Callum. This was meatier, more solid and more masculine in its presentation, and represented a bigger jump in positioning. It, too, proved well judged and successful. Now all eyes are on future Mazda concepts for hints of the fourth-generation MX-5.

MAZDA RX-8

2003–2010 | MEDIUM SPORTS CAR

2.6 ROTARY	
LENGTH	4460 mm (176 in.)
LAYOUT	Front engine, rear-wheel drive
ENGINE	2.6 petrol twin rotor
HORSEPOWER	231
MAX. SPEED	235 km/h (146 mph)
CO_2 EMISSIONS	299 g/km

Since the demise of the NSU Ro80 in 1977, Japan's Mazda has been the sole carmaker to continue using the smooth-running rotary engine pioneered by Dr Felix Wankel. Mazda's RX rotary cars, most of them sports coupés, reached their apogee in 2003 with the RX-8, which lasted in production until killed off by tightening emissions regulations in 2010.

The RX-8 was distinctive for much more than its twin-rotor engine, although the compactness of this engine did allow unusually good accommodation for a coupé. The most talked-about innovation brought by the RX-8 was the one-and-a-half door layout on each side of the coupé-profile cabin: the full-length front door had to be opened first before the half-length rear door, hinged at the rear, could be opened. The result was a pillarless side and far easier entry into the rear seats than would normally be possible in a GT car.

On an aesthetic level, the RX-8 was also one of the first production cars to widen the front fenders and narrow the hood, thus creating separate visual volumes and reducing the apparent mass of the nose. Yet what really sold the RX-8 to its customers was its powerful stance, propelled by a long hood and a short, neat rear.

MERCEDES-BENZ

GERMANY | FOUNDED 1886 | PREMIUM CARS | MERCEDES-BENZ.COM

Although they were not acting together at the time, Gottlieb Daimler and Karl Benz each pioneered feasible, roadworthy automobiles around 1886. Their firms did not join forces until 1926, but the combined Daimler-Benz company can legitimately claim to be the oldest carmaker in the world. The history of Daimler Benz is therefore in large measure the history of the automobile itself.

No company enjoys greater global recognition or possesses a clearer brand image than Mercedes-Benz. Its style has always erred on the side of conservatism, and it has skilfully managed evolutionary change to its main model lines. The company has been acutely aware of the need to keep its choosy and predominantly wealthy clientele on board and to maintain continuity between model generations, so as not to allow previous generations to appear out of date. Even current design head Gorden Wagener insists that Mercedes-Benz designs should last for twenty-five years.

Mercedes-Benz's staple sedan-centred model lines, the C-, E- and S-Class, can trace their ancestry through small but significant steps back to the 170 of 1931, the 'Ponton' 180 of 1953 and the 220SE of 1959 respectively. Its sports cars, which have tended to enjoy longer runs between generations, have needed to make bigger steps with each switch. The contrast between the full and flowing 300SL of 1954 (a landmark design by any standards) and the tight, compact 230SL a decade later is dramatic, while the more extravagant third-generation »SL in 1972 and the fourth in 1989 mark a return to the more emotional design language; nevertheless, the continuity is there for all to see.

Yet with the realization in the 1980s that it needed to broaden its customer base so as to provide protection against market downturns, Mercedes faced the challenge of applying its identity to smaller, and sometimes more utilitarian, cars, and even minibuses and SUVs, without damaging the standing of its core sedan models. There

1954 300SL

1963 230SL 'PAGODA'

2004 A-CLASS THREE AND FIVE-DOOR

HISTORY

1886	Karl Benz develops Patent Motor Car
1893	First production car
1900	Gottlieb Daimler of Mercedes dies
1902	Mercedes trademark registered
1926	Daimler and Benz merge. Launch of Mercedes-Benz marque
1929	Karl Benz and Daimler technical director Wilhelm Maybach die
1946	Post-war production resumes with 170V
1958	Buys Auto Union
1959	Bid to acquire assets of BMW fails
1960	Takes over Maybach Motorenbau
1963	Sells Auto Union to Volkswagen
1985	Acquisition spree: buys MTU, Dornier, AEG
1993	First losses
1994	Restructuring and power struggles
1998	Merges with Chrysler
1999	Peter Pfeiffer replaces Bruno Sacco as chief designer
2000	Takes controlling stake in Mitsubishi
2004	Dissolves partnership with Hyundai
2005	Outsold by BMW. Sells stake in Mitsubishi
2007	Disposes of Chrysler
2008	Gorden Wagener becomes chief designer
2009	Buys 10% of Tesla
2010	Deal with Renault-Nissan on small and electric cars

1995 VARIO CONCEPT WITH INTERCHANGEABLE BODY

1982 190E AND 2010 C-CLASS

2003 F500 MIND CONCEPT

were concerns in the boardroom in 1982 that the compact 190 series would dilute the exclusivity of the two larger model lines; in the event the 190 proved a huge success.

But for the misfortune of the 'elk-test' scandal in the late 1990s, when an example rolled on to its side, the »A-Class would have been just as successful. The most revolutionary design both stylistically and technically in the small-car segment since the original Mini of 1959, the model's looks initially came as a shock, but buyers trusted Mercedes-Benz's technical fixes and were not deterred – evidence that the company's strategy of matching advanced packaging with radical looks was the right one. Yet although the A-Class's clever engineering, with the powertrain below the floor, has been conspicuously not copied by competitors because of high costs, Mercedes will exploit this construction in future hybrid cars and battery- and fuel-cell-powered models, as demonstrated in the 2009 Blue Zero concept.

The Blue Zero is typical of Mercedes concept design, giving precedence to engineering innovation rather than aesthetic beauty. The F700 concept of 2007 was another such landmark, exploring the company's new DiesOtto engine technology as well as dramatically different proportions in its asymmetric luxury-car body. It is not the blueprint for the next S-Class, but will certainly influence it technically. The same exercise had taken place in 1993 when the Vision A concept aired the format and proportion, but not the body language, of the eventual A-Class. At other times Mercedes has used thinly veiled concept versions of upcoming production models to get buyers accustomed to new design features in advance: the 2008 Fascination, a preview of the 2009 E-Class, is one such example.

Although the occasional niche model, such as the 2008 GLK SUV, may jar in its crude design language, Mercedes has developed a very consistent and solid message across its huge span of different vehicle types. This has been achieved through the systematic application of strong, confident design, and the meticulous management of continuity between successive generations to build up a century of brand equity.

2006 GL-CLASS SUV

2007 F700 CONCEPT

PRINCIPAL MODELS

1886	Patent Motor Car
1902	Mercedes Simplex 40 hp
1926	8/38 hp
1928	SSK
1931	170
1953	'Ponton' 180
1954	300SL
1959	220SE (S-Class)
1963	600 Pullman, 230SL 'Pagoda'
1972	S-Class (3rd gen)
1976	240D (W123)
1978	T-series, first station-wagon
1979	G Wagen SUV
1982	190E (W201), first compact Mercedes-Benz
1991	S-Class (W140) (5th gen)
1993	Vision A concept
1995	Vario concept with interchangeable body
1996	SLK (R170) sports car
1997	A-Class (W168), ML-Class leisure SUV; Maybach concept
1999	S-Class (W220) (6th gen); Vision SLR concept
2001	SL (R230) (5th gen)
2002	E-Class (W211)
2003	SLR McLaren; F500 Mind concept
2004	SLK (2nd gen), A-Class (2nd gen)
2005	R-Class, S-Class (W221) (7th gen)
2006	GL-Class SUV
2007	F700 concept
2008	SL (6th gen)
2009	SLS AMG supercar; Blue Zero concept
2010	F800 style concept
2011	SLK (3rd gen)

2009 BLUE ZERO CONCEPT

2008`GLK

MERCEDES-BENZ A-CLASS
2004 | SMALL CAR

MODEL HISTORY 1997 A-CLASS 1ST GENERATION • 2004 A-CLASS 2ND GENERATION

2010 AI60 CDI	
LENGTH	3885 mm (154 in.)
LAYOUT	Front engine, front-wheel drive
ENGINE	2.0 turbo diesel 4-cyl
HORSEPOWER	82
MAX. SPEED	170 km/h (105 mph)
CO$_2$ EMISSIONS	118 g/km

As the most fundamental step forward in small-car architecture since the original Mini of 1959, the Mercedes-Benz A-Class should have had much more influence on car design than it has had. Blame cost: the A-Class's revolutionary construction, which places the engine under the front floor so that passengers can enjoy »S-Class space within the road footprint of a »Volkswagen Polo, entails a complicated sandwich floor structure that is too expensive in today's mainstream market.

Mercedes-Benz's first A-Class, in 1997, proudly proclaimed this new layout with a tall, one-box profile, a high driving position and a distinctive wraparound rear window. It was a rare case of innovation being visible in both design and engineering. The car was not pretty, and the 'elk-test' scandal (when a car rolled on to its side) scarred its early take-up, but Mercedes-Benz's remedial action was swift and decisive, and customers gradually took to it – if not as avidly as Mercedes had hoped.

The second-generation A-Class rolled back on some of the more extreme design points but kept a similar overall profile; by now, acceptance was clear, but it was too late. For its third generation the A-Class will adopt a cheap conventional platform, with the expensive sandwich being reserved for innovative hydrogen, hybrid and electric models, where cost is not such an issue.

1997-GENERATION A-CLASS

MERCEDES-BENZ S-CLASS

2005 | LUXURY CAR

MODEL HISTORY 1959 220SE 1ST GENERATION • 1965 250SE 2ND GENERATION • 1972 S-CLASS 3RD GENERATION • 1979 S-CLASS 4TH GENERATION • 1991 S-CLASS 5TH GENERATION (W140) • 1999 S-CLASS 6TH GENERATION (W220) • 2005 S-CLASS 7TH GENERATION (W221)

2010 500	
LENGTH	5090 mm (201 in.)
LAYOUT	Front engine, rear-wheel drive
ENGINE	5.5 petrol V8
HORSEPOWER	388
MAX. SPEED	250 km/h (155 mph)
CO_2 EMISSIONS	258 g/km

For almost half a century the generic luxury saloon for diplomats, business leaders and celebrities, the Mercedes S-Class can trace its origins back to the so-called 'Ponton' series of the early 1950s. The formal S-Class label began to be used only in the 1970s; prior to that these flagship models carried the SE designation.

Nevertheless, in the eyes of the customer the series remained unbroken. The steady evolution of the design over its seven generations since 1959 is an object lesson to the design community in how to move an essentially conservative formula forward, often in quite bold steps, yet retain continuity of image and the loyalty of a privileged, wealthy and notoriously choosy clientele. Throughout, the image of this, the larger of Mercedes-Benz's two principal saloon lines (the other being the E-Class), has remained constant, to the extent that the S-Class has become a brand in itself.

The famous 'fin-tail' SE of 1959 provided the initial blueprint. The next edition, in 1965, set a trend for the luxury segment with its much cleaner lines, lower waistline and significantly deeper windows: it also established the horizontal tail-light graphic that would feature on many subsequent generations of Mercedes saloons. One of the bigger steps in the S-Class's evolution came with the 1972 version, the first to reflect the thick pillars and generally heavier architecture demanded by the then-new American crash-safety rules.

The influence of aerodynamics became clearer in the smooth and well-received 1979 iteration, but the same could not be said for the now-infamous W140 S-Class of 1991. Developed regardless of cost and incorporating hundreds of technical innovations, it was greatly increased in size and, thanks to its slab sides, in perceived bulk. Unusually for an S-Class, this model attracted near-universal criticism, and its replacement in 1999 by the elegant and much less imposing W220 series was greeted with great relief.

Mercedes-Benz's influence on the rest of the automotive community became clear following the appearance of the seventh S-Class generation: its bulkier, more assertive look and its swollen rear-wheel arches soon set the template for other large cars, and, as with every S-Class generation since the 1960s, its technological innovations raised the bar for the rest of the industry.

1991-GENERATION S-CLASS

MERCEDES-BENZ SL

2008 | LUXURY SPORTS COUPÉ

MODEL HISTORY 1954 300SL 1ST GENERATION • 1963 230SL 'PAGODA' 2ND GENERATION • 1972 350SL 3RD GENERATION • 1989 SL 4TH GENERATION •
2001 500SL 5TH GENERATION • 2008 SL 6TH GENERATION

2010 600: 5.5 V12 BITURBO	
LENGTH	4565 mm (180 in.)
LAYOUT	Front engine, rear-wheel drive
ENGINE	5.5 turbo petrol V12
HORSEPOWER	517
MAX. SPEED	250 km/h (155 mph)
CO₂ EMISSIONS	330 g/km

Although there have been fewer generations of the Mercedes-Benz SL sports car than of the »S-Class sedan, and therefore bigger steps between each generation, the SL is every bit as much of an automotive institution as the S-Class. The story began in memorable fashion in 1954 with the 300SL ('super light'), the thrilling and technically innovative gullwing that was visibly derived from the company's racing cars; it was the supercar of its era and quickly became an icon for the whole brand.

A very much milder 190SL, with similar design cues but feeble performance, followed in 1956 and was a big hit with glamour-seeking celebrities; few, however, were prepared for French designer Paul Bracq's neat, petite style for the 230SL 'Pagoda' that replaced both in 1963. This was much more akin to today's »SLK and lasted until 1972, when it was succeeded by the very much bigger V8-powered, wedge-styled 350SL. By now the SL had abandoned any pretensions to lightness and had become a luxury grand tourer rather than a sports car. This third generation lasted for an astonishing seventeen years before being succeeded by the smooth and flowing fourth generation, which introduced the pop-up rollover hoop; it, too, stayed in the catalogue for a long time – twelve years.

Much had changed by the beginning of the new millennium. The SLK had popularized the rigid folding roof, Jaguar had gained momentum with its »XK and XKR, and BMW was threatening to launch

a new »6 Series; the SL was looking dowdy. So the 2001 500SL brought a more aggressive touch, such as quadruple lights, large wheels and air exit grilles, but also enhanced luxury features, such as the Vario metal folding roof. A clumsy facelift in 2008 did scant justice to the smoothness of the 2001 design, adding awkward lights, body-kit panelling and bigger air intake apron.

Having run for more than a decade and being boxed in by the agile »SLK below and the high-performance SLS AMG above, the sixth-generation SL is likely to be replaced by a model that renews the focus on luxury ahead of ultimate driving thrills.

1989 SL

1963 230SL 'PAGODA'

MERCEDES-BENZ SLK

2011 | MEDIUM SPORTS CAR

MODEL HISTORY 1996 SLK 1ST GENERATION • 2004 SLK 2ND GENERATION • 2011 SLK 3RD GENERATION

2010 200K	
LENGTH	4100 mm (162 in.)
LAYOUT	Front engine, rear-wheel drive
ENGINE	1.8 petrol 4-cyl supercharged
HORSEPOWER	184
MAX. SPEED	236 km/h (146 mph)
CO_2 EMISSIONS	190 g/km

Intense fascination surrounded the first SLK, Mercedes-Benz's answer to the »Porsche Boxster and BMW Z3, in 1996. The item of interest was not so much the car itself, although everything was brilliantly packaged within the compact overall shape; what intrigued everyone was the roof. The first-ever rigid folding top, it emerged out of the trunk lid, unfolded itself and miraculously latched on to the screen as a shiny hardtop; the trunk then shut again to reveal the neat silhouette of what appeared to be a fixed-head coupé.

Crowds would marvel whenever an SLK driver stopped to open or close the top: Mercedes had hit upon the dream of many buyers for the freedom of a convertible combined with the warmth and security of a coupé. The SLK was a huge hit, even though its engine was unrefined and it was no more exciting to drive than a C-Class sedan. This was a Mercedes that appealed across all classes – except to the sporty fraternity.

The second-generation SLK, in 2004, was a much better car, Formula One-influenced in its wedgy shape and astonishingly cleverly packaged to cram (in its top AMG version, at least) a mighty 5.4-litre V8 engine within an overall footprint barely longer than a »Volkswagen Polo's. The third SLK iteration, debuting in early 2011, is longer and more mature-looking, with a more angular grille and a headlamp style reminiscent of the larger »SL, as well as an innovative glass roof that darkens in strong sunlight.

1996-GENERATION SLK

MERCEDES-BENZ SLR MCLAREN

2003–2010 | EXTREME SPORTS CAR

2010 COUPÉ	
LENGTH	4660 mm (184 in.)
LAYOUT	Front engine, rear-wheel drive
ENGINE	5.4 petrol V8 24V
HORSEPOWER	626
MAX. SPEED	334 km/h (207 mph)
CO_2 EMISSIONS	348 g/km

The Mercedes-Benz SLR McLaren was a sports car that promised the world but that in the end disappointed. Its pedigree was perfect: the ruthless quality of Mercedes teamed with the race-winning brilliance of »McLaren, which had just produced the formidable F1 road car – by common consent the finest supercar ever made. Well-heeled enthusiasts began preparing blank cheques as soon as the deal between the two firms was announced.

Yet the SLR McLaren's development period was fraught with rumours of disagreements, and when the car was finally revealed (with the McLaren name pointedly placed last) it was clear that the final design, laden with such equipment as automatic transmission and weighing almost 1800 kilograms (3968 lb) despite its advanced carbon structure, was far less pure than McLaren would have preferred.

Stylistically, too, the SLR failed to engage: it too closely resembled the standard »SL but had a longer hood, sharper nose and more aggressive detailing. Even the forward-swivelling doors were criticized for not having the proper gullwing action.

A cabriolet and a series of increasingly desperate special editions followed, all at prices to make the eyes water. Yet never once did the SLR come close to the magic that its heritage and its many names had led the world to expect.

MERCEDES-BENZ SLS AMG

2009 | EXTREME SPORTS CAR

2010	
LENGTH	4640 mm (183 in.)
LAYOUT	Front engine, rear-wheel drive
ENGINE	6.3 petrol V8
HORSEPOWER	571
MAX. SPEED	317 km/h (197 mph)
CO_2 EMISSIONS	308 g/km

After the unsatisfactory experience of the »SLR McLaren, Mercedes-Benz needed a major success in the ultra-high-performance league to restore its reputation among elite customers. At the same time, emotional pressure was mounting for the firm to come up with a modern-day technological triumph similar to that of the legendary 300SL gullwing in 1954.

Bringing together the very latest in engineering and a body style directly referencing the 1950s brand hero ensured that the SLS would tick all the boxes; the dramatic bonus of upward-opening gullwing doors was a sure-fire guarantee to get every Mercedes loyalist on board.

In almost every aspect, the SLS takes its visual cues from its »SL forebear: the wide, low stance, the long hood and rear-biased glasshouse, the straight-through shoulder line and the wide grille inset with the Mercedes star. Even the side detailing is copied across, most notably the side air outlets crossed by chrome strakes, whose original function was to improve aerodynamic stability. Yet the very authenticity of these features makes for less tolerance of areas where the SLS AMG deviates from its SL mentor, such as the bulbous rear window and the poorly proportioned trunk area, both of which were very neatly resolved on the original. However, while design critics may question the value of this type of blatant retrospection, buyers are queuing up to experience it.

1954 300SL, FOREBEAR OF THE SLS AMG

MERCURY

Mercury was the brainchild of Edsel Ford (son of Henry Ford), who by the mid-1930s had realized that Ford needed a third brand to act as a stepping stone between its mass-market »Ford models and the exclusive »Lincolns at the premium end of the scale.

Early Mercurys were more stylish and slightly more powerful versions of the equivalent Fords and sold well; early post-war models struck the right chords, too – especially with the fans of teen idol James Dean, who drove a 1949 Mercury Coupé in *Rebel Without a Cause* (1955). In 1967 Mercury introduced what was to become its signature model for the baby-boomer generation: the Cougar, a development of the ultra-successful »Ford Mustang but with enough design differentiation to give it a more sophisticated allure.

Mercury's fortunes rose and fell with those of the broader Ford base-model range. All too often, where the Mercury version was differentiated by little more than a different badge, grille and rear appliqué panel, consumers saw through the branding strategy and baulked at paying a higher price for the same product. Mercury could be more successful when it fielded a standalone model or was first in a particular segment; the last such models were the 1993 Villager minivan (coproduced with Nissan) and the 1999 Cougar, which was sold in Europe under the Ford label.

Although Mercury moved its creative centre, along with Lincoln, to California around the turn of the millennium, the brand still appeared to be neglected. Only the largely irrelevant 2003 Messenger V8 coupé concept stands out as an interesting design. Production models remained Ford hand-me-downs, market share dwindled to near zero and, to no one's surprise, Ford pulled the plug in 2010.

HISTORY AND PRINCIPAL MODELS

1938	Mercury founded as 3rd Ford brand. Eight
1949	Coupé
1957	Turnpike Cruiser
1967	Cougar
1985	Merkur XR4Ti (Ford Sierra)
1993	Villager
1996	Mountaineer
1999	Cougar (new gen)
2005	Milan
2010	Ford announces phasing out of Mercury

1967 COUGAR

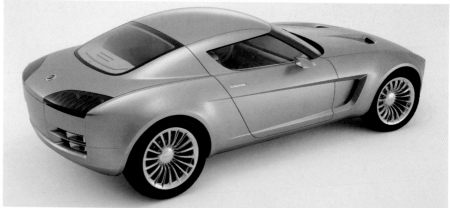

2003 MESSENGER CONCEPT

2005 MILAN

MG ROVER

GREAT BRITAIN/CHINA | FOUNDED 1904 | VOLUME CARS | MGMOTOR.CO.UK

HISTORY AND PRINCIPAL MODELS

1904	Rover builds first car
1905	Austin builds first car
1924	MG founded as sporty adjunct to Morris
1952	Austin and Morris merge to form BMC
1959	Mini is launched
1967	Rover becomes part of British Leyland
1968	BMC merges with BL
1975	BL nationalized
1988	BL renamed Rover, sold to British Aerospace
1994	BMW buys Rover
1998	Rover 75
2000	Rover sold by BMW to Phoenix consortium; soon renamed MG Rover
2004	Shanghai Automotive Industry Corporation (SAIC) buys rights to Rover 75 and 25
2005	Production stops, company collapses. Plant sold to Nanjing Automobile Corp.
2007	Nanjing becomes part of SAIC. MG 7 (former Rover 75) and MG TF built in China
2008	CKD assembly of MG TF in UK
2010	MG 6 built in China. MG Zero concept

2008 MG TF

2010 MG 6

1998 ROVER 75

What was once the world's fourth-largest car company, drawing together a century of history and many of the finest names in British motor manufacturing, fizzled out ignominiously in 2005. In a tiny corner of British Leyland's huge site in Longbridge, near Birmingham (in its heyday Europe's biggest car plant), its remains were picked over by rival Chinese firms and armies of accountants trying to find out what went wrong.

British Leyland, made up of a remarkable confluence of famous marques, had been steadily jettisoning its brands as they became contaminated by the group's declining reputation throughout the 1970s and 1980s. After being swallowed up and spat out by a succession of new owners, only the rump – Rover and MG – were left, set afloat alone and vulnerable in a sea of predatory competitors. It was inevitable that MG Rover would run aground or be eaten up, and with mayday calls to almost every carmaker in the world having been ignored, collapse came, messily, in 2005.

All events prior to that year were now irrelevant. What mattered was that two rival Chinese firms, SAIC and Nanjing Automobile Corporation, had picked up different pieces, the Chinese government had forced them together, and MGs were in production in China alongside Rovers rebranded as »Roewes. Yet even as the dust was settling, SAIC was building up a Britain-based R&D organization to design and develop new models for British and Chinese manufacture. Already revealed have been the Roewe 550 for the Chinese market and its sportier hatchback companion, the MG 6, for Europe. Roewe has also shown its smaller 550 and 350, likely to yield an MG 5, and at the 2010 Beijing motor show the compact and racy MG Zero concept, a British design, was widely applauded.

All point towards a fresh, competitive range of products designed in Europe for European conditions, and perhaps assembled in Europe, too.

GREAT BRITAIN/GERMANY | FOUNDED 1959 | PREMIUM SMALL CARS | MINI.COM

As the first-ever premium small car, BMW's born-again »Mini Cooper seemed a risky proposition when it launched in 2001. Many argued that the number of buyers willing to pay a medium-car price for a car smaller than a »Volkswagen Polo would not be sufficient to make the project viable. History has proved the doubters spectacularly wrong: Mini production is running at almost three times the volume originally planned, the Mini range has mushroomed from a single model to four families, and competitors, from Alfa Romeo and Audi to Citroën and Fiat, are clamouring for a slice of the action. The Mini is, by any standards, a pivotal product – yet it nearly didn't happen at all.

When BMW bought Rover in 1994 it gave top priority to the new Mini project, granting leadership to the British team. Yet it soon became clear that the British and the German sides had very different ideas as to what the new Mini should be. While the British team favoured a radical approach (which would later be revealed in the 1997 underfloor-engined Spiritual concepts), the BMW managers saw the Mini as something more coupé-like, sporting and fashionable, taking stylistic cues from the original but making no attempt to replicate its clever packaging or space efficiency. BMW bosses had rallied round a sketch by »Frank Stephenson, at that time a senior BMW designer, and it was this that evolved into the final Mini concept design shown in a dramatic presentation to journalists prior to the 1997 Frankfurt motor show.

Stephenson's design evoked mixed reactions: excitement from those who loved the idea of a white-roofed sporty fashion statement, cynicism from critics who saw it as too unimaginative and retro, and outright hostility from Mini engineering purists critical of its extravagant size and poor interior space. Behind the scenes and away from the slick presentations, it was a period of tension, misunderstandings and deteriorating relations as control of the

MINI CLASSIC

programme swung back and forth between Britain and Germany. Relief came only in 2000, with BMW's shock decision to dispose of Rover but retain the Mini brand. This meant a hurried juggling of production sites, the Mini shifting from Longbridge, Birmingham, where Rover was to remain, and moving to Cowley, which BMW kept and rebranded Plant Oxford.

By summer 2001 the Mini Cooper had been launched, Frank Stephenson was being feted as a breakthrough designer and Mini-mania was in full swing. The doubters were silenced as orders flooded in, the Cowley plant put on extra shifts to keep pace with demand, and BMW's planners in Munich were beginning to think through their next moves.

Designer »Gert Hildebrand was already installed at Mini when, in 2002, Stephenson was headhunted to join Ferrari. Ideas had already been kicking around for extensions to the Mini line-up, and Hildebrand began looking beyond the 2004 Convertible towards a larger station-wagon model. A series of four concepts at successive motor shows, each slightly different in theme, revealed a slightly larger car with a variety of complex rear-door arrangements and a host of novel stowage ideas; the basic design exaggerated the 2001 car's grille and lights, previewing not just the 2007 Clubman but also the whole second generation.

The 2008 Crossover Mini concept at last gave a glimpse of the company's thinking for

2006 MINI COOPER S

1997 ACV30, ONE OF THE CONCEPTS FOR THE MINI COOPER

HISTORY

1950s	Alec Issigonis of BMC begins developing economy small car
1959	BMC launches Mini
1961	Mini Cooper
1993	Rover group begins work on Mini replacement
1994	BMW buys Rover group, including Mini. Gives new Mini programme the codename R59
1995	Secret 'shootout' (internal competition) decides between designs
1997	ACV30 concept, by BMW Designworks; Mini Cooper concept, by Frank Stephenson; Spiritual concepts, by Rover's Oliver le Grice
2000	BMW disposes of Rover, keeps Mini. Mini manufacturing moves from Longbridge, Birmingham, to Cowley, near Oxford
2001	Mini Cooper launched
2007	Announces 4x4 model will be built by Steyr Motors, Austria
2010	Announces entry into world rallying

FOUR 2006 STATION-WAGON CONCEPTS

2008 CROSSOVER CONCEPT

PRINCIPAL MODELS

1997	Mini Cooper concept presented
2001	Mini Cooper and One go on sale
2002	Mini Cooper S
2003	Mini One D
2004	Convertible
2005–2006	Series of four concepts preview Mini wagon model
2006	Mini GP built by Bertone; Mini Cooper (2nd gen)
2007	Clubman station-wagon
2008	Mini E with electric power; Crossover concept for larger 4x4 Mini
2009	Mini Coupé and Roadster concepts
2010	Countryman crossover; Mini Beachcomber and Rocketman concepts

2009 COUPÉ CONCEPT

a larger car – in this case a station-wagon with optional four-wheel drive. Not everyone liked what they saw: with exaggerated headlamps, a thrust-forward grille and elaborate hinging and sliding doors, it came across as a caricature of the original, although a raft of clever storage solutions ensured it a favourable press. The Crossover concept proved to be an accurate predictor of the 2010 Countryman production car, but it is too early to say whether the same will apply to the two subsequent concepts, the 2009 Coupé and Roadster.

Although the coupé and convertible concepts were familiar in their exaggeration of the original Mini design cues, they adopted more of a wedge profile, with a 'faster' (more steeply raked) windshield and, on the coupé, a so-called bridge roof that appeared to sit heavily halfway down the C pillar, creating an uncomfortable overall proportion. These two models have been confirmed for production at Cowley. If Mini is true to form and stays faithful to the concepts for manufacture, it seems set to stay on its neo-retro design course for some while.

2007 CLUBMAN

MINI COOPER

2006 | SMALL CAR

MODEL HISTORY 2001 MINI COOPER 1ST GENERATION • 2006 MINI COOPER 2ND GENERATION

2010 COOPER	
LENGTH	3700 mm (146 in.)
LAYOUT	Front engine, front-wheel drive
ENGINE	1.6 petrol 4-cyl
HORSEPOWER	122
MAX. SPEED	203 km/h (126 mph)
CO$_2$ EMISSIONS	127 g/km

As in the case of its 1959 precursor, BMW's 2001 Mini Cooper was both a marketing and a social phenomenon almost from the moment of its launch. But while Alec Issigonis's visionary model revolutionized the market by making the idea of a clever but cheap small car acceptable across all levels of society, BMW's twenty-first-century take opted for a more profitable business model: building a straightforward small car and charging much more money for it.

Three key elements guaranteed the Mini Cooper a keen reception in almost every market in which it appeared: the reassurance of the BMW name; the lingering affection for the old Mini, carefully massaged by »Frank Stephenson's brilliantly manipulative retro design; and BMW's invention of the art of personalization, with extra stripes, colours, interiors and wheels that enabled every customer to tailor their individual Mini – and of course spend far more in the showroom than they had originally intended.

First presented in 1997 as a red concept with a white roof, Stephenson's shape initially came across as an unkind caricature of a faithful friend, exaggerating such features as the bug-eyed lights, the upright windshield and, particularly, the ludicrously oversized central speedometer. Yet with its unadorned flanks and neat detailing the Mini Cooper was subtle and appealing at the same time, and by the time production models appeared in 2001 it came across as just how a Mini should be – even though it was almost a metre longer than the Issigonis car.

Having successfully established premium retro in the small-car market and sent rivals scrabbling to compete with the Mini Cooper's enviable price and ability to sell without a discount, BMW faced the dilemma of how to update a retro model – a design oxymoron if ever there was one. Designer »Gert Hildebrand's 2006 answer was to do nothing: the second-generation Mini Cooper is bigger and beefier but otherwise unchanged, except for the raising of the beltline and the further enlargement of the lights, both of which wreck the fine balance of Stephenson's design.

Clubman, Countryman and Coupé derivatives have all turned up the retro volume in order to attract attention. What BMW now needs to take on board is the difference between retro-affection and plain retrograde; new design director Anders Warming has an important task on his hands.

2001-GENERATION MINI COOPER

2010 COUNTRYMAN

MITSUBISHI

JAPAN | FOUNDED 1960 | CARS AND SUVS | MITSUBISHI-MOTORS.COM

Mitsubishi began in the automobile business by assembling Jeeps under licence from the Willys corporation in the early 1950s; by the mid-1960s Mitsubishi had progressed via a series of small cars and trucks to a compact family sedan, the Colt 1500. By the end of the next decade, thanks to such successful designs as the larger Galant sedan and its GTO coupé spin-off, sales of Mitsubishis and its Colt sub-brand were running at over a million a year.

But it was with the sturdy Pajero SUV that Mitsubishi came to be globally recognized. Launched in 1982 as a better-value alternative to the Jeep Cherokee and »Land Rover Discovery, the Pajero – known in some markets as Shogun or Montero – quickly gained a reputation for strength and reliability and, in its later long-wheelbase five-door form, smart looks that appealed to the wealthy rural buyer wishing to haul horseboxes and sports equipment. The Pajero's popularity, coupled with repeated wins in the gruelling Safari rally in East Africa, booming business with Chrysler in the United States and the ultra-sophisticated Galant VR4 in 1987, made this a golden era for Mitsubishi.

The first signs of problems came in the wake of the 1991 deal with Volvo to build a shared family-segment car in The Netherlands. Launched in 1996, the Carisma was, despite its name, a desperately dull design, and dealers were forced for the first time to learn the art of incentives and discounts. Also disappointing was the outcome of a deal with »Pininfarina to build a compact 4x4 in Italy: the 1997 design lacked the flair expected of the Italian coachbuilder, once again betraying the underlying caution of the Japanese design supervisors.

The new millennium saw Mitsubishi swept up in cooperation with DaimlerChrysler as the US–German giant spotted synergies that could bring down the cost of the future four-seater Smart by combining it with a new Mitsubishi Colt. Mercedes-Benz

1969 GALANT

1973 LANCER

managers, including design director Olivier Boulay, filled key positions at the Japanese headquarters, and a fresh and sharper design direction began to emerge. Design was on a roll once more, generating the highly innovative »Mitsubishi 'i' compact car, with its engine under the floor, and the intriguing Se-ro concept. A capsule-like monospace people-carrier finished in polished aluminium and with the curved front almost indistinguishable from the similarly shaped rear, the Se-ro used the underfloor engine to even better effect to provide excellent passenger and load space on a compact road footprint.

The first decade of the new millennium also saw momentum build up behind a raft

1994 3000GT

HISTORY

2006-GENERATION PAJERO

1982 PAJERO

2007 CONCEPT CX

2007 CONCEPT RA

PRINCIPAL MODELS	
1965	Colt 1500
1969	Galant sedan, Delica light commercial
1973	Lancer
1982	Pajero SUV
1987	Galant VR4 with 4-wheel-drive
1994	3000GT
1996	Carisma
2003	Grandis, by Olivier Boulay; 'i' and Se-ro concepts
2005	Concept Sportback, Concept X
2006	Pajero (4th gen)
2007	'i', Lancer (9th gen); Concept cX and ZT
2008	Lancer Evolution X; Concept RA

of new models, including the 2005 Concept X with its dramatically dominating grille; this was intended to be the blueprint for a new mid-size sedan and hatchback to replace the tired – but still rally-winning – »Lancer. Sadly, by the time the Concept X appeared Mitsubishi had split acrimoniously with its DaimlerChrysler parent, Boulay and the Germans had left, and the escalating losses had led many of the more interesting projects to be abandoned.

Deals with France's PSA Peugeot Citroën for crossover SUV production saw Mitsubishi's Outlander morph into the Citroën C-Crosser and Peugeot 4007, losing some of its style in the process; the tiny 'i', converted to running on battery power, was rolled into the limelight as Mitsubishi's ambassador for a new generation of environmentally aware small cars. Deals for Citroën and Peugeot versions followed, making the i-MiEV the first commercially available electric car in Europe. An amusing spin-off was the sporty, bubble-car-like i-MiEV Sport Air concept in 2009.

Yet in its wholesale reprogramming to the amp and the volt, Mitsubishi appeared to have neglected its principal brand hero, the multiple-rally-winning Pajero. Judging by the feeble 2006 revamp of this one-time icon, classical SUVs are no longer a priority.

2008 LANCER EVOLUTION X

2009 i-MiEV SPORT AIR CONCEPT

2007 CONCEPT ZT

2003 SE-RO CONCEPT

MITSUBISHI i

2007 | CITY CAR

2010 0.7 TURBO	
LENGTH	3395 mm (134 in.)
LAYOUT	Mid engine, rear-wheel drive
ENGINE	0.7 turbo petrol 3-cyl
HORSEPOWER	64
MAX. SPEED	135 km/h (84 mph)
CO$_2$ EMISSIONS	114 g/km

After microcar maker »Smart had teamed up with Mitsubishi in 2000 to build the four-seater Forfour and the model flopped in the market because it was seen as too mainstream, many argued that the two partners had chosen the wrong model to work from. A much better choice, they insisted, would have been the Mitsubishi i, first presented as a concept in 2003: this compact city car had all the ingenuity and establishment-challenging imagination that buyers expected of the Smart brand.

What makes that i concept – and subsequent production models – unique is an underfloor engine arrangement that allows the semicircular arc of the passenger cabin to stretch unobstructed for the whole length of the vehicle. A wheelbase longer than that of a »Volkswagen Polo guarantees excellent passenger accommodation and a good ride; it also results in an extreme form of wheel-at-each-corner body design, with zero frontal overhang: the bluff hood rises almost vertically to the big windscreen and the long roof.

The underfloor engine concept has proved its versatility with the battery-powered i-MiEV version and its Peugeot- and Citroën-branded derivatives – and the three-cylinder engine did appear in a Smart after all, as the power unit for the second-generation »Fortwo.

HISTORY

1914	Kwaishinsho Co. begins building DAT car
1934	Nihon Sangyo Co. takes over, renames company Nissan
1952	Technical collaboration with Austin of England
1966	Merges with Prince Motors
1979	Nissan Design International established in USA
1981	Begins using Nissan name on vehicles
1986	Opens first European plant, in UK
1989	Launches Infiniti premium brand in USA
1992	Nissan Micra is first Japanese car to win European Car of the Year award
1999	Forms alliance with Renault
2003	Nissan Design Europe opens in London
2008	Infiniti launches in Europe
2010	Renault-Nissan Alliance to cooperate with Mercedes-Benz on small cars. Electric Leaf model to be made in UK

2009 LEAF

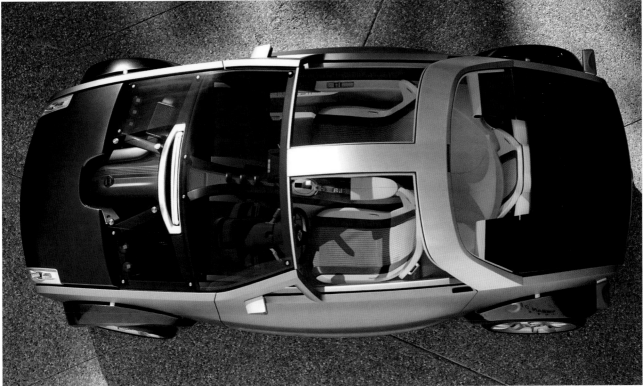

2006 URGE CONCEPT

appeared: »Renault, with its powerful reputation in design. Joining forces with Nissan, Renault set about rationalizing the Japanese company, its hundreds of facilities and its scores of overlapping models. For the first time, Western management practices allowed talented (rather than simply senior) individuals to come to the fore, and with the recruitment of »Shiro Nakamura from Isuzu as chief designer Nissan design once again began to blossom.

The stylish 2001 Chappo concept led directly to the definitive second-generation »Cube the following year, the 2001 'mm' became the next-generation Micra (the first Japanese car to win the coveted European Car of the Year award), and the Murano crossover concept was a showroom hit within a few years. Nissan was at last following up on what it does best: creating original and sometimes wildly imaginative concept cars, and turning them into real cars for customers to buy.

The growing influence of Nissan's European studios was seen in the big success of the »Qashqai, which broke new ground as a crossover aiming to sell against standard hatchbacks. The smaller Qazana concept and its production follow-up, the 2010 Juke, are altogether more polarizing in their approach to the urban youth market.

Unlike its sister company, Renault, Nissan has yet to reveal a specific design identity for the electric cars that are to be its big push in the 2010s. The pioneering »Leaf is disappointingly unadventurous on the outside but has a better resolved interior; further electric models, perhaps inspired by the 2008 Nuvu concept or even the two remarkable swivelling Pivo designs of 2005 and 2007, are promised. And at the opposite end of the scale sits that other defining model of the Nissan brand, the Porsche-taunting »GT-R, a distillation of all the years of Z-car and Skyline history.

2005 ZAROOT CONCEPT

2005 NOTE

2007 QASHQAI

PRINCIPAL MODELS

1930	DAT 91
1932	Datsun type 10
1937	Nissan 70
1957	Prince Skyline
1960	Fairlady roadster
1969	Skyline GT-R; Datsun 240Z, by Albrecht Goertz
1970	Datsun Cherry
1982	Nissan Prairie, Micra/March
1986	ARC-X concept
1987	Be 1, Pao
1989	Figaro, S-Cargo, 300ZX (2nd gen)
1992	Micra/March (2nd gen)
1993	Skyline R33 (4th gen)
1998	Cube
2000	Hypermini concept
2001	Chappo concept
2002	Cube (2nd gen), Micra/March (3rd gen)
2003	Murano crossover
2004	Qashqai concept
2005	Note; Pivo and Zaroot concepts
2006	Urge concept
2007	Qashqai, GT-R replaces Skyline GT-R; Pivo 2 concept
2008	370Z, Cube (3rd gen); Nuvu concept
2009	Leaf, world's first purpose-designed volume-market electric car; Qazana concept
2010	Juke; Townpod concept

2008 NUVU CONCEPT

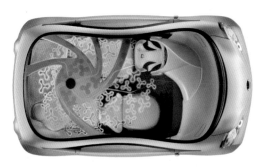

2008 NUVU CONCEPT

NISSAN 370Z

2008 | MEDIUM SPORTS CAR

MODEL HISTORY 1969 DATSUN 240Z • 1978 208ZX • 1984 300ZX • 1989 300ZX 2ND GENERATION • 2002 350Z • 2008 370Z

2010	
LENGTH	4250 mm (168 in.)
LAYOUT	Front engine, rear-wheel drive
ENGINE	3.7 petrol V6
HORSEPOWER	331
MAX. SPEED	250 km/h (155 mph)
CO_2 EMISSIONS	249 g/km

The 370Z is the inheritor of one of the finest traditions of any Japanese automaker. The Z-car cult began in 1969 when Nissan, which at that stage was selling its cars under the Datsun label in the United States, surprised the world with the 240Z, a potent and well-engineered six-cylinder coupé styled with some panache by Albrecht Goertz. It was an instant hit, especially in America, and was followed up by steadily larger and more luxurious Z models.

By the 1980s, however, complacency had set in and the Z series was getting fat and flabby. Recognizing this, Nissan counter-attacked with the excellent 1989 300ZX, a genuinely advanced sports coupé with clever styling that implied it might be mid-engined, as if it were a supercar.

When the 300 was killed off by emissions regulations it seemed as if the Z line had died, too, but after a gap of several years Nissan, by now teamed up with Renault, was applauded for reviving it with the 350Z in 2002. Fast but none too sophisticated, the 350Z tapped into the proportion and the poise of the old Z, but few of its actual design cues. The later 370Z took this a stage further, with a flatter rear screen and a more cab-forward stance.

1989 300ZX

NISSAN CUBE

2008 | COMPACT MINIVAN

2010 1.6	
LENGTH	3890 mm (154 in.)
LAYOUT	Front engine, front-wheel drive
ENGINE	1.6 petrol 4-cyl
HORSEPOWER	110
MAX. SPEED	175 km/h (109 mph)
CO_2 EMISSIONS	151 g/km

Cars that are large, square and very simple are beloved of design professionals, especially those working in occupations outside the automotive community. And of these big and boxy objects of designers' desire, the Nissan Cube is unquestionably the favourite, for in this compact minivan are distilled all the values that designers prize most avidly: purity, efficiency, elegance and clarity of function and purpose.

The first model to bear the Cube name was disappointingly non-cubic: the real story starts with the fabulous Chappo concept at the 2001 Geneva motor show. With its sheer, ice-white body surfaces punctuated only by the semicircular apertures of the wheel arches and windows, it was the design purist's dream; and it was highly practical inside, too.

This design, with the addition of an asymmetric rear door and pillar arrangement, appeared in 2002 as the second-generation Cube, and it is treasured by Cube fanatics as the best of the breed – although the prototype electric Denki-Cube in 2008 took the front-end elegance a step further. By comparison, the third-generation Cube of 2008 has lost its predecessor's compelling simplicity in a complex mess of projecting bumpers and inset lights that spoil the pure cubic nature of the shape.

2008 PROTOTYPE ELECTRIC DENKI-CUBE

NISSAN GT-R

2007 | SPORTS COUPÉ

MODEL HISTORY 1969 SKYLINE GT-R 1ST GENERATION • 1972 SKYLINE GT-R 2ND GENERATION • 1989 SKYLINE GT-R 3RD GENERATION (R32) • 1993 SKYLINE GT-R 4TH GENERATION (R33) • 1999–2002 SKYLINE GT-R 5TH GENERATION (R34) • 2007 GT-R 6TH GENERATION

2010 3.8 V6	
LENGTH	4650 mm (184 in.)
LAYOUT	Front engine, all-wheel drive
ENGINE	3.8 turbo petrol V6
HORSEPOWER	485
MAX. SPEED	310 km/h (192 mph)
CO$_2$ EMISSIONS	298 g/km

Europeans and Americans scoffed openly in 2006 when Nissan first started hinting to enthusiast magazines that the upcoming GT-R sports coupé was being benchmarked against the »Porsche 911 for power, performance and handling. And it wasn't just any 911 that was being targeted, either: it was the Turbo, the crowning glory of the forty-year development story of Europe's top sports-car maker's topmost model. Impossible, presumptive and absurdly ambitious, was the majority European view; Americans, although less narrowly focused on the single Porsche icon, were dismissive too.

In Japan, however, Nissan's plans were taken as a natural next step, for on its own home ground the GT-R is revered as a high-speed icon like no other: nearly forty years of ever-faster Skyline GT-R performance models have built up a massive cult following for the type among affluent enthusiasts, tuning specialists and readers of auto magazines. With these models having only ever been built in right-hand drive (in Japan, cars are driven on the left side of the road), British enthusiasts in receipt of unofficial imports were the only other group truly in on the GT-R secret.

These cult communities were becoming restless following the dropping of the fearsome R34 Skyline GT-R in 2002. The heat was turned up again by a concept in 2005 that abandoned the old Skyline name and was labelled simply GT-R, but it would be a further two years before the definitive production GT-R emerged.

1999 SKYLINE GT-R

1969 SKYLINE GT-R

The design was larger and more clearly coupé-like than before, brutally functional rather than aesthetically satisfying in its powerful stance, and with its surfacing technique of sharp-edged polygons and gentle curves lending it the technical air of a racing car. Yet through this shone two GT-R signature elements that would ensure continuity in the nameplate's line of succession: the recessed quadruple round rear lights and the aggressive rear spoiler.

In design and image terms the GT-R is something quite unusual: an individual model whose aura and reputation completely transcend those of its own brand.

NISSAN JUKE
2010 | COMPACT CROSSOVER

2010 1.5 DCI	
LENGTH	4135 mm (163 in.)
LAYOUT	Front engine, all-wheel drive
ENGINE	1.5 turbo diesel 4-cyl
HORSEPOWER	110
MAX. SPEED	216 km/h (134 mph)
CO_2 EMISSIONS	134 g/km

The design brief for the Nissan Juke was a seemingly simple one: to attract the attention of people even if they are not looking or listening. Created at Nissan's European design centre in London, which had earlier been responsible for the massively successful »Qashqai crossover, the Juke fits into the smaller B segment but, as was the case with the Qashqai, adopts the approach of being different from the mainstream offerings. It is therefore able to sell at a more profitable price point.

The Juke's design, by Matthew Weaver and »Alfonso Albaisa, and previewed by the 2009 Qazana concept, is deliberately challenging and confrontational. It contrives a tough, urban bully look thanks to its big wheels, even bigger wheel arches, high ground clearance and big boulder deflector set into the front apron. A double-frontal face further confuses matters, with huge round lower lights and a smaller secondary set just below the windshield.

The Juke's glass areas are brooding and narrow in relation to the deep, hollowed-out body sides, while at the rear powerful shoulders slim the cabin structure for further dynamic effect. Inside, it is somewhat less frantic, despite door trims shaped like flippers and a centre console sculpted like a motorcycle fuel tank. Deliberately extreme and polarizing, the Juke certainly succeeds in getting itself noticed.

2009 QAZANA CONCEPT PREVIEWING JUKE

2009 QAZANA CONCEPT PREVIEWING JUKE

2010 JUKE

NISSAN LEAF

2009 | ELECTRIC MEDIUM CAR

2010 EV	
LENGTH	4445 mm (176 in.)
LAYOUT	Front engine, front-wheel drive
ENGINE	Electric
HORSEPOWER	109
MAX. SPEED	140 km/h (87 mph)
CO$_2$ EMISSIONS	0 g/km

Remember the original »Toyota Prius, the world's first volume-production hybrid sedan? Dating back to 1997, the dumpy little four-door looked quaintly old-fashioned, totally denying the advanced engineering under its shapeless surface.

It is tempting to see the new Nissan Leaf, the first volume-production electric car, in the same light. Its somewhat soft and shapeless styling does not immediately attract the eye and, unlike in Toyota's later Prius models, the balance of its volumes is that of a conventional B-segment hatchback rather than anything advanced or innovative. The overall stance is droopy, too, a combination of a sagging front topped by complex headlamps raised from the hood surface, and a rear end whose every line and surface draws the attention down to bumper level.

Yet on closer examination the Leaf's detailed design features reveal more interest. The unusual tall and narrow rear lights frame the rear glass and tailgate in two V-shapes. The tranquil, pastel-coloured interior, with its cool blue instruments and information displays and its soft-touch surfaces, conveys the Leaf's innovative engineering far better than does its uninspired external shaping.

NISSAN QASHQAI

2007 | CROSSOVER

2010 2.0	
LENGTH	4315 mm (171 in.)
LAYOUT	Front engine, front-wheel drive
ENGINE	2.0 petrol 4-cyl
HORSEPOWER	141
MAX. SPEED	195 km/h (121 mph)
CO$_2$ EMISSIONS	184 g/km

The instant success of the Qashqai in 2007 surprised most of the auto business – except for Nissan. The company had always been evangelically confident that the best way for a smaller non-premium player to compete in the Volkswagen Golf-size class was not to be cheaper, but to be different. The Qashqai, which took the name, the lofty 4x4 stance and the urban cool of the 2004 concept but little in the way of design cues, was Nissan's answer, promising buyers the status and the command driving position of an SUV but the ease of driving and the low purchase and running costs of a mainstream hatchback.

The formula worked a treat. The simple, smooth-sided design was discreet enough not to appear aggressive, yet the Qashqai's intimations of toughness and 4x4 potential (reinforced by black cladding to the sills and aprons) endeared it to those who wanted to drive something that projected a more adventurous image than an Opel/Vauxhall Astra or a Ford Focus.

A longer-wheelbase seven-seater followed in 2008, along with a facelift that strengthened the Qashqai's frontal appearance and set the seal on its success.

OPEL/VAUXHALL

GERMANY/GREAT BRITAIN | FOUNDED 1899 | VOLUME CARS | OPEL.COM

HISTORY	
1899	First Opel car
1903	First Vauxhall car
1924	Opel pioneers volume production in Europe
1925	Vauxhall bought by General Motors
1929	Opel bought by GM
1936	Opel is Europe's biggest car producer
1980	UK design centre closed
1982	Saragossa plant, Spain
1986	GM Europe established
1996	Opel Omega exported to US as Cadillac Catera
2009	Opel/Vauxhall put up for sale by GM, but retained

1957 VAUXHALL VICTOR

When General Motors began planning its expansion into Europe in the 1920s, the American company first tried to buy Austin, but failed; instead, it was Vauxhall (at that time a respected producer of large and sometimes sporty models) that took the bait in 1925. Opel, the dominant player in Germany, joined the GM fold four years later. Under GM control Vauxhall moved into smaller designs and greater production volumes, reflecting Opel expertise and American styling trends, especially in the larger models.

After the Second World War, Vauxhalls in particular began to look like miniaturized versions of GM's »Chevrolets and »Buicks. Shark-mouth grilles, fins, wraparound windshields and rear windows and elaborate two-tone colour schemes all made the Opels and Vauxhalls of the day highly fashionable, but, as the next fad came in, the cars could quickly look dated. However, in a Europe still recovering from war and deprivation, these brightly coloured, chrome-bedecked fashion statements found a ready audience among the ambitious and those seeking glamour and excitement.

Opels remained differently engineered and styled from Vauxhalls right through into the 1970s, so Vauxhall had no equivalent of, for example, the classic 1968 Opel GT: Vauxhall embraced the Coke-bottle styling ethos of the mid-1960s enthusiastically, with the especially successful 1966 Viva and 1967 Victor. But by 1980 Vauxhall's design department had been closed, its last design the dramatic Equus sports car concept by future GM design chief »Wayne Cherry.

Rationalization had already forced the two brands into a marriage of models with the Chevette, an adapted Opel Kadett, and the Ascona-derived Cavalier in 1975. These models had more than token changes to turn them into Vauxhalls: Cherry turned the so-called droop snoot of the sporty Firenza into a more mildly chiselled nose that became a Vauxhall signifier for the next generation of models.

Yet by the time GM belatedly embraced front-wheel drive with its 1979 Kadett/Astra, any differences had been ironed out in the interests of production efficiency. Now, only badging distinguished one brand from the other. While the »Astra model line swung wildly between progressive

and dull designs as it rolled through the generations, the larger Ascona/Cavalier (later Vectra) stayed resolutely on the cautious side of the dividing line. This worked well at first, with clean and smooth designs – notably the very elegant 1970s Manta coupé and the sophisticated Calibra of 1989 – but the models began to lose sales to premium competitors Audi and BMW, which could offer a classy image and much better interiors than GM's scrappy efforts.

GM's German studio was home to many talented designers, including »Chris Bangle and »Gert Hildebrand. Their work is evident in the aerodynamic Tech 1 concept of 1981 and the small 1983 Junior concept, a key design that later influenced the second-generation Corsa hatchback. Towards the end of the twentieth century GM design was facing further pressure: with value brands such as Hyundai encroaching from below and the booming premium makers increasing their share, Opel/Vauxhall's middle ground was being squeezed and its efforts to build BMW-standard big cars were being ignored by customers. Although some relief came from the United States as GM's struggling Saturn brand turned to Opel for

1966 VAUXHALL VIVA HB

1968 OPEL GT

its products, the concurrent advent of Chevrolet (fielding low-cost Daewoos) as GM's entry brand put further pressure on Opel. In 2009, after GM in America filed for Chapter 11 bankruptcy, Opel/Vauxhall was put up for sale. Eventually the for-sale sign was taken down, and now GM's slimmed-down European management faces big decisions on the style, the positioning and the engineering of its next generation of products. Some not-so-recent city-car concepts (such as the versatile modular Maxx of 1995 and the clever 2003 Trixx) and 2007's Flextreme concept suggest that GM might try being cleverer than everyone else, rather than relying on simply being bigger.

2007 FLEXTREME CONCEPT

OPEL/VAUXHALL ASTRA

2009 | MEDIUM CAR

MODEL HISTORY 1979 ASTRA 1/KADETT D • 1984 ASTRA 2/KADETT E • 1991 ASTRA F • 1998 ASTRA G • 2004 ASTRA H • 2009 ASTRA

2010 1.7 CDTI	
LENGTH	4420 mm (175 in.)
LAYOUT	Front engine, front-wheel drive
ENGINE	1.7 turbo diesel 4-cyl
HORSEPOWER	110
MAX. SPEED	181 km/h (112 mph)
CO_2 EMISSIONS	124 g/km

The history of the Astra makes a fascinating comparison with that of its long-time rival, the »Volkswagen Golf. Over thirty years and numerous generations the pair have evolved in dramatically different ways, the VW building steadily and cautiously from one generation to the next, the Astra chopping and changing its style in response to the whims of the market or the hunches of GM's product planners. What is most striking is that at the end of the three-decade study the Volkswagen has become a near-premium product commanding universal recognition and respect, whereas the Astra, for all the efforts of GM's designers, is still battling for the middle ground and has an uncertain identity among consumers.

The Astra was on the back foot when it first appeared in 1979 to challenge the first-generation Golf, already five years into its production run. The clean-cut first-generation Astra metamorphosed into an aerodynamic second generation in 1984, in response to the scarcely changed second-generation Golf. Both slipped into their third incarnations in 1991, and the Astra's clean and spacious new look could easily have swung buyers disappointed by the clumsy and bulbous new Golf.

Yet, somehow, the opportunity to kick VW when it was down was missed, and by the end of the decade, with the fourth-generation Golf delivering clean lines, a smooth drive and a premium-class interior, the feeble Astra G seemed to be in an altogether lower league.

Two more Astra generations, in 2004 and 2009, saw a determined fightback, first with sharply chiselled lines and then with a curvier, sportier fastback format. The Golf, meanwhile, became steadily more and more Golf and continued handsomely outselling the Astra, despite its higher prices. Design critics might applaud new fashions as they come and go, but the hard truth of the matter is that canny buyers tend to go for models that evolve in an unexciting linear fashion.

1979 ASTRA 1

1984 ASTRA 2

1991 ASTRA F

374

OPEL/VAUXHALL INSIGNIA

2008 | EXECUTIVE CAR

2010 2.8 V6	
LENGTH	4830 mm (191 in.)
LAYOUT	Front engine, front-wheel drive
ENGINE	2.8 turbo petrol V6
HORSEPOWER	260
MAX. SPEED	250 km/h (155 mph)
CO_2 EMISSIONS	256 g/km

Since the »BMW 3 Series and the »Audi A4 became big sellers into the business-car market in Europe, life has been tough for the volume brands in the executive segment. And for none more than Opel/ Vauxhall, squeezed from underneath by the value brands and GM's own Chevrolet, and hemmed in from the top by the premium marques creaming off the most profitable high-specification sales. However good Opel/Vauxhall's products are, buyers seem to head straight for the premium alternative.

With the 2008 Insignia Opel/Vauxhall once again rose to the premium challenge. Unrelated to the imposing 2003 concept of the same name but very directly derived from the later GTC coupé study, the Insignia is a modern, well-shaped family of executive cars distinguished by a strong grille, smooth body surfacing and, on the hatch version, a stylish rear with more than a hint of the »Jaguar XF. A distinctive 'swoosh' in the front door flicks down and then back to fade out just before the rear-wheel arch; Opel/Vauxhall is now standardizing this as a brand identifier.

For many generations Opel/Vauxhall cars were let down by substandard interiors, but here too the Insignia has made major strides towards providing the quality ambience premium buyers expect. The question is, will this be enough to break the jinx?

2003 INSIGNIA CONCEPT

2007 GTC CONCEPT, FORERUNNER OF INSIGNIA

OPEL/VAUXHALL TIGRA

2004–2009 | COMPACT SPORTS CAR

MODEL HISTORY 1994–99 TIGRA 1ST GENERATION • 2004–2009 TIGRA 2ND GENERATION

2009 TWINTOP 1.8 16V	
LENGTH	3920 mm (155 in.)
LAYOUT	Front engine, front-wheel drive
ENGINE	1.8 petrol 4-cyl
HORSEPOWER	125
MAX. SPEED	204 km/h (127 mph)
CO$_2$ EMISSIONS	185 g/km

Opel/Vauxhall's original Tigra of 1994 was a neat two-door coupé based on the Corsa hatchback, featuring a large wraparound rear screen. Disappointingly, it was little better to drive than the Corsa and, although a convertible had also been planned, it was dropped in 1999.

Most believed the Tigra dead – until a new one appeared at the 2004 Paris motor show. This was the ideal location, as Opel/Vauxhall had decided to take a leaf out of Peugeot's book and make the Tigra a coupé-convertible with a rigid folding roof (engineered by French coachbuilder Heuliez).

In terms of style, the new Tigra once again picked up the frontal theme of the Corsa, with a heavy chrome bar substituting for a grille. Roof down, it displayed a sporty-looking rear deck and racy chrome-hooped roll bars behind the occupants' heads; roof up, however, the proportions suffered despite the B-pillar part of the folding structure being picked out in a contrast metal finish.

As in the case of its first-generation predecessor, the second Tigra's dynamics were disappointing. So, too, were the sales figures, and despite the launch-phase flurry of fashionability among women buyers, it was dropped in 2009.

PAGANI

ITALY | FOUNDED 1991 | EXTREME SPORTS CARS | PAGANI.COM

In common with »Koenigsegg of Sweden and »Spyker of The Netherlands, Pagani is a producer of extreme sports cars whose public profile – especially among enthusiast magazines and their petrol-head readers – is out of all proportion to the very low numbers of handmade supercars it sells each year. Yet in a field populated by insanely powerful machines for millionaires, the Pagani Zonda stands out as madder than most: with its low-set nose, quadruple faired headlights, acutely forward-set bubble cabin and huge rear deck covering the massive V12 engine, it has a proportion and a silhouette like nothing else on the road, or the racetrack. And once it has blasted past, the dramatic impression is cemented by that unmistakable Pagani signature: four meaty exhaust pipes grouped together in a chrome circle, set high up in the rear grille above the aerodynamic diffuser. This is a functional car, not an aesthetically beautiful one, and its cluttered, race-car-like interior confirms precisely where its priorities lie.

Such cars are invariably the passion of one man, and so it was with Argentinian Horacio Pagani. A car and motor-racing fanatic from an early age, he managed to enlist the support of Formula One hero Juan Manuel Fangio to get an introduction to Lamborghini in Italy, where he worked and became a specialist in carbon fibre. In 1991 he set up his own business and, again with Fangio's help, struck a deal with Mercedes-Benz for the supply of tuned V12 AMG engines; by 1999 Pagani was able to present the Zonda C12 as a customer-ready car.

All the subsequent, ever more extreme models have evolved from that original. Most of Pagani's design attention appears to have gone on enhancing the Zonda's power and performance and smashing Nürburgring lap records, rather than honing the Zonda's shape. For the extreme sports-car customer, this is just how it should be.

2003 ZONDA ROADSTER

HISTORY AND PRINCIPAL MODELS

1983	Argentinian Horacio Pagani joins Lamborghini
1991	Pagani leaves Lamborghini to set up own business in carbon fibre
1993	Juan Manuel Fangio brokers deal with Mercedes-Benz for V12 engines
1999	Zonda C12 presented at Geneva motor show
2003	Zonda roadster
2007	Zonda R, with 750 hp
2010	Roadster Cinque
2011	Huayra

2007 ZONDA R

2011 HUAYRA

PAYKAN

IRAN | FOUNDED 1967 | VOLUME CARS | IRANKHODRO1016.COM

Strictly speaking a model rather than a brand, the Paykan has been the mainstay of Iran's drivers – and, especially, its taxi drivers – for more than forty years, ever since the pre-revolution government set up a car firm, Iran Khodro, and struck a deal with Britain's Rootes group for the supply of the Hillman Hunter sedan. At the time the Hunter was one of Hillman's latest models, but it was mechanically simple and was supplied to Iran in the form of CKD kits for local assembly. When first Chrysler and then Peugeot took over the Rootes group, the Hunter was dropped and in a series of moves Iran was able to make more and more of the Paykan's parts locally.

The strengthening connection with Peugeot led Iran Khodro to build the 405 from around the turn of the millennium and, later, a locally designed derivative called the Samand. This was part of a government plan to phase out the Paykan, which was seen as thirsty and polluting. By 2005 the almost forty-year-old design was dropped, and Renault had entered the picture with a proposal to build its low-cost Logan. Intense political bargaining surrounded the Renault deal and the situation was never truly clear. Iran Khodro, meanwhile, had pursued its Peugeot technology to come up with a second so-called Iranian national car, the Runna: an enlarged 206 with a trunk.

Iran is a large market, but for Western automakers it is fraught with political difficulties relating to UN sanctions, demands for very high local content and a recent insistence on exports of locally made models. But the Iran Khodro/Peugeot combination, with its 96-plus per cent local manufacture, is better placed than others to benefit from the protected market.

HISTORY AND PRINCIPAL MODELS

1967	Assembly of Hillman Hunter from kits as Paykan
1978	Peugeot takes over Chrysler/Hillman in Europe
1979	Hunter production ends, Paykan production continues in Iran
1996	Samand project for Paykan replacement begins
2001	Samand, based on Peugeot 405
2005	Paykan phased out; pickup version continues
2006	Renault signs deal for Iranian Logan production
2009	Political decision to reduce dependence on the French
2009	Iranian national car no. 2 is Runna, based on Peugeot 206
2010	Launch of Runna, Soren and micro hybrid Samand

1967 PAYKAN / HILLMAN HUNTER

PERODUA

MALAYSIA | FOUNDED 1993 | SMALL CARS | PERODUA.COM.MY

HISTORY AND PRINCIPAL MODELS

1993	Founded as joint venture between Malaysian government, Daihatsu and other Japanese companies
1994	Kancil city car
1996	Rusa minibus
1998	Kembara 4x4
2000	Kenari compact minivan
2001	Kelisa compact car
2005	Builds millionth car. Myvi small car
2007	Viva replaces Kelisa
2008	Nautica 4x4
2009	Alza small minivan

2005 MYVI

2000 KENARI

Perusahaan Otomobil Kedua Sdn Bhd, shortened to Perodua, is Malaysia's second state-controlled automaker and was formed in 1993 as a joint venture between the government and several Japanese companies. Most notable among these was Daihatsu, with a 20 per cent stake; this Japanese builder of small cars, now fully controlled by Toyota, has supplied all the designs and the technologies for the dozen or so models that have appeared under the Perodua label since the brand launched on to the domestic market in 1994.

The launch model was the Kancil, a direct lift of an early-generation Daihatsu Mira city car. The design, although outdated, was simple and straightforward, and the car sold at a keen price on the domestic and, later, export markets. It was followed by the Rusa compact minibus, based on the Daihatsu HiJet van, the Kembara (a version of Daihatsu's Terios compact 4x4 Kembara) and the Kenari, Perodua's interpretation of the boxy and upright Daihatsu Move.

Perodua has chosen the United Kingdom as its bridgehead into Europe: in Britain its products are the cheapest on the market and find favour with older buyers who want a new car for the reassurance of reliability

and are less concerned with technology or style. However, newer Peroduas – especially the Alza small minivan and the Nautica 4x4, based on the seven-seater Daihatsu Luminas and the new Terios respectively – are less dated in their appearance and may well find a broader base of customers.

2001 KELISA

PEUGEOT

FRANCE | FOUNDED 1899 | VOLUME CARS | PEUGEOT.COM

HISTORY

1810	Peugeot brothers open steel foundry
1899	First car bearing Peugeot name
1930	Styling department created under Henri Thomas
1950s	Paul Bouvot becomes styling director
1966	Teams up with Renault and, later, Volvo on engines
1974	Rescues Citroën from bankruptcy
1975	Gérard Welter is head of styling
1976	PSA Peugeot Citroën formed as holding company
1978	Takes over European operations of Chrysler Corporation
1998	New policy of platform and plant sharing
2001	Deal with Ford on diesel engines
2002	Deal with BMW on small petrol engines. Jerome Gallix becomes design co-director
2005	Joint plant with Toyota and Citroën begins production
2008	Jean-Pierre Ploué becomes group design director; Gallix leaves
2009	Gilles Vidal is head of Peugeot design

1955 403

Over Peugeot's 110 years of car manufacture, the company has built up a very strong heritage in design. It was one of the first European manufacturers to follow the American example and set up its own design studio (under Henri Thomas, in 1930) and it has maintained a consistently high standard to the present day, albeit with something of a lapse between 1995 and 2008.

Much, but not all, of Peugeot's design equity has been accumulated as a result of its longstanding relationship with »Pininfarina, which lasted from the mid-1950s 403 to the early-1990s 306. The Italian design house has given Peugeot its absolute classics – the chic 205, the classy 604 and the Ferrari-like 406 coupé – thanks to a strong two-way relationship that allowed Pininfarina to fine-tune the designs to best suit its client.

Nor has Pininfarina been the only style collaborator: very early on Peugeot hit a high note with the smart 1912 Bébé small car, shaped by no less an authority than Ettore Bugatti and a major hit in its day. In the 1930s under Thomas a distinct aerodynamic style began to emerge, the 402 being a powerful example. In the tougher post-war decade a freshly modern image was forged by Pininfarina and given an extra boost by Peugeot's own styling director, Paul Bouvot, who specified for the 1968 504 the slanted headlamps that were to become a key distinguishing feature for Peugeot. Indeed, Peugeot was the first automaker to employ headlamp shape as a major element in its design identity.

Clear and attractive though Peugeot's design identity had become by the mid-1980s, history does reveal two design-related mistakes. In 1987 it released the mid-size 405 sedan, much lauded for its

1938 402

382

1997 406 COUPÉ

1993 306

2004-GENERATION 407

1968 504

PRINCIPAL MODELS	
1896	2-cylinder
1901	Type 36
1912	Bébé, designed by Ettore Bugatti
1924	Lumineuse
1929	201
1938	402
1948	203
1955	403, by Battista Farina
1960	404, by Pininfarina
1965	204, first Peugeot front-drive
1968	504
1975	604
1983	205
1987	405
1988	Oxia concept
1991	106
1993	306
1995	406; Tulip concept for urban electric car
1997	406 coupé, by Pininfarina
1998	206
2001	307
2002	H2O concept
2004	407, 1007
2006	207; 908RC concept
2007	308 RC-Z concept
2008	RC Hybride4 concept
2009	BB1 concepts
2010	508, RC-Z; SR1 concept

2009 BB1 CONCEPT

Pininfarina lines; shortly afterwards came the luxury 605, but this bigger car's style was such a carbon copy of the 405's that it struggled in the market-place. On a much bigger scale was the decision to replace the phenomenally successful 205 of 1983 with not one car but two: the smaller 106 in 1991 and the larger 306 in 1993. Although the 306 was another Pininfarina classic and an excellent car in its own right, 205 owners moved straight to the new »Renault Clio. Peugeot was still struggling to get back into this segment many years later.

Around the turn of the millennium it became clear that all was not well with Peugeot design. The 206 (by »Murat Günak) had failed in its bid to recapture the spirit of the much-loved 205; the tall and inert 307 compared poorly with its agile 306 predecessor; and the overstyled 407 sedan and station-wagon of 2004 imposed a broad, aggressive grille mouth that dominated the entire front. Rolling out this unsubtle caricature of an identity indiscriminately across its entire line-up lured Peugeot into the trap of making all of its models look the same – and equally grotesque. Suddenly the elegance of the Pininfarina styling legacy seemed a long way away, and Peugeot advanced design's output of hectic three-wheelers and ultra-fast supercar concepts irrelevant to the brand did little to stem the impression of confusion and lack of direction.

Enter, in 2008, »Jean-Pierre Ploué, the man who had revitalized Citroën design as style director from 2000, initially through image- and confidence-building concept cars and then through such progressive production models as the Citroën C4 and DS3.

Appointing Gilles Vidal, previously head of concept design at Citroën, to lead Peugeot in late 2009, Ploué signalled the brand's new identity first with the futuristic BB1 urban electric four-seater and the graceful SR1 premium sports-car concept; a matter of months later came the calm and well resolved »508 sedan and the HR-1 urban crossover. All display a restrained and classy frontal face, with the grille (incorporating discreet Peugeot lettering in its top bar) now between the lights to allow a far more relaxed proportion. This is a sign, perhaps, that Peugeot design is back on form.

2010 SR1 CONCEPT

2002 H2O CONCEPT

2007 308 RC-Z CONCEPT

PEUGEOT 207

2006 | COMPACT CAR

MODEL HISTORY 1983 205 • 1998 206 • 2006 207

2010 1.4 VTI	
LENGTH	4045 mm (160 in.)
LAYOUT	Front engine, front-wheel drive
ENGINE	1.4 petrol 4-cyl
HORSEPOWER	95
MAX. SPEED	185 km/h (115 mph)
CO_2 EMISSIONS	140 g/km

1980s 205 AND LATE 1990s 206

Peugeot struck it lucky with the 205 in 1983. The chic little hatchback, one of »Pininfarina's most brilliant designs, had the perfect blend of affordability, smart style and family-friendly practicality, and, as a GTI, it was sensational to drive. It hit the mood of the moment, caught on in a big way and stayed in production until 1998. Peugeot has been struggling to replace it ever since.

Replacing the 205 with two models that were supposed to take over, the small 106 and the medium 306, resulted only in a mass migration of buyers to the Renault Clio. Accepting its mistake, Peugeot readied the 206 for 1998, intent on reviving that 205 spirit, but it, too, disappointed. Its hatchback form echoed the stance of the 205 but the detailing was fussy and the original's clarity had disappeared. The high-performance versions attracted critical reviews, denying the model the sporty cachet in which the 205 had so revelled. This was especially the case with the innovative and popular coupé-cabriolet version, the first low-priced convertible to feature the rigid folding top that had debuted on the »Mercedes SLK just a couple of years earlier.

The step-up to the 207 in 2006 was, in all probability, lost on most people. In profile the new car so resembled the outgoing 206 that it failed the crucial at-a-glance recognition test and went unnoticed; worse, the 207 had been styled around the unsubtle big-mouth front first seen on the »407, and this grille had also just been grafted on to the smaller 107 and the larger 307. This meant that the whole Peugeot small-car range looked the same, and the 207 was never allowed to develop an identity of its own – despite the later addition of station-wagon and retractable-roof CC derivatives.

All eyes are now on new Peugeot design director Gilles Vidal to see how he manages the toughest test of all: replacing the 207 to recapture the magic of the 205.

2007 207 CC

PEUGEOT 407, 508

2004 (407), 2010 (508) | EXECUTIVE CAR

2010 508 1.6 THP	
LENGTH	4790 mm (189 in.)
LAYOUT	Front engine, front-wheel drive
ENGINE	1.6 petrol 4-cyl
HORSEPOWER	156
MAX. SPEED	218 km/h (135 mph)
CO_2 EMISSIONS	149 g/km

The 407 sprang something of a surprise when it was unveiled in the autumn of 2004; to many, it was an unwelcome shock. Peugeot's mid-size, middle-class sedans had always been known for their smart but sober styling; they were conservatively elegant, but never flashy. The preceding 405 and 406 were perfect examples.

The 407, on the other hand, threw discretion to the winds and went off the other end of the scale with a design of dramatically different proportions and graphics. Side on, the 407's diving beltline, strongly swept-back A-pillar and very long front overhang gave it an oddly front-heavy stance. The wagon's C-pillar kicked up at a sharp angle to frame a wide wraparound rear screen, meeting the broad rear lights in a bold arrow shape.

But these graphic devices were nothing compared to the 407's front and the now-infamous grille. The shock has lessened over the years, but in 2004 the gigantic, hungry void of the full-width air intake was greeted with horror and incredulity at seeing a marque known for its refined looks suddenly turning to such an aggressive style. The later 407 coupé would arguably have been a much prettier car but for this unsubtle frontal treatment. The tightly controlled new 508, meanwhile, looks like a return to a more sober style.

407

407 COUPÉ

508

PEUGEOT RC-Z

2010 | MEDIUM SPORTS CAR

2010 1.6 T	
LENGTH	4285 mm (169 in.)
LAYOUT	Front engine, front-wheel drive
ENGINE	1.6 turbo petrol 4-cyl
HORSEPOWER	200
MAX. SPEED	231 km/h (143 mph)
CO_2 EMISSIONS	163 g/km

The Peugeot 308 RC-Z concept of 2007 generated instant and sometimes acrimonious debate as its fervent supporters locked horns with its equally voluble critics. Every aspect was up for discussion: the long and low body and the exaggerated fenders; the long, flat rear deck and the distorted proportions; the very raked rear screen and the double bubble profile of that screen. And there was more: the abbreviated glasshouse, so short that there was hardly a roof, simply a point where the windshield rolled into the rear screen; the polished-metal cant rails that framed this unusual glasshouse; the odd upkick in the beltline above the doorhandle. No one was neutral.

Yet all agreed that this was an exciting incursion into the world of sports cars for Peugeot; that this was a fascinating, if polarizing design; and that if it were put into production it could do for Peugeot what the »Audi TT did for the German automaker.

Peugeot did of course decide to manufacture the RC-Z – at Magna Steyr in Austria – and the signs are that it is beating sales expectations. This is proof, perhaps, that there is just as much appetite for the strange shapes of a Peugeot as there is for the geometric perfection of an Audi.

PETER PFEIFFER

GERMANY | BORN 1943 | CAR DESIGNER AND MANAGER

When he retired in 2008 after thirty years' service, Peter Pfeiffer was just the fourth man in charge of design in the long history of Mercedes-Benz. Rather as in the line of succession in a royal family, Pfeiffer had been given the responsibility of upholding a fine and very public tradition, yet he also needed to ensure that this tradition moved with the times and embraced modern thinking, but without going as far as following passing fashions.

To Pfeiffer must go the credit for striking a skilful balance between advancing design in finely judged (and often quite substantial) steps, and maintaining continuity with past designs so that the heritage is respected and existing customers' cars do not suddenly appear outdated. For Pfeiffer, the kind of wrench caused by the Chris Bangle-designed »BMW 7 Series in 2001 would have been unthinkable; the nearest he came to this was a minor storm over the four-headlamp face of the new E-class in 1995.

Pfeiffer has his fingerprints on almost every Mercedes in current production, as well as several still to come. During his decade in charge he succeeded in making mainstream Mercedes designs more emotional and less architectural, adding characteristic creases and edges and making interiors less stiff and formal. This dynamism was particularly apparent in the new sectors Mercedes entered, such as the small »A-Class, the CLS sports sedan and the emotionally charged »SLS gullwing.

However, although Pfeiffer saw himself as the conductor of the orchestra, the musicians did not always play in tune: such models as the R-class crossover wagon, the GLK SUV and the stretched Maybach limousine did not fit well in the market. Yet, overall, Pfeiffer's achievement in adding spirit and excitement to Mercedes design without scaring away customers or straining the evolutionary chain is a remarkable one.

1995 MERCEDES-BENZ E-CLASS

2004 MERCEDES-BENZ CLS

2005 MERCEDES-BENZ S-CLASS

PININFARINA

ITALY | FOUNDED 1930 | CAR DESIGN, DEVELOPMENT AND MANUFACTURE | PININFARINA.IT

The history of Pininfarina is in almost every sense the history of car design itself; it is also a large part of the history of many marques, such as Ferrari, Alfa Romeo, Peugeot, Lancia, Fiat, Austin and Morris. That's how closely the Italian design house is intertwined with the biographies of many of the world's most prominent automakers, especially during the formative decades after the Second World War, when cars first began to be seen as objects of aesthetic design rather than simply anonymous cladding stretched over the necessary mechanical substructure.

1955 ALFA ROMEO GIULIETTA SPIDER

More than any other company, Pininfarina could be said to have invented universal car design, setting a style agenda that other companies were obliged to emulate or, at their commercial peril, ignore. It made car design a talking point – and, more importantly, a selling point – among volume-market car customers, not just the elite of wealthy enthusiasts.

In an unmatched bloodline of elegant showcars, pioneering research studies and production models of often breathtaking beauty, Pininfarina has marked the waypoints of automobile evolution for eight decades. Its designs, while clearly pushing certain boundaries, have always shared a classical elegance and grace. This has differentiated Pininfarina's output from more provocative and confrontational designs of longstanding rival »Bertone and the fresher, more modernist offerings of its more recent competitor, »Giorgetto Giugiaro's »Italdesign. Throughout, Pininfarina has been highly visible as the first-choice design house for almost every Ferrari production model and a substantial proportion of Alfa Romeos, Lancias and Peugeots, several of which the firm also manufactured. It is hardly surprising, then, that Pininfarina is generally regarded as first among the world's independent design studios.

It could be argued, too, that Pininfarina owes its current pre-eminence to the

1983 PEUGEOT 205

1992 FERRARI 456 GT

392

HISTORY

1906	Giovanni Farina sets up coachbuilding shop in Turin
1911	Younger brother Battista 'Pinin' designs grilles for Fiat Zero
1930	Pinin Farina breaks away to set up Carrozzeria Pininfarina
1931	Coachbuilding on Lancia, Alfa Romeo, Hispano Suiza chassis
1945	Manufacture of Lancia Aprilia Bilux
1946	Excluded from Paris motor show; displays two cars outside
1947	Cisitalia 202; is displayed in New York's Museum of Modern Art in 1951
1952	Begins cooperation with Ferrari
1955	Manufacture of Alfa Romeo Giulietta Spider. Begins working with Peugeot
1958	New manufacturing plant completed
1960	Aerodynamic Fiat Abarth Monoposto breaks speed records
1961	Pinin Farina hands firm over to son Sergio
1966	Pinin Farina dies
1972	Wind tunnel opened
1987	Design work now includes trains, trams, watches
1991	Pininfarina Deutschland set up to undertake engineering
1997	Agreement with Mitsubishi to build Pajero Pinin small SUV
2003	Acquires Matra's testing and prototyping business
2004	Signs contract to build Ford Focus convertible
2006	Andrea Pininfarina, grandson of founder, becomes CEO
2007	Five Pininfarina models presented at Shanghai auto show
2008	Andrea Pininfarina dies in traffic accident
2009	Manufacture and distribution of Pininfarina BlueCar electric car, produced with Bolloré of France

2003 ENJOY CONCEPT

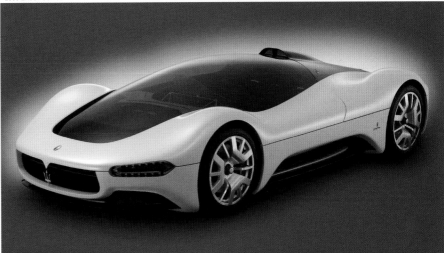

2005 MASERATI BIRDCAGE 75 CONCEPT

PININFARINA

2010 ALFA ROMEO DUETTOTTANTA CONCEPT

continued support of these Italian marques throughout the difficult period of the 1950s and 1960s, when coachbuilders had to shift their focus from craft-level construction of personalized one-off designs for wealthy clients to the creation of more accessible models for volume carmakers to build. This is the step that the equivalent French and British coachbuilders failed to make; yet the two major Italian design houses, Pininfarina and Bertone, went a step further to set up their own manufacturing plants. This was initially successful, but later became a serious burden when demand for outsourced manufacturing vanished after the turn of the millennium.

Pininfarina's highlights, shaped under a succession of chief designers who include Sergio Pininfarina, son of founder Battista 'Pinin' Farina, are far too many to cite individually. Nevertheless, the 1955 Alfa Romeo Giulietta Spider stands out as a miniature masterpiece; the consistently good work for Peugeot and BMC brought style to middle-class motoring in the 1950s and 1960s; and the 1978 Jaguar XJ Spider

design study was an elegant response to the ungainly standard model. The Peugeot 205 was a true classic, never bettered by subsequent in-house designs. Indeed, both Peugeot and BMW lost their way stylistically when they stopped using Pininfarina.

In more recent times the Spider and coupé designs for Alfa Romeo have stood out, as has – of course – each successive new model for Ferrari. Yet Pininfarina's in-house concepts such as the tiny Metrocubo, the Ethos series and the Birdcage 75, for Maserati's seventy-fifth anniversary, have also marked high points. The late 2000s saw a shift in Pininfarina's business, towards engineering services and other product sectors as well as pure design. Tragedy struck in 2008 when CEO Andrea Pininfarina, grandson of Pinin Farina, died in a traffic accident.

The second decade of the new millennium will see Pininfarina expand in a new direction and become a car marque in its own right, selling the attractive »BlueCar battery vehicle jointly produced with Bolloré of France.

2008 SINTESI CONCEPT

PININFARINA BLUECAR

2009 | ELECTRIC CITY CAR

2010	
LENGTH	3650 mm (144 in.)
LAYOUT	Front engine, front drive
ENGINE	Electric motor
HORSEPOWER	67
MAX. SPEED	130 km/h (81 mph)
CO2 EMISSIONS	0 g/km

Anyone who thinks that electric cars – and small electric city cars at that – can't be classy and sophisticated should take a look at the Pininfarina BlueCar. The first car to be marketed under the legendary design house's own name, the BlueCar is an object lesson in how to make a small car graceful, practical and beautiful.

While »Pininfarina did not want to produce a design that was too radical, for fear of alienating those still uncertain about battery power, the gentle wedge profile uses simple but elegant surfacing to bring dynamism to the small four-seater. The body mass is subtly squeezed in the centre so as to lessen its visual weight, and the wide-set wheels give a secure stance on the road. The blue of the front grille and roof derives from solar cells, highlighting the car's electric status and recharging the batteries, which are positioned under the passenger compartment.

With the BlueCar, Pininfarina is presenting a highly attractive face for battery power, one that could make electric driving both fashionable and fun. It promises to be that most desirable of purchases: a powerful style statement and an environmental message wrapped into a shape that is hard to resist.

JEAN-PIERRE PLOUÉ

FRANCE | BORN 1962 | CAR DESIGNER AND MANAGER

Having always been renowned as a bold innovator, France's Citroën found its fortunes waning towards the end of the 1990s as its products lost their distinctiveness and consumers turned to other mainstream brands. With ten years' experience at Renault, during which he had a hand in the innovative Twingo and shaped the influential Argos and Laguna concept cars, Jean-Pierre Ploué was the natural choice as a new design director who could reanimate the brand and restore Citroën's reputation for originality and excitement. In addition, he knew about quality from his time at Volkswagen.

Ploué's antidote to Citroën's brand stagnation was a strong series of concept vehicles, beginning with the glasshouse-like Osmose urban taxi in 2001. These soon fed into such production models as the C4 and C4 Picasso, which were welcomed for restoring a sense of individuality to the brand. Stand-out designs include the dramatic C-Métisse concept of 2006, the 2008 Hypnos concept with its stunning interior, and the »C4 and »C3 Picasso minivans that at last regained the initiative from Renault.

Promoted in 2008 to lead the design of the Peugeot brand too, Ploué began working on creating a distinct identity for each marque and restoring momentum to »Peugeot. The 2009 BB1 concept was a well-received cross between two scooters and an urban electric car, and early indications of a new design language were signalled with the elegant SR1 sports coupé concept the following spring.

Despite Peugeot's historic success with »Pininfarina-penned models, Ploué remains determined to keep Peugeot design in-house. He has displayed skilful judgement in bringing the individuality back to Citroën, while resisting any tendency towards the bizarre. He now needs to show the same sure touch and restore clear design values to the lion brand.

2001 CITROËN OSMOSE CONCEPT

2006 CITROËN C4 PICASSO

2008 CITROËN C3 PICASSO

2008 GTbyCITROËN CONCEPT

2006 CITROËN C-MÉTISSE CONCEPT

PONTIAC

UNITED STATES | 1926–2009 | VOLUME CARS | PONTIAC.COM

Pontiac is one of the famous General Motors brand names terminated in the wake of the American giant's post-2000 rationalization, along with Oldsmobile, »Saturn and »Hummer. While Oldsmobile had been linked with innovation and Saturn with a fair deal for the consumer, Pontiac's associations are overwhelmingly those of a vibrant, sporty brand with high-powered muscle cars, aggressive design and a generally provocative character. It is an image that derives from the brand's big hits of the 1960s, when it can lay claim to having produced the first muscle car, the GTO.

Shamelessly stealing the designation of a much-revered Ferrari, Pontiac engineers (including John DeLorean, who later launched his own car company) created the GTO by breaking internal company rules and fitting a big V8 engine reserved for large cars into a special edition of the mid-size Tempest; this proved a sure-fire magnet for affluent, horsepower-obsessed younger buyers, and the nameplate continued until 1974.

The second model line fuelling the sporty Pontiac image was the Firebird, first launched as a parallel model to the Chevrolet Camaro in 1967. This was one of GM's most successful Coke-bottle designs and worked even better as a Pontiac than a Chevrolet. Instead of a separate bumper bar, the Firebird had its whole grille surrounded by a thinner chrome strip, reinforcing the impression of a car lightened for competition. Later Firebirds went even further, with a soft frontal moulding linking quadruple square lamps with what would become the classic 'dual port' split Pontiac grille.

The evaporation of the muscle-car boom in the face of the fuel crises of the 1970s posed something of a problem for GM's product planners. Pontiac's sporty models rolled back on power and speed, although there was little dilution of the aggressiveness of body design and detailing, especially with the sinister razor-edged shovel nose of the second-generation Firebird in its

1953 FIREBIRD I CONCEPT

1963-GENERATION GTO

1984 FIERO

Trans Am incarnation. By the time of the third generation, in the 1980s, interest was waning, and even the more imaginative 1993 fourth generation, showing influence from Chevrolet's 1986 Corvette Indy concept, failed to stir up the old magic.

Pontiac had already spread to other segments, with the dramatic Trans Sport minivan, complete with nose reminiscent of a high-speed train, and a deal with Toyota to build a Corolla-based compact minivan in California appeared to put an end to Pontiac as an enthusiast brand. The disastrous Pontiac Aztek of 2001, which was said to have inspired more jokes than buyers, seemed to seal Pontiac's fate. A minivan-based crossover aimed at a hip youth audience, the Aztek's scarcely believable ugliness cast the judgement of GM's planners into doubt, and, despite heavy incentives, sales reached only one third of their targets. Unquestionably, the brief episode damaged the brand.

Bob Lutz, the self-styled product tsar who rejoined GM in 2001 (having previously worked there in the 1960s) vowing to get things done and not to let bureaucratic processes stifle initiative, had different ideas for Pontiac. He proclaimed it a sporty brand once again, showing the inspirational Solstice concept for a two-seater sports roadster in 2002 and rolling out a series of potent rear-wheel-drive muscle cars, such as the reborn GTO in 2004 and the G8 in 2008. They posed as American icons, but both were imported from Australia (one of the few markets still to favour rear-wheel drive) as rebadged versions of the Holden Commodore.

Unlike the GTO and the 2006 Torrent, Pontiac's first SUV and a version of the Chevrolet Equinox, the »Solstice was not

1999 CONCEPT GTO

2001 AZTEK

2006 TORRENT

2004 G6

2008 G8 GXP

PRINCIPAL MODELS	
1941	Torpedo coupé
1953	Parisienne Dream Car; Firebird I concept, first of several Firebird concepts
1959	Bonneville
1963	GTO – first muscle car
1967	Firebird
1968	Banshee concept
1973	Grand Am
1984	Fiero sports car
1989	Trans Sport
1999	Concept GTO
2001	Aztek; Vibe concept
2002	Solstice roadster concept
2004	GTO is rebadged Holden Commodore; G6 sports sedan
2005	Solstice
2006	Torrent – first Pontiac SUV
2008	G8, G8 GXP sports truck

an exercise in badge engineering or brand tinkering. True to Lutz's word, GM invested in the wholly new light rear-drive Kappa platform for the Solstice, also spawning the reborn Opel GT in Germany and the short-lived Saturn Sky.

The 2005 Solstice gained much good press for Pontiac, but it was already too late. None of the GM numbers added up, and with its other marginal brand, Buick, saved by its growing and profitable presence in China, it was Pontiac that GM culled in its post-bankruptcy reorganization.

PONTIAC SOLSTICE

2005–2009 | COMPACT ROADSTER

2009	
LENGTH	3995 mm (158 in.)
LAYOUT	Front engine, rear-wheel drive
ENGINE	2.4 petrol 4-cyl 16V
HORSEPOWER	173
MAX. SPEED	220 km/h (136 mph)
CO$_2$ EMISSIONS	–

Originally shown as a concept in 2002, the Solstice was the first proof that General Motors' charismatic 'car-guy' vice president, Bob Lutz, had meant what he'd said when he promised to get great new cars into production quickly in order to have the giant GM corporation firing on all cylinders again.

The concept for this compact, lightweight two-seater roadster proved wildly popular; within a few years Lutz had stirred up the notoriously sluggish GM engineering machinery and developed a new platform to animate it. All was kept pure and simple, as it was in the »Mazda MX-5 the Solstice was aimed at. Clothing the hydroformed rear-wheel-drive chassis and 2-litre engine was a smooth body of gentle, rounded forms and soft but simple details; the twin Pontiac grilles were no more than smooth honeycomb mesh wrapped round the curve of the nose.

Although the Solstice was joined by a »Saturn version, the Sky, as GM desperately sought to revive that brand, neither were destined to last long. GM pulled the plug on both marques in 2009 and also stopped supplies to Opel/Vauxhall, who had sold the model as the GT.

PORSCHE

GERMANY | FOUNDED 1948 | PREMIUM CARS | PORSCHE.COM

HISTORY

1900	Ferdinand Porsche develops Lohner Porsche electric car
1923	Designs Mercedes Kompressor sports car
1931	Sets up own design bureau
1933	Develops V16 Auto Union racer
1934	Designs Volkswagen Beetle
1948	Beetle-based 356 is first Porsche-badged car
1950	Porsche begins building sports cars
1951	Ferdinand Porsche dies
1970	Wins Le Mans 24 Hours and 2nd sports car championship
1971	Weissach technical centre opens
1984	First of 3 F1 world championships as engine supplier
1992	CEO Wendelin Wiedeking steers Porsche away from bankruptcy
1998	Takes decision to launch SUV as 3rd model line
2005	Begins building stake in VW
2008	Lifts VW stake to 74%
2009	Bid fails; VW takes 49.9% of Porsche
2011	Closer integration into VW Group

Porsche is one of the few car marques about which it is hard to be neutral. So much is evoked by the smooth, sweeping Porsche silhouette, so powerful is the howl of the flat-six engine, and so sophisticated is the finely honed precision engineering. To a petrol-head these are irresistible signals that immediately send the pulse racing; to the ecological campaigner they represent all that is worst about arrogant power and speed and the antisocial behaviour of the rich. Extreme reactions, perhaps, but equally valid nonetheless, for

each is a response not to an actual car but to a stereotype. That is how powerfully symbolic the Porsche profile has become.

Such archetypes do not arise overnight. They are the outcome of many generations of messages that are consistent and uninterrupted, and on a brand level this means a clear line of evolution with small and sensible steps between generations so as to preserve the all-important continuity over time. The Porsche »911 is the textbook example of this: the latest incarnation is unmistakably a direct descendant of the 1964 original, and you don't have to see any intermediate generations to make the connection. The 911 has the clearest image and the greatest brand equity that any single model has ever had, but this in turn has its drawbacks. So strongly is the Porsche image centred on this brand champion that, as the company found out to its cost in the 1970s with the 924 and 928, models that diverge from this icon tend to be ignored or, worse, rejected.

What those models had tried to do was to reinvent the Porsche sports car in a different format, one that would allow for better handling and greater development potential than the 911. With its rear engine, just as in the original VW-derived 356 of the 1950s, the 911 has unique proportions, its taut waistline stretched rearward from the headlamps and the arched roofline sweeping smoothly rearwards to cover the

1948 356

2005 BOXSTER

1977 928

engine. With their front engines, long hoods and glassy rear hatchbacks, the 924 and 928 had a completely different aesthetic. Buyers weren't keen, so Porsche played safe and kept developing the 911 in parallel before dropping the other two.

Having learned its lesson, Porsche played safe with its next line, the »Boxster: with a mid- rather than rear-mounted engine, this again had a different proportion, but by cleverly keeping the nose and rest of the body language the same as the 911's, it ensured the loyalty of the Porsche buyer. And for its second generation, in 2005, the Boxster repeated the 911's trick of barely perceptible changes to such details as lights and vents, again guaranteeing continuity.

A tougher design challenge was posed by Porsche's decision to enter two additional market sectors. The 2002 Cayenne luxury SUV sought to present the Porsche take on a Range Rover rival, and in 2009 the Panamera appeared as a luxury sedan. Porsche's recipe for the high-riding SUV's frontal identity was a double-deck nose with a sloping hood set between 911-style streamlined lights; below this was a lower layer of very deep air intakes. The rest of the vehicle was soft and bulky and, overall, the design was poorly received. The »Panamera, designed under »Michael Mauer, is similarly cautious, with classic 911-shaped headlights and a very gentle rise in waistline to the bulky hatchback rear window. The effect is that of a 911 widened and stretched in length, but the greater height results in much visual mass around the rear doors and a disappointing lack of tension. That said, the nose is very clearly designed to advertise the 911 connection.

Further design challenges lie ahead as Porsche is drawn closer into the Volkswagen Group, and shared platforms bring not only the likelihood of smaller and cheaper Porsche sports cars but also the need to differentiate possible Audi and VW models built on the same architecture. The 918 concept shows a more fluid, more emotional design language in a neat supercar format, and Porsche designers will relish the task of addressing a younger and more open-minded audience with fresh designs that jump into the future rather than evolve from a long-running stereotype, however sacred that stereotype has been.

2002 CAYENNE

1997 911

PRINCIPAL MODELS	
1948	356
1953	550 Spyder
1964	911, initially 901
1967	914 VW-Porsche
1975	924 with front engine
1977	928
1985	959 with 4-wheel-drive
1993	Boxster roadster concept
1996	Boxster
1997	911 adopts water cooling
2002	Cayenne is first Porsche SUV
2003	Carrera GT
2005	Cayman is coupé Boxster
2009	Panamera sports sedan
2010	911 GT3-R flywheel hybrid racer; 918 concept

2010 918 CONCEPT

PORSCHE 911

2004 | LUXURY SPORTS CAR

MODEL HISTORY (KEY LANDMARKS) 1963 901 • 1964 911 • 1973 'G' SERIES • 1979 911SC • 1988 911 (964) • 1993 911 (993) • 1997 911 (996) • 2004 911 (997)

2010 3.6 FLAT 6	
LENGTH	4435 mm (175 in.)
LAYOUT	Rear engine, rear-wheel drive
ENGINE	3.6 petrol 6-cyl
HORSEPOWER	345
MAX. SPEED	289 km/h (179 mph)
CO_2 EMISSIONS	242 g/km

FERDINAND ALEXANDER PORSCHE, GRANDSON OF PORSCHE FOUNDER, AND 1963 901

It's likely that more column-inches have been written about the Porsche 911 than any other car, old or new. Over a succession of generations and nearly fifty years it has transcended any role it might have had as just another sports car in the Porsche catalogue. Instead it has become an archetype for speed, status and engineering prowess that is recognized worldwide, a phenomenon that has developed a life of its own over and above any input from Porsche designers and technicians.

For the past thirty years the 911 has been the benchmark against which magazines, customers and even other sports-car makers have chosen to compare rival products; most recently, Nissan declared that its GT-R, a coupé completely different in every way to the 911, was being engineered to beat the 911 Turbo. Within Porsche the 911 long ago acquired the status of the company crown jewels, a sacred text that could not be rewritten, merely fine-tuned. The upshot has been a slow-motion evolution of the car's external design such that in purely aesthetic terms today's car is a comparatively modest step forward from its 1964 forebear. Compare this with how Ferrari has advanced the design of its most comparable model, the 1969 Dino 246, into today's »Ferrari 458 Italia, and the scale of the difference is clear.

None of this means that the 911's development is in any way less valid, merely that it has taken place in more of a vacuum than would have been the case with other, less linear carmakers. Advances tend to be

advances in Porsche terms, closely focused on the demands of its devoted clientele; owners and commentators tend to see these steps as technical progress rather than aesthetic enhancements.

Yet the summation of all these advances has made the 911 a vastly more capable machine than its inherently problematic rear-engined layout should in theory allow. This is a triumph of systematic development. Only in recent years has that focus been allowed to expand to other model lines.

It did seem for many years that Porsche could not control the 911, and that it was the 911 that controlled Porsche. Soon, however, that unquestioned icon will be allowed to get on with its job of being a great sports car while Porsche makes its plump profit margins on heavyweight 4x4s and luxury sedans instead.

1993 911 TURBO

2004 911 TURBO S

2010 911 SPEEDSTER

PORSCHE BOXSTER, CAYMAN
2005 | MEDIUM SPORTS CARS

MODEL HISTORY 1996 BOXSTER 1ST GENERATION • 2005 BOXSTER 2ND GENERATION • 2005 CAYMAN

2010 BOXSTER S	
LENGTH	4340 mm (172 in.)
LAYOUT	Rear engine, rear-wheel drive
ENGINE	3.4 petrol 6-cyl
HORSEPOWER	310
MAX. SPEED	274 km/h (170 mph)
CO$_2$ EMISSIONS	230 g/km

2005-GENERATION BOXSTER AND 1960 718 RS SPYDER

In the early 1990s Porsche was effectively a single-model company, totally dependent on the expensive »911, and it had come close to bankruptcy after the American market for luxury sports cars collapsed. A new generation of managers prescribed an additional line of smaller models sharing some of their parts with a re-engineered 911: all would benefit from reduced costs and, thanks to advice from Toyota, more efficient production.

The smooth and compact Boxster concept at the 1993 Detroit motor show was the first outward evidence of the new strategy: penned by Dutch designer Harm Lagaay, it evoked the mid-engined RS racing cars of the 1950s and was symmetrical in its gentle front and rear contours. The interior was particularly imaginative; one unusual feature was that the grilles within each cabin air vent allowed for a glimpse of bright metal fan blades.

The production Boxster emerged as a two-seater roadster that was slightly larger and more assertive, but no less charming. The dashboard was notably more adventurous than anything Porsche had done before, and in engineering terms the move to a mid-mounted and now water-cooled flat-six was significant. So too was the fact that the engine, such a point of pride among Porsche customers, was hidden under a panel and could not be seen by the owner.

Priced at little more than half the cost of the 911 but just as well made, the Boxster gained rave reviews for its handling and balance, and it became such a sell-out hit

that Porsche had to subcontract some of the production to an outside manufacturer. Steadily more powerful versions followed, with a second generation in 2005. Espousing the philosophy of gradual change, the second series was so subtly updated that only owners could tell the difference.

The Cayman introduced an interesting stylistic twist: adding a fastback coupé glasshouse to the lower body of the Boxster. The proportions became overlaid with those of the 911, moving the visual centre forward and creating greater tension in the design. As it was for the 911, the way forward for these mid-market Porsche models is likely to be a process of gradual evolution, with the innovative thinking reserved for future still-smaller models yet to come.

2010 BOXSTER SPYDER

2005 BOXSTER

2010 BOXSTER SPYDER

PORSCHE CARRERA GT

2003–2006 | EXTREME SPORTS CAR

2006	
LENGTH	4615 mm (182 in.)
LAYOUT	Mid engine, rear-wheel drive
ENGINE	5.7 petrol V10
HORSEPOWER	612
MAX. SPEED	330 km/h (205 mph)
CO_2 EMISSIONS	–

If it is possible to have a mid-engined supercar with an exotic brand name, ten cylinders, 600-plus horsepower and a top speed of more than 200 mph, but precious little aesthetic emotion, then the Porsche Carrera GT is it.

First previewed as a concept at the 2000 Paris auto show, the Carrera GT was well received and Porsche decided on a limited-run production at its newly opening Leipzig centre, with each of the 1500 examples to be priced at around US$450,000.

Away from the euphoria of the show stand, it became clear that the appeal of the Carrera GT was much more closely focused on its technology and its crushing performance than on its aesthetics. The external shape is purely functional, with little attention paid to warmth or passion: the nose is little more than a copy-across of »911 design cues, and, as on the »Boxster, the rear fenders wrap simply round the tail – indeed, the GT's proportion is that of a stretched and squared-up Boxster.

Interest, where it occurs, is largely technical: on the Carrera GT's extended rear deck, for example, where the double-hoop rear roofline fights uncomfortably with the nacelles over the long engine, and the bridge spoiler, which changes its angle depending on speed through the use of hydraulics, stretched between the rear fenders.

PORSCHE PANAMERA

2009 | LUXURY CAR

2010 4.8T V8	
LENGTH	4970 mm (196 in.)
LAYOUT	Front engine, rear-wheel drive
ENGINE	4.8 turbo petrol V8
HORSEPOWER	500
MAX. SPEED	303 km/h (188 mph)
CO$_2$ EMISSIONS	286 g/km

With no visual heritage in the luxury sedan class, Porsche could not afford to take the patient Lexus route and gradually build up a fresh corporate identity to rival that of BMW and Mercedes-Benz. Instead, it decided to take the image that it is most famous for, the »911 sports car, and trade on it.

This becomes clear at first glance. Front-on, the Panamera is a 911 but with the proportion dramatically widened; from the side, it is again 911 front and rear, but with a long centre section added to stretch the proportion and give the long, shallow window graphic of a limousine. From the rear, especially from a higher vantage point, it is pure 911 in the rounded shapes, the rear lights and the long slope of the rear screen.

Overall, while the exercise may be successful in signalling Porsche's arrival as a sedan brand, in design terms it has resulted in an unimaginative shape with a weighty look and awkward angles. Only the Panamera's interior stands out as a design highlight. Overall, »Aston Martin has done a much better job with the »Rapide. Yet, as always, the customers have the final word, and the long waiting lists show that, with Porsche, brand is more powerful than design.

MAREK REICHMAN

GREAT BRITAIN | BORN 1966 | CAR DESIGNER

Marek Reichman is best known as the designer who helped to bring James Bond's favourite marque, »Aston Martin, to the attention of a worldwide audience – not merely in terms of customers (the exclusive brand's annual output still remains in four figures only) but also in terms of visual identity and brand recognition. Reichman successfully expanded the template set by his predecessors »Henrik Fisker and »Ian Callum to encompass extreme sports cars, racing coupés and a luxurious four-door coupé, the Rapide.

Reichman began his career at Rover, then moved to BMW Designworks in California in 1995. Following then-CEO Jacques Nasser's reorganization of Ford, which involved a new studio in Irvine, California, Reichman joined »Gerry McGovern to take on responsibility for both Lincoln and Mercury. This creative period yielded a series of concepts that sought to cultivate a premium image for »Lincoln and to differentiate »Mercury from Ford. The Messenger, reminiscent of an early 1960s Corvette, is one such concept. Yet these initiatives fell apart when Ford refocused on its core brand after the resignation of Nasser as CEO.

Arriving at Aston Martin in 2005 with the »DB9 already established and the smaller »V8 Vantage just launching, Reichman began exploring a broadening of the Aston portfolio. The most dramatic of these extensions has been the »Rapide four-door coupé, shown to great acclaim as a concept in 2006; the following year Ford sold Aston Martin to a syndicate of Middle Eastern interests. It was strongly suspected within the design community that it was pressure from these investors that led to the creation of the brash and poorly received 2009 Lagonda concept for a large SUV. This is the only blot on Reichman's portfolio of classically elegant (if very similar) luxury sports cars that vie with Ferrari for status and instant recognition.

2003 MERCURY MESSENGER CONCEPT

2003 LINCOLN NAVICROSS CONCEPT

2002 RANGE ROVER

2006 ASTON MARTIN RAPIDE CONCEPT

2010 ASTON MARTIN ONE-77

RENAULT

FRANCE | FOUNDED 1898 | VOLUME CARS | RENAULT.COM

Any student of the automotive industry seeking evidence of the importance of design to a company's fortunes need look no further than Renault. Engineering, marketing, handling, economy: all have played secondary roles to that of design in those Renault products that have enjoyed the biggest success over the years.

With Renault, design goes much deeper than the mere embellishment of a set of mechanical components. While others might style cars to look good, the best Renault designs spring from new ways of doing things or new user needs to cater for. That's why so many of Renault's designs over the years have pioneered new market segments and changed the way we think about our cars.

The roll-call of Renault game changers is impressive. The small and stylish Dauphine in the 1950s showed that cheap cars could be chic; the R4 of 1961 was a back-to-basics car/van/estate with simple charm; the R16 of 1965 invented the idea of the family hatchback. The fresh and smart R5 (1972) kicked off the trend for supermini hatchbacks, later to be taken up by the Volkswagen Polo and Ford Fiesta, while the 1980 Fuego, a smoothly contoured coupé, showed that sporty cars could be practical, too. The really influential ones, however, were the »Espace in 1984 (no explanation needed), the 1992 »Twingo and, in 1996, the »Scénic – the first car to be truly shaped around the needs and budget of the everyday family. By distilling the practicality of the large Espace into a convenient and affordable mid-size design, Renault discovered a huge groundswell of demand, forcing all its competitors to rush back to their drawing boards to develop cars to combat the Scénic.

The Kangoo the following year added a friendly face to the humble light van, thus making the passenger-carrying version attractive to families and prompting the appearance of yet another segment: that for low-cost utilitarian station-wagons. Later,

BRIGITTE BARDOT AND 1959 FLORIDE

1956 DAUPHINE

1972 R5 AND 1985 R5

HISTORY

1898	Renault brothers produce first cars
1901	Marcel Renault dies in accident
1911	Billancourt factory opens
1914	Renault taxis take troops into combat
1925	First win in Monte Carlo Rally
1940	Occupation of France by Germans; 4CV engine designed in secret
1944	Louis Renault dies
1945	State ownership
1952	Flins plant opens
1974	Buys Berliet trucks
1975	Buys American Motors Corporation. Robert Opron becomes head of styling
1977	Enters F1, first win in 1979
1978	Wins Le Mans 24 Hours
1986	CEO Georges Besse murdered
1987	Sells AMC. Patrick le Quément becomes head of design
1990	Alliance with Volvo
1992	Louis Schweitzer becomes CEO
1998	Technocentre opens
1999	Renault-Nissan Alliance. Takes control of Dacia, Romania
2000	Buys Samsung, Korea
2005	Carlos Ghosn becomes CEO. F1 world champion
2009	Laurens van den Acker becomes head of design

2006 NEPTA CONCEPT

2003 BEBOP CONCEPTS

the versatile Modus would try with rather less success to bring Scénic values into the small-car segment, hampered by the perceived toy-like style of its upright shape.

The Espace predated »Patrick le Quément's arrival as Renault design director in 1987, but everything since has sprung from his belief that design should be a central instrument in strategic planning, not just the icing on an already-baked cake. In particular, he insisted that design should be represented at board level with equal weight to engineering.

The first evidence of le Quément's activities was a rush of concept cars, imaginative and ambitious and stretching the Renault brand in many unexpected

2008 ONDELIOS CONCEPT

directions, such as sports cars (Laguna concept, 1990) and luxury cars (Initiale, 1995). The charming 1992 Twingo city car was first to bring the fresh thinking into the showrooms, but it was the first Mégane generation, starting in 1995 and with five eventual versions, each tailored to a different user group, that showed design and industrial planning truly working together.

The astonishing success of the Scénic has been well documented, but the jury is still out on the follow-up Mégane hatch in 2002: with its provocative rear-end design it had a certain shock value when first released, after which it sold well before fading quickly. Le Quément counts this as one of his disappointments and is open about the others, in particular the eccentric Avantime coupé-minivan and the stately Vel Satis, which failed in its bid to persuade customers of German luxury brands to switch to a French-flavoured alternative.

Renault design appeared to flounder badly towards the end of the decade, with dull follow-ups to the large Laguna and small Twingo especially disappointing; the third-generation members of the Mégane family were more me-too in their design, no longer the clear leaders in their segments; even the key Scénic ceded the advantage to its Citroën rival, the C4 Picasso.

With the appointment of »Laurens van den Acker as head of design in 2009 there is evidence of a new clarity, and of a new momentum around electric vehicles and the fresh Renault face, first seen on the warm and sensuous DeZir coupé concept at the 2010 Paris auto show. The quality and imagination shown in this concept, and in the two key electric models Twizy ZE and Zoe ZE, give every confidence that Renault design can continue to be the most influential in the volume-car segment. The subsequent 2011 Captur and R-Space concepts – a muscular crossover and an imaginative minivan respectively – confirm that Renault is once again back on track.

2008 MÉGANE COUPÉ CONCEPT

2010 DEZIR ELECTRIC CONCEPT

2009 TWIZY ZE CONCEPT

2009 ZOE ZE CONCEPT

PRINCIPAL MODELS	
1898	Voiturette
1905	AG taxi
1929	Reinastella 8-cylinder
1937	Juvaquatre
1946	4CV, in production until 1961
1956	Dauphine
1959	Floride, by Ghia and Frua
1961	Renault 4, in production until 1992
1965	R16
1971	R15, R17
1972	R5
1980	Fuego
1984	Espace, R25; SuperCinq, by Marcello Gandini
1988	Mégane concept
1990	Clio; Laguna concept
1991	Scénic concept
1992	Twingo; Zoom concept
1994	Argos concept
1995	Mégane hatchback, Spider; Initiale concept
1996	Scénic; Fiftie concept
1997	Kangoo
1998	Clio (2nd gen); Vel Satis concept
2001	Avantime
2002	Mégane hatchback (2nd gen), Vel Satis; Ellypse concept
2003	Espace (4th gen); Bebop concept
2004	Modus, Dacia Logan
2005	Clio (3rd gen); Zoe concept
2006	Nepta concept
2007	Twingo (2nd gen)
2008	Mégane hatchback (3rd gen); Mégane coupé and Ondelios concepts
2009	Scénic (3rd gen); Zoe ZE and Twizy ZE concepts
2010	Wind roadster; DeZir electric supercar concept
2011	R-Space and Captur concepts

RENAULT CLIO

2005 | COMPACT CAR

MODEL HISTORY 1990 CLIO 1ST GENERATION • 1998 CLIO 2ND GENERATION • 2005 CLIO 3RD GENERATION

2010 1.6	
LENGTH	4030 mm (159 in.)
LAYOUT	Front engine, front-wheel drive
ENGINE	1.6 turbo petrol 4-cyl
HORSEPOWER	110
MAX. SPEED	190 km/h (118 mph)
CO₂ EMISSIONS	160 g/km

The Renault 5, in production since it had invented the so-called supermini class in 1972, was a hard act to follow. More than fifteen years after it was introduced, and even though it was technically tired, the design still held a certain classy flair, which Renault needed to retain in the R5's replacement while simultaneously moving the game on.

The 1990 Clio did this admirably, thanks to its clean and contemporary style, its roomy interior and its well-organized dashboard. The second generation followed in 1998 with a more rounded and voluminous expression of the same theme, adding a key external distinguishing feature: a rear screen rolling round into the roof, in the style of the 1994 Ludo small-car concept. This concept previewed many small-car themes, not just the general style of the Clio but also Smart's later Tridion exoskeleton structure. An astute facelift in 2004 then gave it further momentum, with larger, more upright headlights, a divided grille and a very much stronger personality.

Much of this identity went to waste with the third-generation Clio in 2005. A busy style with oversized headlights and a pronounced shoulder running forward from the rear lights made the Clio hard to read, and appeared to be intended to make the car look bigger. A facelift in 2009 did bring a superficial resemblance to the larger »Mégane, but it also introduced Peugeot's much-debated open-mouthed frontal style.

2011 CLIO

1996 CLIO

1999 CLIO

2005 CLIO

2004 CLIO

RENAULT ESPACE

2003 | LUXURY MINIVAN

MODEL HISTORY 1984 ESPACE 1ST GENERATION • 1991 ESPACE 2ND GENERATION • 1996 ESPACE 3RD GENERATION • 2003 ESPACE 4TH GENERATION

2005 2.2 DICE 16V	
LENGTH	4660 mm (184 in.)
LAYOUT	Front engine, front-wheel drive
ENGINE	2.2 turbo diesel 4-cyl
HORSEPOWER	150
MAX. SPEED	190 km/h (118 mph)
CO$_2$ EMISSIONS	206 g/km

Espace-type vehicles are now so universally accepted and appreciated that today, thirty years on from the launch of the Espace, it is hard to believe how controversial it originally was. The impetus for the Espace did not come from within Renault, but the French carmaker made the idea its own and expanded it imaginatively to take in all shapes and sizes of highly practical single-volume vehicles.

The Espace has gone on an upmarket journey, growing from its initial sharp-edged train style, through a softer and more aerodynamic 1990s shape, to the most recent, a more intricate and more obviously styled body with expressive contours and elegant details. All the while, the versatile flat floor and removable and repositionable individual seats have remained; travel comfort has stepped up from good to outstanding; and game-changing innovations, such as repositioning the instruments to the dashboard centre, and placing the bulky heating and air conditioning modules under the floor to save space, have been notched up en route.

The Espace has done more than just change the course of car design. It has also opened up our horizons when it comes to travel and transport.

FOUR GENERATIONS OF ESPACE

RENAULT MÉGANE

2008 | MEDIUM CARS

MODEL HISTORY 1995 MÉGANE 1ST GENERATION • 2002 MÉGANE 2ND GENERATION • 2008 MÉGANE 3RD GENERATION

2010 2.0 TCE	
LENGTH	4295 mm (170 in.)
LAYOUT	Front engine, front-wheel drive
ENGINE	2.0 turbo diesel 4-cyl
HORSEPOWER	180
MAX. SPEED	225 km/h (140 mph)
CO$_2$ EMISSIONS	178 g/km

The unassuming and slightly flimsy-feeling Mégane five-door hatchback that emerged from Renault in the autumn of 1995 was the start of something much bigger. It has had a deep influence on the way the automobile industry develops, designs, markets and manufactures its cars.

The Mégane hatch was the first of a family that would later encompass five further versions, each sharing the same technical architecture and components, thus saving development time and reducing the cost of manufacture. By coordinating the design of the hatchback, coupé, sedan, station-wagon, convertible and, in 1996, the breakthrough »Scenic medium minivan, Renault was able to flood the market with new products and keep its factories running at peak capacity and efficiency, improving its profit margins in the process.

In terms of design, the Méganes were different but clearly related, with a shared theme of rounded details set against the background of simple, easy-to-read body shapes. Interior themes and components were generally shared.

The arrival of the bold second-generation Mégane in 2002 was one of the biggest shocks inflicted on the car business. The three- and five-door hatchbacks shared the same lean, neatly chamfered lower body, and each had a vertical wraparound rear window (modelled on the Vel Satis concept of 1998) above what was unflatteringly referred to as a fat butt of a trunk. The hatchbacks differed in the architecture of the greenhouse: the five-door used upright

pillars, while the three-door had a dramatic semicircular profile to its side windows, leaving the C-pillar as a large point-down triangle. Some loved it; many began by hating it but eventually became admirers.

The attractive wagon and coupé-convertible followed a similar style at the front, leaving the awkward-tailed sedan as the runt of the litter.

The Mégane third generation in 2008 brought high expectations but disappointing design. The main five-door hatch and three-door coupé-hatch adopted a much bulkier and harder-to-read look, with a ridged-edge hood standing proud of the headlamps and a heavy, drooping stance at the front. The rear lost its focus, too, looking excitingly sporty from some angles but clumsy and ungainly from others.

2002 MÉGANE

1995 MÉGANE

426

RENAULT SCÉNIC

2009 | MEDIUM MINIVAN

2010 1.9 DCI	
LENGTH	4345 mm (172 in.)
LAYOUT	Front engine, front-wheel drive
ENGINE	1.9 turbo diesel 4-cyl
HORSEPOWER	130
MAX. SPEED	195 km/h (121 mph)
CO_2 EMISSIONS	149 g/km

If there is a single model that defines the shift in car-design priorities over the past two decades, it is the Renault Scénic. Prior to the Scénic, cars tended to be either luxurious, sporty or utilitarian. Post-Scénic, those same cars have become more intelligent, more adaptable and more practical for everyday tasks. What the Scénic has added is the human touch, the realization that rather than forcing ourselves to fit in with our cars, our cars should adapt to us.

It all began in 1991 with the truly visionary concept that launched not only the Scénic name but also the idea of travel as an adventure for the whole family. This roomy mini-Espace, built on a mid-size platform, housed five 'continents' (the seats, each upholstered in different colours to represent different continents) as well a wealth of new ideas for stowage, comfort and safety.

The potential was clear, and a compact »Espace-type vehicle at a family-friendly price was factored into Renault's plans for the 1995 »Mégane. The Scénic version appeared in 1996 to instant acclaim: buyers immediately took to its high build, progressive good looks and outstanding practicality. Its success was well beyond Renault's expectations, and other carmakers rushed to ready new designs to compete.

Only Citroën, with the Xsara Picasso, managed to come up with a plausible answer. Soon afterwards Renault brought out its second-generation Scénic, now a model in its own right, along with a new trump card: the seven-seater Grand Scénic,

designed to bridge the growing price jump to the luxury Espace. Once again, Renault was ahead, but not for long. Citroën's 2006 C4 Picasso, also in two sizes, outsmarted the now tired-looking Scénic, and Renault lost market leadership for the first time.

Renault's counterstroke, the third-generation Scénic of 2009, missed its target, failing to move the minivan design game on in the way the C4 Picasso had done. With this series, Renault tried to cultivate a difference between the sportier five-seater and the longer, more luxurious seven-passenger models. Yet, uncharacteristically, Renault designers appeared to have run out of imagination, leaving the initiative in Citroën's hands.

2003 SCÉNIC

1996 SCÉNIC

RENAULT TWINGO

2007 | SMALL CAR

MODEL HISTORY 1992 TWINGO 1ST GENERATION • 2007 TWINGO 2ND GENERATION

2010 TWINGO 1.2 T	
LENGTH	3600 mm (142 in.)
LAYOUT	Front engine, front-wheel drive
ENGINE	1.2 turbo petrol 4-cyl
HORSEPOWER	100
MAX. SPEED	185 km/h (115 mph)
CO_2 EMISSIONS	138 g/km

For a car that was so small, so simple and so cheap, the Renault Twingo made a very big impact when it was wheeled out at the 1992 Paris auto show.

The Twingo, the first all-new design under ambitious design director »Patrick le Quément, brought something entirely new: the idea of a small car as a warm and cuddly family pet, a faithful friend to everyone in the household. The design, by a team including »Anne Asensio and future PSA Peugeot Citroën group design director »Jean-Pierre Ploué, was deliberately human in its expression, with big friendly 'eyes' set into a warm and smiling 'face'. Yet its overall format, as a single-volume micro-»Espace, was highly advanced, as were its versatile seating arrangements and the new feeling of interior space (gained through a windshield pushed far forward and instruments minimized into a small display in the centre of the dash). Picking out minor controls in a bright contrasting colour added to the playful feeling, and Renault's decision to offer only one engine and chassis specification made it cheap to buy, too.

Yet after its impressive fifteen years in production the first-generation Twingo was followed up for its second generation by a disappointing, mainstream and unimaginative design. Bringing back the original Twingo's inspirational streak should be high on the to-do list of new design director »Laurens van den Acker.

1992 TWINGO

1975 CAMARGUE COUPÉ

1980 SILVER SPIRIT

the final split in 2003, there was a Bentley equivalent too. Neither was to remain in production long: Vickers sold the two marques to Volkswagen in 1998. VW retained Bentley and the Crewe headquarters; the rights to Rolls-Royce, from the beginning of 2003, went to BMW for £50 million.

BMW had bought the Rolls-Royce name, the double-R logo and the 'flying lady' mascot, but no cars, no designs, no factories and no customer lists. The challenge it faced was the complete reinterpretation for the new millennium of a globally cherished automobile institution. Having asked BMW designers worldwide to submit proposals for the new Rolls-Royce identity, design chief »Chris Bangle assembled an international team under Briton Ian Cameron to work on the new model in conditions of great secrecy, in a former National Westminster bank premises in London's upmarket Mayfair district. Early

2004 100EX CONCEPT AND 2003 PHANTOM

PRINCIPAL MODELS

1907	Silver Ghost
1925	Phantom
1936	Phantom III with V12 engine
1949	Silver Dawn
1955	Silver Cloud
1965	Silver Shadow
1975	Camargue coupé, by Pininfarina
1980	Silver Spirit
1998	Silver Seraph
2003	Phantom
2004	100EX V16 convertible concept
2006	101EX coupé concept
2007	Phantom drophead coupé
2008	Phantom coupé
2009	200EX concept, becomes Ghost

2008 PHANTOM COUPÉ

2003 PHANTOM

on, BMW had identified the 1950s Silver Cloud as the model that best epitomized the Rolls-Royce ethos to be revived for the twenty-first century: its stature and sheer scale, its stately curves, its sweeping tail and its tall, temple-like grille, were all much admired.

Yet there were gasps as the »Phantom was unveiled in 2003. Cameron's design was bold and imposing, bordering on the severe with its Parthenon grille, big square lights, huge 21-inch wheels and massive C-pillars to provide privacy for rear-seat passengers. BMW had specified an imposing, bold presence, and the Phantom surely delivered it. It was certainly clever in its classical-looking interior, with such modern necessities as the sat-nav screen hidden away behind exquisitely veneered wooden panels; the rear doors were hinged at the back for more graceful entry and exit.

Following the Phantom in 2004 was the 100EX concept, precursor to the Phantom convertible of 2007. Although similar in theme, this introduced the polished-metal contrast engine cover and the distinctly vintage touch of front doors hinged at the rear and closed from the inside by a push button. The related coupé (2008) introduced another much-admired innovation: the 'starlight' roof, an interior roof lining custom-wired with thousands of light fibres to resemble the sky at night.

The latest chapter in the Rolls-Royce saga is the smaller and less imposing »Ghost. By going for a lower build, more steeply sloped screens front and rear and a more curved bodyside section, the design team has been able to give the car a more dynamic stance. This is exactly what is needed for modern customers who might just want to take the wheel themselves.

2009 200EX CONCEPT

2007 PHANTOM DROPHEAD COUPÉ

ROLLS-ROYCE GHOST

2009 | SUPER-LUXURY CAR

2010	
LENGTH	5400 mm (213 in.)
LAYOUT	Front engine, rear-wheel drive
ENGINE	6.6 turbo petrol V12
HORSEPOWER	570
MAX. SPEED	250 km/h (155 mph)
CO_2 EMISSIONS	317 g/km

Labelled 'the baby Rolls' by the media throughout its gestation period, the Rolls-Royce Ghost is a baby only on the RR scale of measurement: just 430 mm (17 in.) less from stem to stern than the stately standard-wheelbase Phantom, it is longer than any »BMW 7 Series or »Mercedes-Benz S-Class.

The brief to chief designer Ian Cameron was to come up with a modern and more dynamic Rolls-Royce that had all the hallmarks of the great cars of the past but in a less imposing, more engaging package. The skill of the Ghost's design can be seen in how the car looks so much handier and shorter, even though the difference against the tape measure is not that great.

The Ghost's classic RR Parthenon grille, slightly angled back, has its effect amplified as its surround wraps into the air intake below. A short front overhang and wide-set wheels plant the Ghost securely on the road, and the combination of more steeply sloped A- and C-pillars lends a lower, more agile look to the glasshouse, the DLO being highlighted by a bright trim surround. The final expert touch is the subtle slant to the rear deck and tail panel, combining dignity with a discreetly rakish style that will have Bentley worried.

ROLLS-ROYCE PHANTOM

2003 | SUPER-LUXURY CAR

2010	
LENGTH	5834 mm (231 in.)
LAYOUT	Front engine, rear-wheel drive
ENGINE	6.75 petrol V12
HORSEPOWER	460
MAX. SPEED	240 km/h (149 mph)
CO_2 EMISSIONS	377 g/km

There can have been few design assignments more daunting – or more exciting – than that given to Ian Cameron by BMW Group bosses at the end of the 1990s: to re-create for the twenty-first century the identity of the proudest and most conspicuous automobile marque in the world, Rolls-Royce, which the German company had just acquired in a three-way deal with Volkswagen.

Armed with no more than the rights to the double-R emblem and close study of RR heritage, the embryo Rolls-Royce design team identified a key theme for any new Rolls-Royce as a feeling of superior status through sheer size and presence. Also, the driver and passengers had to sit high up in relation to the occupants of everyday vehicles.

The 2003 Phantom proved to be even more imposing and more stately than many had expected. Largely composed of straight lines, especially at the front, it showed little of the flowing elegance of the 1950s Silver Cloud that was its role model: only in the tapering tail could a hint of affection be seen. Critical reaction was divided, but the world's super-rich were unanimous: majestic splendour had been restored, Rolls-Royce was once again the best car in the world, and the Phantom was the car in which to be seen.

SAAB

SWEDEN | FOUNDED 1947 | PREMIUM CARS | SAAB.COM

In an automotive business overflowing with surplus capacity and aspiring premium-car brands, it could be argued that no one needs Saab and the 100,000-odd cars it builds in a good year. But the enormous outcry that arose when General Motors was about to shut Saab down in late 2009 shows a very different sentiment: dealers, owners, prospective customers and scores of fanatically loyal fan clubs around the world all desperately want Saab to stay because its cars have an individuality and a strength of character not seen in any other carmaker's products.

The resilience of that character is clear to see. The popular picture of Saab as a nonconformist, an offbeat innovator and a builder of quirky and confident cars has survived intact through twenty years of GM control, despite the American giant's best efforts to constrain Saab's eccentricities and force it into a convenient standard-sized corporate box.

With the nail-biting last-minute rescue of the stalled Swedish carmaker by bespoke supercar maker »Spyker of The Netherlands, an automotive icon has been saved and cultural commentators can relax. Spyker CEO Victor Muller is brimming with confidence that, thanks to independent management and a return to freethinking design, more than enough current and former Saab owners will invest in a new-era Saab to push the Trollhättan plant into profitable production. But what, precisely, will these comeback customers be buying into?

First and foremost, Saab's heritage derives from its origins as an aircraft maker: the original 92 of 1949 was very light and extremely aerodynamic, and its successors, the 95 wagon and 96 sedan, were clever in their use of space. In 1968 the idea moved to the middle ground with the larger 99, but Björn Envall's design was no less individualistic for it: the engine sat on top of the gearbox, the ignition key was next to the gear lever and the wraparound

1949 92

1960 96

1977 99 TURBO

1986 900 CONVERTIBLE

2006 AERO-X CONCEPT

443

windshield hid under a heavy beetle brow. This was a car whose appeal was confined to the cognoscenti, but it was Saab's next big move – the turbocharger – that brought the brand near-universal recognition. With its long combi-coupé tail, distinctive alloy wheels and searing performance, the black 99 Turbo was the car of the moment in the late 1970s, and it quickly became the defining model for the Saab brand. The 900 that followed was an intelligent evolution, with bigger bumpers and the first of Saab's fabulously clear aircraft-style interiors; it built upon the character of the 99.

No such continuity could be claimed for the 1984 9000 Turbo. Styled by Giugiaro and part of a four-car common structure deal with Fiat, Lancia and Alfa Romeo, this immensely roomy car could have been a corporate conformity disaster. But Saab's engineers managed again to imbue it with dynamic character, even if the quirkiness was limited to the aircraft instrument panel and the ignition switch being positioned on the floor, alongside the handbrake.

It all started to go wrong in 1990 when GM, piqued at being pipped at the post by Ford to buy Jaguar, swooped on Saab as its European premium brand. The second-generation 900 looked much like the old one but, following the GM dictum that it had to take thirty hours to make (rather than 110 as had been the case previously), it was built on the outdated Opel/Vauxhall Ascona platform. Its dynamics suffered, and Saab loyalists hated it. A rebranding as the 9-3 a few years later moved the ignition switch to the floor as a peace offering, but the car still failed to convince. A new platform and a new style in 2002 resulted in a much better car, but the style could equally well have been that of a BMW or Toyota, so again it failed the fans' test.

The larger 9-5, replacing the 9000 and also built on an outmoded GM platform, showed more character when decision-makers chose the most radical proposal for the station-wagon version, yet still there was the underlying feeling that this was not the car the Saab people really wanted to build. The new 2009 9-5 shares less with Opel/Vauxhall, but the dull hand

2009-GENERATION 9-5 SPORTWAGON

2008 9-X BIOHYBRID

2009 9-5

of GM's caution has quashed any real character in its shape.

The growing trend towards distinctive premium small cars presents a great opportunity for Saab to succeed with a model that repackages the 96's individualistic appeal in a more modern format. The next 9-3 in 2012 could incorporate inspiration from »Anthony Lo's remarkable 2006 Aero-X concept, a design that has been something of a beacon of hope for Saab loyalists. An engine deal with BMW gives further cause for confidence – provided, of course, that Saab's financial backers hold their nerve until these promising new models reach the showroom.

2011 9-4X

SAAB 9-3 CABRIOLET
2003 | LUXURY CONVERTIBLE

MODEL HISTORY 1986 900 1ST GENERATION • 1994 900 2ND GENERATION • 1998 9-3 1ST GENERATION • 2003 9-3 2ND GENERATION

2010 2.0 16V	
LENGTH	4635 mm (183 in.)
LAYOUT	Front engine, front-wheel drive
ENGINE	2.0 turbo petrol 4-cyl
HORSEPOWER	150
MAX. SPEED	210 km/h (130 mph)
CO$_2$ EMISSIONS	192

So many Saab models from the 1980s and 1990s could have filled this slot, but in a book devoted to twenty-first-century car design only the Cabriolet does the job of linking today's bland, General Motors-guided 9-3 and 9-5 with the powerful characters of the 99 and 900 Turbo that forged Saab's unique pre-GM personality.

Miraculously, the Saab 9-3 Cabriolet (Convertible in North America) has clung to the classy yet unorthodox aura put out by the very first version way back in the 1980s as a car for freethinkers and those who cared. Somehow, the driver of a Saab Cabrio, even a Turbo, was seen as being a more sympathetic individual than the driver of the equivalent BMW or Mercedes. Yet the earliest Cabriolets, proofed against arctic conditions, were in truth somewhat shaky on poor roads. The second generation was little better, and it took until the current iteration in 2003 for the dynamics of the Cabriolet to match up to its by then sky-high reputation.

Saab's new owner, Dutch supercar maker »Spyker, is keen to develop new models that tap into the emotions of great Saabs of the past. The 96, introduced in 1960, is top of the list for reinterpretation, and it's a fair bet that a thoroughly modern Cabriolet is not far behind.

1998 SAAB 9-3 CABRIOLET

SALEEN

UNITED STATES | FOUNDED 1983 | EXTREME SPORTS CARS AND PERFORMANCE PARTS | SALEEN.COM

Racing driver Steve Saleen began in the 1980s developing and selling performance parts for Ford models, especially the Mustang, for both street and track use. Before long he had begun to sell complete tuned vehicles to which he gave his own model designations. He gradually moved into other Ford models, including the XP8 Explorer SUV, which he described as the world's first performance utility vehicle.

By the mid-1990s Saleen's ambitions were widening beyond the confines of tuner cars, and he engaged collaborators to develop a mid-engined supercar of his own design. The Saleen S7, unveiled at California's Laguna Seca raceway in 2000, used a modified version of a Ford NASCAR race engine. Priced at more than $600,000, it attracted much media interest, not least among those who shared Saleen's ambition of seeing an all-American supercar challenging the dominance of the Italian brands at the most exotic level of car design. In 2002 Saleen again became news as the company selected by Ford to build the prestigious »Ford GT supercar for its centenary, and contracts to build showcars for Ford followed. Saleen also built cars for films, such as *Transformers* (2007).

The Saleen S7, meanwhile, was steadily increasing in speed and power, with a twin-turbo version at more than 1000 horsepower claiming the title of the world's most powerful production car in 2006. Yet production was never great enough to sustain the business. The lighter and much more elegantly styled S5S Raptor that replaced the extravagant S7 never got off the ground, and after Steve Saleen's exit in 2007 the company reverted to its original business of supplying fearsomely fast Mustangs and performance parts for Ford models.

HISTORY AND PRINCIPAL MODELS

1983	Performance parts for Ford models
1995	S351 Speedster
1998	Explorer XP8
2000	S7 supercar
2002	Assembly of Ford GT
2004	S7R beats Lamborghini. Ferrari, Maserati in Imola, Italy
2006	S7 twin turbo exceeds 1000 hp
2007	Steve Saleen leaves company
2008	S5S Raptor concept shown at New York motor show
2009	Acquired by MJ Acquisitions
2011	S281 Mustang

2011 S281 MUSTANG

SAMSUNG

KOREA | FOUNDED 1998 | VOLUME CARS | RENAULTSAMSUNGM.COM

Korean giant Samsung was the fourteenth-largest industrial company in the world in 1996 when it announced its intention – against the advice of banks, commentators and competitors – to enter the market for cars and to become a global top-ten player by 2010. To get its automotive operation off to a smooth start it enlisted the cooperation of Nissan, which was eager to get a foothold in the notoriously closed-off Korean market. Yet by the time Samsung launched its three-car range in 1998 the market was saturated and the Asian crisis was beginning to take hold. Just 52,000 cars had been built before the automotive operations fell into receivership the following year.

This suited Renault, which had just formed an alliance with Nissan and saw Samsung as a useful base for production, design and monitoring. Within a year Renault Samsung Motors (RSM) had been formed and a mid-term development plan drawn up. Production resumed in 2002 with lightly facelifted versions of the SM3 medium car and the larger SM5, a sedan based on the Nissan Teana. In 2004 the launch of the much more luxurious SM7, a variant of the SM5, signalled RSM's longer-term intentions of forging a semi-premium position midway between the domestic Korean producers and the pricey imported brands.

The next phase of RSM's development has been its integration into Renault-Nissan's international network of design, development and manufacturing. The SM3 is being exported under two Nissan nameplates (Sunny and Almera), and the freshly developed crossover SUV built on the »Nissan Qashqai platform is sold in Europe as the Renault Koleos. The latest twist in this saga is Renault's new Latitude sedan, destined to be the company's flagship: it is to be built in Korea as a derivative of the new-generation Samsung SM5, which is itself based on the architecture of the Renault Laguna.

2011 SM7 CONCEPT

HISTORY AND PRINCIPAL MODELS

1998	Samsung enters Korean market with Nissan-derived models
1999	Market collapses and Samsung Motors enters receivership
2000	Renault wins control with 80% stake
2001	Reveals mid-term development plan
2002	SM3
2004	SM7 luxury car
2005	New SM5
2006	SM3 exported under Nissan brand
2007	QM5 crossover SUV
2008	QM5 exported to Europe as Renault Koleos
2009	New SM3; eMX concept at Seoul auto show
2010	New SM5 on Laguna architecture
2011	SM5 exported to Europe as Renault Latitude. SM7 concept

2009 SM3

2007 QM5

2008 XB

2004 TC

2008 XB

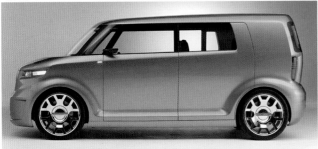

2005 T2B CONCEPT

SEAT

SPAIN | FOUNDED 1950 | VOLUME CARS | SEAT.COM

For the first quarter-century of its existence SEAT was a well-kept industry secret, building its versions of Fiat models under a very restrictive licence purely for the protected Spanish domestic market, and visible only to tourists picking up rental cars for their holidays. But after the death of dictator Francisco Franco in 1975 the Spanish market opened up to foreign competition, Fiat began to let SEAT export its products (which at that stage were still restyled versions of Fiats) and the Spanish automaker began to make inroads as an entry-level brand in many European markets.

Finally freed from the shackles of its historical deal with Fiat, in the early 1980s SEAT shopped around Europe for the best available consultants to shape its planned new model range, and it signed up »Giorgetto Giugiaro for design and Porsche for engine work. The Ibiza supermini launched in 1984 was a real turning point for the brand. Giugiaro's lines were strikingly elegant and pure, and the System Porsche branding for the engine (for which SEAT paid DM7 – about £3 – per vehicle) added exceptional credibility for a small car.

One person who was particularly impressed was Volkswagen's then boss, Carl Hahn. SEAT already had a contract to distribute VW and Audi vehicles in Spain; Hahn was able to persuade the Spanish government to sell some of the country's stake in SEAT, and by 1986 VW had gained control and was planning how to expand the company's output and integrate it into VW's international operations.

Giugiaro was commissioned to come up with a trio of concepts for medium-sized cars to complement the Ibiza. Of these, from today's perspective the smooth mono-volume Proto C stands out as being much the most advanced; but it was the notchback Proto TL that went on to become the 1991 Toledo, and it was joined two years later by the second-generation Ibiza – a disappointingly heavy, high-waisted design.

2005 LEON

Sensing that SEAT was still not pulling its weight in VW's international empire, the German bosses began dispatching their big guns to Spain; this included Erwin Himmel, who had a line of Audis to his credit, to set up a new design centre in Sitges, along the coast from Barcelona. Himmel shaped the 1998 Bolero concept and the related 1999 Leon hatchback, but it was with the snatching of »Walter de'Silva from Alfa Romeo (he had styled the acclaimed 156) that SEAT design began to be more widely noticed. The 2000 Salsa concept was his statement of intent. With a high build and a smooth sweep from the front bumper, over the hood, windshield and roof and back down over the rear window to the back bumper, it was a dramatic new silhouette, and with its floating trapezoidal central grille it established a new frontal identity that would stay with the brand for a decade.

Sadly, however, two of the three production models spun off from the Salsa were destined to bomb in the market, further aggravating SEAT's reputation as

2008 IBIZA

2010 IBE CONCEPT

the problem child within the VW network. The Altea and new Toledo both incorporated the new front, but their exaggerated height created an awkward overall proportion that no amount of sculpting of the sides was able to balance; the later long-wheelbase Altea had much better visual equilibrium. The 2005 Leon, a more conventional low-rise hatchback, made the most attractive use of the Salsa's genes, although at the expense of poor visibility for the driver.

By this stage »Luc Donckerwolke, from Lamborghini, had come on board to replace de'Silva, who had been called to Germany to oversee Audi as well as the Italian and Spanish brands. Donckerwolke's influence was first seen in the 2007 Tribu concept for a compact SUV, and in the 2008 Ibiza, complete with fashionable broken waistline and sculpted sides. The coupé version of this has the better proportions, and the theme was distilled even more compellingly in the small and engaging 2010 IBE electric coupé, again a show concept.

Considering that many excellent SEAT concepts have failed to make production (for example, the fabulous little Tango roadster of 2001), it is paradoxical that the wheel should have turned full circle for the company. In 2008, in a bid to buy credibility in the executive sedan market, SEAT launched the Exeo, a warmed-up previous-generation Audi A4 built on Audi machinery shipped over from Germany.

2007 TRIBU CONCEPT

2000 SALSA CONCEPT

2001 TANGO CONCEPT

SKODA

CZECH REPUBLIC | FOUNDED 1905 | VOLUME CARS | SKODA-AUTO.COM

HISTORY

1895	Vaclav Laurin and Vaclav Klement begin making bicycles
1905	Build first cars
1924	Fire destroys works; weapons maker Skoda takes over
1945	Becomes state owned under planned economy
1991	Establishment of joint venture with VW Group
1993	Dirk van Braeckel appointed chief designer
1999	Thomas Ingenlath is head of design
2006	Jens Manske is head of design
2008	Jozef Kaban becomes head of design

1934 POPULAR

1936 RAPID

Skoda is unusual among automakers, appearing almost as often in business textbooks as it does in car magazines and newspapers. It rose seemingly effortlessly from unreliable and outmoded four-wheel joke in the 1980s to admired quality product and top customer-satisfaction provider little more than a decade later, making it a perfect case study for any MBA student wanting to demonstrate the effectiveness of well-thought-out design and marketing strategies in rehabilitating a brand. More recently, Skoda's strategy to push its brand still higher into a clearer quality role is also attracting interest from business academics.

Not long after Volkswagen had gained management control of Skoda in 1991 (outsmarting Renault, which had been interested too) the then CEO Ferdinand Piëch, explained his positioning strategy for the group's two new brands: he wanted »SEAT to be a competitor to Alfa Romeo, while Skoda would move into the same league as Volvo – in other words, become a byword for quality, practicality and respectability. At the time the Skoda plan seemed much the

1996-GENERATION OCTAVIA

PRINCIPAL MODELS	
1929	422
1934	Popular
1936	Rapid
1959	Octavia, Felicia convertible
1964	Rear-engined M100 replaces Octavia
1981	Rapid coupé
1987	Favorit is first front-drive Skoda
1994	Felicia, first all-new car under Volkswagen
1996	Octavia, on VW Golf platform
1999	Fabia replaces Felicia
2001	Superb, on stretched VW Passat platform
2003	Roomster concept
2004	Octavia (2nd gen)
2005	Yeti concept
2006	Roomster; Joyster concept
2007	Fabia (2nd gen)
2008	Superb (2nd gen)
2009	Yeti

2006 ROOMSTER

2008 SUPERB

more implausible. Now, with a line-up ranging from the sturdy Fabia hatchback to the large and genuinely luxurious Superb estate, it is the Czech firm that has come the closest to attaining Piëch's target.

Skoda's first design under its new owners was the 1994 Felicia, similar in size and proportion to the previous mainstay model, the Favorit, but based on the »Volkswagen Polo platform and clearly much better built. The big step up came two years later with the Octavia. Reviving another famous Skoda name, »Dirk van Braeckel's five-door hatchback on the »Volkswagen Golf platform was precisely what was needed to bring confidence and trust to the brand: simple, solid and practical, it had a modern but not trendy profile and a secure stance on the road. A big trunk and a well-resolved interior helped, too. The model and its wagon derivative were such successes that VW Golf sales were affected as consumer magazines advised that the Octavia was in effect a Golf without VW's premium price.

The smaller Fabia, Skoda's equivalent of the Polo, brought the Skoda range fully up to date in 1999, and the brand stretched higher two years later with the Superb – again a revival of an old name. Although outwardly following the theme of the Octavia, the Superb was in fact built on a lengthened »Volkswagen Passat platform, once more frightening the opposition with its combination of keen price, roominess, build quality and classy looks.

With these three models well established and with Volkswagen's well-stocked parts warehouse allowing every combination of powertrain, body style and trim, Skoda had achieved respectability and completely banished any memories of its bad old models. Now it could afford to expand the brand upward and outward, and it began to explore niches with such key show concepts as the offbeat Roomster high-roofed leisure wagon, the playful Yeti light SUV and the innovative Joyster, a high-rise coupé with a fold-out tailboard that turned into a picnic bench. Often overlooked is the 2002 Ahoj! study, an attractively simple compact hatchback in the »Fiat Panda/ »Renault Twingo mould. When the Skoda Roomster and »Yeti reached the showrooms, they were larger and softer than the showcars, but in other respects retained the same shape and feel. The Joyster and Ahoj! did not make production.

When the Fabia was renewed in 2007, it adopted a consciously more youthful tone with a Mini-like contrast-colour roof and a range of customization options. This did not sit happily with what had come to be accepted and respected as Skoda's Ikea approach to design: decent and attractive products at moderate cost. This down-to-earth approach has made Skoda one of the big successes of recent times, and has enabled it to be perceived as something unique: a superior offering within the value-brand segment.

2007 FABIA

2005 YETI CONCEPT

2007 FORD MONDEO

2010 FORD FOCUS

465

SPYKER

THE NETHERLANDS | FOUNDED 2000 | EXTREME SPORTS CARS | SPYKERCARS.NL

HISTORY AND PRINCIPAL MODELS

2000	Victor Muller revives Spyker name for supercar venture. C8 Spyder prototype
2001	C8 competes at Le Mans 24 Hours for the first time
2004	Spyker floated on stock market
2005	C12 LaTurbie with W12 engine
2006	Profitable. Buys Midland F1 team. D12 Peking-to-Paris SSUV concept
2007	Sale of Spyker F1 team agreed. C12 Zagato shown; later postponed
2008	Lotus cooperates on D12 development. C8 Aileron
2009	Spyker assembly transferred to UK
2010	Spyker buys Saab

2000 C8 LAVIOLETTE SWB

2006 D12 PEKING-TO-PARIS CONCEPT

For a company that has made fewer than three hundred cars in its born-again existence, Spyker has perfected the art of punching above its weight, both in terms of the scale of the tasks it takes on and in the publicity it manages to generate.

Founded by financier, entrepreneur and car collector Victor Muller in 2000 after he had offered to help a designer friend to make a home-built supercar ready for the road, Spyker revives an honourable Dutch name from motoring's golden era, when large cars were handmade for wealthy clients who did not have to ask the cost. The original Spyker ceased production in 1926.

Today's Spyker Aileron is lower, more agile, more sophisticated and, with a turbocharged Audi engine giving more than 400 horsepower, very much faster than the original cars were. Yet it is still hand-built and beautifully crafted using the finest materials, and still draws its customers from a wealthy elite. That's why Spyker's sales – at more than €300,000 per car – remain in double figures, and only once, in 2006, has the company declared a profit.

Already a regular participant at the Le Mans 24 Hours and in other long-distance races with its road-derived cars, Spyker bought the Midland Formula One team in the same year, only to sell it again a year later in the face of huge losses.

Spyker's so-called super-sports utility vehicle concept, the D12 Peking-to-Paris, was presented in 2006. Powered by an Audi W12 engine and with the allure of a supercar on steroids, it was aimed at wealthy clients in countries where the roads were too poor for the super-fast Aileron. Critics gave it the thumbs down and the project was postponed. In 2010 Muller and Spyker hit the headlines for very different reasons: as the successful saviours of »Saab. Such is Muller's confidence in his new acquisition that it is easy to imagine Saab eventually having to save Spyker.

2009 C8 AILERON SPYDER

2008 C8 AILERON

SSANGYONG

KOREA | FOUNDED 1986 | SUVS | SMOTOR.COM

Even by the erratic standards of Korean car companies, SUV maker Ssangyong is unusually strike- and bankruptcy-prone. It has spent many periods in its twenty-five-year history at a standstill or in the limbo of receivership, the latest being a long period of uncertainty following the acrimonious collapse of relations with its one-time Chinese majority shareholder, Shanghai Automotive Industry Corporation (SAIC), which had previously given Ssangyong some much-needed stability after its 2002 bankruptcy. That deadlock had in turn come about as a result of the spectacular crash of »Daewoo, which had acquired Ssangyong and other companies in 1997 in a mad rush to expand, just as the Asian bubble was about to burst.

Small wonder, then, that Ssangyong's product development has been sporadic and unconventional. Its models throughout have been defined by the Mercedes-Benz technology licensed from 1991 onward; only recently has it been able to break away from this, with the new 2010 Korando, the first Ssangyong with modern componentry.

The 2010 Korando continues a Ssangyong nameplate that first appeared in 1988 on a compact, Jeep-like SUV. Unusually for a Korean company, Ssangyong's models, the work of Briton Ken Greenly, are all distinctive rather than bland in their styling. The 1993 Musso was notable for its droopy, pointed front; incredulity greeted the 2004 Rodius, a bizarre large station-wagon looking as if two different models had been welded together; and the 2005 SUV trio of Actyon, Kyron and Rexton II still draw puzzled glances.

For the 2010 Korando Ssangyong took a very different tack, employing the talents of »Giorgetto Giugiaro to come up with an attractive and much calmer-looking crossover SUV well suited to a broad spectrum of markets. With this design in place and »Mahindra of India at the controls, Ssangyong no longer has such awkward questions to answer.

HISTORY AND PRINCIPAL MODELS

1986	Ssangyong Business Group buys Dong-A Motors
1988	Korando utility SUV
1991	Mercedes-Benz investment
1993	Musso luxury SUV, by Ken Greenly
1997	Bought by Daewoo; models rebranded Daewoo
2000	Goes into receivership with Daewoo
2001	Rexton medium SUV
2003	Creditors invite bids for Ssangyong
2004	SAIC of China takes 51% stake. Rodius large wagon
2005	Actyon, Kyron, Rexton II, all by Greenly
2009	Receivership; production halted
2010	Mahindra of India declared preferred bidder. Korando II, by Giorgetto Giugiaro
2011	Mahindra takes control

1993 MUSSO

2004 RODIUS

2010 KORANDO

FRANK STEPHENSON

MOROCCO | BORN 1959 | CAR DESIGNER

1999 BMW X5

Car designers don't come more cosmopolitan – or more broadly experienced – than Frank Stephenson. Born in Morocco of Norwegian and Spanish parents on the same day in 1959 as the original BMC Mini was launched, Stephenson was destined forty years later to design the all-new BMW »Mini Cooper that would relaunch Mini mania. Celebrated as something of an expert in rekindling the emotion of past favourites in a modern form, he would later lead the design team that produced the spectacularly successful Fiat 500. It says something about Stepheson's standing in popular automotive mythology that these are by far his best-known designs, even though he also penned the original »BMW X5 and the »Alfa Romeo MiTo,

supervised several Ferraris and Maseratis, and is now in charge of design at McLaren.

Inspired as a schoolboy by a glimpse of a Ferrari Dino, Stephenson caught the car-design bug that would lead him to the Art Center College of Design in California, then to Ford and on to a job at BMW. As lead designer on the 2001 Mini programme, Stephenson's fame was assured; a call came from no less a legend than Ferrari, where his skill in supervising the work of retained design agency »Pininfarina resulted in the fabulous F430 and the »Maserati Quattroporte.

Greater acclaim was in store at Fiat, where Stephenson led the team that developed the Bravo in less than 18 months and the 500 in rather more. The »Fiat 500 has been widely lauded for the sensitive way it reinterprets key design points of the 1957 original in a modern context, but by the time it was launched Stephenson had already left the Fiat group. His destination was McLaren, where the 2011 »MP4-12C is the first of several supersports car designs on the stocks.

2001 MINI COOPER

2004 MASERATI MC12

468

PETER STEVENS

GREAT BRITAIN | BORN 1945 | CAR AND TRUCK DESIGNER AND CONSULTANT

1989 LOTUS ELAN

2002 ROVER TCV CONCEPT

Known in the car-design world as something of a guru, Peter Stevens is by any standards unusual. Throughout his working life he has managed to remain an independent freelance operator, even during the years when he was design director for »MG Rover, and he has maintained a strong relationship with the Royal College of Art in London, where he was the first graduate of the vehicle-design course and where he continues to teach as a visiting professor.

In the broader car business, however, Stevens is best known as the man who shaped the front-wheel-drive 1989 Lotus Elan and the 1992 McLaren F1, at that time easily the fastest car ever built. He was faced with the challenge of clothing a very unusual engineering package, where the driver sat in the centre of the vehicle with the two passengers alongside, but further back. Stevens's solution for the 360-km/h (224-mph) rocket was simple, elegant and above all compact, resisting the standard supercar clichés of large aerodynamic add-ons and excess detailing.

Stevens was fortunate in already having experience in ultra-high-performance car design in the shape of the Jaguar XJR-15, effectively a roadgoing version of the Jaguar Le Mans-winner. He also shaped BMW's 1999 Le Mans car, but it was his later work with the struggling MG Rover group that shows him as such a highly skilled designer. On a minimal budget, Stevens facelifted sober-looking Rovers into sporty sharp-suited MGs, which sold well; he updated the MGF roadster to become the TF; and he produced the imaginative TCV sport-wagon concept to some acclaim at the 2002 Geneva auto show. This versatile and stylish vehicle predated such current sports minivans as the Ford S-Max, and was exhibited with a washing machine upright in the cargo bay to demonstrate its roominess.

2002 MG TF

1992 MCLAREN F1

SUBARU

JAPAN | FOUNDED 1953 | CARS AND CROSSOVERS | SUBARU-GLOBAL.COM

Subaru's modern-day image is dominated by one model: the fire-breathing Impreza WRX turbo, itself a direct descendant of the spectacular bright blue rally-winning Imprezas of the 1990s. The sudden appearance of the first Impreza turbo in 1993 was something of a surprise on the automotive scene. Up to that point Subaru had been thought of as an oddball but not especially sporty manufacturer, best known for its characterful flat-four engine, all-wheel-drive chassis and the occasional eccentric styling touches that led some commentators to label it the Japanese Citroën. Examples include the acutely wedge-shaped 1985 XT Alcyone coupé – complete with crazy interior controls – and the appealing but unsuccessful SVX, a big flat-six-powered GT coupé styled by »Giorgetto Giugiaro.

Subaru's L-series Leone that preceded the Impreza was unusual for more than the detail of its design or its boxer engine: this was a neat, compact station-wagon with four-wheel drive, and it proved popular in mountainous areas on both sides of the Atlantic. As such, it was the precursor of today's generation of crossover SUVs. It would spawn the Brat 4x4 pickup version as well as the bigger Forester and Outback crossovers.

As for the Impreza, the focus has tended to remain on the linear development of the turbo version towards ever more powerful engines and wilder body kits; Subaru's two restyles – in 2000 and 2007 – were not well received by the model's fanatical customer base, nor was the ugly B9 Tribeca luxury SUV, aimed at rivalling the BMW X3.

Now in the orbit of its biggest shareholder, Toyota, Subaru is co-developing the FT86 rear-drive sports car, with Subaru power, which might add much-needed design flair to the line-up.

2003 B9 SCRAMBLER CONCEPT

1985 XT ALCYONE

1991 SVX

HISTORY AND PRINCIPAL MODELS

1953	Fuji Heavy Industries established out of former Nakajima aircraft maker
1954	First car is P1 1500
1957	Subaru 360 is Japan's first minicar
1965	First flat-four boxer engines
1972	Leone (L-Series) with 4-wheel drive and flat-four. Brat is pickup version of L-series
1985	XT Alcyone sports coupé
1989	Legacy sedan and wagon
1990	Enters world championship rallying
1991	SVX luxury performance coupé, by Giorgetto Giugiaro
1992	Impreza
1996	Forester
1997	Outback crossover
1999	GM takes 20% stake
2000	Impreza (2nd gen)
2003	B9 Scrambler sports car concept
2005	GM sells stake, Toyota takes 8.7%. B9 Tribeca luxury SUV
2007	Impreza (3rd gen)
2008	Flat-four diesel is world first. Toyota increases stake, announces sports-car cooperation

2007 IMPREZA

SUZUKI

JAPAN | FOUNDED 1909 | SMALL CARS AND SUVS | GLOBALSUZUKI.COM

Suzuki is perhaps the quietest and most cautious of the Japanese automakers, but it has been the most consistently successful over the years. It has achieved this by sticking to what it knows best – small cars and small-to-medium 4x4s – and by making itself invaluable to other automakers by providing them with a handy supply of off-the-shelf models to fill gaps in their line-ups. A current example of this is the Nissan Pixo: it is in fact a Suzuki Alto, built in India by »Maruti Suzuki, and an exact twin of the Maruti A-Star. The European Opel/Vauxhall Agila, likewise, is a Suzuki Splash, made by Suzuki in Hungary.

There is little room for design finesse in all this, although post-2007 models are notably sharper and fresher in style than the boxy mainstream products of earlier eras. That said, Suzuki's smaller SUV models, such as the Jimny, have always stuck to an appealingly honest and functional look that has brought them a clear identity, and the Cappuccino sports car of 1991 is a miniature masterpiece.

For Suzuki the big change came in 2004 with the Swift: previously a dull shrinking violet, it was suddenly transformed into something solid, strong and surprisingly Mini-like. This is one Suzuki model that has not been diluted from concept to production, unlike the flashy 2007 Kizashi concept, which went through two further concept stages before emerging as a disappointingly bland 2010 production model.

By Suzuki standards the Kizashi is a large car, and it confirms one long-standing observation about the brand: the most vibrant and engaging Suzuki design is to be found in the myriad micro models buzzing around Tokyo streets, and not in the mainstream models sent for export or overseas production.

1991 CAPPUCCINO

2002 ALTO LAPIN

2004 SWIFT

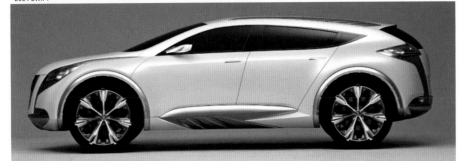

2007 KIZASHI CONCEPT

HISTORY AND PRINCIPAL MODELS

1907	Michio Suzuki opens loom works
1952	Moves into auto business with 32cc motorcycle
1955	Suzulight 360 cc 2-stroke minicar
1965	Fronte 800 2-stroke passenger car
1970	Jimny 4x4 debuts as 360 cc 2-stroke
1977	Jimny 8 has 800 cc 4-stroke
1979	Alto debuts as 550 cc minicar
1981	Tie-up as General Motors takes stake
1982	Agreement with Indian government to produce Suzuki cars
1983	Swift 1.0
1988	Vitara/Escudo leisure 4x4
1990	Agreement for production in Hungary
1991	Cappuccino mini roadster
1998	Agreement with GM to develop compact vehicles in Europe. Wagon R miniwagon
2002	Takes majority stake in Maruti of India. Alto Lapin compact car
2004	Swift hatchback (2nd gen)
2006	SX4 crossover co-developed with Fiat
2007	Splash small hatchback; Kizashi concept
2008	New Alto
2009	Volkswagen takes 20% stake
2010	Swift (3rd gen)

THINK

NORWAY | FOUNDED 1991 | ELECTRIC CITY CARS | THINKEV.COM

HISTORY AND PRINCIPAL MODELS

1991	PIVCO founded in Oslo
1992	First prototype built
1994	PIV2 prototypes built
1995	PIV3, limited production
1999	Ford buys a 51% stake. City series production begins
2003	Ford withdraws. Think bought by Swiss microelectronics firm
2004	Th!nk public concept
2006	Receivership. Bought by Norwegian investors, renamed Think Global
2007	Open convertible concept
2008	Ox concept
2009	Production restarts at Valmet Automotive's facility in Finland
2010	Think Global announces plans for production with partners in the USA and Japan. City electric car
2011	Declares bankruptcy

2008 OX CONCEPT AND 2010 CITY

Backed by a grant from the Norwegian government and venture capital, Oslo-based start-up PIVCO (Personal Electric Vehicle Company) aimed to create small lightweight cars using thermoplastic body panels over a spaceframe construction. These could have been petrol-, diesel-, fuel-cell or hybrid-powered, but the company decided to start with a battery concept, and stuck with it.

Under founding chairman Jan Otto Ringdal, PIVCO put its first prototype on the road in 1992, following up with an improved PIV2; ten were built for demonstration at the 1994 Winter Olympics in Lillehammer. PIV3, the City Bee/Citi, with a range of up to 145 kilometres (90 miles) and a top speed of 105 km/h (65 mph), took part in field trials, forty cars going to a programme in San Francisco.

PIV4, the first to take the Th!nk name (with exclamation mark), was further advanced with consultancy from Lotus; its appealingly personable bug-eyed face and outline by Stig Olav Skeie gave it a personality it had previously lacked. However, PIVCO had run out of money and went into receivership. Ringdal led a management buy-back and looked for investment from a bigger carmaker. Ford, which was interested in the construction concept, stepped up and took a 51 per cent stake in 1999, funding series production at a purpose-built factory in Aurskog and supplementing engineering work at its British technical centre.

Ford displayed the »Think City, as it was now called, at the 2002 Los Angeles and Detroit motor shows. It announced its intention to market a series of electric products under the Think brand, but pulled

the plug on the programme just a year later. Ford's shares were sold to the Swiss Kamcorp Microelectronics; a concept for an electric microbus, the Think public, was created, but production stalled and by 2006 Think was again in receivership.

Revived by a consortium of enthusiastic Norwegian investors, the company rebranded as Think Global (now officially minus the exclamation mark) and rethought its strategy. Its new name, and the Ox (five-seater) and Open (convertible) concepts, hinted at its expansion plans. Before Think once again declared bankruptcy in summer 2011, production at the Valmet facility in Finland had enabled a scaling up of output, and the firm exported widely across Europe, mostly in bulk deals for rental fleets, car clubs and other car-sharing groups.

THINK CITY
2010 | ELECTRIC CITY CAR

2010	
LENGTH	3140 mm (124 in.)
LAYOUT	Front engine, front-wheel drive
ENGINE	Electric
HORSEPOWER	40
MAX. SPEED	110 km/h (68 mph)
CO_2 EMISSIONS	0 g/km

The Think City evolved from prototypes built by PIVCO (Personal Independent Vehicle Company) of Oslo, trialled in the early 1990s. Thanks to »Ford investment in the Think brand, the very first Think made its series-production debut in 1999 (although Ford cancelled its programme in 2003) and was the first electric car to achieve homologation to European crash-safety standards. Its suspension and crumple-zone impact-absorption structures are accommodated within a high-tensile steel lower frame; its aluminium upper spaceframe is clad with thermoplastic moulded panels, unpainted and fully recyclable.

The City's form is determined entirely by its function: it was developed specifically to be a tough, user-friendly and easy-to-own runaround. Its short nose and deep glass tailgate give good all-round visibility and ease of parking; its 2+2-seater cabin is versatile and its body panels stand up well to the inevitable scratches and scrapes incurred in urban life. Prominent wheel arches (in which, unusually, the side indicators are mounted) and broad bumpers give it a squat stance and an attitude sometimes lacking in compact city cars.

Until the Norwegian consortium that produced the City declared bankrupcy in 2011, the car featured lithium-ion batteries that gave a much-improved range between recharges, and was in its fifth iteration, although it still owed much – including its switchgear and some suspension components – to Ford's earlier input.

FREEMAN THOMAS

UNITED STATES | BORN 1957 | CAR DESIGNER

Freeman Thomas, along with »J. Mays and »Peter Schreyer, is one of a now-celebrated coterie of designers who worked on the original »Audi TT and whose careers took off spectacularly, largely as a result of the design community's feting of the TT as an icon of modern design. Thomas is credited with having drawn the key sketch that led to the 1995 TT concept, mixing cues from pre-war German sports cars and the post-war Porsche 356 in a new design language dominated by circles and smooth, carefully calculated radii.

Very much the same themes had been evident the year before, although in a more upright form, as Mays and Thomas unveiled the Volkswagen Concept 1. Conceived in VW's Simi Valley studio in California, the Concept 1 was an instant success and led to the production New Beetle in 1998. The later Microbus concept was not taken up for manufacture.

Moving to Chrysler's Pacifica studio, also in California, in 1999, Thomas hoped to repeat the TT trick with a new compact sports car, the »Chrysler Crossfire; the 2001 concept, with its novel central spine feature, was well received. A key theme pushed by Thomas at Chrysler was that of the 'noble American sedan'. This led directly to the »Chrysler 300C concept and a very successful production model. Also memorable is Thomas's spectacular Dodge Tomahawk concept, a V10-engined car–motorcycle hybrid.

Hired by his former colleague J. Mays to head Ford's strategic design in 2005, Thomas arrived in the middle of the design process for the unusual Reflex compact hybrid sedan concept. Much more European than American in flavour, it encouraged Thomas to promote further compact concepts such as the 2009 Lincoln C, seating six within the footprint of a »Ford Focus, and the Start, unveiled at the 2010 Beijing auto show.

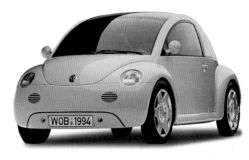

1994 VOLKSWAGEN CONCEPT 1 (NEW BEETLE)

2001 CHRYSLER CROSSFIRE CONCEPT

2003 DODGE TOMAHAWK CONCEPT

2000 JEEP COMMANDER

TOYOTA

In 1929, Kiichiro Toyoda travelled to Europe and the United States on a research mission: he was considering expanding his family's loom-making business and going into the automotive industry. A year later, the firm began developing gasoline engines, and it produced its first vehicle prototypes in 1935. The initial cars produced by the new Toyota Motor Company (the 'd' of Toyoda was changed to a 't' for easier pronunciation and depiction in Japanese characters) owed much to Western influence. The mechanicals of the A1 car and the related G1 truck were said to be rather similar to those of contemporary Fords, and the A1's streamlined body panels to have been inspired by the Chrysler Airflow.

The Jeep-style BJ (later renamed Land Cruiser) did much to establish Toyota's reputation for durability and solidity, but the company struggled to distinguish itself in design terms. The heavy-bodied Crown and more elegant Corona of the 1950s again mimicked the lines and details of popular American cars, although the smaller »Corolla and Publica of the 1960s were more European in flavour, with marked references to the workaday Austins and entry-level Fords of the time. Not that this mattered very much: Toyota was happily selling growing numbers of its unpretentious, plain-clothes products to buyers unconcerned about striking a pose.

Perceptions were challenged with the 1965 unveiling of the 2000 GT, hailed as Japan's first supercar. Influenced by designer Albrecht von Goertz's proposal for a sports coupé for Nissan (a precursor to the Datsun 240Z) but also paying homage to the Jaguar E-Type, Toyota designer Satoru Nozaki came up with a swooping, low-slung and muscular two-seat GT, pop-up headlights high on its bonnet and driving lamps behind sheets of Plexiglas. Expensive to build, and with a high price tag attached, the 2000 GT was an image-booster for Toyota – and the Japanese automotive

1966 COROLLA

1970 CELICA

2002 AYGO

2011 FT-86-II

1984-GENERATION MR2

industry as a whole – rather than a commercial success, but it did much to prepare consumers for the more accessible Celica and the hot-rod Supra. The marketing of these much-loved and long-running model series was backed up by Toyota's rallying activities, which culminated in Carlos Sainz's World Rally Championship wins of the 1990s before Toyota turned to Formula One instead.

Therein lies the dichotomy inherent in Toyota's product line-up for the last decades of the twentieth century: on the one hand, motorsport credentials and a worthy sports-car heritage; on the other, a series of terminally uninspiring family cars and subcompacts with only reliability to commend them, and a well-respected but ageing series of 4x4s, SUVs and trucks (although the RAV4 'soft-roader' was a genre-definer at its debut).

In more recent years, Toyota has addressed this problem by the application of technology – most notably in the »Prius hybrid – and the introduction of more adventurous small cars. These include the European-designed Yaris supermini, the city-friendly »Aygo produced in a joint venture with PSA Peugeot Citroën, and the cleverly packaged »iQ, an ingenious and intrinsically Japanese creation rather than a bland Euro-clone.

Indeed, much of Toyota's most imaginative thinking is in the city-car and urban-mobility spheres, as demonstrated by concepts such as the 2001 Pod, 2003 PM and 2005 i-unit, although it has also teased its intentions to build a more eco-friendly type of high-performance car with such concepts as the exotic hybrid Alessandro Volta and the FT-HS. And while the firm has recently come under harsh criticism and media pressure for alleged engineering faults, and has been forced to carry out extensive product recalls, Toyota continues to capitalize on its position as the foremost manufacturer of hybrid vehicles. As the Prius family of related vehicles expands, and hybrid, electric or fuel-cell models are added to existing ranges, the boundaries between Toyota's niche offerings and its mainstream products will become increasingly blurred.

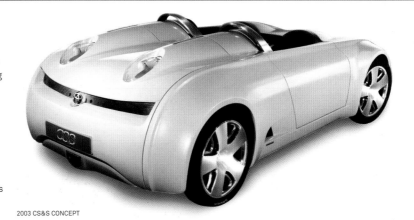

2003 CS&S CONCEPT

2005 i-UNIT CONCEPT

2007 FT-HS

PRINCIPAL MODELS

1935	G1; A1 concept
1936	AA
1951	Land Cruiser (BJ)
1955	Crown, Crown Deluxe and Master (taxi)
1957	Corona
1966	2000 GT, Corolla
1970	Carina, Celica
1971	Century GT45 gas turbine concept
1979	Supra; CX-80 concept
1981	Soarer (Lexus SC)
1984	MR2
1990	Sera
1991	AXV-IV concept
1994	RAV4
1995	Tacoma
1997	Prius; eCom concept
1998	Yaris, Harrier (Lexus RX)
1999	Tundra
2001	Pod concept
2002	Aygo
2003	CS&S and PM concepts
2004	Alessandro Volta concept
2005	Endo and i-unit concepts
2006	RAV4 (3rd gen)
2007	Auris, FT-HS, RiN and Hybrid-X concepts
2008	iQ, Corolla/Auris (10th gen); A-BAT concept
2009	Land Cruiser (10th gen), Prius (3rd gen); FT-EV and FT-86 concepts
2010	FT-CH concept
2011	Yaris (3rd gen), FT-86-II

2009 FT-EV CONCEPT

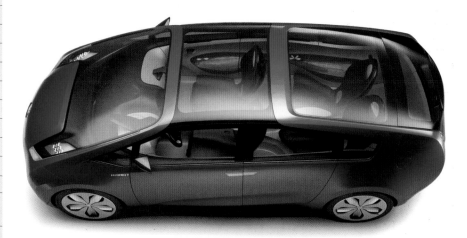

2007 HYBRID-X CONCEPT

2001 POD CONCEPT

2010 FT-CH CONCEPT

485

TOYOTA COROLLA/AURIS

2008 | MEDIUM CAR

MODEL HISTORY 1966 COROLLA 1ST GENERATION • 1970 COROLLA 2ND GENERATION • 1974 COROLLA 3RD GENERATION •
1979 COROLLA 4TH GENERATION • 1983 COROLLA 5TH GENERATION • 1987 COROLLA 6TH GENERATION • 1991 COROLLA 7TH GENERATION •
1997 COROLLA 8TH GENERATION • 2001 COROLLA 9TH GENERATION • 2008 COROLLA/AURIS 10TH GENERATION

2010 1.6	
LENGTH	4220 mm (167 in.)
LAYOUT	Front engine, front-wheel drive
ENGINE	1.6 petrol 4-cyl
HORSEPOWER	132
MAX. SPEED	195 km/h (121 mph)
CO$_2$ EMISSIONS	153 g/km

2010 AURIS HYBRID

No single model defines the Toyota brand better than the Corolla. Indeed, this unchanging formula of basic, easily understood design, a simple driving experience and near-total reliability has made the Corolla the world's bestselling nameplate. Over ten generations since 1966 this small car has grown steadily in size and stature but has always remained technically and stylistically conservative, giving it an image as a sensible but unexciting car for older buyers – a legacy it still struggles with today.

Corolla style lagged behind the mainstream design trends in the 1960s and 1970s. The biggest break came with the fifth generation, in 1983, when Toyota at last adopted front-wheel-drive and a sharper, Volkswagen Golf-like body language emerged. The sixth generation, in 1987, took on a sportier, more rounded look inspired by Toyota's Celica coupé of the time, but by the time of the ninth redesign, in 2001, the body had swelled into the medium-size class and any sense of freshness or aesthetic appeal had been sacrificed in the interests of not offending any buyer group.

Conscious that this blandness was translating into sliding sales in key image-conscious markets, Toyota ditched its most hallowed name for Europe, relabelling it Auris for the tenth generation. Yet the design remained stodgy, the middle-of-the-road stigma stuck, and Toyota was left wondering whether such a conservative approach to design was still fit for the twenty-first century.

1997 COROLLA

2001-GENERATION COROLLA

486

TOYOTA YARIS

2011 | SMALL CAR

MODEL HISTORY 1998 YARIS 1ST GENERATION • 2005 YARIS 2ND GENERATION • 2011 YARIS 3RD GENERATION

2010 TS	
LENGTH	3785 mm (150 in.)
LAYOUT	Front engine, front-wheel drive
ENGINE	1.8 petrol 4-cyl
HORSEPOWER	147
MAX. SPEED	200 km/h (124 mph)
CO2 EMISSIONS	164 g/km

Judged European Car of the Year in 2000, the Yaris subcompact (known as the Echo and Vitz outside Europe) set a new benchmark in its class. Safe, practical, versatile and easy to drive, it was also much more stylish than its predecessor, the long-running Starlet.

The work of Sotiris Kovos, who trained at London's Royal College of Art before working at Toyota's European Office of Creation (EPOC) in Brussels, the Yaris was deliberately European in feel and much influenced by German models; Kovos cited solidity, strength and functionality as important attributes to convey in this small vehicle. He aimed for simplicity of design, and it worked. Although unconvincing as a sporting choice, the Yaris became a bestseller for Toyota, at one point accounting for one in four of all Toyotas sold in Europe.

The watchword for development of the second-generation models was big-car thinking. Repositioning of the exhaust enabled a fully-flat floor, enhancing versatility and interior space, especially for rear-seat passengers. Otherwise, Toyota wisely resisted tampering much with Kovos's clean lines, and although the Yaris now looks very conservative next to newer rivals, it has not dated too badly at all.

2011 YARIS HSD CONCEPT

2005-GENERATION YARIS

1998-GENERATION YARIS

TVR

GREAT BRITAIN | 1947–2006 | SPORTS CARS | TVR.CO.UK

Trevor Wilkinson saw the potential of glass fibre-reinforced plastic (GFRP) as an effective way to make a striking-looking sports car. First came the Jomar, created to order for an American client, but the first real TVR was the Mk1, later called Grantura, in 1958. This set Wilkinson's blueprint for a powerful front-engined/rear-wheel-drive car, with a long hood and the engine mounted as far back as possible to give a near 50:50 weight distribution, a high power-to-weight ratio, a GFRP body and a backbone chassis.

TVR has tampered little with this formula since, although in the 1960s Turin's Carrozzeria Fissore was tasked with creating a steel- and aluminium-bodied prototype coupé called Trident; two fastbacks were displayed at the 1965 Geneva motor show, but TVR went into receivership. The car went on to be sold as the Trident Clipper, but TVR's new owners, dealer Martin Lilley and his father Arthur, did not get the rights to its production.

Further concepts, the sleek Hillman Imp-based Tina fastback and spider, were proposals for more affordable sportsters to broaden the range, again styled at Fissore by Trevor Fiore. These also failed to come to fruition, partly because of problems finding a mass-production partner. However, their Italianate lines and sharp-edged angles informed the subsequent ranges, right up to the radical 'wedge' of the Tasmin in 1980; this emphatically polarized opinion, and proved so expensive to develop that the company had to be sold again.

Under the ownership of Peter Wheeler in the 1980s and 1990s, curvier designs returned; the lacklustre reception given to the Tasmin-derived Speed Eight concept (featuring the much-loved Buick-Rover V8) sealed the decision, and the aggressively rounded car that revived the Griffith name from the 1960s received a far more positive response. TVR widened and diversified its range, fitted its home-grown engines and attracted a new generation of enthusiast

1991 V8 S

1992 GRIFFITH

1993 CERBERA

HISTORY AND PRINCIPAL MODELS

1947	Trevor Wilkinson founds Trevcar Motors in Blackpool, Lancashire
1949	Company renamed TVR Engineering. First car built
1958	Mk1 (Grantura)
1963	Griffith. Works starts on Trident prototype
1965	TVR bought by Arthur and Martin Lilley
1966	Tina concept
1967	Tuscan, Vixen
1971	Causes a stir at the London motor show with naked models on the Tuscan V8
1980	Tasmin
1981	Peter Wheeler buys the company
1986	S-series
1989	Speed Eight prototype
1991	V8 S
1992	Griffith
1993	Chimaera, Cerbera
1999	Tuscan
2001	Tamora
2003	T350C, T-series, Sagaris
2004	Company bought by Nikolai Smolensky. Typhoon
2006	Receivership
2007	Smolensky buys back Blackpool Automotive and TVR trademark. Rumoured new Typhoon concept
2008	Sagaris 2 previewed to TVR Club members
2010	Smolensky promises production will restart 'in 2012'

customers for its increasingly wild designs. Yet by 2004 it was in financial trouble again. Young Russian entrepreneur Nikolai Smolensky stepped in, but split the company into three units prior to its going into administration.

Smolensky has since regained control of the manufacturing rights and TVR brand name, and has outlined three new cars. First up (in 2012) is said to be the Corvette-engined MD-1, based on the Tuscan convertible and relatively traditional in its styling, although a bolder model is also promised.

1993 CHIMAERA

1999 TUSCAN

2003 SAGARIS

UAZ

RUSSIA | FOUNDED 1941 | TRUCKS AND SUVS | UAZ.RU

HISTORY AND PRINCIPAL MODELS

1941	Automaker ZIS evacuated from Moscow to Ulyanovsk
1943	Factory renamed UAZ
1953	GAZ/UAZ light truck
1965	452
1967	Work starts to expand plant
1973	469
1974	Builds millionth vehicle
1980	Makes electric prototype
1983	Makes amphibious prototype for Soviet Army, wins state-sponsored awards
1993	3150-series
1997	3160-series
2000	Severstal Avto becomes major shareholder. Simbir (3162)
2001	Patriot

As German troops advanced on Moscow during the Second World War, Soviet leader Joseph Stalin ordered the relocation of various key industries, and the car-builder ZIS (later ZIL) was evacuated to Ulyanovsk, on the banks of the Volga River almost 900 kilometres (555 miles) east of the capital. This site was soon designated as the Ulyanovsky Avtomobily Zavod (automobile factory), although it continued to build ZIS models for the Soviet military. The GAZ/UAZ 69, a rugged off-roader influenced by the Willys »Jeep, was exported to twenty-two countries, and was also built under licence by Romanian carmaker Aro.

A dedicated UAZ design centre was built at the facility, in parallel with a massive modernization programme to automate and mechanize production, and talented young engineers were recruited. The first in-house 450-series models, all-purpose trucks with

distinctive circular headlights and a chassis easily adapted to support a variety of body styles, emerged from the late 1950s. The best-known is the go-anywhere 452, used by police and military across the former Soviet Union as well as by farmers and residents of Russia's most remote regions. Its essential design has changed little, and it remains in production today in a variety of guises, including pickup truck, minibus and crew-cab, still with its smoothed-off, near-vertical snub nose and round front lamps. The early-1970s 469, successor to the 69, also remains in production. It continues to be used by the Russian military, along with a more refined Hunter derivative, and both have a civilian following among owners who like their utilitarian retro-Soviet chic.

UAZ vehicles built up an enviable reputation for durability and all-terrain capability in inhospitable climates, from the heat of Cuba to the cold of Siberia; these qualities were promoted by mountain-climbing stunts and participation in endurance rallies. However, the 'new-look' SUV-style models of the 1990s, and the more recent Simbir and Patriot (hated even at launch) proved less reliable and never captured the public's affection in the same way. UAZ has been unable to compete against imports coming on to the Russian market after the fall of the Iron Curtain.

Since takeover by Sollers (formerly Severstal Avto), the distributor of Fiat, Isuzu and Ssangyong in Russia, the UAZ plant has been assembling CKD kits of Isuzu trucks, and is due to start production of the Ssangyong Actyon. The long-term future of its own-brand vehicles is uncertain.

1973 469

1965 452

2001 PATRIOT

GEOFF UPEX

GREAT BRITAIN | BORN 1955 | CAR DESIGNER

1998 ROVER 75

2002 RANGE ROVER

2004 RANGE STORMER CONCEPT

2005 RANGE ROVER SPORT

Quiet, methodical and frequently self-effacing, Geoff Upex has remained loyal throughout his design career to a single employer: the MG Rover group and the many incarnations of its constituent companies that resulted from its absorption by BMW in 1994 and its subsequent splitting up and selling off. Upex, who retired in 2006, will always be associated with the dramatic renaissance of »Land Rover after the turn of the millennium. It was his determination to avoid the mistakes of the past, when Land Rover and Range Rover models were updated only half-heartedly, that helped Land Rover to move from being a nostalgia brand to a flourishing, thoroughly modern premium competitor. The 2004 »Land Rover Discovery/LR3, in particular, showed great design skill in making a large family-orientated vehicle fresh, classy and elegant, and yet distinct from the parallel top-premium Range Rover line.

The big breakthrough had occurred with the 2002 Range Rover, developed under BMW's ownership. Upex specified an exceptionally high-class interior, with design cues drawn from luxury yachts and particularly accomplished use of wood. In parallel with the Range Rover programme, Upex had had a supervisory role in the much acclaimed design of the Rover 75, and served as a steadying hand in reconciling the conflicting factions vying for influence in the »Mini Cooper project.

Land Rover's renewal kicked off in earnest in 2004, when Upex presented the brand's first concept car, the Range Stormer. This racy low-rider proposed the then-novel idea of a sporty Range Rover; the concept was so well received that it evolved into the 2005 »Range Rover Sport, which was a huge commercial success. The 2006 Land Rover Freelander 2/LR2 showed a similar sureness of touch.

497

DIRK VAN BRAECKEL

BELGIUM | BORN 1958 | CAR DESIGNER

2002 BENTLEY CONTINENTAL GT

1991 AUDI CABRIOLET

2007 BENTLEY BROOKLANDS

1996 SKODA OCTAVIA

There was much unease among older members of the establishment in the United Kingdom in April 1999 when Volkswagen announced that it had appointed Dirk van Braeckel to be director of styling and design at »Bentley, the aristocratic British marque that it had bought the previous year. Not only was Van Braeckel not English, but also he had for the past six years been designing »Skodas, a low-cost brand that had for a long time been regarded as a joke. The unspoken fear was that Bentleys would soon come to resemble Skodas; what was conveniently overlooked was the remarkable turnaround in Skoda's fortunes, sales and reputation that had resulted from Van Braeckel's finely judged and discreetly stylish 1996 Octavia.

Van Braeckel had been groomed for the key Skoda role by VW Group head Ferdinand Piëch on the strength of his earlier work at Audi, especially the 80 Avant and the elegant Cabriolet, a design that has still

not dated. So when it came to selecting an architect for his next big project, the modernization of Bentley into a high profile super-luxury brand, Piëch's choice once again fell on the Belgian.

Van Braeckel's big moment came in 2002 with the launch of the »Bentley Continental GT, the first of a new family of slightly smaller but much sportier Bentleys. His lithe, muscular and well-grounded coupé shape made a dramatic contrast with the old-fashioned standard Bentleys, and it was very well received by customers, although less so by traditionalists. The Continental worked less well as a sedan, but Van Braeckel scored a bullseye in 2007 with the truly elegant Brooklands coupé, the last Bentley on the old chassis. The same theme, allied to a new front with distinctive large round headlights, was developed for the 2009 »Bentley Mulsanne flagship sedan, again discreetly sporting and crafted with great sensitivity to Bentley tradition.

LAURENS VAN DEN ACKER

THE NETHERLANDS | BORN 1965 | CAR DESIGNER AND MANAGER

2006 MAZDA NAGARE CONCEPT

2003 FORD MODEL U CONCEPT

2010 MAZDA5

While »Patrick le Quément succeeded in building up Renault's dynamic, design-led image, it now falls to his successor, Laurens van den Acker, to maintain the momentum and evolve the brand's identity for the second decade of the twenty-first century. Expectations are high: le Quément's design renaissance totally rejuvenated the brand, and Van den Acker comes with a powerful track record of reshaping and revitalizing another once-stagnant brand, Mazda.

The design world is waiting to see how the Dutchman plans to move »Renault's image on, and an early glimpse has been provided by the sensuous DeZir electric sports-car concept announced in 2010.

Prior to Ford and then Mazda, Van den Acker's early car-design career was illuminated by his involvement with »J. Mays's »Audi TT team. Moving to California to join Mays at Ford in 1998, Van den Acker then produced two utilitarian concepts, the back-to-basics Model U and the urban-cool Synus, and drew the Escape SUV. A major increase in his responsibilities came in 2006, when he crossed the Pacific to take charge of global design for »Mazda, and it was at this Japanese brand that he produced his most imaginative work.

A series of remarkable concept cars began pouring out of Mazda studios worldwide, each themed around the notion of Nagare, or flow; each explored a different market segment and interpretation of the theme, and it was clear that Mazda was building up a tremendous reservoir of design ideas. However, the only production car truly to embody Nagare thinking is the 2010 Mazda5 minivan; after Van den Acker's departure to Renault, Mazda announced that the Nagare theme was being set aside.

Few yet know the fresh design direction Van den Acker has in mind for Renault, but given his fertile imagination and the French automaker's fondness for creativity, great results must be on the cards.

2010 RENAULT DEZIR CONCEPT

ADRIAN VAN HOOYDONK

THE NETHERLANDS | BORN 1964 | CAR DESIGNER AND MANAGER

CV	
1988	Studies industrial design at Delft University of Technology
1992	Graduates from Art Center Europe, Vevey, Switzerland. Joins BMW, Munich, as designer
2000	Moves to BMW Designworks, California
2001	President of Designworks
2004	Head of brand studio, BMW
2009	Head of design, BMW Group

KEY DESIGNS	
1997	Mini ACV 30 showcar
1999	BMW Z9 concept, exterior
2001	BMW 7 Series (E65) (4th gen)
2003	BMW 6 Series (2nd gen)
2007	BMW CS concept
2008	BMW 7 Series (5th gen); BMW M1 Hommage concept
2009	BMW 5 Series (6th gen), 5 Gran Turismo, Z4 (2nd gen); BMW Vision EfficientDynamics concept

2008 BMW 7 SERIES

2007 BMW CS CONCEPT

2009 BMW 5 GRAN TURISMO

So completely did »Chris Bangle dominate all debate and all coverage of post-2000 »BMW design that the other members of the design team tended to be left in the background: it was Bangle who took all the criticisms and defended such divisive designs as the 2001 E65 »BMW 7 Series. Later, it emerged that the 7 Series was actually the work of Dutchman Adrian van Hooydonk; the BMW Z9 concept of 1999 had been his, too.

Van Hooydonk, who after the departure of Bangle in 2009 became director of design for the entire BMW Group, including »Mini, »Rolls-Royce and motorcycles, joined BMW in the same year as Bangle and the two

worked closely together. Van Hooydonk's 1997 Mini ACV 30 concept coupé showed that BMW was serious about introducing a modern Mini and provided key cues, such as the contrast roof, the twin round headlights and large central speedometer. Two years later the Z9 big-coupé concept once again provided clues to the upcoming »BMW 6 Series and 7 Series. Towards the end of the new millennium's first decade, with Van Hooydonk already having been in full charge of BMW design following Bangle's elevation to a supervisory role, the first post-Bangle cars began to emerge: the elaborate M1 Hommage concept as a fresh tribute to the 1978 original and the big CS coupé-sedan concept, with the oversized grilles that would appear on the new »5 Series and 7 Series that followed.

These, along with the new X3, the X1 SUV and the revised »BMW Z4 sports car, all show bolder grille graphics but a toning down of the flame-surfacing language associated with Bangle. Yet the clearest indication of one promising direction Van Hooydonk could take is the stunning and futuristic 2009 Vision EfficientDynamics concept, a glass-roofed coupé with complex folded, wrapped and layered bodywork.

2009 BMW VISION EFFICIENTDYNAMICS CONCEPT

2008 BMW M1 HOMMAGE CONCEPT

VENTURI

FRANCE | FOUNDED 1985 | ELECTRIC SPORTS CARS AND NICHE VEHICLES | VENTURI.FR

HISTORY AND PRINCIPAL MODELS

1984	Godfroy Ventury concept, with Volkswagen Golf GTI engine, shown at Paris auto show
1985	Manufacture de Voitures de Sport established
1987	Venturi 200
1989	MVS renamed Venturi
1990	Venturi Prototype Paris-Dakar; 280 SPC
1992	260 Atlantique
1993	260 LM, 500 LM, 600 LM, 400 GT
1994	Venturi bought by Scotsman Hubert O'Neill
1996	Bankruptcy. Venturi bought by Thai investors Nakarin Benz
2000	Declared bankrupt again
2001	Monegasque Gildo Pallanca Pastor takes over
2002	Fétish electric coupé and Grand Prix concepts
2004	Fétish roadster concept
2006	Heritage GT3; Eclectic and Astrolab concepts
2008	Volage and Eclectic 2.0 concepts
2009	Jamais Contente fuel-cell streamliner
2010	Jamais Contente electric streamliner sets record with 495 km/h (308 mph). Pastor buys French motorcyle-maker Voxan. Nouvelle Fétish; America and Antarctica concepts

Former Heuliez engineers Claude Poiraud and Gérard Godfroy set up Manufacture de Voitures de Sport (MVS) in the mid-1980s with the aim of producing a world-beating, exclusive French GT. The Venturi 200 started a series of high-performance fibreglass-bodied coupés and convertibles featuring a mid-mounted, turbocharged version of the Peugeot-Renault-Volvo V6.

The company went on to make nearly seven hundred cars in its first twenty years, increasing power outputs and offering such variations on the original theme as the stripped-out Atlantique. Collaboration with Larrousse saw a Formula One entry but, scoring just one point in the 1991 season, this was short-lived. Instead, Venturi turned to GT racing, developing the Kevlar/carbon-fibre-bodied Trophy for a one-make series.

Godfroy designed a much-needed update for the brand with the Antlantique 300, a road-going, roomier version of the Trophy car. The related, more hard-core, 400 GT was the world's first production car to feature carbon brakes, and was also the fastest-yet French production vehicle. Profitability continued to elude Venturi, however, until it was rescued by Monaco-based Gildo Pallanca Pastor in 2001.

Under Pastor, Venturi has taken a very different turn and has created far more eco-friendly, mostly electrically driven models. Paris-based designer Sacha Lakic set the new tone with the Fétish, an exotic, ultra-exclusive electric coupé. His 2008 Volage concept, a small sports coupé, appears to be a highly appropriate contender for production, and the doorless America coupé-buggy is a serious proposition. The Eclectic (first an open-bodied golf cart, but for production, an enclosed commuter car) is slated to hit the road shortly. The solar-panelled Astrolab speedster was purely a showcar, although the drive-by-wire, tracked Antarctica is actually set to work as a support vehicle at a polar research centre.

All these striking and specifically targeted vehicles, and the Jamais Contente land-speed record-breakers, mainly serve as demonstrators of Venturi's electric-vehicle ingenuity and engineering skills, advertising its bread-and-butter business of developing and converting vehicles for major clients.

2008 ECLECTIC CONCEPT

2008 VOLAGE

1996 ATLANTIQUE 300

502

VOLGA

RUSSIA | 1956–2010 | VOLUME CARS | GAZGROUP.RU

HISTORY AND PRINCIPAL MODELS

1956	GAZ M21 Volga sedan enters production
1958	Second series of M21, with vertical 'shark' grille. Display at Brussels Expo
1961	'Made in Belgium' Ghia Volga displayed at Brussels auto show
1962	Third series of M21, in production until 1970
1968	GAZ 24 Volga sedan, taxi, ambulance
1977	24 second series
1982	Third series of 3102 and 24-10
1992	31029. GAZ is privatized
2004	31105
2005	GAZ Group is restructured
2006	Deal with DaimlerChrysler to build a car based on the Chrysler Sebring/ Dodge Stratus. GAZ Group buys UK vanmaker LDV
2010	Production of 3102 ends

Volga – named after Russia's great river – was the name given by »GAZ (Gorky Avtomobily Zarod, or Gorky Automobile Factory) to its model line of large sedans and related models intended for mid-ranking Communist Party officials. In the 1950s the factory at Nizhny Novgorod (known as Gorky during the Soviet era) replaced its popular GAZ M20 Pobjeda ('Victory') with the M21 Volga. Body designer Lev Eremeev was said to have been particularly influenced by the big Fords of the time, but the Western flavour was quite deliberate as exports of this car were also planned.

The launch of the lightly made-over second-series M21 at the 1958 Brussels Expo, and subsequent rally successes (a win in the 1000 Lakes Rally, Finland, and third place in the Acropolis Rally of Greece), brought this conservative but attractive sedan to notice beyond the Iron Curtain.

Assembly from exported kits (plus the fitment of diesel engines from Perkins, Rover and then Peugeot) was carried out in Antwerp, Belgium, where the local importer went so far as to commission a front-end redesign from Ghia for cars to be sold in the Benelux countries. Back home, Soviet state apparatchiks had top priority on the long waiting lists for the car, and exclusive rights to the V8 version, while patient civilians had to stick with the four-cylinder. Yuri Gagarin, the first person in space (in 1961), was presented with an M21 by the government.

The GAZ 24-series Volga of 1968 carried over its predecessor's benefits on the same basic platform: sturdy construction, high ground clearance and heavy-duty suspension, to deal with Russia's poor rural roads. The body was squarer, more contemporary, although its three-box outline dated rapidly. It formed the basis for two distinct successors, the 3102 (initially destined for state officials only) and the more workaday, accessibly priced 24-10, an increasingly aged-looking, unrefined and uncompetitive product offering little of the 3102's desirability.

Further attempts were made to create cars that at least looked more modern even if they were archaic under their sheet metal, but it was the 3102 and its KGB associations that endured, thanks to the decision of parent company RusPromAvto to try to market it as a 'heritage' product. The car lasted right up to 2010, when it finally gave way on the production lines to the Siber, based on the Chrysler Sebring/Dodge Stratus.

2004 31105

VOLKSWAGEN

GERMANY | FOUNDED 1937 | VOLUME CARS AND SUVS | VOLKSWAGEN.COM

In 1933, German chancellor Adolf Hitler briefed engineer Ferdinand Porsche to develop an affordable, economical and versatile 'people's car' – a *Volkswagen*, a term used to describe numerous vehicles created in the 1920s and 1930s. Porsche had earlier made a proposal for a similar car to German motorbike-maker NSU, and many of the features of that Type 32 made it into the Series 3 prototype he presented in 1935, including the rear-mounted, air-cooled flat-four, independent suspension and backbone chassis. Neither the format nor the curved, beetle-like body shape were by any means unique (Czechoslovakia's Tatra, in particular, had gone down that path) but the KdF-Wagen, as Hitler called it, went on to become the Beetle, a well-documented mass-market success, and the foundation of Volkswagen as a company.

The basic blueprint produced by Porsche (aided by body designer and long-time colleague Erwin Komenda) spawned diverse vehicles: the amphibious Schwimmwagen; pretty coupés and roadsters styled by Italian design house Ghia and built by German coachbuilder Karmann; Type 3 Variant station-wagons; the much-loved Transporter and Microbus camper van; and even a Baja-racing dune buggy. Manufacturing in exponentially increasing numbers in more and more countries around the world, Volkswagen neglected to look beyond this successful formula, and by the 1960s it relied entirely on a range based on a single, hopelessly dated platform. The eventual retirement of managing director Heinrich Nordhoff allowed a radical overhaul of the company's product planning, enabled by the purchase of Auto Union and NSU in the late 1960s: »Audi and NSU models formed the basis of VW's new-age front-engined, water-cooled line-up.

»Giorgetto Giugiaro's »Italdesign studio was engaged to style the state-of-the-art »Volkswagen Passat, »Scirocco and »Golf, the start of a long relationship. Italdesign's

1938 TYPE 60 KDF-WAGEN ('BEETLE')

1955 KARMANN GHIA

wedge-shaped, De Tomaso-esque Tapiro super-coupé concept (based on the Porsche 914/916) and the Cheetah roadster (which predated the style of the later Fiat Z1/9) were not taken up, nor the Orbit compact minivan. Much later, its four prototypes showcasing VW's outrageous W12 engine – the W12 Syncro, the Roadster, the Nardo and the Record – were very credible proposals for a Volkswagen supercar. Italdesign also developed the Tarek off-roader, VW's Paris-Dakar endurance rallier (2003). However, the bulk of Volkswagen's

design work since has been in-house, under the leadership of »Hartmut Warkuss, who headed the design team for nearly three decades, until the appointment of »Murat Günak in 2003.

Many concepts, from early eco-friendly experiments such as the Student and Chico to the super-sporty GX3 and EcoRacer, have demonstrated fuel-efficient technologies and alternative powertrains. The most extreme of these concepts has been the teardrop-shaped, tandem-seat 1-litre concept of 2002, capable of going 100 kilometres

HISTORY

1937	Gesellschaft zur Vorbereitung des Deutschen Volkswagens established
1938	Renamed Volkswagenwerk. Type 60 KdF-Wagen ('Beetle') goes into production
1939–45	Volkswagen factory makes Kübelwagen and Schwimmwagen military vehicles
1945	Factory placed under direction of the British military government; Major Ivan Hirst oversees resumption of car production
1948	VW reformed under state ownership. Former Opel manager Heinrich Nordhoff recruited as managing director
1955	Millionth Beetle made. Volkswagen of America formed
1964	VW buys 50% of Audi, taking full control following year; new factory in Emden
1969	VW buys NSU
1972	Beetle sets the record for highest-production car, beating Ford Model T
1985	VW forms joint venture to manufacture in China; becomes Europe's largest carmaker
1986	VW takes 51% stake in SEAT, later 75%; owns it outright from 1990
1987	50 millionth Volkswagen built
1991	VW acquires Skoda
1998	Volkswagen Group acquires Lamborghini, Bentley and Bugatti brands
1999	VW makes its 100 millionth vehicle
2003	Beetle production ends
2005	Porsche begins building stake in VW but fails to take it over completely
2007	25 millionth Golf built
2009	VW takes a 49.9% stake in Porsche; merger agreed but still under negotiation. Takes a 20% stake in Suzuki
2010	VW acquires Italdesign design house

2011 BULLI CONCEPT

2001 MICROBUS CONCEPT

1974 MICROBUS (SECOND GENERATION)

505

on a litre of fuel (282 mpg); others, such as the one-box, gullwing-doored Futura IRVW of 1989 and Noah of 1977, have explored packaging and the future of cabin layouts. Most, however, have previewed production vehicles – although sadly for nostalgics, the next-generation Lupo city car will not have the rear-engined layout of its Up! concept precursor. A production version of the ecstatically received Microbus showcar (2001, the work of Volkswagen's studio in California) has not been forthcoming, either, but rumours persist that this may yet happen.

In the first ten years of the twenty-first century Volkswagen's range has diversified further, not always to acclaim or commercial advantage. From the luxury-laden Phaeton of 2001, a putative rival to the »Mercedes-Benz S Class and »BMW 7 Series that could never transcend its relatively humble badge despite its superb engineering, to the back-to-basics Fox of 2005 (which lacked the character of the Lupo it replaced), the brand has a model in most sectors. This includes a huge SUV (Touareg), a coupé-like compact-executive sedan (Passat CC), a folding-roof coupé-convertible (Eos) and now a pickup truck (Amarok). But with efforts concentrated on developing these products, Volkswagen's core mainstream models, the Polo and Golf, have arguably been neglected, losing ground to their competitors.

Internal Volkswagen Group politics are said to have accelerated the departure of advanced design chief »Peter Schreyer (New Beetle, Golf fourth generation, Eos, Concept R); and Murat Günak (Concept A, Tiguan, Iroc, Passat CC, Golf fifth generation) left suddenly in 2007 after then-CEO Dr Wolfgang Bernhard was ousted in a management reshuffle. Incoming design chief »Walter de'Silva, a former colleague at Audi of new VW Group CEO Martin Winterkorn, has since been upfront about his philosophy of going back to the company's roots, simplifying and re-evaluating what a Volkswagen should be. He first toned down Günak's aggressive Iroc for the production Scirocco, and then came up with a quickly facelifted sixth-generation Golf with less ornamentation and fewer fussy details. It

1998 W12 ROADSTER

2009 L1 CONCEPT

was surely no coincidence that cuts in the cost of Golf production had to be made at the same time.

Volkswagen model programmes specific to North America and China are under way, previewed by the NCC (New Coupé Concept) and NMS (New Midsize Sedan) to be built in Tennessee, and the Shanghai-designed Lavida. De'Silva and the head of VW brand design, Klaus Bischoff, have an interesting challenge ahead to redefine Volkswagen's proposition, and in addition to their overhaul, Italdesign will be involved again. Volkswagen recently bought a 90.1 per cent stake and majority control of the design house and its facilities, and has confirmed collaboration to bring the Up! model family to production.

2011 XL1 CONCEPT

PRINCIPAL MODELS

1938	Type 60 KdF-Wagen ('Beetle')
1940	Type 62 Kübelwagen
1950	Type 2 Microbus
1955	Type 14 Karmann Ghia
1961	Type 34 Karmann Ghia; Type 3 1500
1967	Transporter 2
1968	411
1970	Buggy; K70, the first water-cooled Volkswagen. Volkswagen-Porsche Tapiro concept, by Italdesign
1971	Cheetah concept, by Italdesign-Karmann
1973	Passat
1974	Scirocco, Golf (Rabbit)
1975	Polo
1976	Golf GTI
1979	Transporter 3, Jetta
1981	Auto 2000 concept, with three-cylinder direct-injection diesel engine
1982	Student concept
1986	Scooter design study; Orbit concept, by Italdesign
1989	Futura IRVW concept
1991	Vario concept
1992	Chico hybrid concept
1995	Sharan
1997	W12 Syncro and Noah concepts
1998	New Beetle, Lupo, W12 Roadster
1999	Concept D study
2001	Microbus and W12 Nardo concepts
2002	Phaeton, Touareg, Touran; 1-litre and W12 Record concepts
2003	Concept R, GX3 concept
2004	Concept T
2005	Fox, Eos; EcoRacer and Beetle Ragster concepts
2006	Concept A, Iroc and NanoSpyder concepts
2007	Tiguan; Up! and Space Up! concepts
2008	Passat CC, Scirocco (3rd gen), Golf (6th gen), Study Amarok pickup
2009	Polo (5th gen); L1, BlueSport, E-Up! and Up! Lite concepts
2010	Passat (7th gen); NCC and NCS (Jetta) concepts
2011	Bulli and XL1 concepts

2007 SPACE UP! CONCEPT

2003 GX3 CONCEPT

2009 BLUESPORT CONCEPT

VOLKSWAGEN GOLF

2008 | MEDIUM CAR

MODEL HISTORY 1974 GOLF 1ST GENERATION • 1983 GOLF 2ND GENERATION • 1991 GOLF 3RD GENERATION • 1997 GOLF 4TH GENERATION • 2003 GOLF 5TH GENERATION • 2008 GOLF 6TH GENERATION

2010 2.0 TDI	
LENGTH	4200 mm (166 in.)
LAYOUT	Front engine, front-wheel drive
ENGINE	2.0 turbo diesel 4-cyl
HORSEPOWER	140
MAX. SPEED	209 km/h (130 mph)
CO$_2$ EMISSIONS	126 g/km

2008-GENERATION GOLF R

The state-of-the-art Golf of 1974 was different in every way from the archaic Beetle it was intended to replace. Angular where the Beetle was curved, its water-cooled engine up front under the hood, »Giorgetto Giugiaro's two-box Golf was the car Volkswagen desperately needed, and a car the world eagerly wanted. It was neither Volkswagen's first front-wheel-drive car nor its first practical hatchback – the larger, more conservatively styled »Passat had paved the way – but it effectively marked a new beginning for the company and it went on to become a bestseller.

In a range spanning hot-hatch GTIs and economical diesels, a cabriolet bodied by coachbuilding firm Karmann, the Jetta sedan, the Caddy pickup and regionally targeted variations including the Rabbit and Caribe, the well-engineered, well-thought-out and cleverly marketed Golf was smart, fun to drive and highly desirable. The second generation, in 1983, tweaked by Volkswagen's in-house design team and developed for fully robotized production, was smoothed out a little, lengthened and better equipped. It lost a little of its initial character but none of its class.

However, the unadventurous third-generation Golf and the smarter fourth of 1997 became progressively heavier, more lumpen in their handling and duller of demeanour, as Volkswagen attempted to turn the car into more of a comfort-orientated, premium-priced compact luxury option. The then-radical »Ford Focus hit it hard, and buyers also migrated to the growing

array of compact SUVs and more versatile crossovers on offer. The fifth-generation Golf, in 2003, marked a return to form, with more striking detailing, a nod to the range's heritage, and a GTI worthy of the name once more.

Under the leadership of »Water de'Silva, Klaus Bischoff's sixth-generation Golf has evolved to lose many fussy details (a move made not least to cut the cost of its production). The philosophy has been to zoom in on core elements of historical 'DNA' and simplify the finish, drawing a clear, clean line of descent from Giugiaro's classic and leaving most of the drama to the born-again Scirocco coupé with which it shares its underpinnings.

Unpretentious, unostentatious and undeniably still the aspirational choice in this sector, the Golf continues to exemplify all the values of Volkswagen.

1997 GOLF

1974 GOLF

2008 GOLF GTI

VOLKSWAGEN PASSAT

2010 | EXECUTIVE CAR

MODEL HISTORY 1973 PASSAT 1ST GENERATION • 1981 PASSAT 2ND GENERATION • 1988 PASSAT 3RD GENERATION • 1993 PASSAT 4TH GENERATION • 1996 PASSAT 5TH GENERATION • 2005 PASSAT 6TH GENERATION • 2010 PASSAT 7TH GENERATION

2010 1.8 TFSI	
LENGTH	4765 mm (188 in.)
LAYOUT	Front engine, front-wheel drive
ENGINE	1.8 turbo petrol 4-cyl
HORSEPOWER	160
MAX. SPEED	220 km/h (136 mph)
CO$_2$ EMISSIONS	172 g/km

In many ways more revolutionary for Volkswagen than the »Golf, the Passat owed its engineering to Audi (under Volkswagen control since 1964) and followed the related 80 saloon on sale. The first of a series of »Giorgetto Giugiaro-designed models from the »Italdesign studio, the 1973 Passat took a hatchback body style with sloped fastback tailgate, a bold move in a class still dominated by sedans with separate trunks. A sedan called Santana followed for some markets, however, along with a roomy station-wagon. The Passat's design development has roughly mirrored that of the Golf; second-generation models retained the elegance of Giugiaro's original; the third generation (which was controversial for its lack of a front grille, a trend at the time) became curvier but more generic; the fourth generation even less distinguished, although its interior set new standards for quality.

Echoing design cues of the Golf, Eos, Tiguan and other all-new Volkswagens, the sixth generation (2005) was the most clearly differentiated Passat in decades. The 2010 seventh generation (by Klaus Bischoff and VW Group design director »Walter de'Silva) is the most upmarket yet, with subtle chrome highlights, LED daytime running lights and more aggressive contouring. These all draw a connection with the Passat CC four-door coupé, which was added to the sixth-generation line-up in 2007 to provide a more clearly premium alternative.

2007 PASSAT CC

1973 PASSAT

VOLKSWAGEN POLO

2009 | SMALL CAR

MODEL HISTORY 1975 POLO 1ST GENERATION • 1981 POLO 2ND GENERATION • 1994 POLO 3RD GENERATION • 2002 POLO 4TH GENERATION • 2009 POLO 5TH GENERATION

2010 1.6 TDI	
LENGTH	3970 mm (157 in.)
LAYOUT	Front engine, front-wheel drive
ENGINE	1.6 turbo diesel 4-cyl
HORSEPOWER	105
MAX. SPEED	190 km/h (118 mph)
CO$_2$ EMISSIONS	109 g/km

One of the first so-called superminis, the Polo started life as the Audi 50 in 1974. The last car developed by chief engineer of Audi Ludwig Kraus before his retirement, the 50 was born from the programme to replace the old two-stroke DKWs and NSUs of the Auto Union with an all-new cutting-edge line-up. Along with the 80 and 100, it was penned by Claus Luthe, creator of the futuristic and utterly unique NSU Ro80, and later the chief designer at BMW; clearly, however, the 50 was inspired by »Giorgetto Giugiaro's »Volkswagen Golf and »Scirocco. Italian influence also came from »Bertone's Nuccio Bertone, who was consulted for the finishing touches. Badge-engineered and with a cheaper interior, it became the first-generation Volkswagen Polo in 1975. This outsold the more expensive Audi so comprehensively that the 50 was soon discontinued.

The second-generation Polo, in 1981, brought a sedan (Derby) as well as the hatch, now labelled Coupé, but most familiar in many regions was the mini-wagon, an impressively practical small car. Loved for its solidity and durability, the economical and long-running second-generation Polo was deservedly popular, to a degree never achieved by Volkswagen's later entry-level cars, the Lupo and Fox, which were launched to fill the niche that opened as the Polo was positioned further upmarket.

As in the case of the VW Golf and »Passat, the Polo grew larger and heavier in its third-generation incarnation and successive updates, and became often overlooked in favour of its close relatives, the SEAT Ibiza (sportier-looking and more youthful in its appeal) and Skoda Fabia (more utilitarian of image, and better value for money). Indeed, with little to distinguish the Polo from these two other than its Volkswagen badge and some different (expensive) engine options, there was nothing to recommend it over its cheaper sister models.

The fourth-generation Polo's twin circular headlamps brought a welcome note of personality back to its face, while a facelift in 2005 delivered a more imposing look, with larger headlights and a grille that linked with the lower air intake for a premium impression. But only with »Walter de'Silva's Passat-alike fifth generation in 2009 did the Polo again become one of the classier subcompacts on the block.

1994 POLO

1975 POLO

VOLKSWAGEN SCIROCCO

2008 | SPORTS COUPÉ

MODEL HISTORY 1974 SCIROCCO 1ST GENERATION • 1982–88 SCIROCCO 2ND GENERATION • 2008 SCIROCCO 3RD GENERATION

2010 2.0 TDI	
LENGTH	4255 mm (168 in.)
LAYOUT	Front engine, front-wheel drive
ENGINE	2.0 turbo diesel 4-cyl
HORSEPOWER	140
MAX. SPEED	207 km/h (128 mph)
CO$_2$ EMISSIONS	134 g/km

Developed and designed alongside the »Golf, with which it shared its underpinnings, the Scirocco of 1974 owed much to »Giorgetto Giugiaro's Audi Karmann Asso di Picche (Ace of Spades) coupé, an angular concept commissioned by German coachbuilder Karmann in 1973. Karmann failed to clinch the deal to make an Audi coupé, but it did secure the contract from Volkswagen to make a much-needed successor to the voluptuous Beetle-based Karmann Ghia.

Volkswagen went on to sell half a million first-generation Sciroccos, and although the square-headlamped second generation of 1982 was less of a sensation, demand kept it in production until the early 1990s.

The Scirocco's successor, the Corrado of 1988, was a more focused, more expensive sports car and never enjoyed the same appeal, and after a long interlude VW went back to the original blueprint. The reborn, third-generation Scirocco of 2008 (previewed by VW designer Robert Lesnik's deep-grilled Iroc concept) was again an accessible, functional four-seater with useful load space.

Yet while the brief was similar, the new Scirocco (styled for production by Marc Lichte) was deliberately forward-looking, with only minimal retro nods to the original. Visual tricks make it look far longer and lower than the »VW Golf, although its wheelbase is the same and its roof just 100 millimetres (less than 4 in.) lower, and its broad-shouldered stance makes it much more muscular-looking than the slender first and second generations.

1974 SCIROCCO

VOLVO

SWEDEN | FOUNDED 1927 | NEAR-PREMIUM CARS | VOLVOCARS.COM

1956 AMAZON

1974 240 ESTATE

1988 440

Volvo's first series-production car, the ÖV4 of 1927, came only in dark blue with black wings. The 'Jakob', as it was nicknamed, was functional rather than fashionable, and its construction was to the tried-and-tested format of a sheet-metal body mounted on to a wooden frame. The primary concern of company founders Assar Gabrielsson and Gustaf Larson was quality, and as a result the Jakob was by no means the cheapest car of its type, but Swedish car-buyers quickly took to this home-grown product, which was tough enough to withstand harsh winters and Sweden's then very poor road surfaces.

The larger and grander six-cylinder models of the 1930s, including the upright TR-series (*Trafikvagn*) taxis, and the more forward-looking and aerodynamic PV36 'Caricoca', were little more innovative or aesthetically pleasing, despite experiments such as designer Gustaf Ericsson's Venus-Bilo concept car of 1933, a radical streamliner.

By the Second World War, however, Volvo was noting the increasing popularity of small imported German cars. Sweden's neutrality during the war enabled it to develop a car using the latest construction methods, styled as the first distinctive Volvo product. The PV444, unveiled in Stockholm in 1944, was an instant hit, with its unitary construction, short-stroke engine, fastback rear end and independent suspension, and such features as its laminated windshield helped to establish Volvo's growing reputation for safety.

Independently coachbuilt versions included vans and even convertibles, but also a new type of car: the PV445 Duett, a small station-wagon. Styled by long-serving chief design engineer Jan Wilsgaard, who had begun his career at Volvo in 1950, it was the start of a long line of Volvo wagons, load-carriers aimed at families seeking versatility rather than at commercial users. Wilsgaard was heralded by Volvo as 'the man who turned the van into a station-wagon', and the tone was set by his philosophy:

'Follow the laws of nature and don't complicate matters! Functional and simple designs are often the best-looking.'

Not that the Volvos of the 1950s and 1960s were purely utilitarian. Wilsgaard's immensely successful 'pontoon'-bodied Amazon (121/122S) nodded to fashion with its tiny tail fins, and has its modern equivalent in the long-running »V70, while the 1956 Sport P1900 introduced a new proposition: a Volvo sports car. The reception given this limited-run two-seat roadster with fibreglass-reinforced polyester body and tubular chassis encouraged the follow-up volume-production P1800, best known for its starring role alongside Roger Moore in the TV series *The Saint*. Created at the studio of Italian stylist Pietro Frua, but credited to Pelle Petterson, son of Volvo's engineering consultant Helmer Petterson, the P1800 was later updated by Wilsgaard as the P1800 ES with shooting brake-type tail end, but Wilsgaard's most influential work in this era was on the 140- and 240-series sedans and estates, which for many remain the definitive Volvos.

Volvo's punt at the luxury coupé market, the angular 1977 262C built by »Bertone, is today viewed as something of a curiosity, as is the Bertone-penned, America-orientated 1985 780 two-door. The 480 ES, Volvo's first front-wheel-drive, transverse-engined model and featuring fashionable pop-up headlights, was more of a practical small hatch than a serious sports car. It took until the mid-1990s for Volvo to come up with a

2007 XC60 CONCEPT

515

successful coupé again, the C70 developed
in collaboration with Tom Walkinshaw
Racing (TWR). Design director »Peter
Horbury, who took over from Wilsgaard in
1991, led a programme to sport up the
brand's conservative image and make it
desirable for more than just safety and
durability. Sports-tuned R models, Touring
Car racing, the sleek »S60 sedan and a
series of advanced experimental concept
cars were all attempts to overcome such
perceptions and (from 1999) to achieve new
owner Ford's ambition of building the Volvo
brand into a premium-level marque on a par
with BMW, Audi and Mercedes-Benz.

Ford bundled Volvo into its Premier
Automotive Group and embarked on a
platform-sharing strategy. This was most
successful at the entry-level end of the
range, the Ford Focus-related S40, V40/V50
and later, »C30, all much more dynamic to
drive and more attractive-looking than the
dowdy Dutch-built 440 and 460 models they
replaced. But while the XC90 and »XC60
SUVs have enticed buyers new to the brand,
Volvo has lost touch with some of its faithful
following, its drive upmarket coming at the
expense of practicality and utility: the 2010
V60, for example, is a 'sportwagon', Volvo
insists, and not an estate at all.

The 3CC and Tandem concepts, from
Volvo's Monitoring and Concept Centre in
California, hint at a different side to the
brand's thinking, however. The same applies
to such concepts as the 2004 YCC (Your
Concept Car), a hybrid coupé developed
by an all-female team that showcased a
number of imaginative new interior finishes
and packaging solutions, and a
quintessentially Scandinavian approach.
Now under Chinese ownership, and with
Horbury restored to his position after a
lengthy stint at Ford USA, Volvo will need
to reconnect with its roots in order to
determine its identity again.

2001 SCC CONCEPT

2009 S60 CONCEPT

PRINCIPAL MODELS

1927	ÖV4 'Jakob', PV4
1935	TR701-704, PV36 'Carioca'
1944	PV444 prototype unveiled
1949	PV445
1953	PV445 Duett; Elisabeth I concept, by Michelotti-Vignale
1956	Sport P1900, 120-series Amazon
1958	PV544
1961	P1800
1962	P220 Amazon wagon
1966	140-series
1971	1800 ES
1972	VESC (Volvo Experimental Safety Car) concept
1974	240- and 260-series
1976	340-series
1977	262C
1979	Tundra concept, by Bertone
1982	760-series
1985	780, 480 ES
1988	440
1991	850 (sedan later known as S70)
1992	ECC concept (Environmental Concept Car) with hybrid gas-turbine powertrain, styling anticipates S80
1995	S40, V40
1996	V70, C70
1997	ACC (Adventure Concept Car, an SUV)
1998	S80
2000	S60
2001	SCC (Safety Concept Car), styling influences C30
2002	XC90
2003	S40, V50; VCC concept
2004	YCC (Your Concept Car); 3CC and Tandem concepts
2006	C30
2007	V70 (3rd gen)
2008	XC60
2009	S60 concept
2010	S60 (2nd gen), V60

1992 ECC CONCEPT

2003 VCC CONCEPT

VOLVO C30

2006 | COUPÉ

2010 2.5 T	
LENGTH	4250 mm (168 in.)
LAYOUT	Front engine, front-wheel drive
ENGINE	2.5 turbo petrol 5-cyl
HORSEPOWER	230
MAX. SPEED	240 km/h (149 mph)
CO_2 EMISSIONS	203 g/km

With the C30 came an entirely new proposition for Volvo buyers: a compact but high-quality hatchback to rival the »Audi A3 and BMW 1 Series, a sporty model that didn't even pretend to be a practical family car. Signalling the company's intent to break away from the legacy of its boxy estates, the C30 is three-door only, and its two rear seats are just nominally usable; for functionality, look to the related V50.

Intended to appeal to a fresh demographic of younger buyers new to the brand (or to catch older empty-nesters downsizing), the C30 is the result of much market research and consumer focus-grouping, and is more a lifestyle accessory than a load-lugger. Cues such as the vertical grille and V-shaped hood emphasise that this is a Volvo (and not the Ford Focus it essentially is beneath the surface).

The work of Canadian Simon Lamarre, who trained in Montreal as an industrial designer, the C30's outline and many of its features were trialled in the wide-shouldered 2001 SCC (Safety Concept Car) concept, an exercise in ergonomics and all-round outward vision. The SCC, with its wide all-glass tailgate, in turn nodded to Volvo's 480 and classic 1800 ES coupés. Neither the C30 nor the SCC come near to the elegance of the 1800 ES, however.

VOLVO S60

2010 | EXECUTIVE CAR

MODEL HISTORY 2000 S60 1ST GENERATION • 2010 S60 2ND GENERATION

2010 3.0 T	
LENGTH	4630 mm (183 in.)
LAYOUT	Front engine, front-wheel drive
ENGINE	3.0 turbo petrol 6-cyl
HORSEPOWER	304
MAX. SPEED	250 km/h (155 mph)
CO$_2$ EMISSIONS	239 g/km

Volvo design director »Peter Horbury gave pretty clear directions to his team as to the shape the brand-new S60 saloon should take: he started by taking a C70 coupé to the studio and marking off a pair of rear doors with sticky tape. The result, in 2000, was a striking and convincingly sporty four-door, albeit one with rather cramped rear seats, and it was Volvo's first credible contender in the compact-executive sector.

Some ten years later, Horbury – who had in the meantime departed Volvo for Ford North America, but had returned in time for the launch of the second-generation S60 – judged the original to be bit too minimalist and applauded the work done in his absence. The new S60 concept developed under the direction of Steve Mattin was far more dramatic and extrovert, with aggressive side sculpting, deeper angles to the hood's V and an enlarged, higher-set Volvo emblem. The production model was little toned down, aside from the loss of its glass roof and clamshell doors.

Some gentler, more subtly Scandinavian themes remained in the S60, however; programme chief for the exterior, Örjan Sterner, cited his love of sailing as an influence on the wave-like forms and flowing aerodynamics that calmed Mattin's more macho tendencies.

2000 S60

VOLVO V70

2007 | STATION-WAGON

MODEL HISTORY 1996 V70 1ST GENERATION • 2000 V70 2ND GENERATION • 2007 V70 3RD GENERATION

2010 2.5 T	
LENGTH	4825 mm (191 in.)
LAYOUT	Front engine, front-wheel drive
ENGINE	2.5 turbo petrol 5-cyl
HORSEPOWER	231
MAX. SPEED	210 km/h (130 mph)
CO$_2$ EMISSIONS	209 g/km

The V70 may be the quintessential Swedish station-wagon, but in fact its design roots are in California, at Volvo's Camarillo car monitoring and concept centre, where Briton »Peter Horbury oversaw the creation of the ECC (Environmental Concept Car) in 1992. The ECC's hybrid gas-turbine powertrain may not have seen production, but this 850-based prototype previewed a new design direction for Volvo: most obviously, it foreshadowed the good-looking S80 saloon and the V70 estate, which shared the same front-end layout.

A curvier update to the boxy 850, with more exaggerated grooves to its hood and character lines on its flanks, the V70 marked Volvo's first concerted efforts to move away from sheer utilitarianism, although its inherent relationship between flair and functionality was always a little uneasy. This was underlined by Horbury's later wry comments about 'the front end of an E-Type Jaguar married to the back end of a Ford Transit van'.

In the end, duty won out over dynamism: the third-generation V70 of 2007 got a new, more upright tailgate to address the loss of load space in its predecessor, and the natural order was restored.

2000 V70

1996 V70

VOLVO XC60

2008 | CROSSOVER SUV

2010 2.4 D	
LENGTH	4630 mm (183 in.)
LAYOUT	Front engine, front-wheel drive
ENGINE	2.4 turbo diesel 5-cyl
HORSEPOWER	163
MAX. SPEED	205 km/h (127 mph)
CO_2 EMISSIONS	183 g/km

For Steve Mattin, Volvo's design director at the time, the 2008 XC60 was all about 'turning up the visual volume', charging Volvo with more energy and bringing brand identity to the fore. Hence the bold detailing, the huge headlamps, the gaping black grille and the massive Volvo ironmark logo. The XC60 is not so much a smaller counterpart to the conservative, predictable XC90 as a Volvo hot hatchback on stilts and steroids.

It was claimed at the XC60's launch that the car personified modern Scandinavian design, but there was little about it that was subtle, simple or understated apart from some pale-wood interior trim (and, in the concept, Orrefors crystal). This was a bold, brash compact crossover aimed fairly and squarely at the North American market.

The first (and in the end, only) clean-sheet car Mattin developed for Volvo, the XC60 is as expressive and extreme as intended, and is clearly distinct in identity from the many other similarly sized SUVs offered within the wider Ford family to which Volvo belonged at the time. However, whether or not it has the character of a Volvo is arguable, and comments made soon afterwards by new CEO Stefan Jacoby about Volvo recognizing its true roots appear to signal a return to designs that pay more attention to function than fashion.

HARTMUT WARKUSS

GERMANY | BORN 1940 | CAR DESIGNER AND MANAGER

CV

1964	Joins Mercedes-Benz design department
1966	Moves to Ford, Cologne
1968	Audi design office
1976	Head of Audi design centre
1993	Head of design, Volkswagen Group
2004	Retires

KEY DESIGNS

1969	Audi 100S Coupé
1972	Audi 80
1982	Audi 100
1991	Audi Avus quattro and Quattro Spyder concepts
1994	Audi A8
1996	Volkswagen Passat (5th gen)
1997	Volkswagen Golf (4th gen)
2002	Volkswagen Phaeton and Touareg
2003	Volkswagen Golf (5th gen)
2005	Volkswagen Passat (6th gen), Bugatti Veyron 16.4

Hartmut Warkuss worked for the Volkswagen Group for almost forty years, during thirty of which he was in charge of design, first at Audi and then at Volkswagen. He began with »Audi just as it was beginning to establish its own identity, Warkuss helping to pen arguably the first mature Audi, the 100S Coupé of 1969. His pivotal streamlined 100 of 1982 marked the dawn of the aerodynamic era, and he designed the first aluminium luxury car, the »Audi A8, in 1994.

When Ferdinand Piëch became CEO of the Volkswagen Group in 1993 Warkuss was asked to take charge of VW design. One of his first missions was to respond to Piëch's desire to take »Volkswagen into the luxury segment, so he began to sketch concepts

1969 AUDI 100S COUPÉ

1994 AUDI A8

1991 AUDI QUATTRO SPYDER CONCEPT

2002 VOLKSWAGEN TOUAREG

for what would later become the Phaeton limousine, the Touareg luxury SUV and the »Bugatti Veyron 16.4 supercar. Yet two models, the 1996 »VW Passat and the following year's fourth-generation »Golf, symbolize the Warkuss/Piëch era better than any others. Each marked a quantum step up in quality and, above all, interior design, so that buyers felt they were getting a car from a more luxurious segment. These two models helped to cement VW's status as a superior volume-car maker.

Warkuss's visual style was always characterized by a calm Bauhaus simplicity, which meant gently rounded forms, smooth surfaces and a very clean, pure look. This is evident from the smallest VW Lupo to the most luxurious Phaeton; and even the million-euro, 400-km/h (250-mph) Bugatti Veyron 16.4 has a simple curved form unadorned by distracting detail.

It is significant that following Warkuss's retirement in 2004 his successor tried to find ways of adding more emotion into VW's products (often with clumsy chrome grilles) but that this policy was swiftly reversed when Martin Winterkorn took charge of the group in 2007.

1991 AUDI AVUS QUATTRO CONCEPT

2005 BUGATTI VEYRON 16.4

ED WELBURN

UNITED STATES | BORN 1951 | CAR DESIGNER AND MANAGER

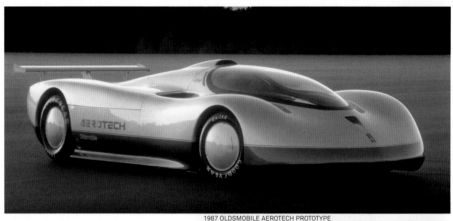

1987 OLDSMOBILE AEROTECH PROTOTYPE

2007 CHEVROLET VOLT CONCEPT

2007 CADILLAC SRX

One of relatively few African Americans to hold a top design management position in an American car company, Edward Welburn, son of a Philadelphia repair-shop proprietor, has risen to what is perhaps the most important job in the world of automotive design. In 2003 he was appointed vice president of design of »General Motors, at that time the world's largest automaker, with a stable of eight brands, eleven studios in ten countries and some 1500 designers worldwide. Welburn is just the sixth GM design chief since the corporation was founded in 1908, and several of his predecessors have become legends in the automotive world.

Car-mad from a very early age, Welburn only ever wanted to work for GM: indeed, he wrote to the company at the age of eleven seeking advice on how to become a car designer. Following the advice he received and armed with the recommended degree in product design and sculpture, he began working in GM's advanced studio, the first black person to do so.

A fast riser within GM's ranks, Welburn has been responsible for literally scores of production and concept cars, and has witnessed huge shifts in the auto industry. From the turn of the millennium product tsar Bob Lutz infused new enthusiasm for exciting products within GM, bypassing the corporation's notorious bureaucracy to get models to market faster. Welburn presided over the rise – and then decline – in heavyweight SUVs and pickups, and helped to make such small cars and and eco-models as the »Chevrolet Spark and »Volt attractive to customers. He also modernized »Cadillac and »Buick, but by the end of the decade Oldsmobile, »Pontiac, »Saturn and »Hummer had all been forced to close, slimming GM down to just four core brands – Buick, Cadillac, Chevrolet and trucks division GMC.

2009 CHEVROLET CAMARO

2007 CHEVROLET GROOVE, BEAT AND TRAX CONCEPTS

2010 CHEVROLET VOLT

WESTFIELD

HISTORY AND PRINCIPAL MODELS

1983	Westfield Sportscars founded to make XI lightweight sports-car kit
1986	7SE
1991	SEIGHT
2000	Megabusa, Megablade
2001	XTR2
2004	Relaunch of XI kit
2005	2000 S
2006	Westfield bought by Potenza Sports Cars
2007	Potenza buys GTM and integrates its operations with Westfield's. Aerosport
2010	Launch of electric iRacer at Geneva motor show

2001 XTR2

2007 AEROSPORT

2004 XI

In 1983 historic motorsport enthusiast Chris Smith decided to build a fibreglass-bodied replica of his all-time favourite car, »Lotus Le Mans 24 Hours contender the 1956 Eleven. His re-creation was so well received that he formed Westfield Cars to manufacture kits for sale to other Lotus fans and enthusiasts. Moving on to make a Lotus Seven-inspired kit (to the annoyance of Lotus, which took legal action), the company moved to progressively larger premises, expanded its remit to offer turnkey cars as well as kits for DIY assembly, and ran one-make race series. It went on to fit powerful superbike engines in its lightweight, stripped-out roadsters to give explosive acceleration and high-revving racing performance.

The Westfield story, in common with so many small-scale British kit-car makers, could have ended there, but in 2006 Smith sold out to Potenza Sports Cars, which has also bought British firm GTM Cars and a Swedish maker of AC Cobra replicas, Roadster Bil. Under new management, Westfield has – V8-engined Cobra kits apart – gone green: it has partnered with a team at the University of Warwick to develop a hybrid

racer, with a view to offering hybrid-drive upgrade kits, and is working on an all-electric car, the 600-kilogram (1323-lb) iRacer.

The featherweight iRacer, intended to star in its own race series, is made from composites, recyclable plastics and, strikingly, a stretched Lycra 'skin' over an aluminium framework for its body panels; its centre of gravity is lower than that of an Formula One car, says Westfield. Styled by young Royal College of Art graduate Elliott Hawkins, the iRacer is undergoing final evaluation before hitting the track in 2011.

Already exporting worldwide, Westfield has also recently announced a joint venture with a Malaysian carmaker to manufacture a new product line of eco-friendly and affordable sports cars, with a view to both local and international sales. The majority of its sales are now of turnkey cars, and the company has achieved European Type Approval status for its Vauxhall Corsa VXR-engined Sport Turbo, the first niche vehicle manufacturer to do so. Now making more than four hundred cars a year, this small British firm is thinking big, and with increasing originality.

WIESMANN

GERMANY | FOUNDED 1988 | BESPOKE LUXURY SPORTS CARS | WIESMANN.COM

Brothers Martin and Friedhelm Wiesmann, with backgrounds in engineering and industry respectively, have basically followed their childhood dream. After a visit to the Essen motor show had inspired them to build their own car, they built their first prototype in their spare time while continuing their day jobs, and in 1988 they unveiled their Roadster. All subsequent models, powered by the latest top-end BMW engines and featuring glass fibre-reinforced composite bodyshells, have evolved from the Roadster.

Wiesmann builds sports cars for those who feel that a »BMW Z4 or even a »Mercedes-Benz SL is just too common and unimaginative, or too contemporary-looking. The boutique carmaker from Dülmen, north-east Germany, promises individuality, exclusivity and hand-built craftsmanship, and combines traditional values and classic styling with modern technology. Each car – of the handful made each year to bespoke customer specification – is unique, says the company. Since 2008 every aspect of the car's manufacturing, from making the body moulds to constructing wiring harnesses and tanning the leather for the upholstery, is done in-house at a similarly unique glass factory built in the shape of Wiesmann's gecko logo.

Wiesmann carefully treads the perilous path between timeless design and retro pastiche, redeemed by the relative simplicity of its outlines (reminiscent of the modern-day »Morgans, themselves part-throwbacks) and the quality of its workmanship. The company's strategic partnership with luxury-goods brand Loewe, and clever PR, including the live-build of a car at the 2009 Frankfurt motor show, underline its status as more than just an expensive nostalgia merchant.

HISTORY AND PRINCIPAL MODELS

1986	Martin and Friedhelm Wiesmann start to design their car
1987	First prototype built
1988	Wiesmann Roadster presented
1993	Production of Roadster MF3 begins
2005	GT MF4 launched
2008	New 'glass factory' opens in Dülmen. GT MFG unveiled. Brand partnership formed with Loewe
2009	Roadster MF4 and GT MF5 launched
2010	BMW's twin-turbo 4.4 V8 fitted in MF5

2005 GT MF4

2009 ROADSTER MF4

2009 GT MF5 AND ROADSTER MF4

ZAGATO

ITALY | FOUNDED 1919 | CAR DESIGN AND COACHBUILDING | ZAGATO.IT

2010 ALFA ROMEO TZ3

1963 ALFA ROMEO GIULIA TZ

1986 ASTON MARTIN V8 ZAGATO

2007 ZAGATO DIATTO OTTOVU

HISTORY

1919	Coachbuilding firm founded by Ugo Zagato
1920s	Builds sports and racing bodies on a variety of chassis
1930	Builds Alfa Romeo racing cars and aerodynamic models
1946	Opens new factory
1960s	Manufactures special editions for Alfa Romeo, Lancia and Osca
1962	Opens new factory
1970s	Manufactures Lancia Beta Spyder
1980s	Expands into vehicle development
1990s	Third generation as grandson Andrea Zagato assumes control

KEY DESIGNS

1938	Lancia Aprilia Sport Aerodinamica
1949	Maserati 1500Z Panoramica
1957	Alfa Romeo Giulietta SZ
1960	Aston Martin DB4 Zagato
1962	Osca 1600 GTZ
1963	Alfa Romeo Giulia TZ
1966	Lancia Fulvia Sport Zagato
1986	Aston Martin V8 Zagato
1989	Alfa Romeo SZ
2002	Aston Martin DB7 Zagato
2007	Zagato Diatto Ottovu
2008	Bentley Continental GTZ
2010	Alfa Romeo TZ3

Of the principal Italian coachbuilding and design houses, Zagato has always been the most adventurous, the most extreme and the most controversial in its designs. Its founder, Ugo Zagato, was an early aeronautical engineer who used his knowledge of lightweight materials and advanced construction techniques to great effect in the 1920s and 1930s. Before long he was building racing cars for Alfa Romeo and extravagant streamlined bodies on conventional chassis for wealthy private clients.

By the 1950s the firm was building more affordable sports cars, often elegant miniature masterpieces, on Fiat and other chassis, although still largely by hand using craft methods. The 1960s brought the realization that volume manufacture was here to stay. The company invested in a new factory to make the numerous special-bodied Lancias, Alfa Romeos, Fiats and even Aston Martins that client companies were demanding.

This was in many ways Zagato's heyday: such classics as the Alfa Romeo Giulia TZ, the Aston Martin DB4 Zagato and the Lancia Fulvia Sport Zagato are all highly collectable cars today. What most of Zagato's designs shared was a soft, rounded and sometimes bulbous form language, often with details that surprised the onlooker and strange window and grille shapes that, for their time, were seen as shocking and not altogether attractive. Small wonder, then, that Zagato was regarded as the eccentric, the bête noire among the Italian *carrozzerie*.

Among Zagato's most regular customers have been »Alfa Romeo and »Aston Martin. The British firm has commissioned three distinct generations of limited-edition Zagato-bodied sports cars, while the 1989 SZ coupé for Alfa Romeo has the distinction of being the first production car to have been designed entirely on computer.

Most recently of all, the 2010 Alfa Romeo TZ3, a racing coupé built to commemorate its namesake of the 1960s, marks a stunning return to form for the company.

ZIL

RUSSIA | 1916–2009 | LARGE SEDANS AND LIMOUSINES | AMO-ZIL.RU

HISTORY AND PRINCIPAL MODELS

1916	AMO (Automobile Moscow Society) founded
1918	Unfinished facility is nationalized following the Russian Revolution
1924	First truck assembled on 1 November, marks birth of the Soviet auto industry
1931	Factory renamed after Stalin: Zavod imeni Stalina (ZiS). First production-line assembly
1939	101 Sport
1946	110 limousine
1951	112 prototype, a three-seater with experimental 6.0 V8 engine
1956	Factory renamed Zavod imeni Likhacheva (ZiL)
1958	111 replaces 110
1967	114
1976	4104
1985	41041, 41047
1988	4102 prototype
1992	ZiL privatized following collapse of Soviet Union; renamed AMO ZiL
1997	Shareholders approve sale of stock to pay off creditors
2002	ZiL restructured; small-scale truck production continues
2005	ZiL becomes a supplier of parts for Russian assembly of Renault Logan
2009	Production slows to three days a week
2010	Rumours of a new ZiL limousine

1967 114

ZiL predates the Soviet Union; founded just prior to the Russian Revolution, the company was initially intended to build trucks under licence from Fiat, but was nationalized and renamed ZiS (Zavod imeni Stalina) in honour of Soviet leader Joseph Stalin. In the mid-1930s it added carmaking to its portfolio. Early models drew heavily on the large cars of Buick and Packard, although the 101 Sport of 1939, a voluptuous cabriolet based on the 101-A sedan's chassis, was hailed as one of the most attractive Russian cars ever made.

For all that the Soviet Union wanted to promote the technological advances of Communism, the large cars from ZiS were remarkably American in flavour. The creators of the 101 Sport had clearly been studying the work of Harley Earl at General Motors and his dream cars, especially the Buick Y-Job. The huge, spaceship-like 112 concept was uncannily similar in appearance to the 1951 Buick LeSabre. ZiS – ZiL, from 1956 – did better with its more functional products, developing a huge range of simple, tough, easy-to-maintain

trucks, coaches, minibuses and specialist working vehicles.

Yet ZiL limousines and large sedans (exported, usually in armoured form, to Africa and the Middle East) played an important role in the Soviet hierarchy. Used by high-ranking officials and for ceremonial duties, they became symbols of state power and authoritarian rule. Their dated technology barely mattered. With the fall of the Iron Curtain and an influx of far more appealing Western luxury cars, demand first dwindled, then petered out.

The ZiL tale might not be over, however. Russian president Dmitry Medvedev is said to be considering a plan to revive the brand and rid diplomatic and governmental fleets of unpatriotic Mercedes-Benz, Audis and BMWs. Concepts have been sketched by a former ZiL designer, and images have appeared on the Internet showing CAD drawings of an angular, long and low sedan with an upright front grille and mean demeanour. Reports suggest that discussions are under way to put this into production.

WHO OWNS WHOM

*The world's automobile brands: ownership, control
and cooperation*

The first decade of the twenty-first century has seen rapid
and profound changes in the world of car brands. The 1990s
witnessed a scramble by major volume carmakers, such as
Ford, General Motors and Volkswagen, to snap up independent
premium brands. Barely a decade later, as the large and
unwieldy American groups struck trouble, those same
premium brands were dispersed among a variety of new
owners. Aston Martin went to Middle Eastern interests,
Jaguar and Land Rover to India's Tata, Saab to Dutch
supercar maker Spyker, and Volvo to Geely of China.

The financial crisis that began in 2008 took its toll on
brands both major and minor: GM has closed no fewer than
three big nameplates, Ford has shut Mercury, Chrysler has
come under the control of Fiat, and Porsche and Italdesign
have become part of the Volkswagen Group. Yet at the same
time, as an indication of the shift in the auto industry's
centre of gravity, Chinese manufacturers and their partners
announced a dozen or more new brands.

The web of cross-ownerships and technical collaboration
agreements between companies is even more complex. Here
we list the main manufacturing groups and the brands they
own (with dormant brands indicated by an asterisk), and
give the principal links between groups, whether in the form
of shareholdings or management control. The picture is a
constantly evolving one, and this mid-2011 freeze-frame is
sure to change as the second decade of this century unrolls.

BMW GROUP
BMW
Mini
Riley*
Rolls-Royce
Triumph*

CHERY
Chery
Kary
Rely
Riich

CHRYSLER GROUP
(controlled by Fiat)
Chrysler
De Soto*
Dodge
Hudson*
Imperial*
Jeep
Nash*
Ram

DAIMLER GROUP
Maybach
Mercedes-Benz
Nissan *(3.1% stake)*
Renault *(3.1% stake)*
Smart
Tesla *(10% stake)*

FIAT AUTO
Abarth
Alfa Romeo
Autobianchi*
Chrysler *(51% stake)*
Ferrari
Fiat
Innocenti*
Lancia
Maserati

FIRST AUTO WORKS
FAW Besturn
Hongqi

FORD
Ford
Lincoln
Mazda *(technical
    collaboration)*
Mercury*

GAZ GROUP
LDV*
Siber
Volga

GEELY
Englon
Gleagle
Shanghai Emgrand
Volvo

GENERAL MOTORS
Buick
Cadillac
Chevrolet
Corvette
Daewoo
GM
GMC
Holden
Hummer*
Oldsmobile*
Opel
Pontiac*
Saturn*
Vauxhall

HONDA
Acura
Honda

HYUNDAI
Asia Motors*
Hyundai
Kia

MAHINDRA
Ssangyong

PROTON
Lotus
Proton

PSA PEUGEOT CITROËN
Citroën
Hillman*
Humber*
Panhard*
Peugeot
Simca*
Singer*
Sunbeam*
Talbot*

RENAULT-NISSAN ALLIANCE
Alpine*
AvtoVAZ (Lada)
Dacia
Daimler *(3.1% stake)*
Datsun*
Infiniti
Nissan *(15% stake
    in Renault)*
Renault *(43% stake
    in Nissan)*
Renault Sport
Samsung

**SAIC (SHANGHAI
AUTOMOTIVE INDUSTRY
CORPORATION)**
Austin
MG
Morris
Nanjing
Roewe
Wolseley

SPYKER
Saab

SUZUKI
Maruti *(control)*
Suzuki
3% stake in Volkswagen

TATA MOTORS
Daimler*
Indicar
Jaguar
Land Rover
Rover*
Tata

TOYOTA
Daihatsu
Lexus
Scion
Subaru *(control)*
Tesla *(stake)*
Toyota
Will*

VOLKSWAGEN GROUP
Audi
Auto Union*
Bentley
Bugatti
DKW*
Horch*
Italdesign
Lamborghini
NSU*
Porsche *(takeover
    during 2011)*
SEAT
Skoda
Suzuki *(19.9%
    stake)*
Volkswagen
Wanderer*

**INDEPENDENT MARQUES
AND DESIGN HOUSES**
AC
Artega
Aston Martin
    (Lagonda)
Austin-Healey*
AviChina
Beijing
Bertone
Bitter
Brilliance
Bristol
BYD Auto
Caterham

Chang'An
Dongfeng
Donkervoort
EDAG
Elfin
ETUD
Farboud
Fenomenon
Fioravanti
Fisker Automotive
Great Wall
Hafei
Heuliez
Hindustan
Hongqi
I.DE.A
Inovo
Invicta
Irmscher
Isuzu
Izh
Jensen*
Joss
Koenigsegg
KTM
Lightning
LTI
McLaren
Magna Steyr
Marcos
Mitsubishi
Mitsuoka
Morgan
Noble
Pagani
Panoz
Paykan
Perodua
Pininfarina
Rinspeed
Saleen
Sivax
Stola
Tesla
Think
Tramontana
TVR*
UAZ
Venturi
Westfield
Wiesmann
Zagato
ZAZ
ZIL

* = dormant brand

GLOSSARY OF DESIGN TERMINOLOGY

A comprehensive glossary of vehicle design terms, expressions and techniques used by the international design community, compiled by David Browne, course director for automotive design at Coventry University.

The icon » indicates a cross-reference to a term described in the glossary.

This glossary first appeared in How to Design Cars Like a Pro *(Motorbooks, 2010), updated from material originally presented on cardesignnews.com. It is adapted and reproduced by kind permission of David Browne, Motorbooks and cardesignnews.com.*

BELTLINE (UK English: **waistline**)
The line directly underneath the side windows of the car created by the junction of the »greenhouse and the »shoulder or body side (literally, the side of the body). The position and inclination of the beltline affects the appearance and proportion of a car, as well as its character and »stance. A car with a low beltline and tall greenhouse may look delicate, elegant or modern. A car with a high beltline and shallow greenhouse will tend to look tough and mean. A rising beltline provides the long-fashionable wedge appearance and imparts a dynamic sense of purpose and direction.

BONE LINE
As in the case of the »crease line, the »feature line and the »swage line, the bone line's principal purposes are variously to create definition, to add emphasis, visual interest and design organization, and to direct – or even deceive – the viewer's eye. A bone line is a hard, positive only, linear 'peak' in a car's body side; it is more prominent than a crease line. There can be a subtle distinction between some of these terms, and this has led to a certain interchangeability of terminology.

BONNET *see* »hood

BULKHEAD *see* »firewall

CAB FORWARD
Cab-forward design, first seen on the 1987 Portofino concept car by Chrysler (which coined the term), led to the production of a family of cab-forward products, including the 1993 Dodge Intrepid and the 1994 Chrysler LH and New Yorker. The benefit to the overall »package was space: by moving forward the screen, driver and passenger, space was liberated for the rear compartment.

CANT RAIL
The structural member that usually sits squarely on top of the B-pillar (*see* »pillars), forming the top edge of the door-frame aperture, and that may run (visually) seamlessly into the A- and C-pillars.

CILL *see* »sill/cill

CKD (Completely Knocked Down)
The assembly of finished vehicles from kits supplied from another plant, often in another country.

CREASE LINE
The pressed or folded line created by the meeting of two different planes or surfaces. Unlike »feature lines, a crease is integral to a design, and cannot simply be applied to a surface, but is commonly the means of defining major surfaces and elevations. A crease may be positive or negative. *See also* »bone line, »swage line.

CROWN
Crown in a panel is compound curvature – usually convex: in one plane it would simply be 'curvature'. To the engineer, crown provides inherent stiffness; to the designer, it enables the control of highlights and lightlines.

DAYLIGHT CATCHER *see* »light catcher

DLO (daylight opening)
The term is used to describe the graphic shape of a car's side glass. The DLO is the strongest and most important graphic element of a car's design, as it provides the opportunity to create a major contrasting surface that can be employed to flatter or accentuate a form.

DRG (down the road graphics)
The design features and characteristics of the front end or 'face' of a car that enable the marque to be immediately identified from a distance.

DRIVELINE
The mechanical elements of the vehicle that convey the power from the engine to the front, rear or all four wheels. Includes the clutch, gearbox, driveshafts, differential and axle(s). *See also* »powertrain.

FEATURE LINE
A simple line in a car's body surface. The best feature lines will be sympathetic to the design of a car, but some may simply have been introduced to relieve otherwise dull or large areas of plain sheet metal. They can also be used to accentuate the form, and to tie in an array of items. Any and all body panels may have feature lines. *See also* »bone line, »crease line, »swage line.

FENDER (UK English: **wing**)
Those panels near the wheels that are legally required to wrap or cover the wheels, protecting the bodywork – and sometimes the occupants – and other road users from spray, dirt, stones and anything else thrown up by the revolving tyres. In their early, simplest form, fenders closely followed the shape of the wheel, as bicycle mudguards do.

FIREWALL (UK English: **bulkhead**)
The structural panel that separates the engine compartment from the passenger compartment. Its principal functions include sound and heat insulation, but the firewall may also support such items as the battery.

FORM LANGUAGE (or **surface language**)
A term that may refer to the manipulation of the form of any individual vehicle, or to the visual feel or identity that characterizes and unites a manufacturer's entire range.
  Usually, the way in which the principal surfaces of any car's exterior – and interior – are treated will help to confirm its nature or purpose. A small city car, intended to be non-threatening and friendly, may have soft curves, generous radii, a happy 'face' and 'playful' interior detailing. Sports cars' surfaces should help to make them look athletic and powerful, and 4x4s will tend to be chunky and apparently unsubtle and unrefined.

Deployed corporately, surface language is a form of individual brand or marque identity, referring to the manner in which designers from different companies will treat the sculptural journey from broadly similar points A to points B.
  Audi designs, for example – epitomized by the original TT – have highly disciplined geometric surfaces and detailing. This cerebral designing characterizes the entire range and creates a unified family identity.

GREENHOUSE (or **glasshouse**)
The upper, glazed, part of the passenger compartment that sits on the bodywork. This conjunction is referred to as the »beltline (or waistline). As front and rear screen angles have become ever 'faster' or more steeply raked, and »tumblehome more pronounced, conspiring to increase solar gain, this piece of terminology is finally coming into its own.

HARD POINTS
Points on a »package drawing indicating the position of component parts or extremities that cannot be moved, and that must therefore be accommodated or designed around. These include the engine, suspension, fuel tank, wheel centres and »wheelbase (and therefore inner wheel arches), and pedals – maybe a whole shared »platform – and therefore exert considerable influence on both exterior and interior designs.

HAUNCH
The name given to the emphatic sculpting of the »fender panel above the rear »wheel arches, which evokes the skin tightly stretched over the well-toned muscles and sinews of an athlete, and therefore implies power and performance. Haunches have been an essential ingredient of the generic rear-wheel-drive coupé from the 1950s and are often associated with Jaguar, which has used this device as a key part of its »form language since that time.

HOOD (UK English: **bonnet**)
The exterior body panel that covers the engine compartment of front-engined cars (it's called an engine cover on rear-engined cars) and which can usually be lifted or opened to provide access to the engine. Most Land Rovers and Saabs have signature 'clamshell' hoods that effectively incorporate the tops of the front »fenders, moving the shut lines to the body sides.

INSTRUMENT PANEL (IP) (also known as **facia, dashboard, dash**) A hugely important, multifunctional 'platform' that contains information displays relating to a car's performance, well-being and geographical location; major and minor controls, switches and so on; heating and ventilation outlets; storage access; and, of course, the obligatory cup-holder. It also conceals a number of functions, such as the passenger airbag, and the air-conditioning/ventilation/screen-demisting systems and their associated trunking, as well as the important structural cross-member.

JEWELLERY
The collective name for those bright component parts applied to the main exterior body surfaces (grille, wheels and even painted brake calipers, head and tail lamps, side repeaters, door handles, bright trim and badges) or in the interior (sometimes switches, instruments, vents, local metallized details and so on).

The impact will depend on contrast with body colour: jewellery will stand out against dark colours, and be discreet against silver. Lighting has become serious jewellery, with projector and LED technology enabling anything designers can dream up.

Mercedes-Benz used to be the most consummate user of chrome, employing it to define form rather than merely decorate it, and turning its use into a Teutonic art form with the 1963 600 limousine.

LIGHT CATCHER (or **daylight catcher**)
As in the case of a »feature line, this styling device is intended to add surface interest, but the light catcher is deliberately positioned so as to reflect light from an area normally in shadow; it is typically found on a car's lower body side, doors or »sills.

The introduction of an upward-facing detail in a part of the body section that would usually reflect ground tones creates bright 'sky' reflections of the same value as those on the upper body surfaces. This simultaneously draws the eye downward, lowers the visual centre of gravity to below the wheel centres, and helps to plant a car on the ground, giving it a more positive, emphatic »stance.

OVERHANG
Those parts of a car that project forward of the front wheels and extend rearward of the rear wheels, and that incorporate the crumple zones, the parts that crunch up during a minor crash.

The relationship between overhang and »wheelbase is critical in achieving an overall visual balance: too much overhang is undesirable. Fortunately, the visual perception of excessive overhang can be reduced by the judicious use of »plan shape.

PACKAGE / PACKAGE DRAWING
A package is the basic layout of a car. Typically, package drawings are delivered, via engineering, as an assembled collection of largely non-negotiable »hard points in the form of the car's unclothed functional contents.

This specification will include recommended length, width and height, wheel centres, engine, »driveline and fuel tank location, screen position and angle, and maximum and minimum percentile manikin positions (with sightlines); the last will also impact on the interior's design, as will inner wheel arch intrusion.

PILLARS
Pillars fulfil a number of primary functions: they are important structural members; doors are hinged off them and/or close on to them; they support the roof and cage and protect the occupants; and they visually frame the windows. Pillars may be 'removed'

graphically by being matt-blacked out, by being 'wrapped' by the side or rear glass, or by internal masking to achieve the required »DLO graphic.

The **A-pillars** (or A-posts) are the upright structural supports either side of the windshield, which is usually bonded to them. A-pillars invariably flow visually seamlessly into the »cant rail.

The **B-pillars** of most four- and five-door cars are not visible until their doors are opened. What we refer to as B−pillars are in fact the adjacent uprights of the front and rear side-window frames, which sit over, and hide, the actual B-pillar. The real B-pillar is invariably a hefty, vertical, structural member on to which the front doors latch and off which the rear doors are hinged.

C-pillar, D-pillar (rearmost pillars): while an A-pillar might have elegance, and a B-pillar is largely plain, functional and anonymous, a C-pillar may have style. Some, such as BMW's so-called Hofmeister kink (named after BMW's design director of the 1960s), have become important marque signifiers. Strictly speaking, for a car with three windows along the side (such as an estate car, SUV or MPV), the C-pillar is the third pillar – that is, the rear-door pillar. In these cars, the rearmost pillar is therefore the D-pillar.

PLAN SHAPE

A term that refers to the amount of curvature in body sides, and particularly front and rear ends, as seen from above, *i.e.* in plan view.

Cars have predominantly constant curvature in plan, but these days this curvature will become noticeably more pronounced towards the front and rear ends, leading into much more generously radiused corners – or, in some cases, effectively no corners at all. Clever use of plan shape provides the best opportunity to disguise the greater »overhangs required by ever-tougher impact testing.

PLATFORM

It is possible to think of a platform as a latter-day chassis – a basic structural and mechanical architecture subsequently clad in the visible sheet metal of the bodywork. It is the invisibility of the elements of the platform – typically »powertrains, suspensions and structural pressings, such as floorpans and »firewalls – that enables the widespread practice of platform sharing and the massive economies of scale to be achieved.

POWERTRAIN

The engine, clutch, gearbox, driveshafts, differential(s)

and axle(s) of a vehicle. *See also* »driveline.

SHOULDER / SHOULDERLINE

The shoulderline basically runs the length of a car's upper body side where it folds over to meet the side windows, and its nature will reflect the essential character of the car. The surface between the shoulderline and the »beltline directly below the side windows is referred to, reasonably, as the shoulder; amusingly, it is therefore below the beltline.

SILL / CILL (or **rocker panel**)

The visible structural member that runs between the front and rear »wheel arches below the doors. Some doors overlap, and hide, their sills. As the outline that defines the lower body, the sill is also a strong visual element, and its shape is quite likely to reinforce the character of a car. The lower sill is usually part of a continuing line, indexed through the wheel arches, running round the car.

STANCE

Stance confers presence, suggests attitude, intent and ability, and is equally identifiable whether a car is stationary or on the move. Stance is largely defined by the

body-to-wheel and the overall vehicle-to-ground relationships, which are important in all cars but vital in those for which attitude is critical. Wheels that fill a car's »wheel arches in depth as well as diameter will suggest a confident stability. Wheels and wheel arches pulled out from the body sides will imply performance and even aggression, as will minimal ground clearance. Conversely, generous ground clearance is both a physical and a visual requirement for an off-roader vehicle.

SURFACE LANGUAGE *see* »form language

SWAGE LINE

The term is often used generically for any raised, continuous, pressed body-side »crease line or »feature line. Swaging is a technique in which cold metal is formed over a grooved tool, or swage.

TUMBLEHOME

A nautical term that was introduced to automotive design with the advent of curved side glass and the need to describe the convex inward curvature of the side of a car above the »beltline.

WAISTLINE *see* »beltline

WHEEL ARCH

Circular apertures in the body sides that admit the road wheels and, importantly, frame them. At their simplest, wheel arches appear to have been surgically cut out of the body sides. The relationship of wheel to wheel arch is critical, and designers attempt to make the former fill the latter as fully as possible.

WHEELBASE

The distance between the front and rear wheel centres, and a crucial dimension in the quest for internal space efficiency and optimized accommodation. Successive models in all manufacturers' ranges tend to be incrementally bigger than their predecessors, but the biggest dimensional gain is invariably to the wheelbase.

WING *see* »fender

PICTURE CREDITS